Cheeky Angel

Vol.1
Story and Art by
Hiroyuki Nishimori

Cheeky Angel
Vol. 1
Action Edition
Story and Art by
HIROYUKI NISHIMORI

Translation/Joe Yamazaki
English Adaptation/Gary Leach
Touch-Up Art & Lettering/Gabe Crate
Cover and Interior Design/Izumi Evers
Editor/Michelle Pangilinan

Managing Editor/Annette Roman
Editor-in-Chief/Alvin Lu
Production Manager/Noboru Watanabe
Sr. Director of Licensing & Acquisitions/Rika Inouye
VP of Marketing/Liza Coppola
Executive VP/Hyoe Narita
Publisher/Seiji Horibuchi

CHEEKY ANGEL is rated "T+" for Older Teens. This volume contains violence, adult language and suggestive situations.

Printed in the U.S.A.

Published by VIZ, LLC
P.O. Box 77010
San Francisco, CA 94107

Action Edition
10 9 8 7 6 5 4 3 2 1
First printing,
June 2004

storeviz.com

Contents

Chapter 1: Meeting at Full Speed

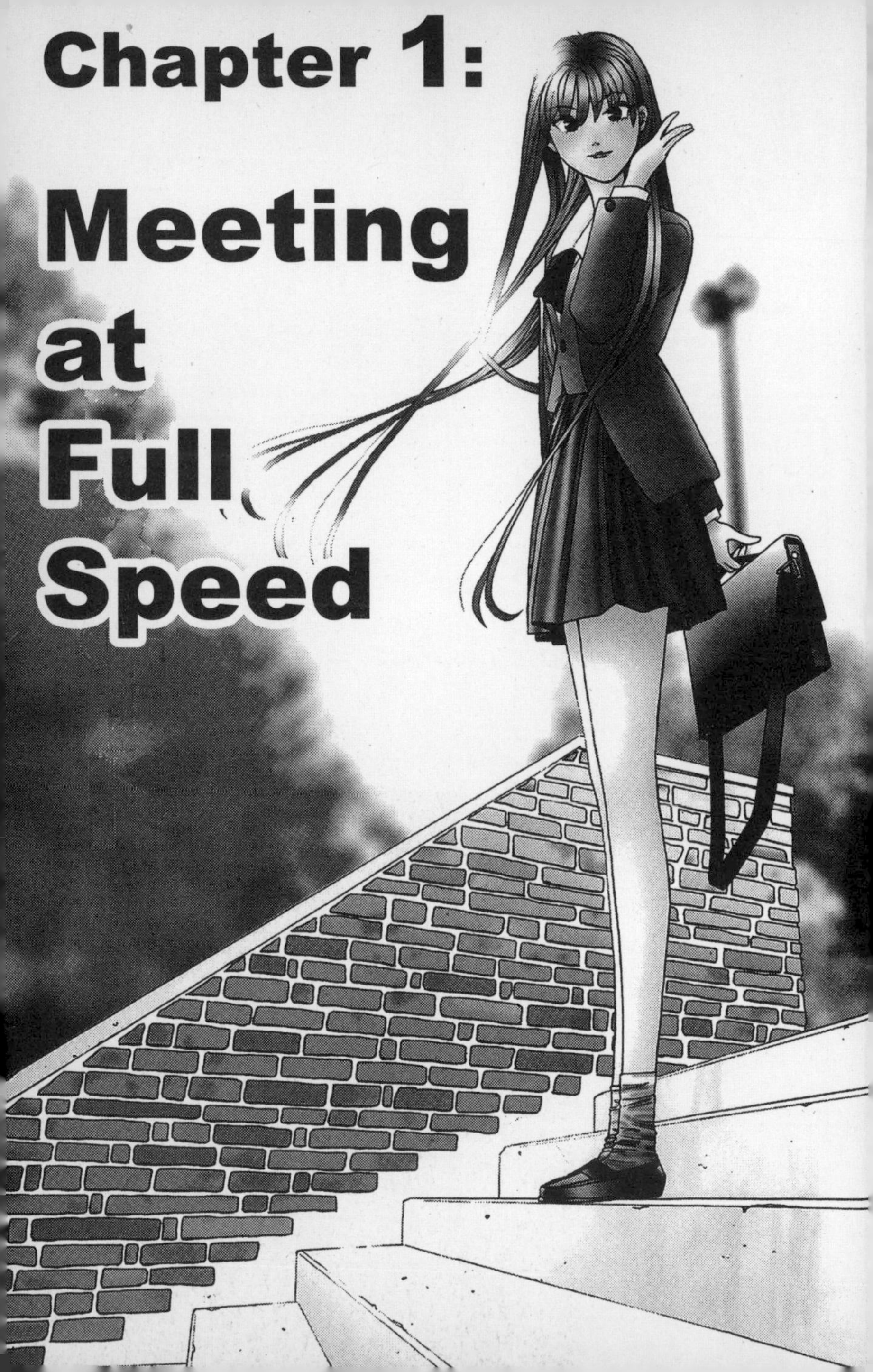

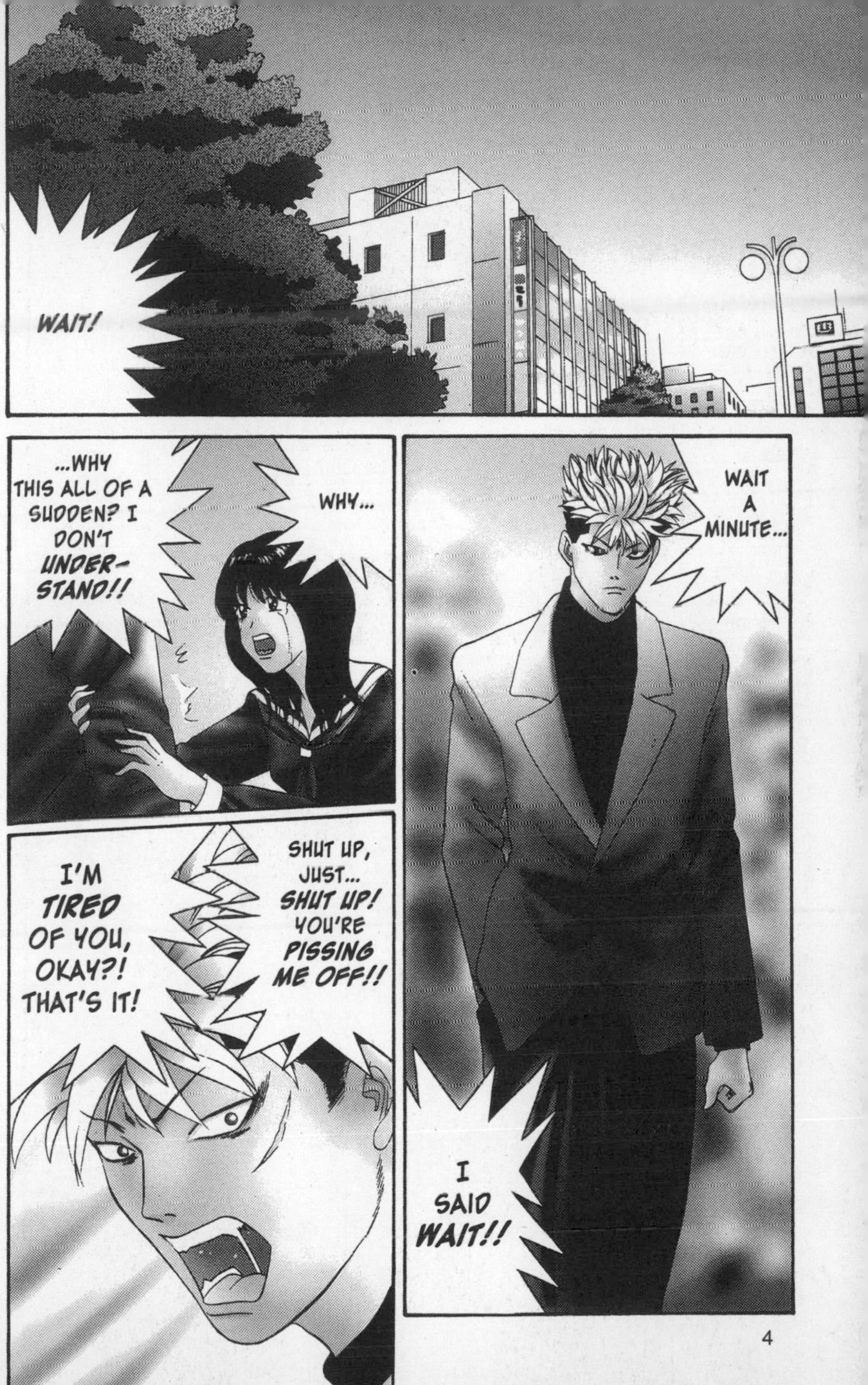
WAIT!
WAIT A MINUTE...
I SAID WAIT!!
WHY...
...WHY THIS ALL OF A SUDDEN? I DON'T UNDERSTAND!!
SHUT UP, JUST... SHUT UP! YOU'RE PISSING ME OFF!!
I'M TIRED OF YOU, OKAY?! THAT'S IT!

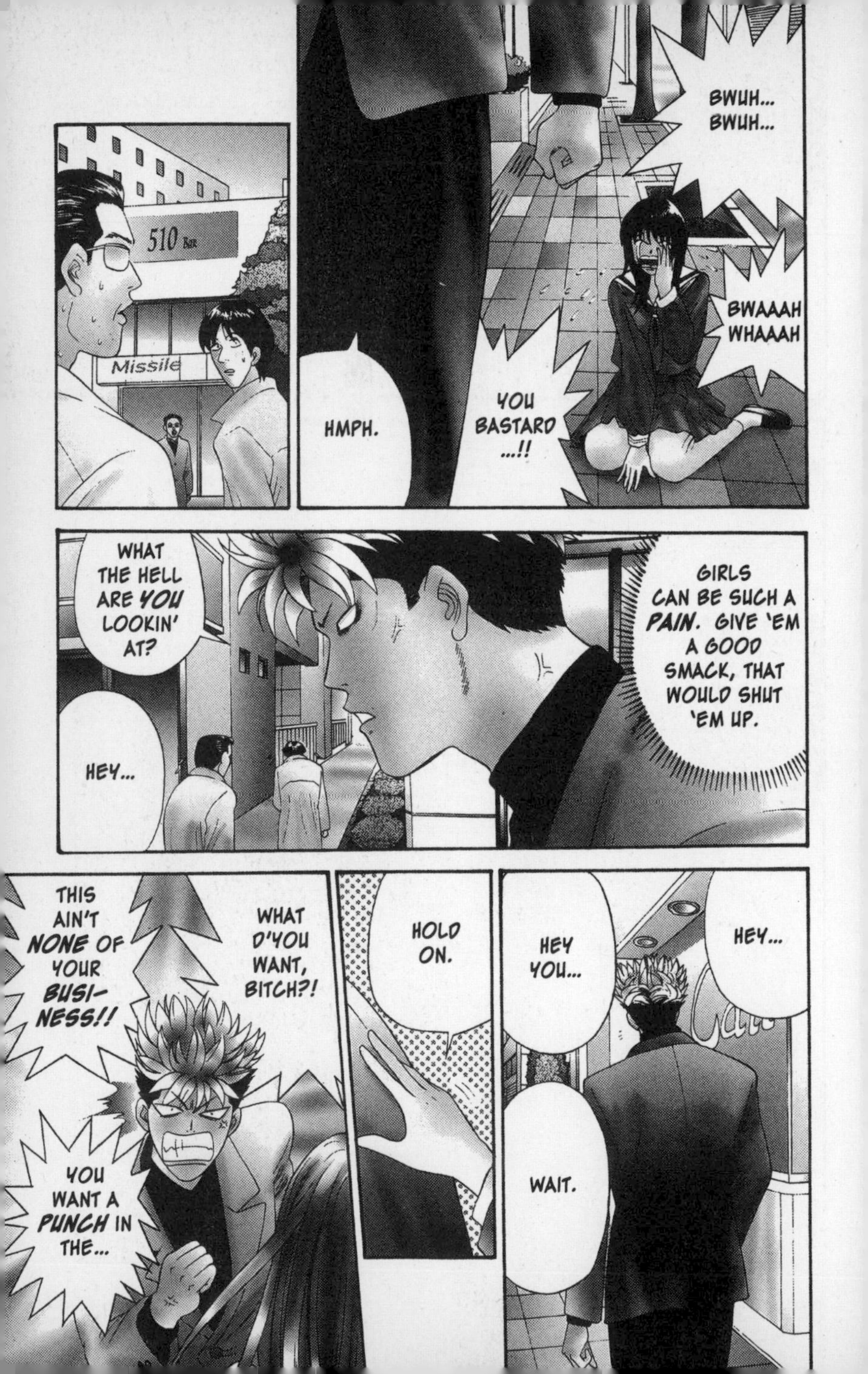
BWUH... BWUH...
BWAAAH WHAAAH
YOU BASTARD ...!!
HMPH.
510 Bar
Missile
GIRLS CAN BE SUCH A PAIN. GIVE 'EM A GOOD SMACK, THAT WOULD SHUT 'EM UP.
WHAT THE HELL ARE YOU LOOKIN' AT?
HEY...
HEY...
HEY YOU...
WAIT.
HOLD ON.
WHAT D'YOU WANT, BITCH?!
THIS AIN'T NONE OF YOUR BUSI-NESS!!
YOU WANT A PUNCH IN THE...

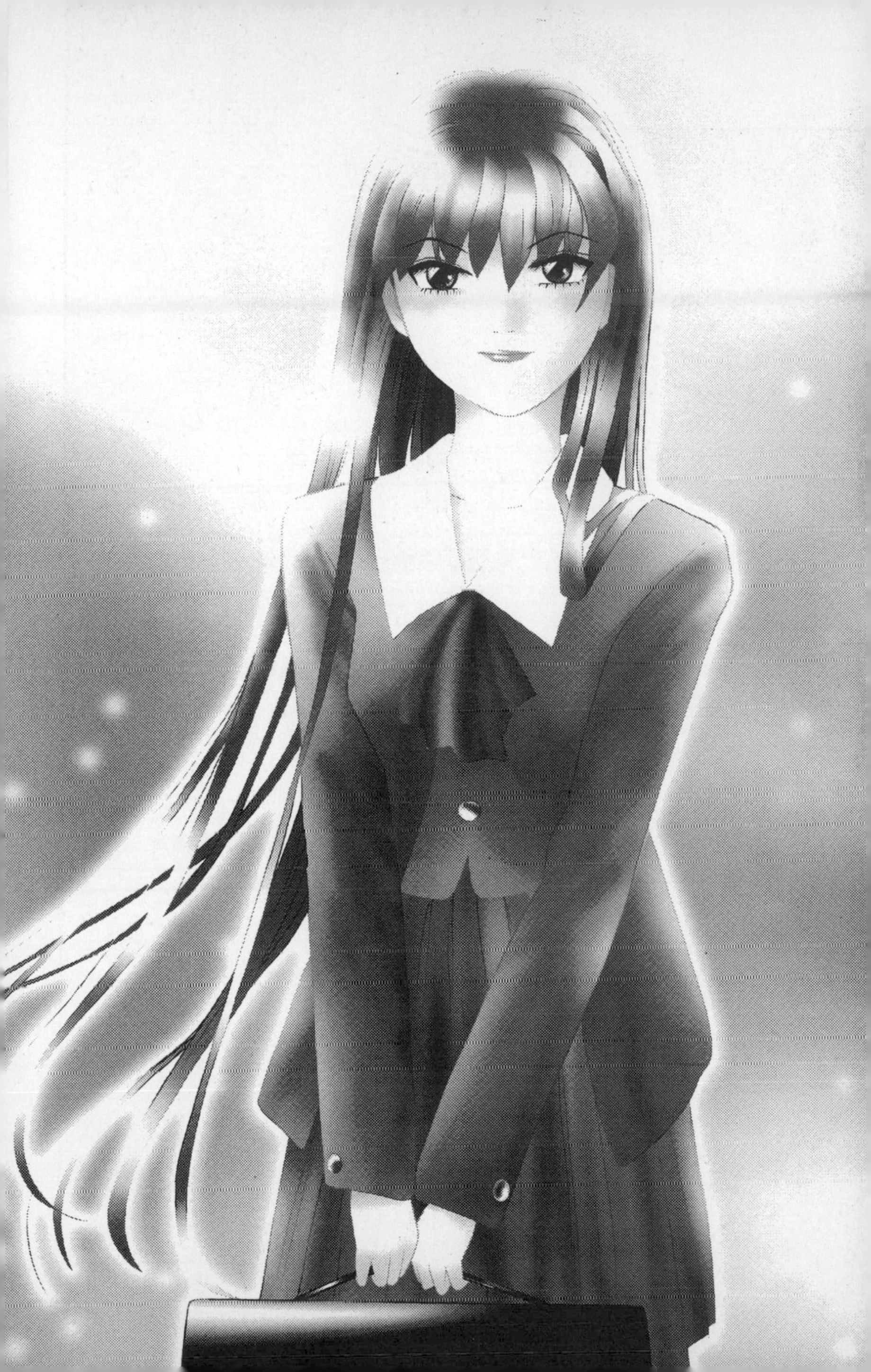

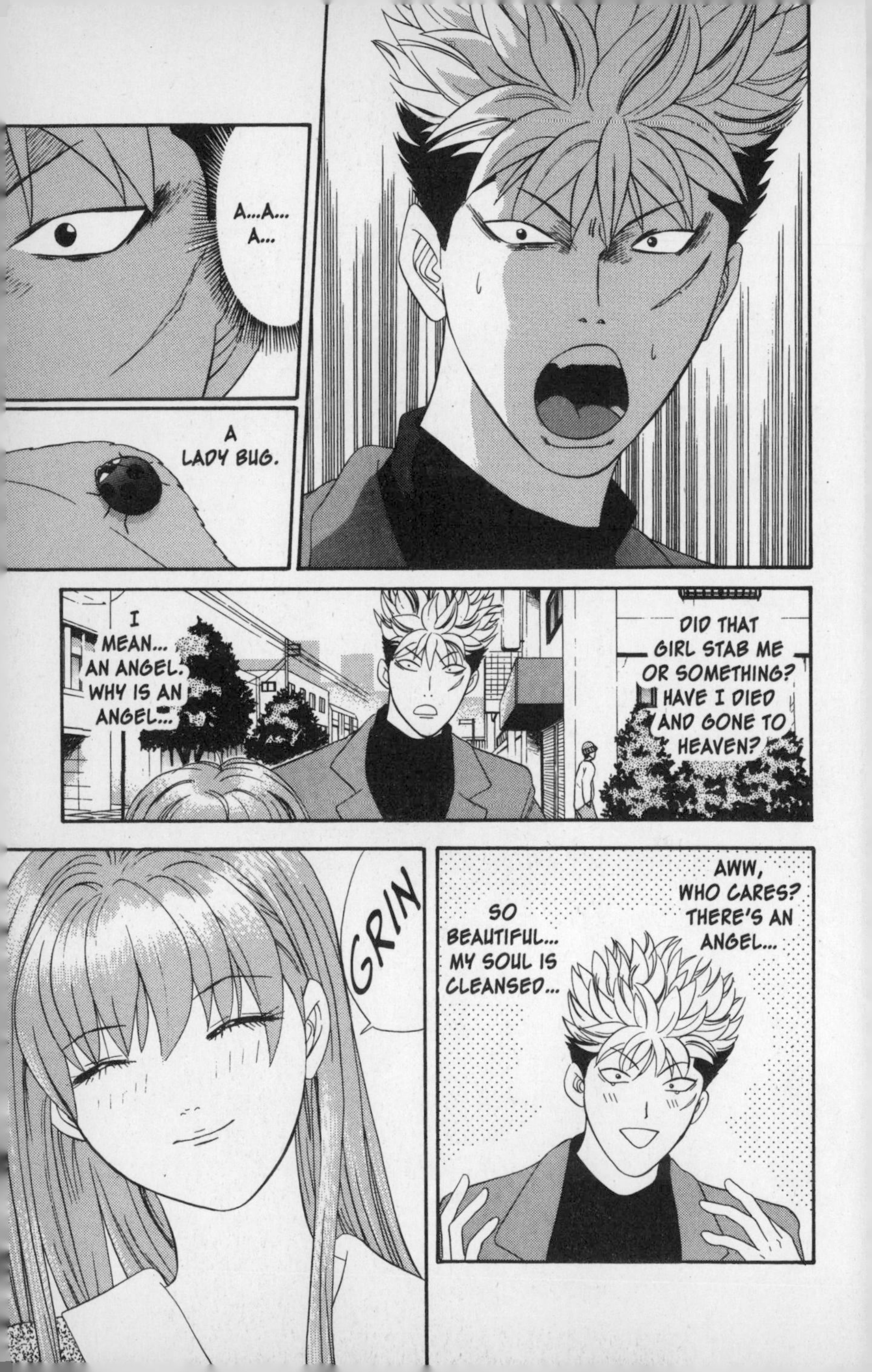
A...A... A...
A LADY BUG.
DID THAT GIRL STAB ME OR SOMETHING? HAVE I DIED AND GONE TO HEAVEN?
I MEAN... AN ANGEL. WHY IS AN ANGEL...
AWW, WHO CARES? THERE'S AN ANGEL...
SO BEAUTIFUL... MY SOUL IS CLEANSED...
GRIN

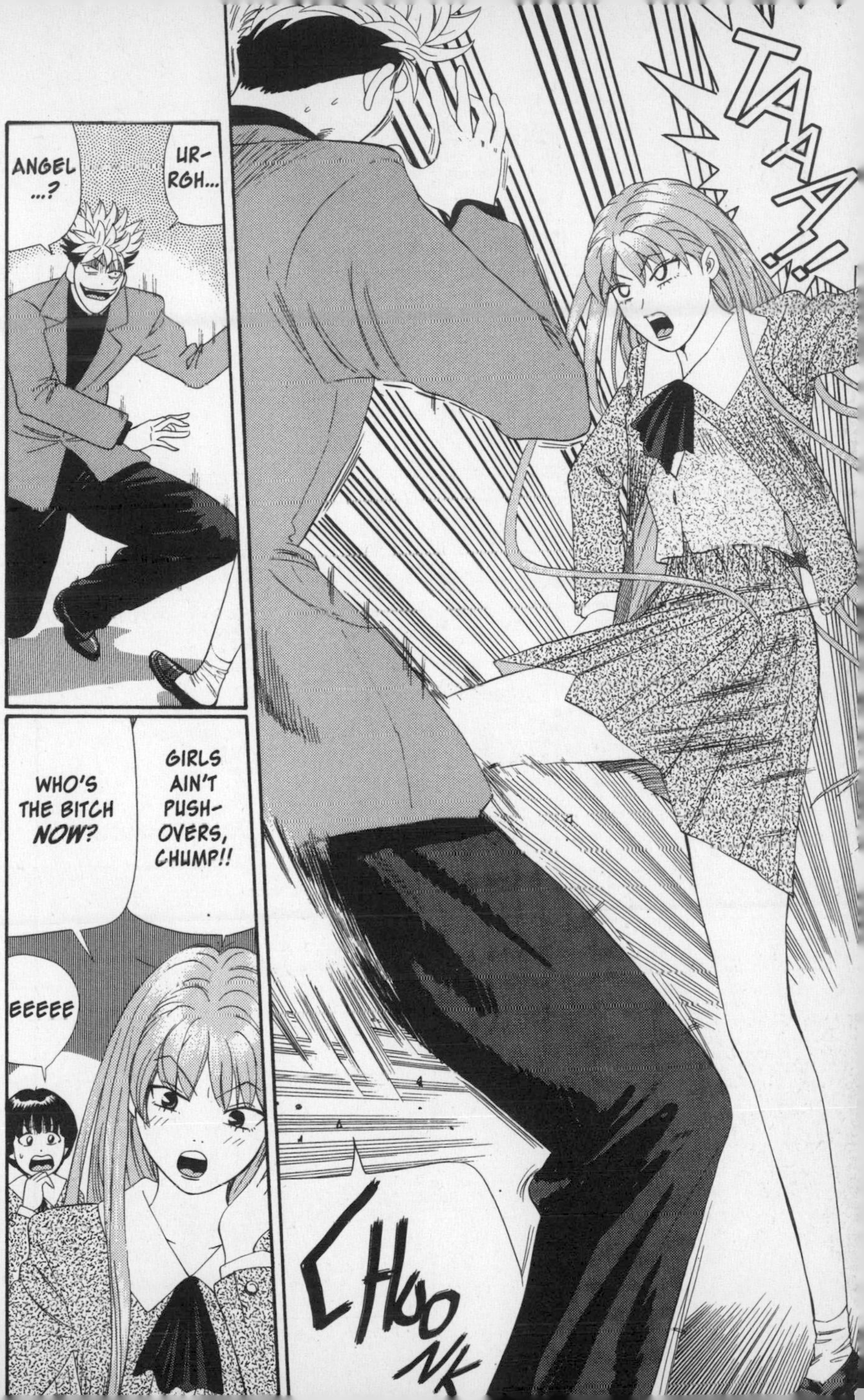
TAAA!!
CHOONK
UR-RGH...
ANGEL ...?
GIRLS AIN'T PUSH-OVERS, CHUMP!!
WHO'S THE BITCH NOW?
EEEEE

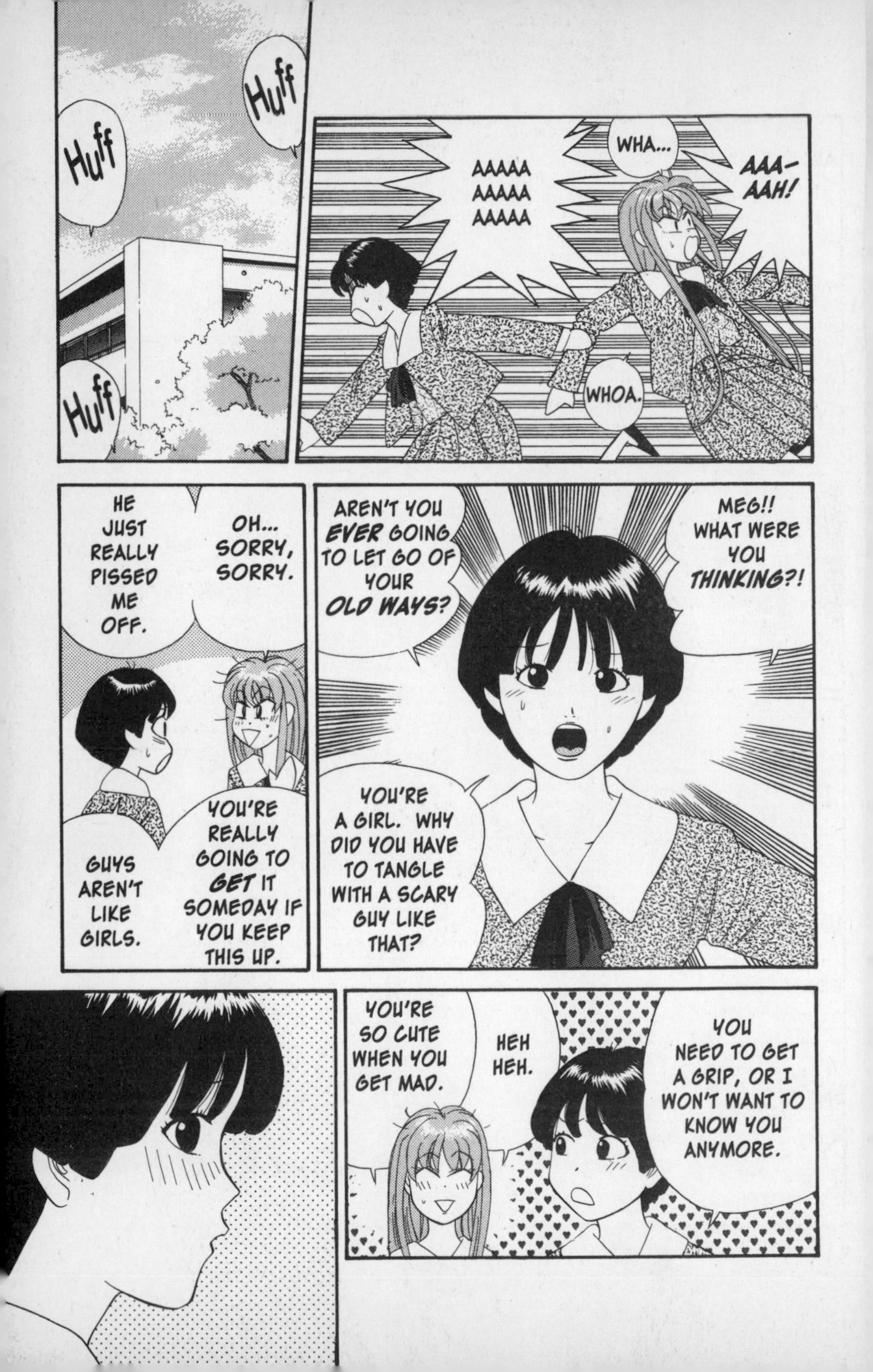
AAA-AAH!
WHA...
AAAAA AAAAA AAAAA
WHOA.
Huff
Huff
Huff
MEG!! WHAT WERE YOU THINKING?!
AREN'T YOU EVER GOING TO LET GO OF YOUR OLD WAYS?
YOU'RE A GIRL. WHY DID YOU HAVE TO TANGLE WITH A SCARY GUY LIKE THAT?
OH... SORRY, SORRY.
HE JUST REALLY PISSED ME OFF.
YOU'RE REALLY GOING TO GET IT SOMEDAY IF YOU KEEP THIS UP.
GUYS AREN'T LIKE GIRLS.
YOU NEED TO GET A GRIP, OR I WON'T WANT TO KNOW YOU ANYMORE.
HEH HEH.
YOU'RE SO CUTE WHEN YOU GET MAD.

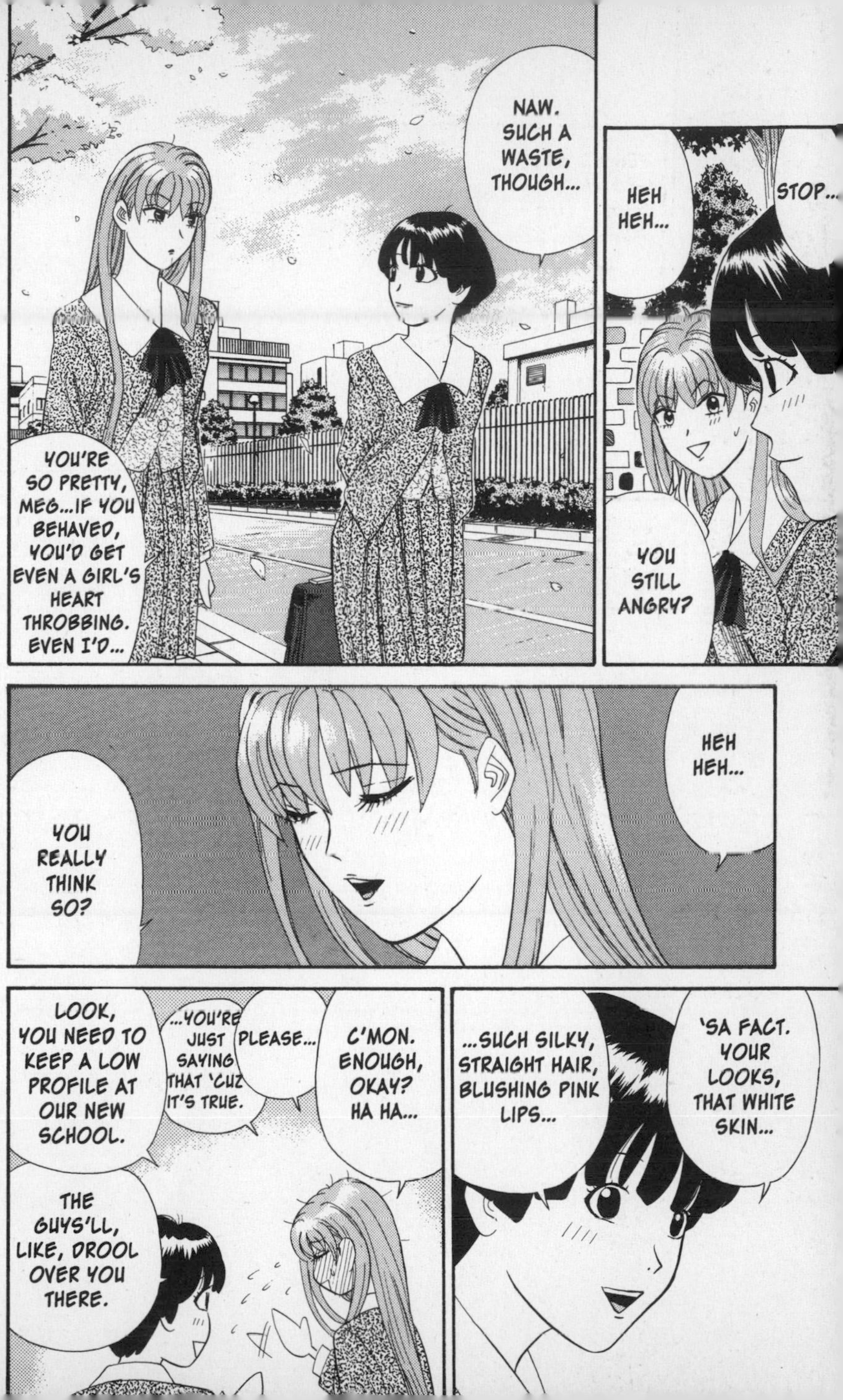
STOP...
HEH HEH...
YOU STILL ANGRY?
NAW. SUCH A WASTE, THOUGH...
YOU'RE SO PRETTY, MEG...IF YOU BEHAVED, YOU'D GET EVEN A GIRL'S HEART THROBBING. EVEN I'D...
HEH HEH...
YOU REALLY THINK SO?
'SA FACT. YOUR LOOKS, THAT WHITE SKIN...
...SUCH SILKY, STRAIGHT HAIR, BLUSHING PINK LIPS...
C'MON. ENOUGH, OKAY? HA HA...
PLEASE...
...YOU'RE JUST SAYING THAT 'CUZ IT'S TRUE.
LOOK, YOU NEED TO KEEP A LOW PROFILE AT OUR NEW SCHOOL.
THE GUYS'LL, LIKE, DROOL OVER YOU THERE.

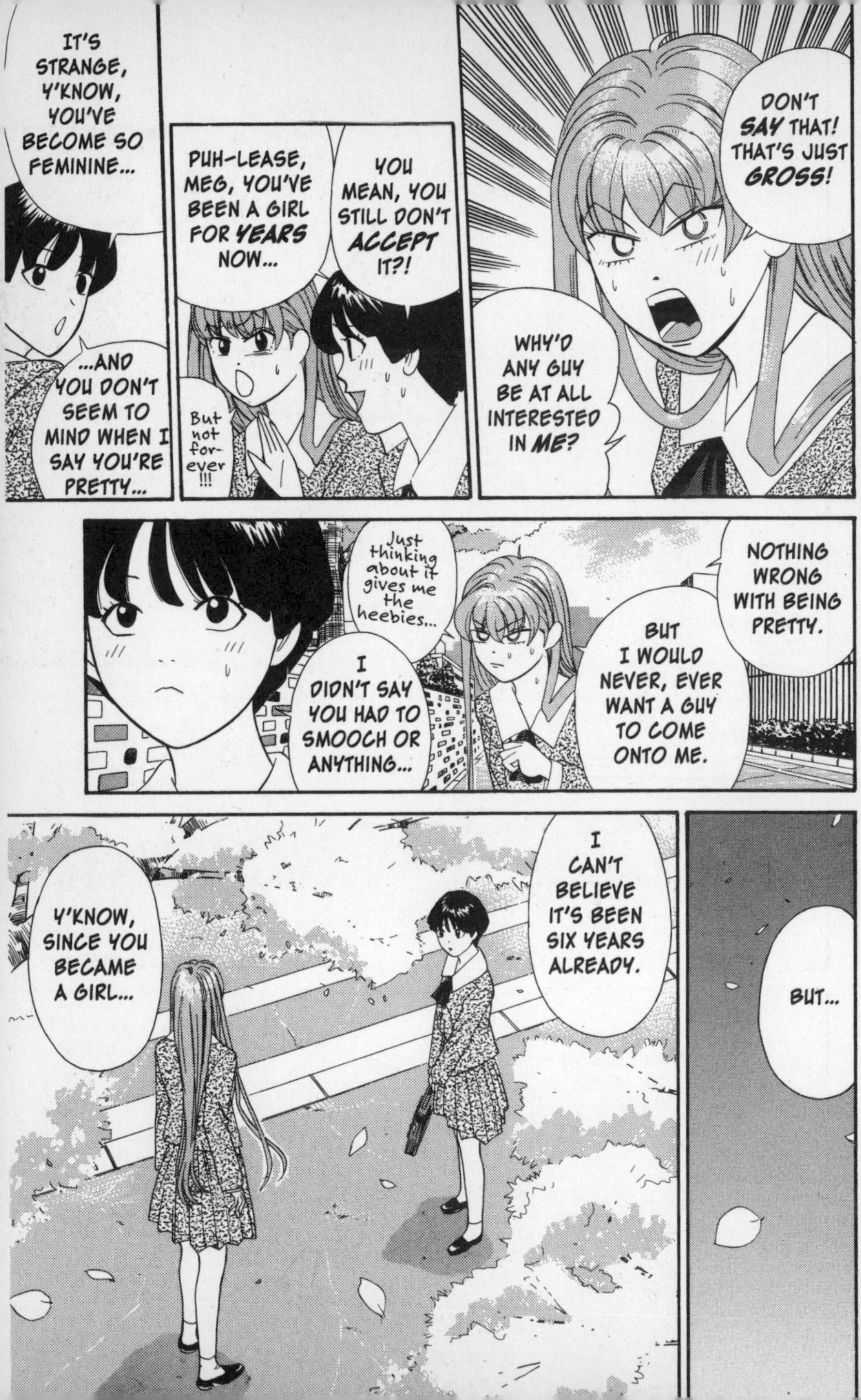
DON'T SAY THAT! THAT'S JUST GROSS!
WHY'D ANY GUY BE AT ALL INTERESTED IN ME?
YOU MEAN, YOU STILL DON'T ACCEPT IT?!
PUH-LEASE, MEG, YOU'VE BEEN A GIRL FOR YEARS NOW...
But not for-ever!!!
IT'S STRANGE, Y'KNOW, YOU'VE BECOME SO FEMININE...
...AND YOU DON'T SEEM TO MIND WHEN I SAY YOU'RE PRETTY...
NOTHING WRONG WITH BEING PRETTY.
BUT I WOULD NEVER, EVER WANT A GUY TO COME ONTO ME.
Just thinking about it gives me the heebies...
I DIDN'T SAY YOU HAD TO SMOOCH OR ANYTHING...
BUT...
I CAN'T BELIEVE IT'S BEEN SIX YEARS ALREADY.
Y'KNOW, SINCE YOU BECAME A GIRL...

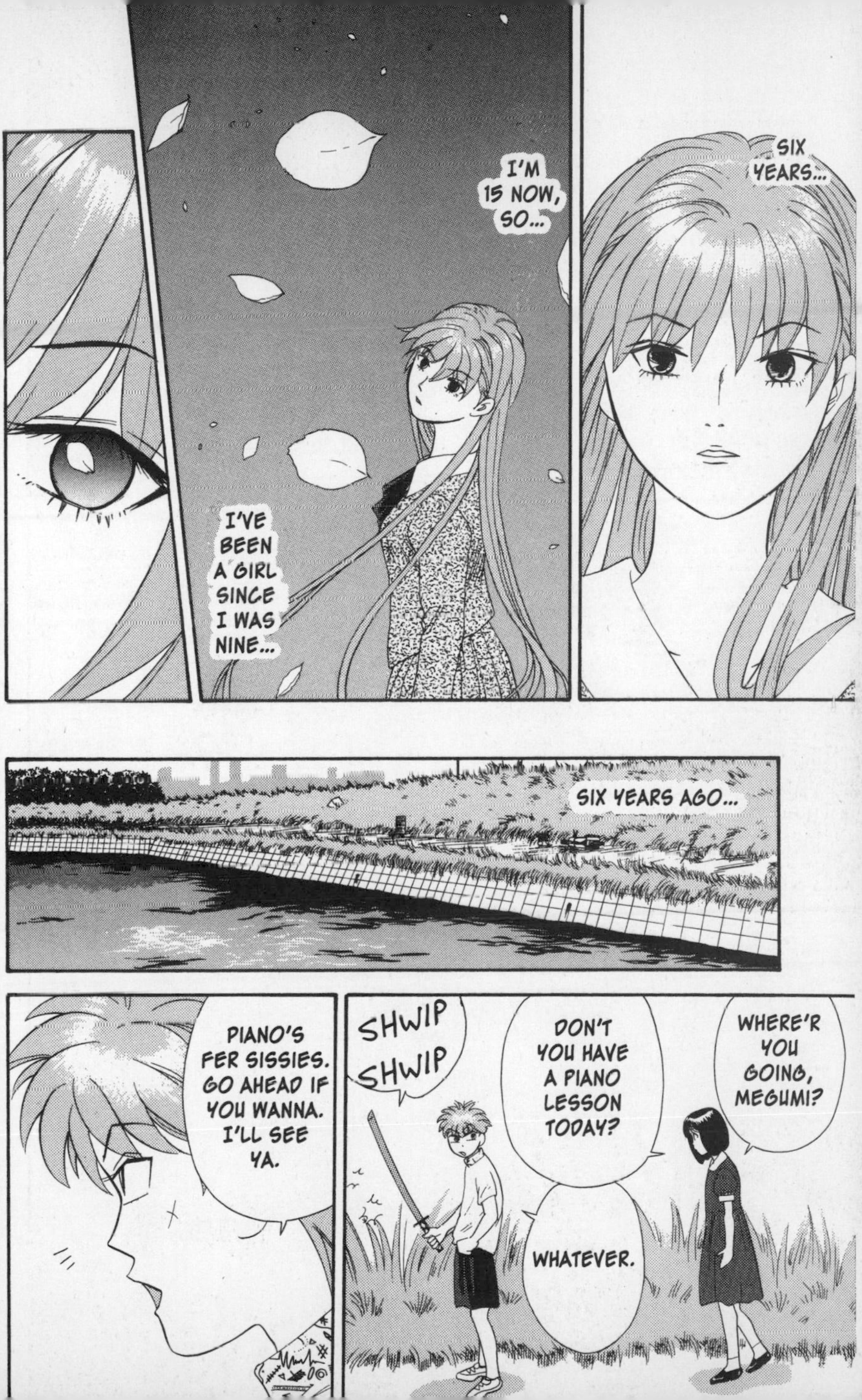
SIX YEARS...
I'M 15 NOW, SO...
I'VE BEEN A GIRL SINCE I WAS NINE...
SIX YEARS AGO...
WHERE'R YOU GOING, MEGUMI?
DON'T YOU HAVE A PIANO LESSON TODAY?
SHWIP SHWIP
WHATEVER.
PIANO'S FER SISSIES. GO AHEAD IF YOU WANNA. I'LL SEE YA.

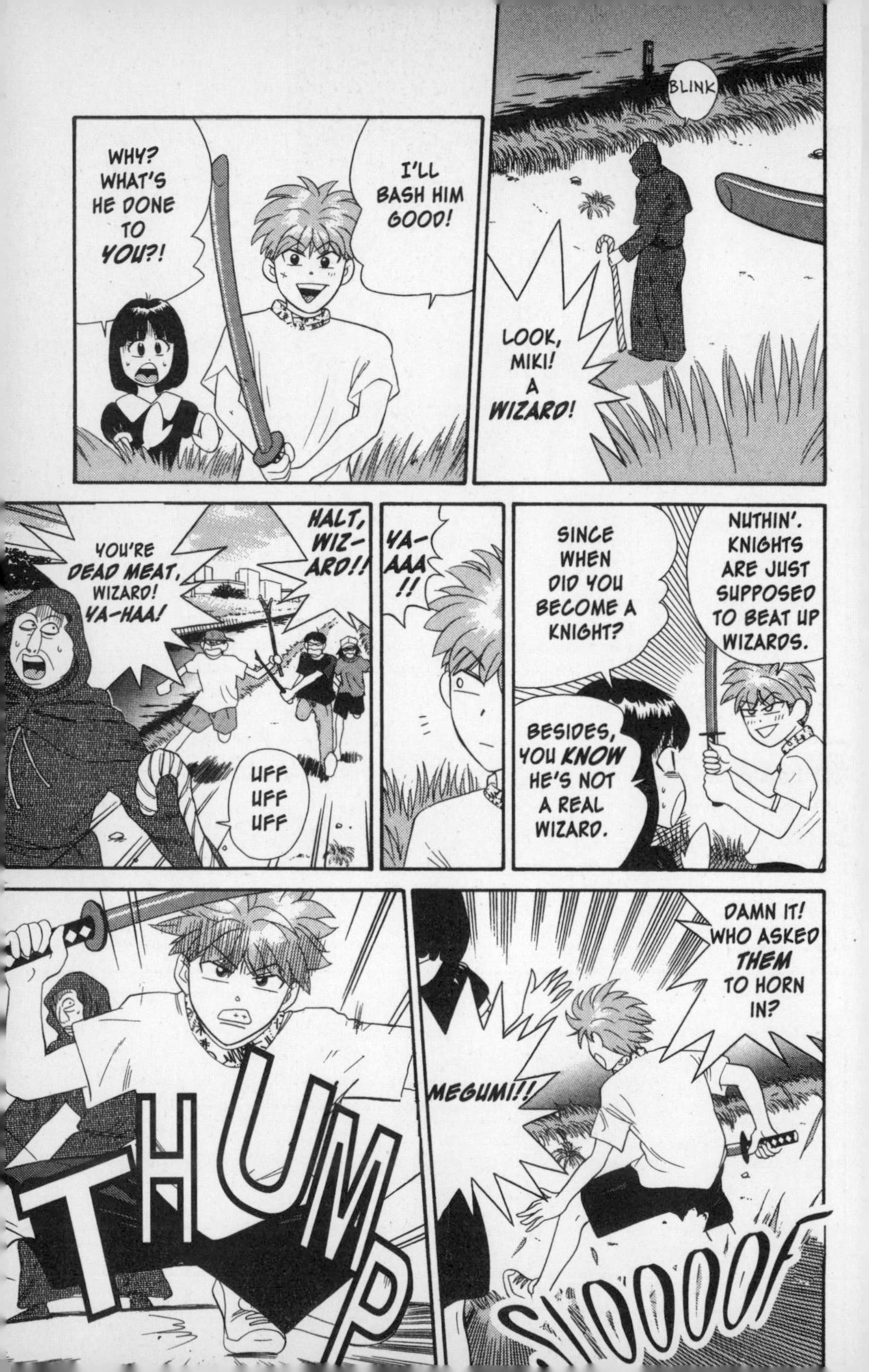
BLINK
LOOK, MIKI! A WIZARD!
I'LL BASH HIM GOOD!
WHY? WHAT'S HE DONE TO YOU?!
SINCE WHEN DID YOU BECOME A KNIGHT?
NUTHIN'. KNIGHTS ARE JUST SUPPOSED TO BEAT UP WIZARDS.
BESIDES, YOU KNOW HE'S NOT A REAL WIZARD.
YA-AAA!!
HALT, WIZ-ARD!!
YOU'RE DEAD MEAT, WIZARD! YA-HAA!
UFF UFF UFF
DAMN IT! WHO ASKED THEM TO HORN IN?
MEGUMI!!
SHOOOOF
THUMP

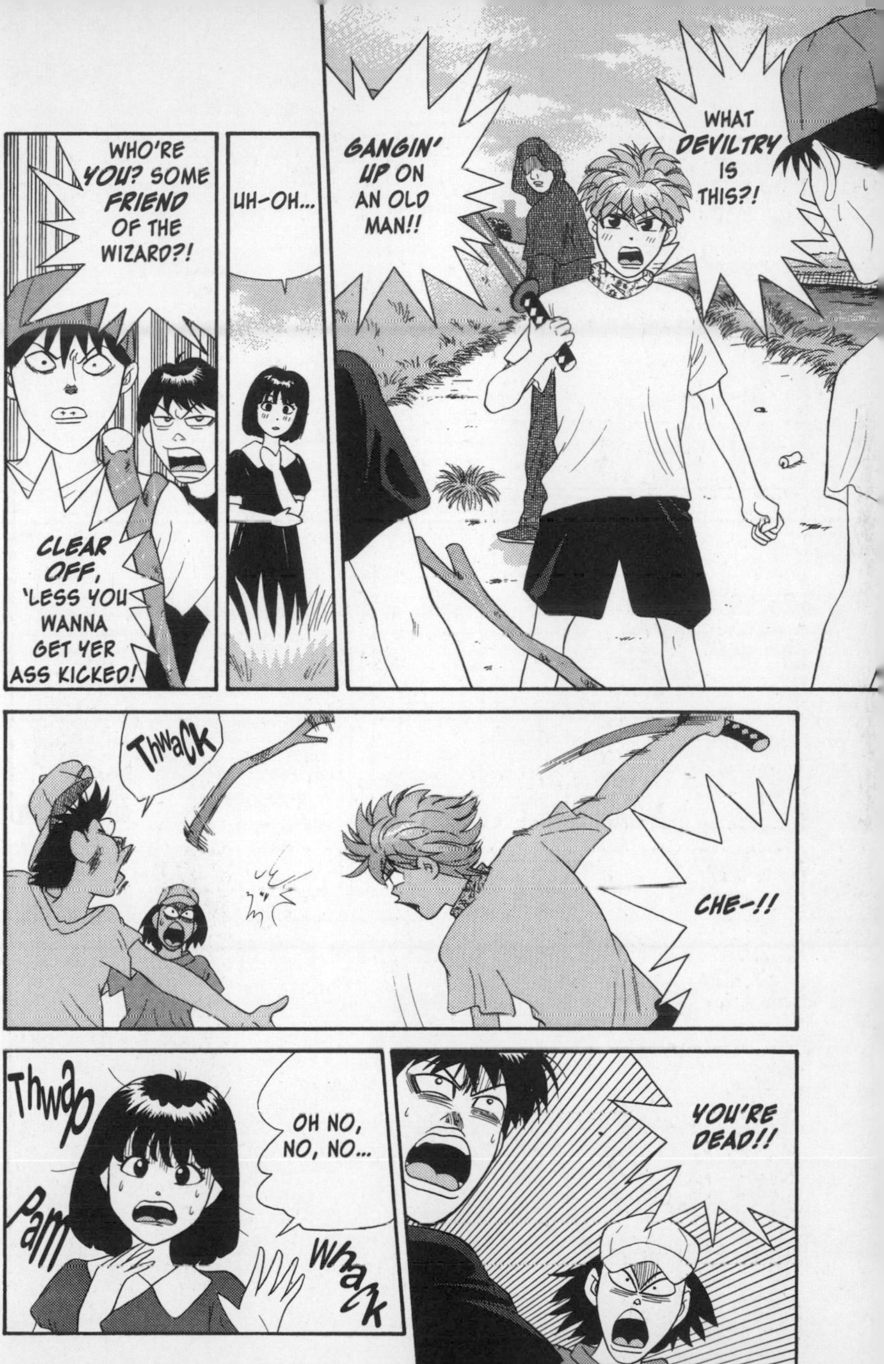
WHAT DEVILTRY IS THIS?!
GANGIN' UP ON AN OLD MAN!!
UH-OH...
WHO'RE YOU? SOME FRIEND OF THE WIZARD?!
CLEAR OFF, 'LESS YOU WANNA GET YER ASS KICKED!
CHE-!!
Thwack
YOU'RE DEAD!!
OH NO, NO, NO...
Thwap
Pam
Whack

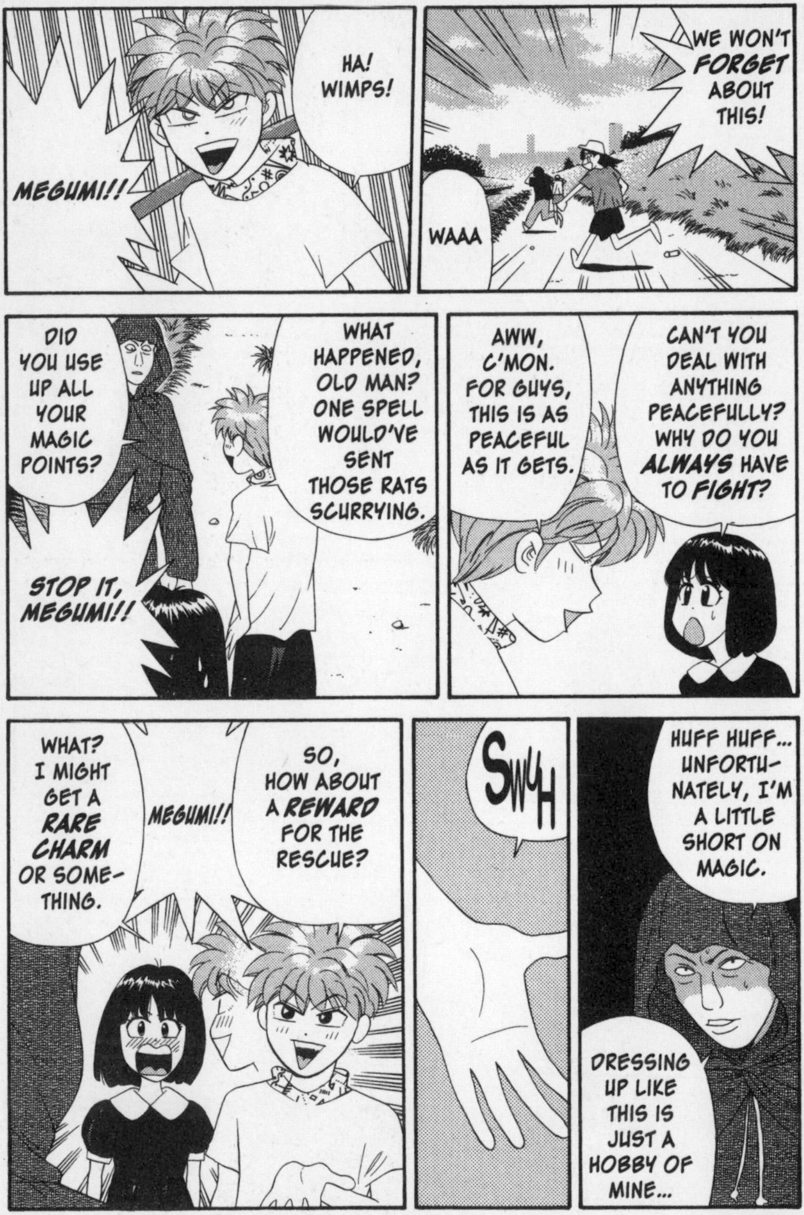
WE WON'T FORGET ABOUT THIS!
WAAA
HA! WIMPS!
MEGUMI!!
CAN'T YOU DEAL WITH ANYTHING PEACEFULLY? WHY DO YOU ALWAYS HAVE TO FIGHT?
AWW, C'MON. FOR GUYS, THIS IS AS PEACEFUL AS IT GETS.
WHAT HAPPENED, OLD MAN? ONE SPELL WOULD'VE SENT THOSE RATS SCURRYING.
DID YOU USE UP ALL YOUR MAGIC POINTS?
STOP IT, MEGUMI!!
HUFF HUFF... UNFORTU-NATELY, I'M A LITTLE SHORT ON MAGIC.
DRESSING UP LIKE THIS IS JUST A HOBBY OF MINE...
SWUH
SO, HOW ABOUT A REWARD FOR THE RESCUE?
MEGUMI!!
WHAT? I MIGHT GET A RARE CHARM OR SOME-THING.

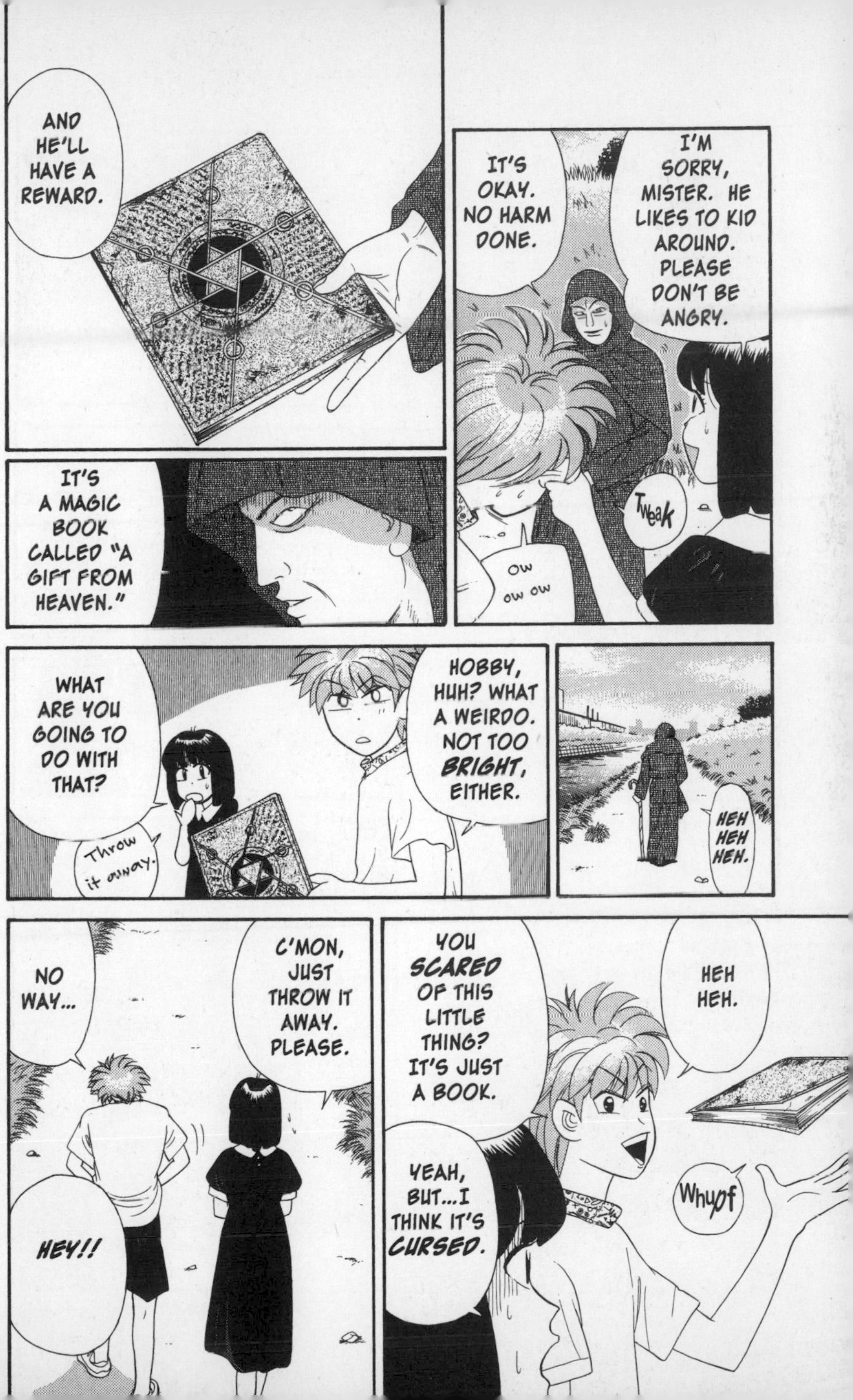
I'M SORRY, MISTER. HE LIKES TO KID AROUND. PLEASE DON'T BE ANGRY.
IT'S OKAY. NO HARM DONE.
Tweak
OW OW OW
AND HE'LL HAVE A REWARD.
IT'S A MAGIC BOOK CALLED "A GIFT FROM HEAVEN."
HEH HEH HEH.
HOBBY, HUH? WHAT A WEIRDO. NOT TOO BRIGHT, EITHER.
WHAT ARE YOU GOING TO DO WITH THAT?
Throw it away.
HEH HEH.
YOU SCARED OF THIS LITTLE THING? IT'S JUST A BOOK.
Whupf
YEAH, BUT...I THINK IT'S CURSED.
C'MON, JUST THROW IT AWAY. PLEASE.
NO WAY...
HEY!!

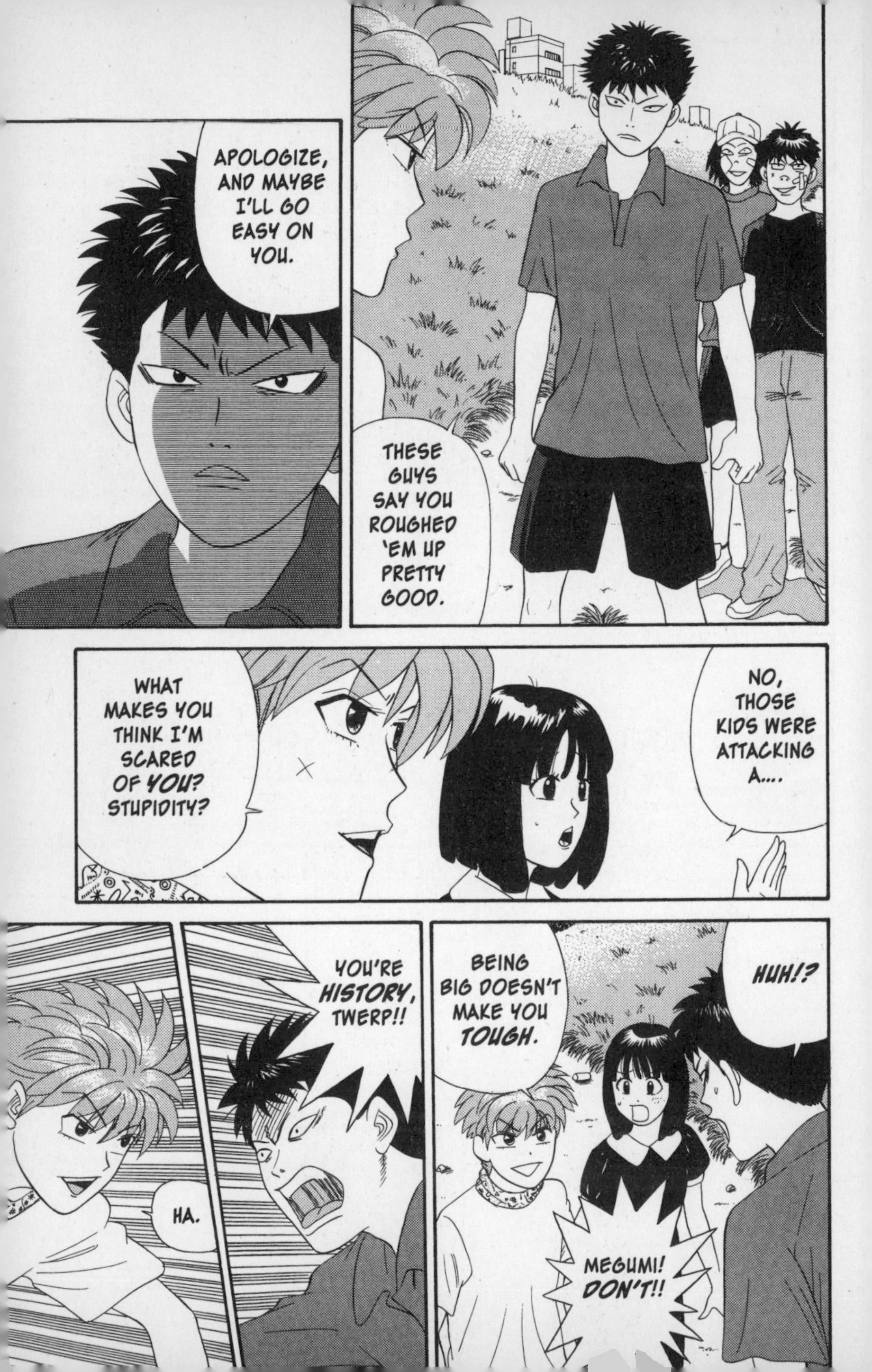
THESE GUYS SAY YOU ROUGHED 'EM UP PRETTY GOOD.
APOLOGIZE, AND MAYBE I'LL GO EASY ON YOU.
NO, THOSE KIDS WERE ATTACKING A....
WHAT MAKES YOU THINK I'M SCARED OF *YOU*? STUPIDITY?
HUH!?
BEING BIG DOESN'T MAKE YOU *TOUGH*.
MEGUMI! *DON'T!!*
YOU'RE *HISTORY*, TWERP!!
HA.

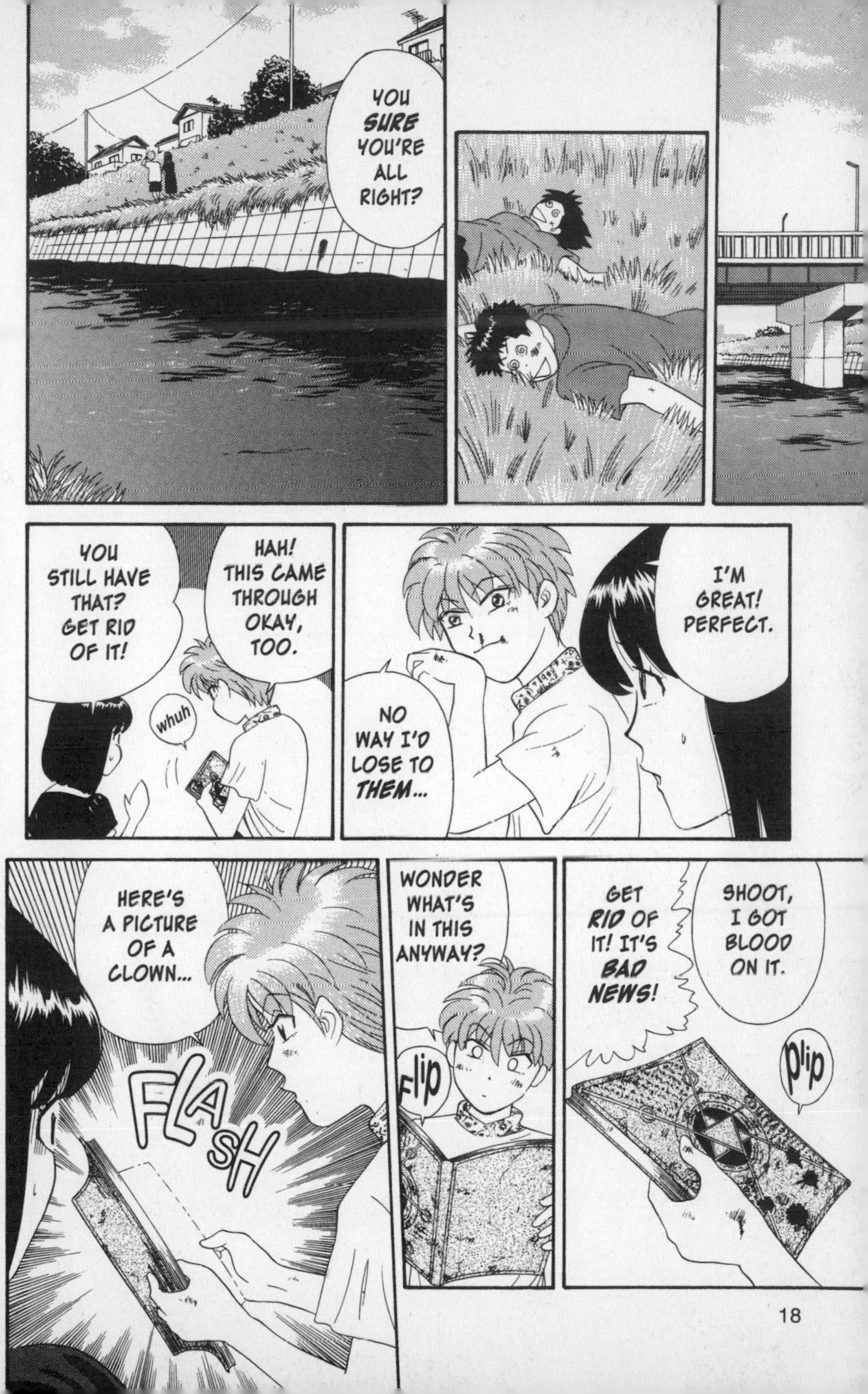
YOU SURE YOU'RE ALL RIGHT?
I'M GREAT! PERFECT.
NO WAY I'D LOSE TO THEM...
HAH! THIS CAME THROUGH OKAY, TOO.
YOU STILL HAVE THAT? GET RID OF IT!
whuh
SHOOT, I GOT BLOOD ON IT.
GET RID OF IT! IT'S BAD NEWS!
plip
WONDER WHAT'S IN THIS ANYWAY?
Flip
HERE'S A PICTURE OF A CLOWN...
FLASH

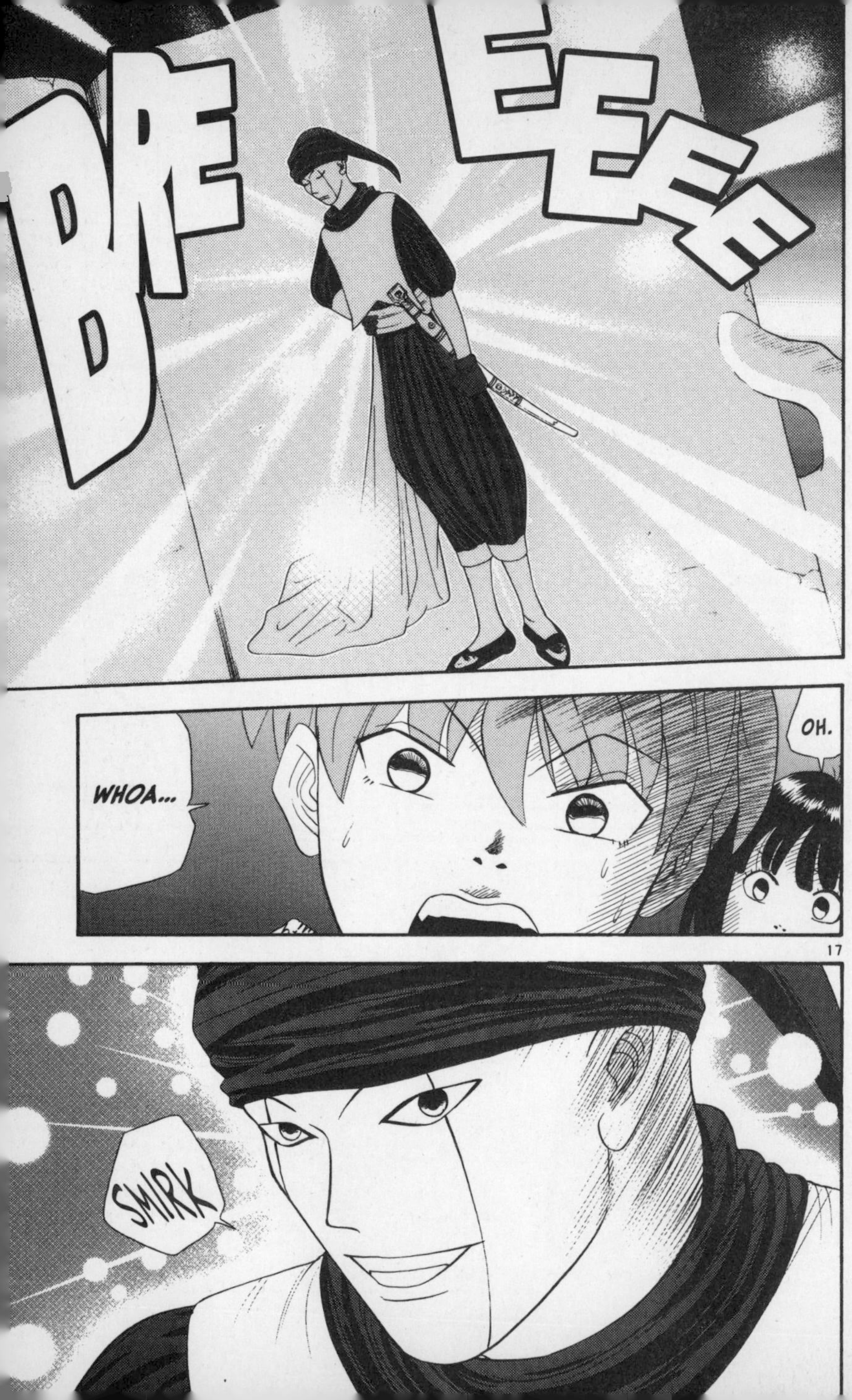
BRE
EEEE
OH.
WHOA...
SMIRK

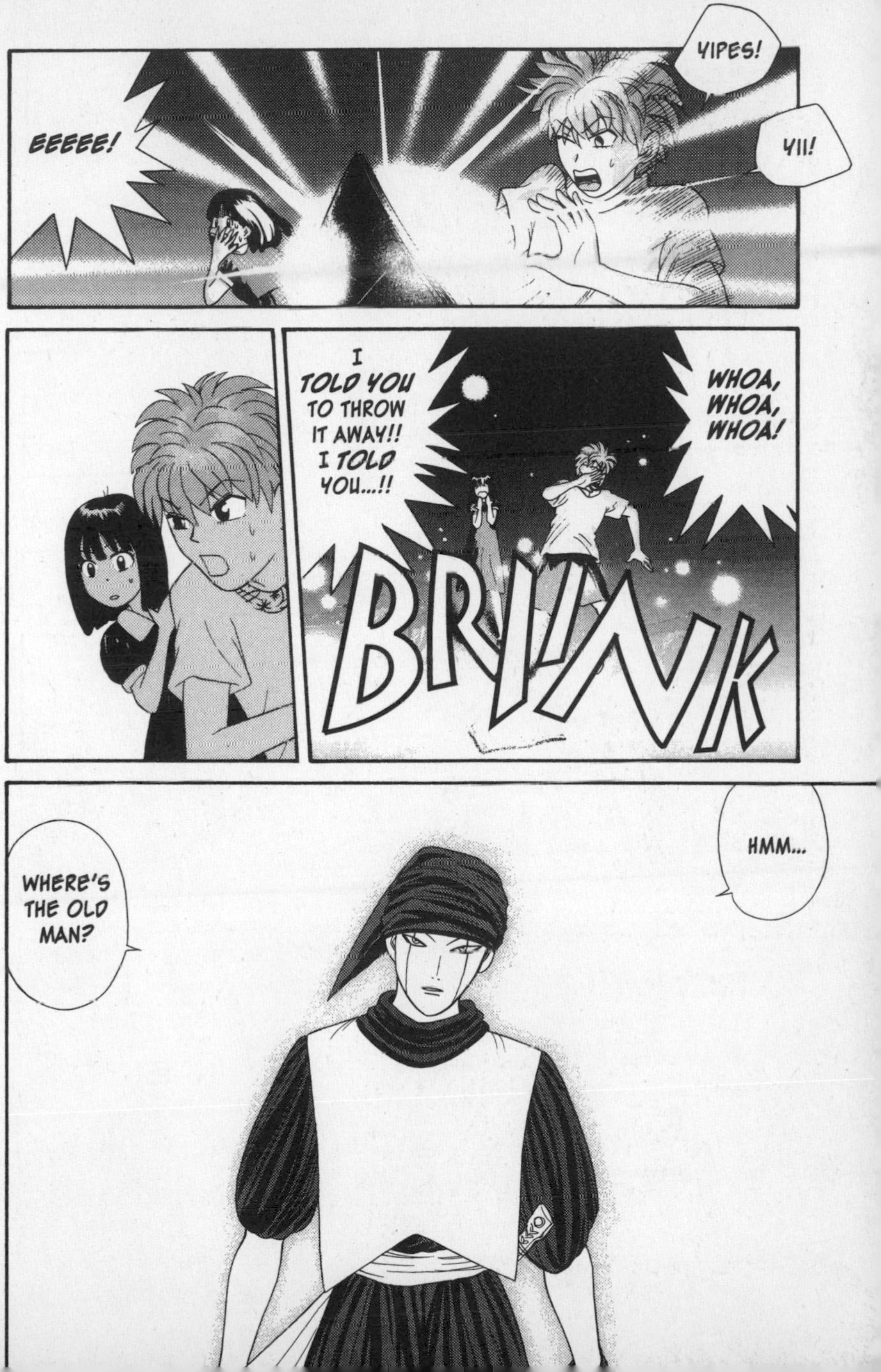
YIPES!
YII!
EEEEE!
WHOA, WHOA, WHOA!
I TOLD YOU TO THROW IT AWAY!! I TOLD YOU...!!
BRIIINK
HMM...
WHERE'S THE OLD MAN?

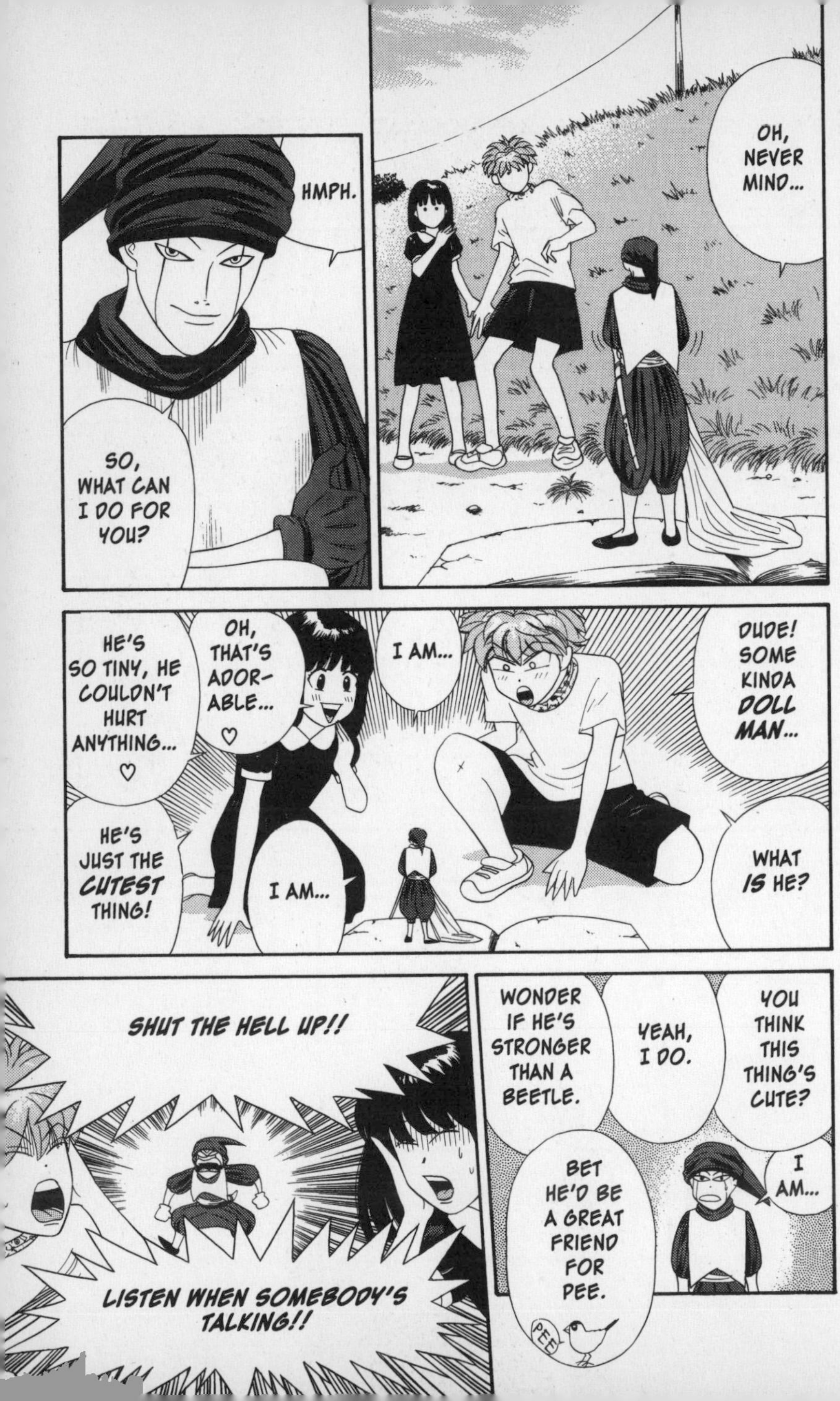
OH, NEVER MIND...
HMPH.
SO, WHAT CAN I DO FOR YOU?
DUDE! SOME KINDA DOLL MAN...
WHAT IS HE?
I AM...
OH, THAT'S ADOR-ABLE... ♡
HE'S SO TINY, HE COULDN'T HURT ANYTHING... ♡
I AM...
HE'S JUST THE CUTEST THING!
YOU THINK THIS THING'S CUTE?
YEAH, I DO.
WONDER IF HE'S STRONGER THAN A BEETLE.
I AM...
BET HE'D BE A GREAT FRIEND FOR PEE.
PEE
SHUT THE HELL UP!!
LISTEN WHEN SOMEBODY'S TALKING!!

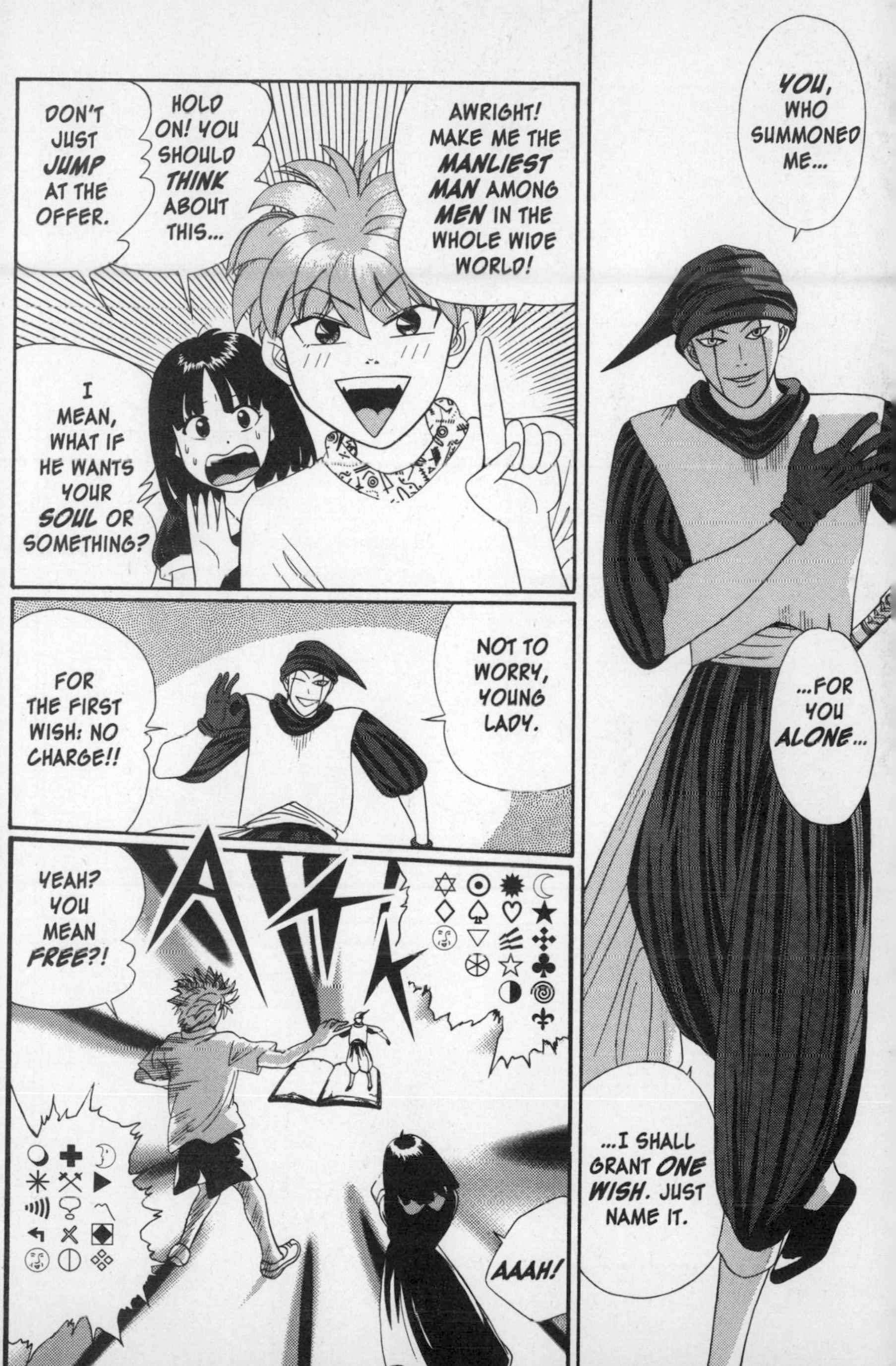
YOU, WHO SUMMONED ME...
...FOR YOU ALONE...
...I SHALL GRANT ONE WISH. JUST NAME IT.
AWRIGHT! MAKE ME THE MANLIEST MAN AMONG MEN IN THE WHOLE WIDE WORLD!
HOLD ON! YOU SHOULD THINK ABOUT THIS...
DON'T JUST JUMP AT THE OFFER.
I MEAN, WHAT IF HE WANTS YOUR SOUL OR SOMETHING?
NOT TO WORRY, YOUNG LADY.
FOR THE FIRST WISH: NO CHARGE!!
YEAH? YOU MEAN FREE?!
AAAH!

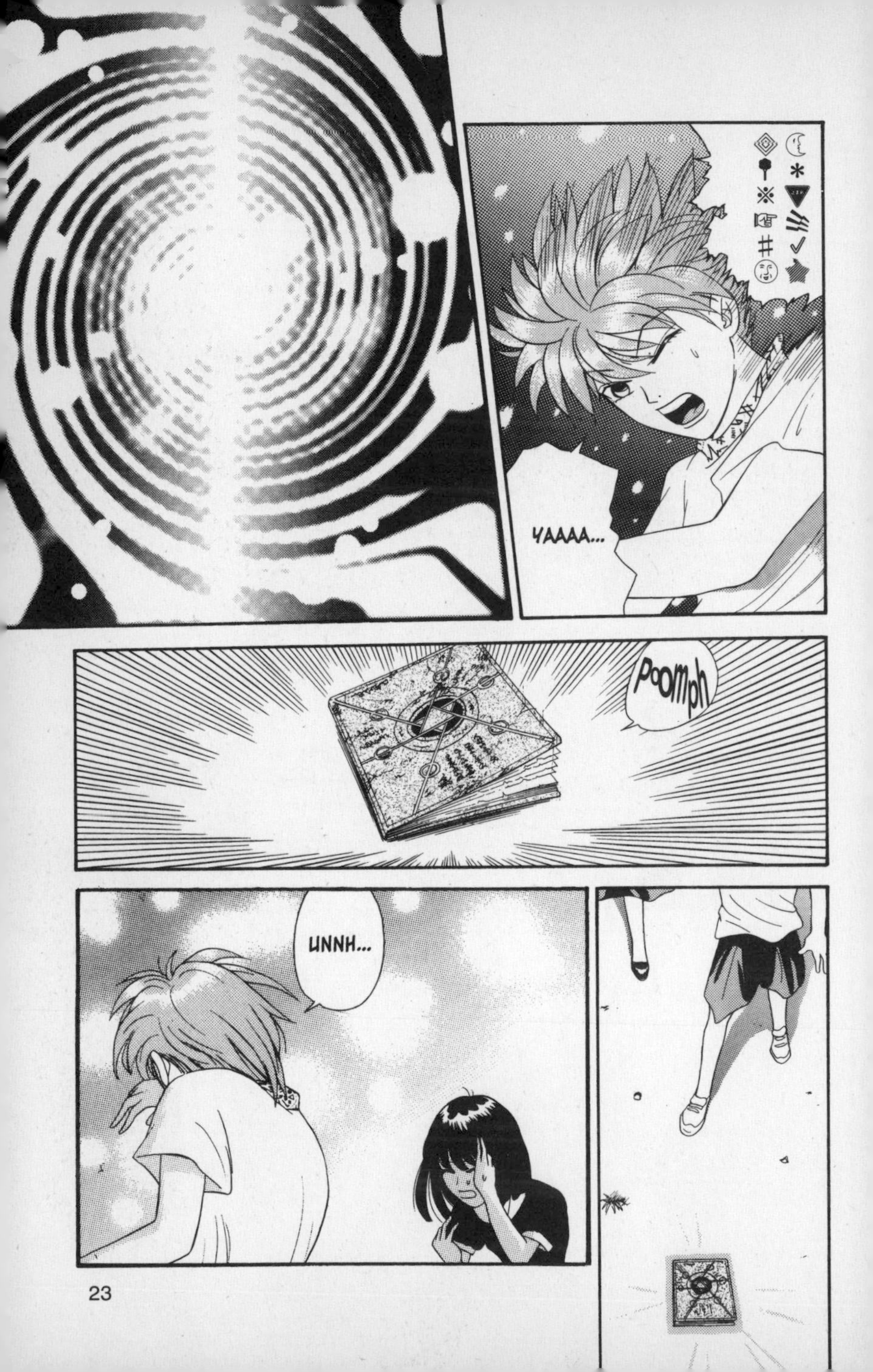
YAAAA...
Poomph
UNNH...

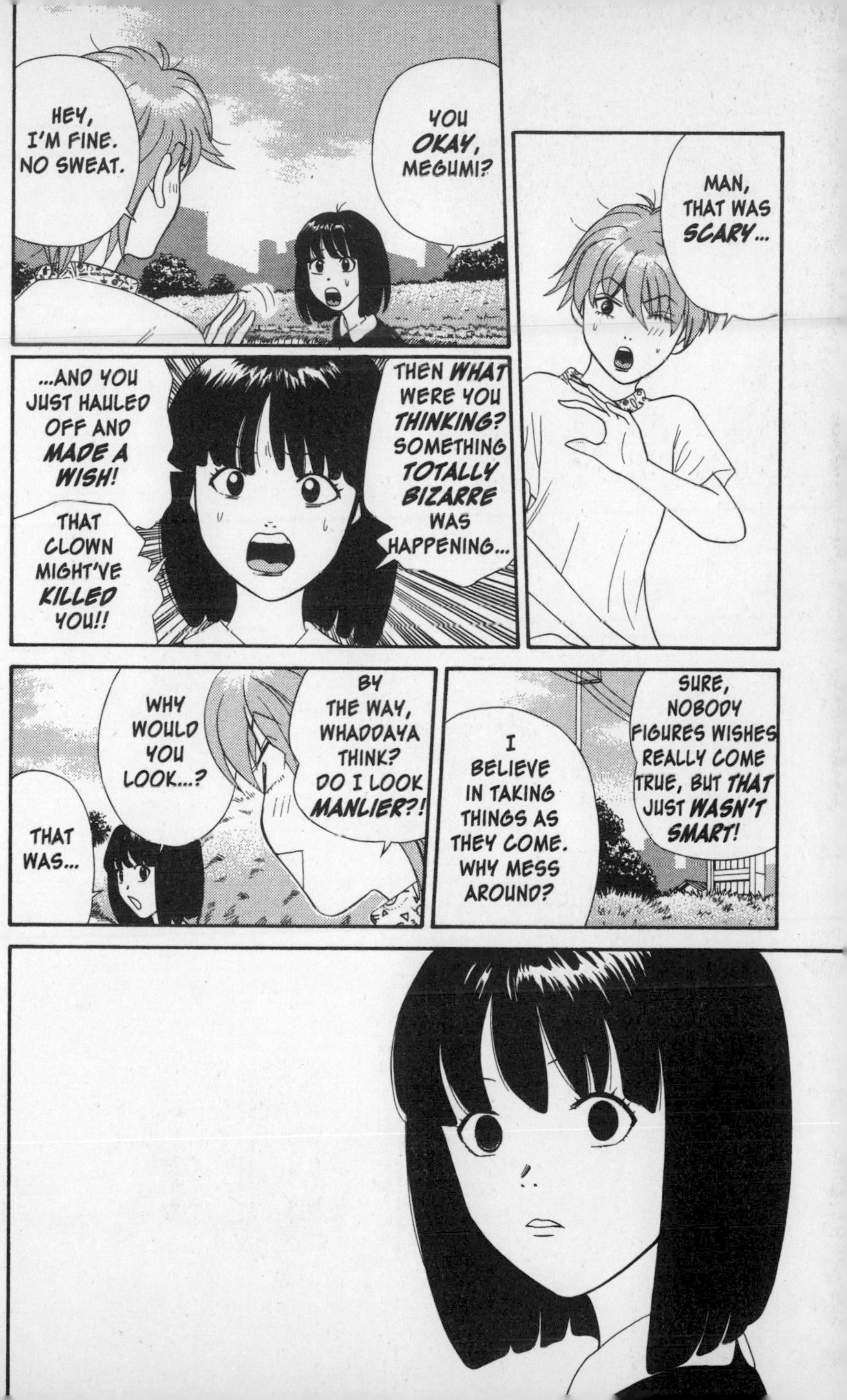
MAN, THAT WAS SCARY...
YOU OKAY, MEGUMI?
HEY, I'M FINE. NO SWEAT.
THEN WHAT WERE YOU THINKING? SOMETHING TOTALLY BIZARRE WAS HAPPENING...
...AND YOU JUST HAULED OFF AND MADE A WISH!
THAT CLOWN MIGHT'VE KILLED YOU!!
SURE, NOBODY FIGURES WISHES REALLY COME TRUE, BUT THAT JUST WASN'T SMART!
I BELIEVE IN TAKING THINGS AS THEY COME. WHY MESS AROUND?
BY THE WAY, WHADDAYA THINK? DO I LOOK MANLIER?!
WHY WOULD YOU LOOK...?
THAT WAS...

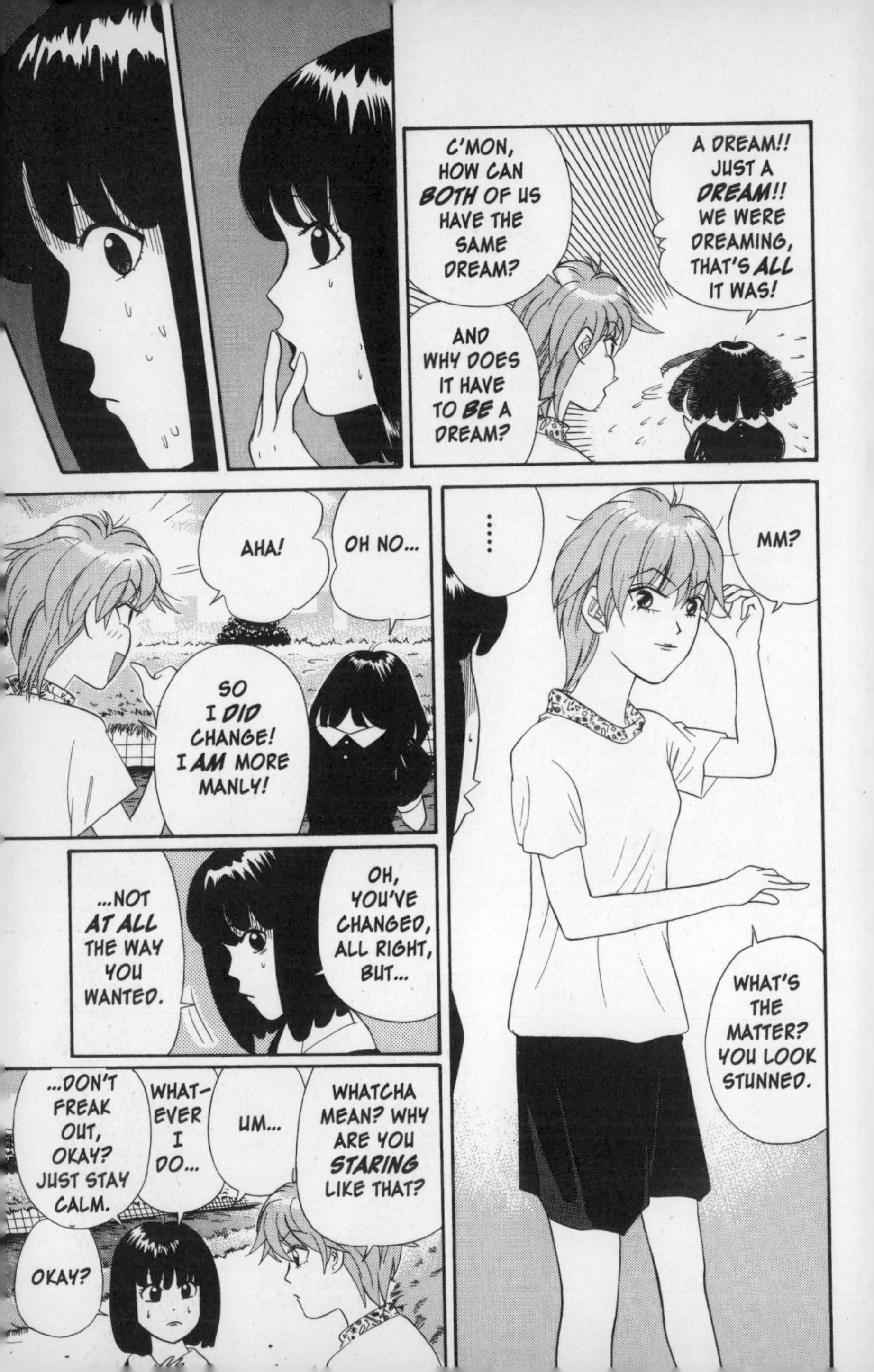
A DREAM!! JUST A DREAM!! WE WERE DREAMING, THAT'S ALL IT WAS!
C'MON, HOW CAN BOTH OF US HAVE THE SAME DREAM?
AND WHY DOES IT HAVE TO BE A DREAM?
MM?
......
WHAT'S THE MATTER? YOU LOOK STUNNED.
OH NO...
AHA!
SO I DID CHANGE! I AM MORE MANLY!
OH, YOU'VE CHANGED, ALL RIGHT, BUT...
...NOT AT ALL THE WAY YOU WANTED.
WHATCHA MEAN? WHY ARE YOU STARING LIKE THAT?
UM...
WHAT-EVER I DO...
...DON'T FREAK OUT, OKAY? JUST STAY CALM.
OKAY?

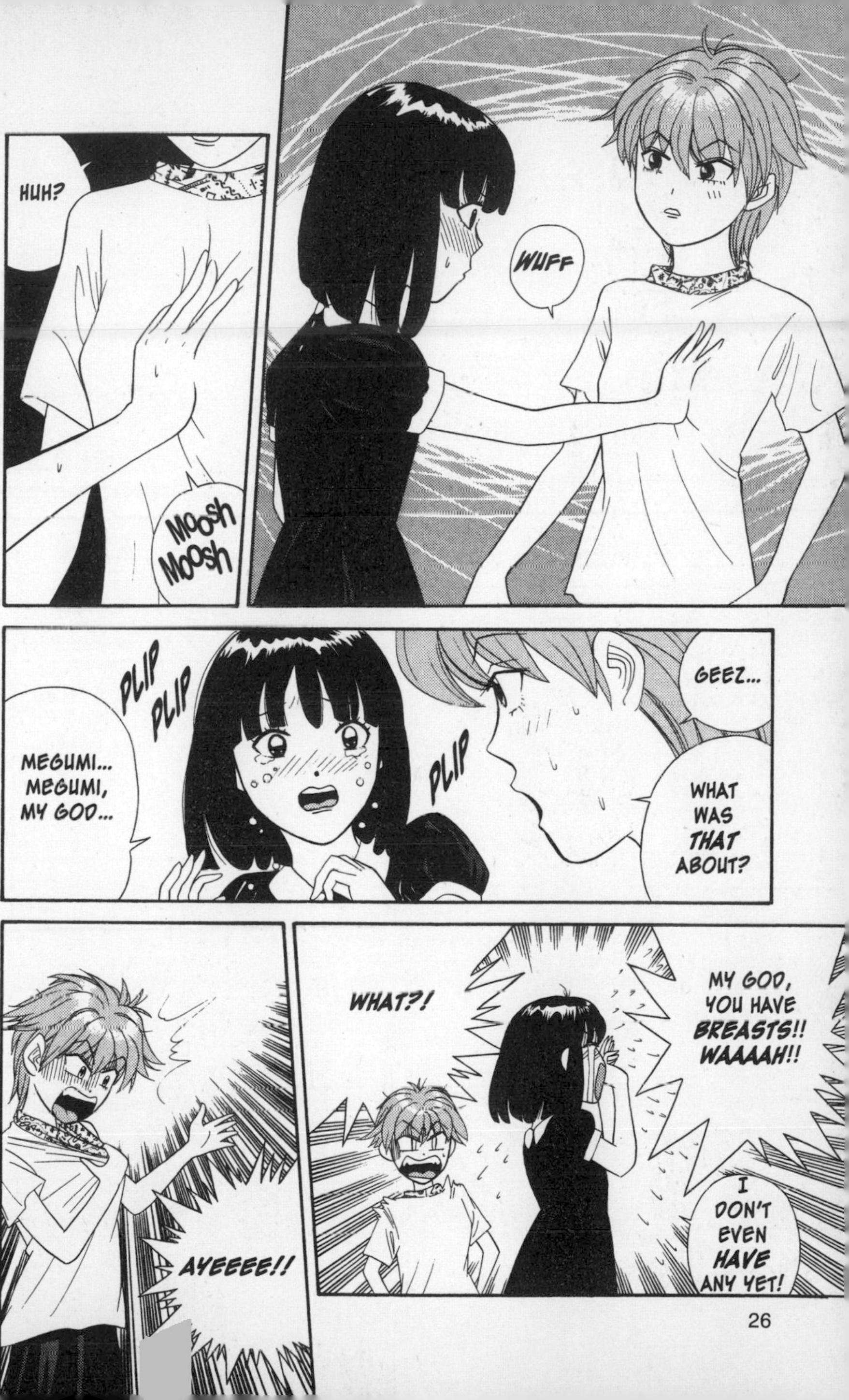
WUFF
HUH?
Moosh Moosh
GEEZ...
WHAT WAS THAT ABOUT?
PLIP
PLIP PLIP
MEGUMI... MEGUMI, MY GOD...
MY GOD, YOU HAVE BREASTS!! WAAAAH!!
WHAT?!
I DON'T EVEN HAVE ANY YET!
AYEEEE!!

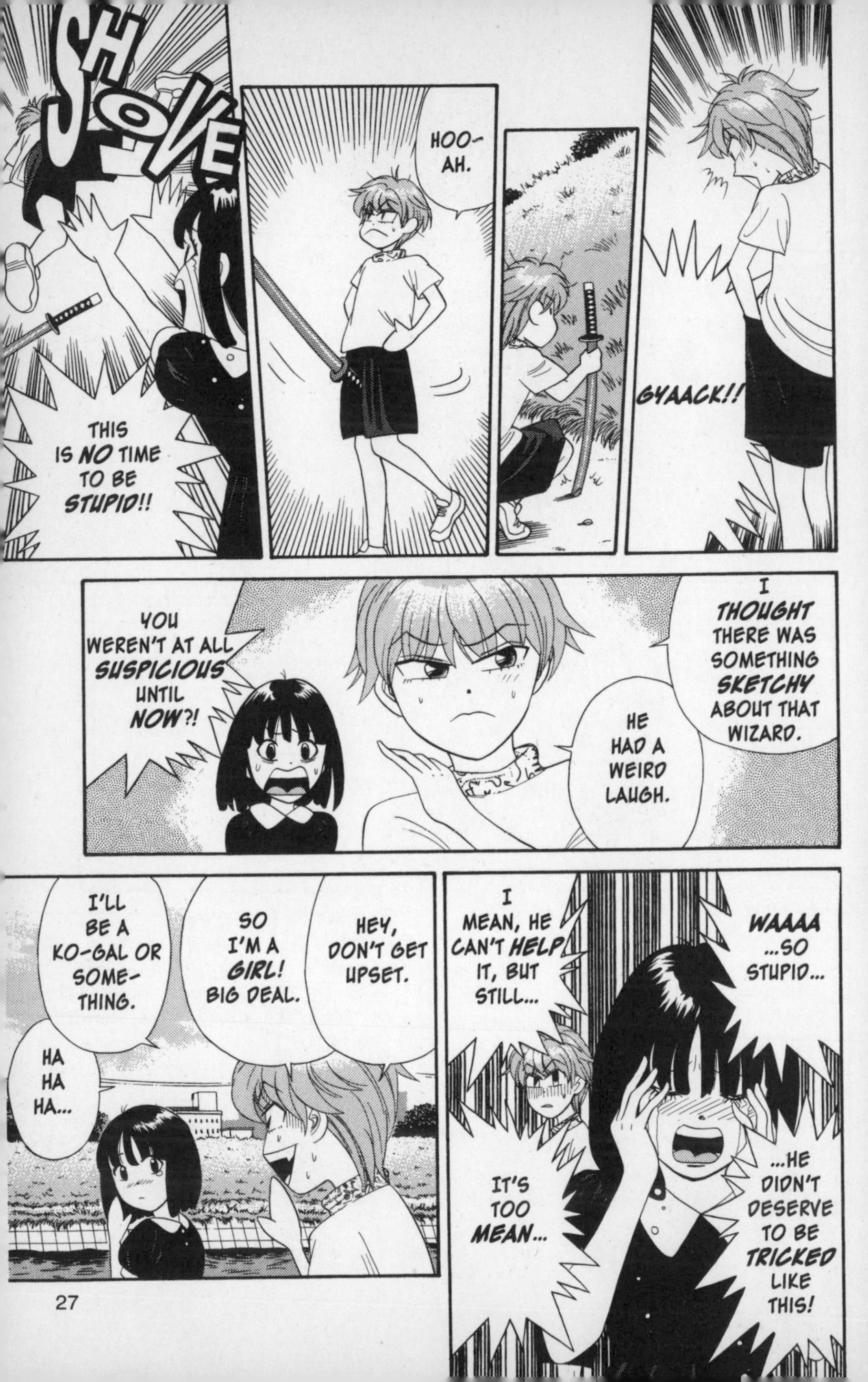
GYAACK!!
HOO-AH.
SHOVE
THIS IS NO TIME TO BE STUPID!!
I THOUGHT THERE WAS SOMETHING SKETCHY ABOUT THAT WIZARD.
HE HAD A WEIRD LAUGH.
YOU WEREN'T AT ALL SUSPICIOUS UNTIL NOW?!
WAAAA ...SO STUPID...
I MEAN, HE CAN'T HELP IT, BUT STILL...
...HE DIDN'T DESERVE TO BE TRICKED LIKE THIS!
IT'S TOO MEAN...
HEY, DON'T GET UPSET.
SO I'M A GIRL! BIG DEAL.
I'LL BE A KO-GAL OR SOME-THING.
HA HA HA...

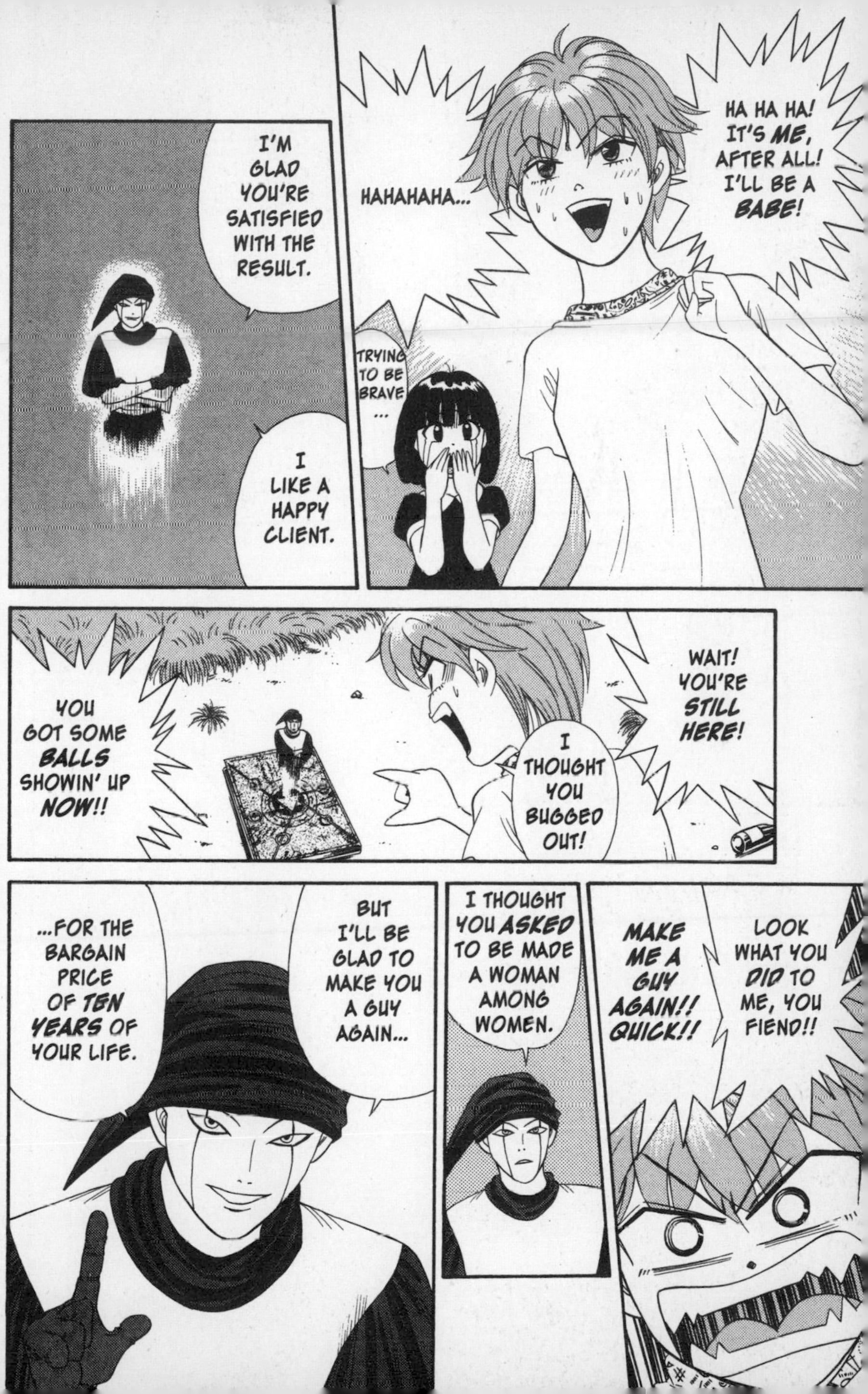
HA HA HA! IT'S ME, AFTER ALL! I'LL BE A BABE!
HAHAHAHA...
TRYING TO BE BRAVE ...
I'M GLAD YOU'RE SATISFIED WITH THE RESULT.
I LIKE A HAPPY CLIENT.
WAIT! YOU'RE STILL HERE!
I THOUGHT YOU BUGGED OUT!
YOU GOT SOME BALLS SHOWIN' UP NOW!!
LOOK WHAT YOU DID TO ME, YOU FIEND!!
MAKE ME A GUY AGAIN!! QUICK!!
I THOUGHT YOU ASKED TO BE MADE A WOMAN AMONG WOMEN.
BUT I'LL BE GLAD TO MAKE YOU A GUY AGAIN...
...FOR THE BARGAIN PRICE OF TEN YEARS OF YOUR LIFE.

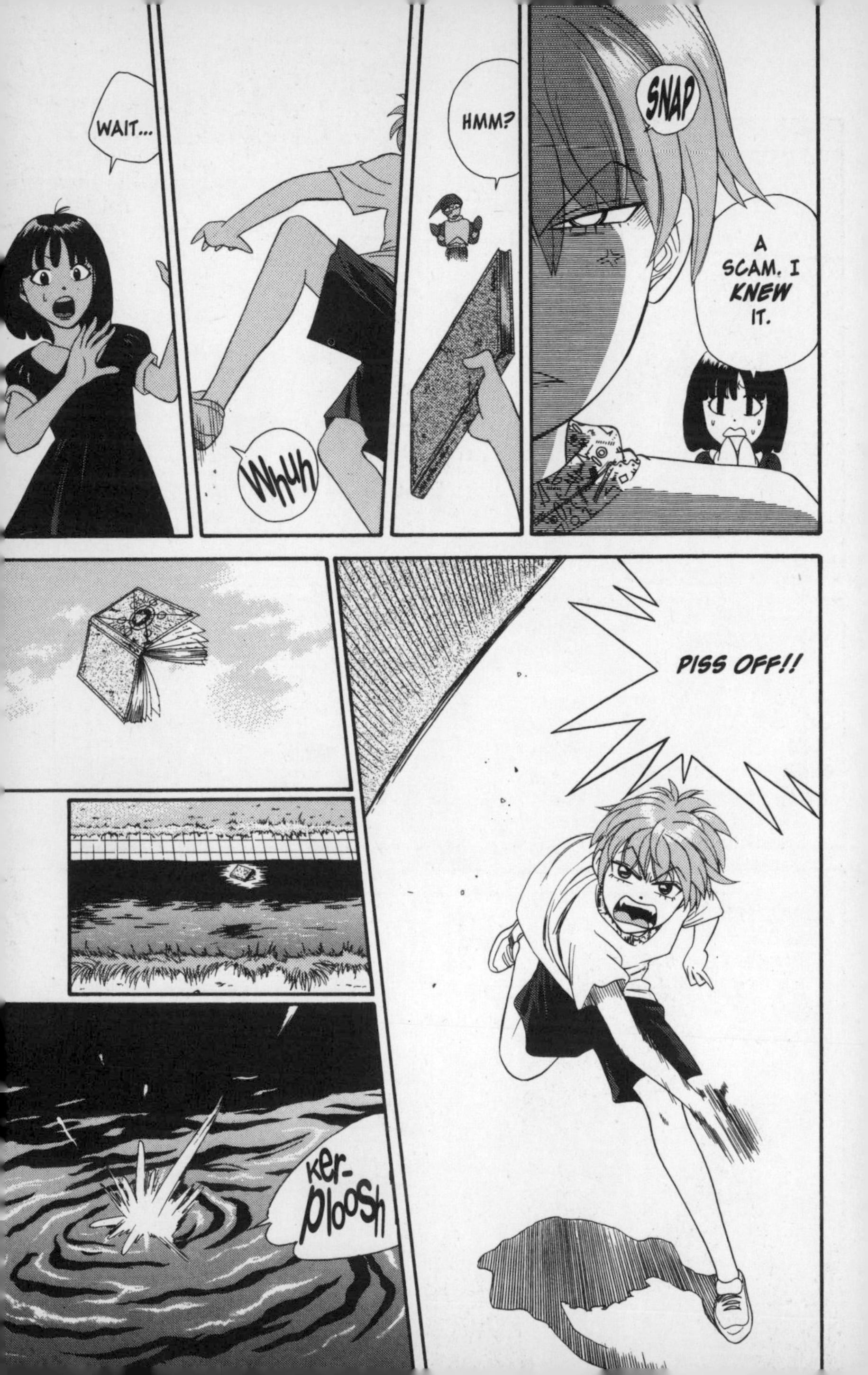
SNAP
A SCAM. I KNEW IT.
HMM?
Whuh
WAIT...
PISS OFF!!
ker-ploosh

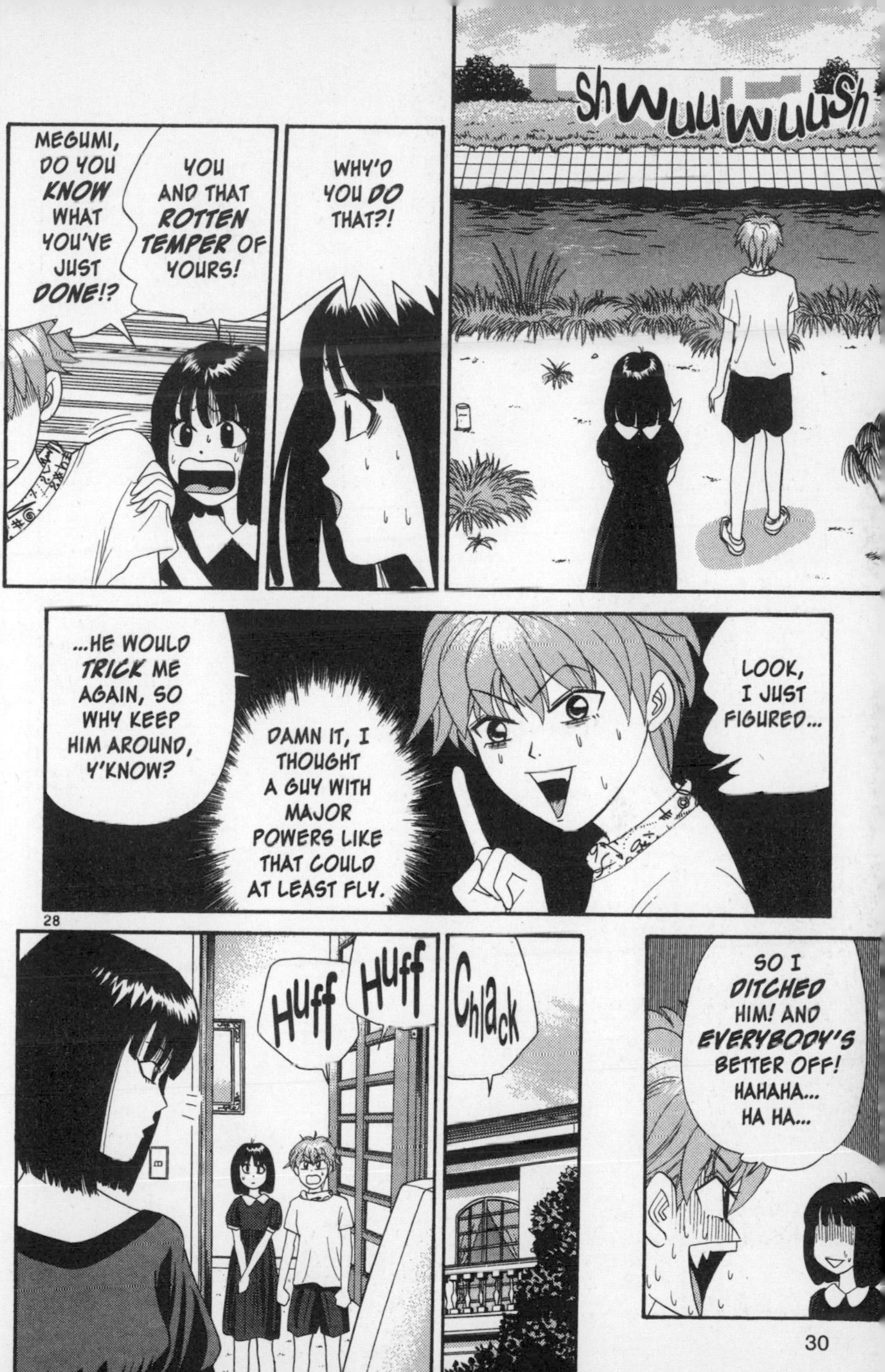
Shwuuwuush
WHY'D YOU DO THAT?!
YOU AND THAT ROTTEN TEMPER OF YOURS!
MEGUMI, DO YOU KNOW WHAT YOU'VE JUST DONE!?
LOOK, I JUST FIGURED...
DAMN IT, I THOUGHT A GUY WITH MAJOR POWERS LIKE THAT COULD AT LEAST FLY.
...HE WOULD TRICK ME AGAIN, SO WHY KEEP HIM AROUND, Y'KNOW?
SO I DITCHED HIM! AND EVERYBODY'S BETTER OFF! HAHAHA... HA HA...
Chlack
Huff
Huff

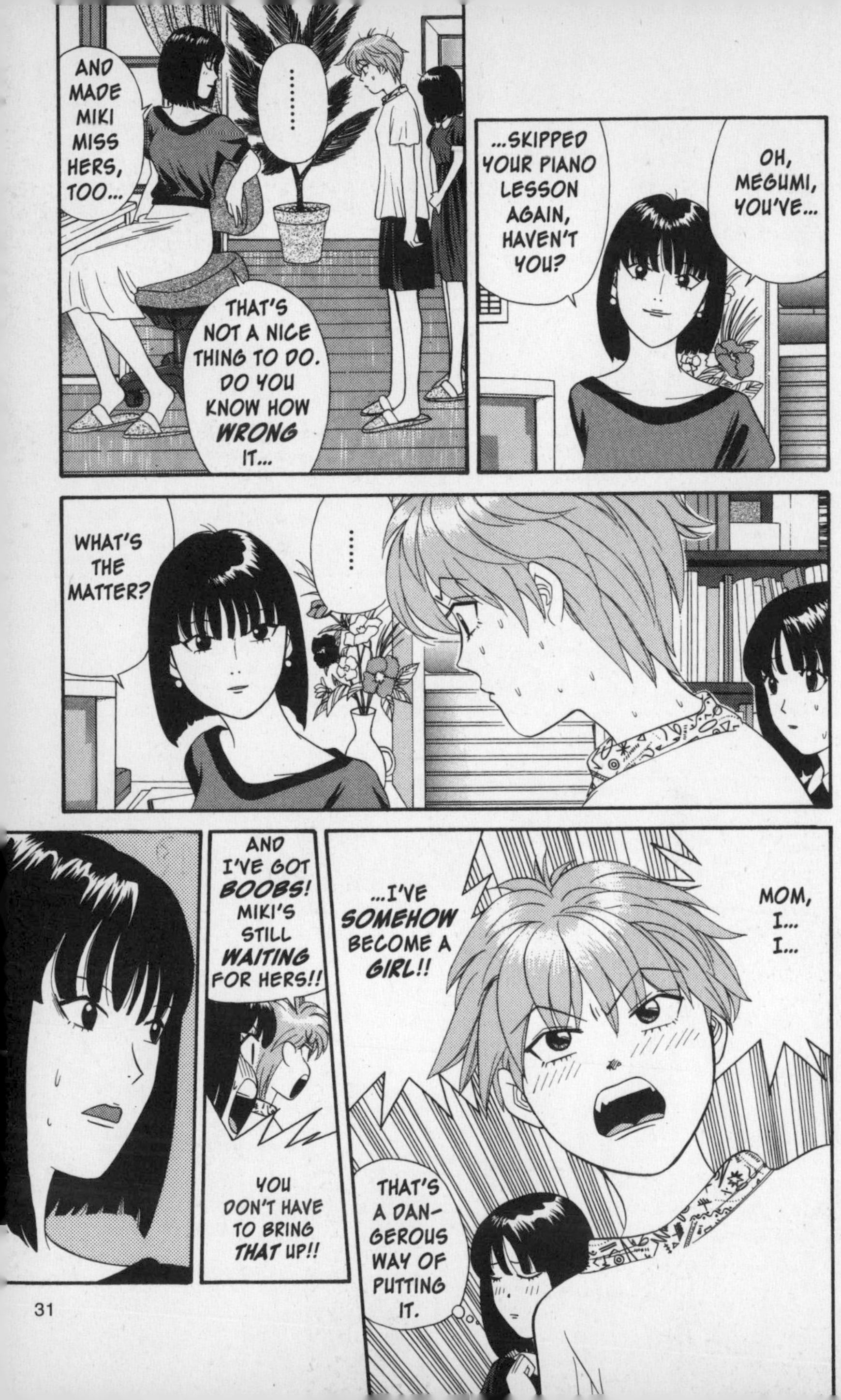
OH, MEGUMI, YOU'VE...
...SKIPPED YOUR PIANO LESSON AGAIN, HAVEN'T YOU?
......
AND MADE MIKI MISS HERS, TOO...
THAT'S NOT A NICE THING TO DO. DO YOU KNOW HOW WRONG IT...
......
WHAT'S THE MATTER?
MOM, I... I...
...I'VE SOMEHOW BECOME A GIRL!!
THAT'S A DAN-GEROUS WAY OF PUTTING IT.
AND I'VE GOT BOOBS! MIKI'S STILL WAITING FOR HERS!!
YOU DON'T HAVE TO BRING THAT UP!!

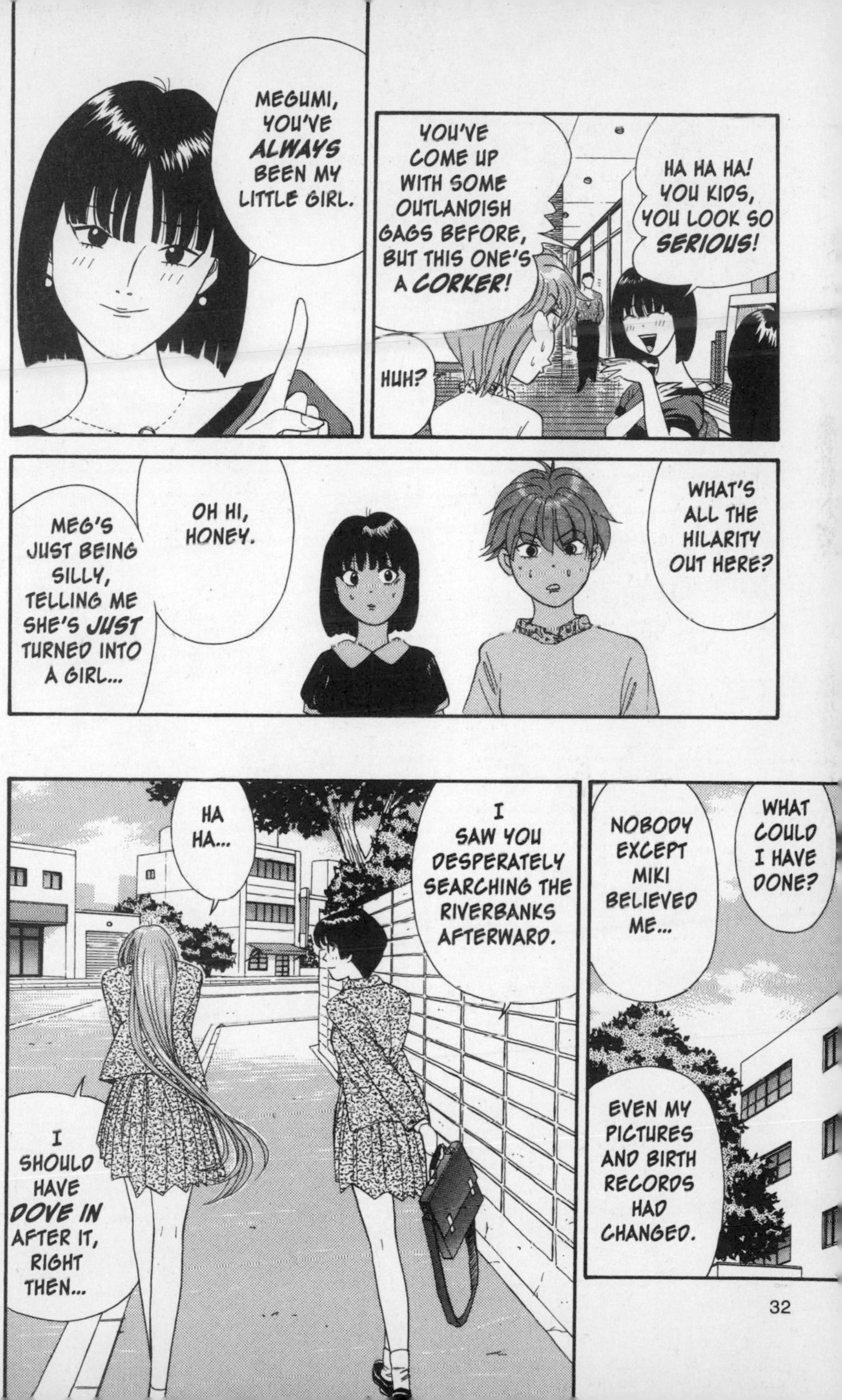
HA HA HA! YOU KIDS, YOU LOOK SO *SERIOUS!*
YOU'VE COME UP WITH SOME OUTLANDISH GAGS BEFORE, BUT THIS ONE'S A *CORKER!*
HUH?
MEGUMI, YOU'VE *ALWAYS* BEEN MY LITTLE GIRL.
WHAT'S ALL THE HILARITY OUT HERE?
OH HI, HONEY.
MEG'S JUST BEING SILLY, TELLING ME SHE'S *JUST* TURNED INTO A GIRL...
WHAT COULD I HAVE DONE?
NOBODY EXCEPT MIKI BELIEVED ME...
EVEN MY PICTURES AND BIRTH RECORDS HAD CHANGED.
I SAW YOU DESPERATELY SEARCHING THE RIVERBANKS AFTERWARD.
HA HA...
I SHOULD HAVE *DOVE IN* AFTER IT, RIGHT THEN...

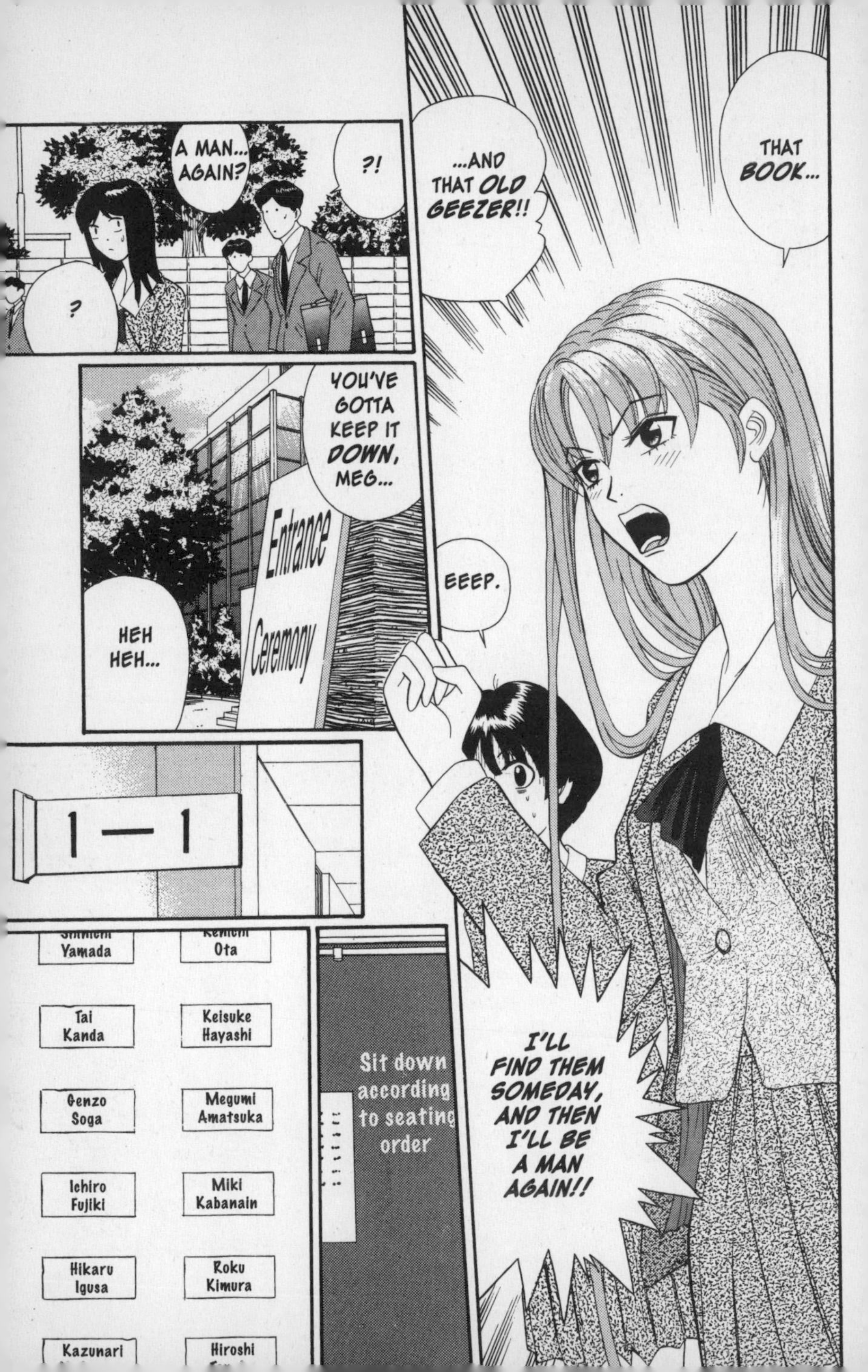
THAT BOOK...
...AND THAT OLD GEEZER!!
EEEP.
I'LL FIND THEM SOMEDAY, AND THEN I'LL BE A MAN AGAIN!!
?!
A MAN... AGAIN?
?
YOU'VE GOTTA KEEP IT DOWN, MEG...
Entrance Ceremony
HEH HEH...
1—1
Sit down according to seating order
Yamada
Ota
Tai Kanda
Keisuke Hayashi
Genzo Soga
Megumi Amatsuka
Ichiro Fujiki
Miki Kabanain
Hikaru Igusa
Roku Kimura
Kazunari
Hiroshi

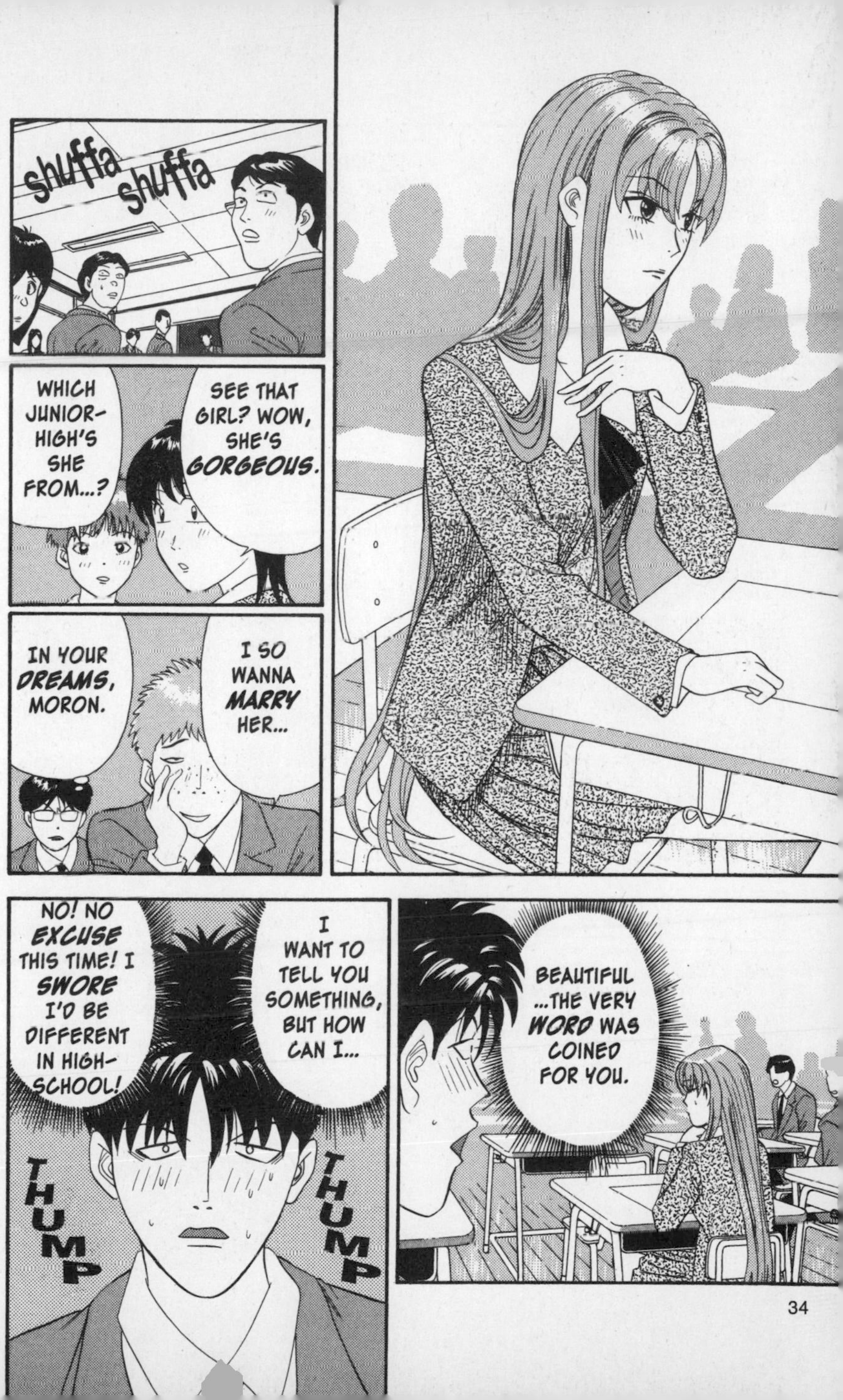
shuffa shuffa
SEE THAT GIRL? WOW, SHE'S GORGEOUS.
WHICH JUNIOR-HIGH'S SHE FROM...?
I SO WANNA MARRY HER...
IN YOUR DREAMS, MORON.
BEAUTIFUL ...THE VERY WORD WAS COINED FOR YOU.
I WANT TO TELL YOU SOMETHING, BUT HOW CAN I...
NO! NO EXCUSE THIS TIME! I SWORE I'D BE DIFFERENT IN HIGH-SCHOOL!
THUMP
THUMP

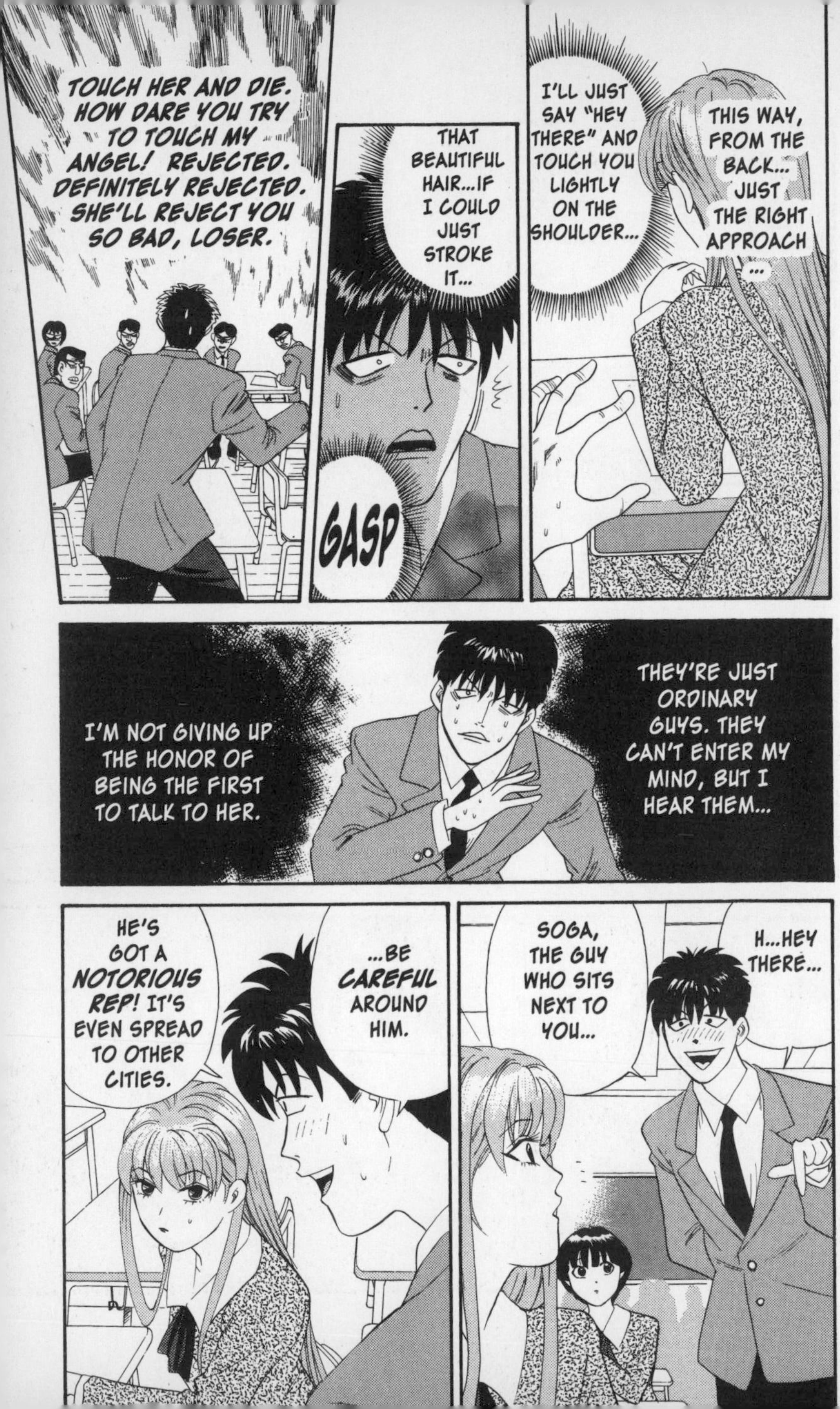
THIS WAY, FROM THE BACK... JUST THE RIGHT APPROACH ...
I'LL JUST SAY "HEY THERE" AND TOUCH YOU LIGHTLY ON THE SHOULDER...
THAT BEAUTIFUL HAIR...IF I COULD JUST STROKE IT...
GASP
TOUCH HER AND DIE. HOW DARE YOU TRY TO TOUCH MY ANGEL! REJECTED. DEFINITELY REJECTED. SHE'LL REJECT YOU SO BAD, LOSER.
THEY'RE JUST ORDINARY GUYS. THEY CAN'T ENTER MY MIND, BUT I HEAR THEM...
I'M NOT GIVING UP THE HONOR OF BEING THE FIRST TO TALK TO HER.
H...HEY THERE...
SOGA, THE GUY WHO SITS NEXT TO YOU...
...BE **CAREFUL** AROUND HIM.
HE'S GOT A **NOTORIOUS REP!** IT'S EVEN SPREAD TO OTHER CITIES.

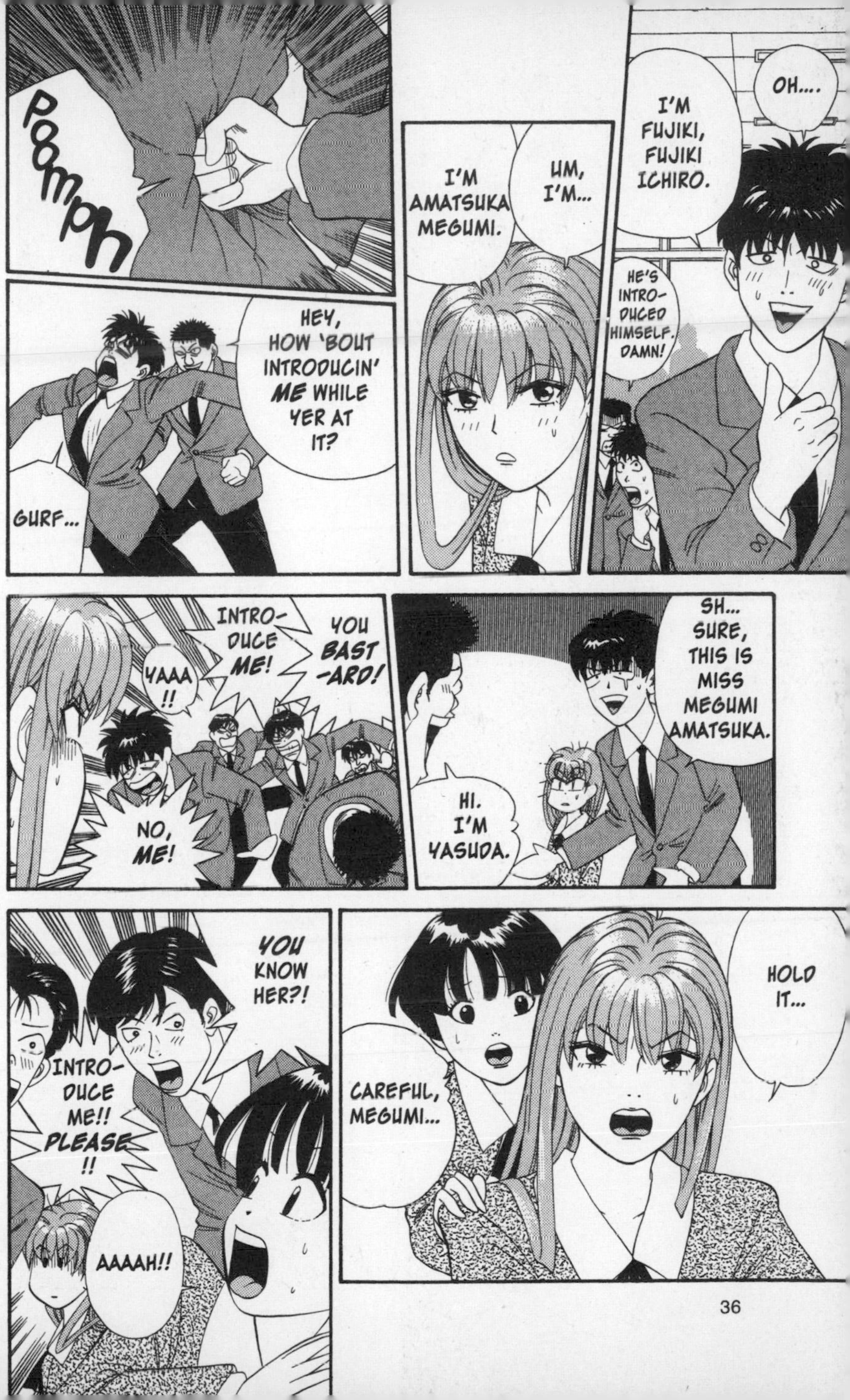
OH....
I'M FUJIKI, FUJIKI ICHIRO.
HE'S INTRODUCED HIMSELF. DAMN!
UM, I'M...
I'M AMATSUKA MEGUMI.
Poomph
HEY, HOW 'BOUT INTRODUCIN' ME WHILE YER AT IT?
GURF...
SH... SURE, THIS IS MISS MEGUMI AMATSUKA.
HI. I'M YASUDA.
YOU BASTARD!
INTRODUCE ME!
YAAA!!
NO, ME!
HOLD IT...
CAREFUL, MEGUMI...
YOU KNOW HER?!
INTRODUCE ME!! PLEASE!!
AAAAH!!

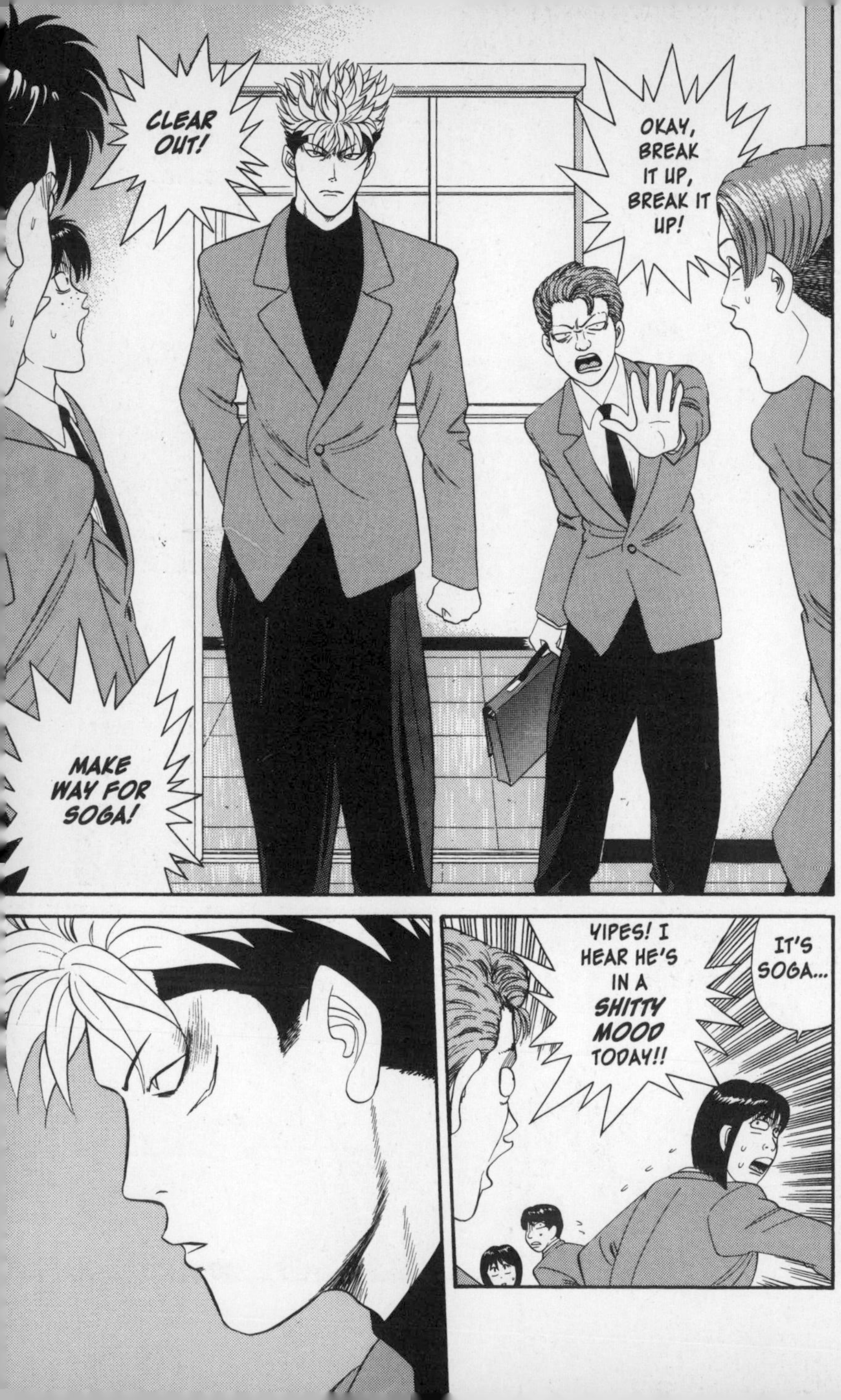
OKAY, BREAK IT UP, BREAK IT UP!
CLEAR OUT!
MAKE WAY FOR SOGA!
IT'S SOGA...
YIPES! I HEAR HE'S IN A SHITTY MOOD TODAY!!

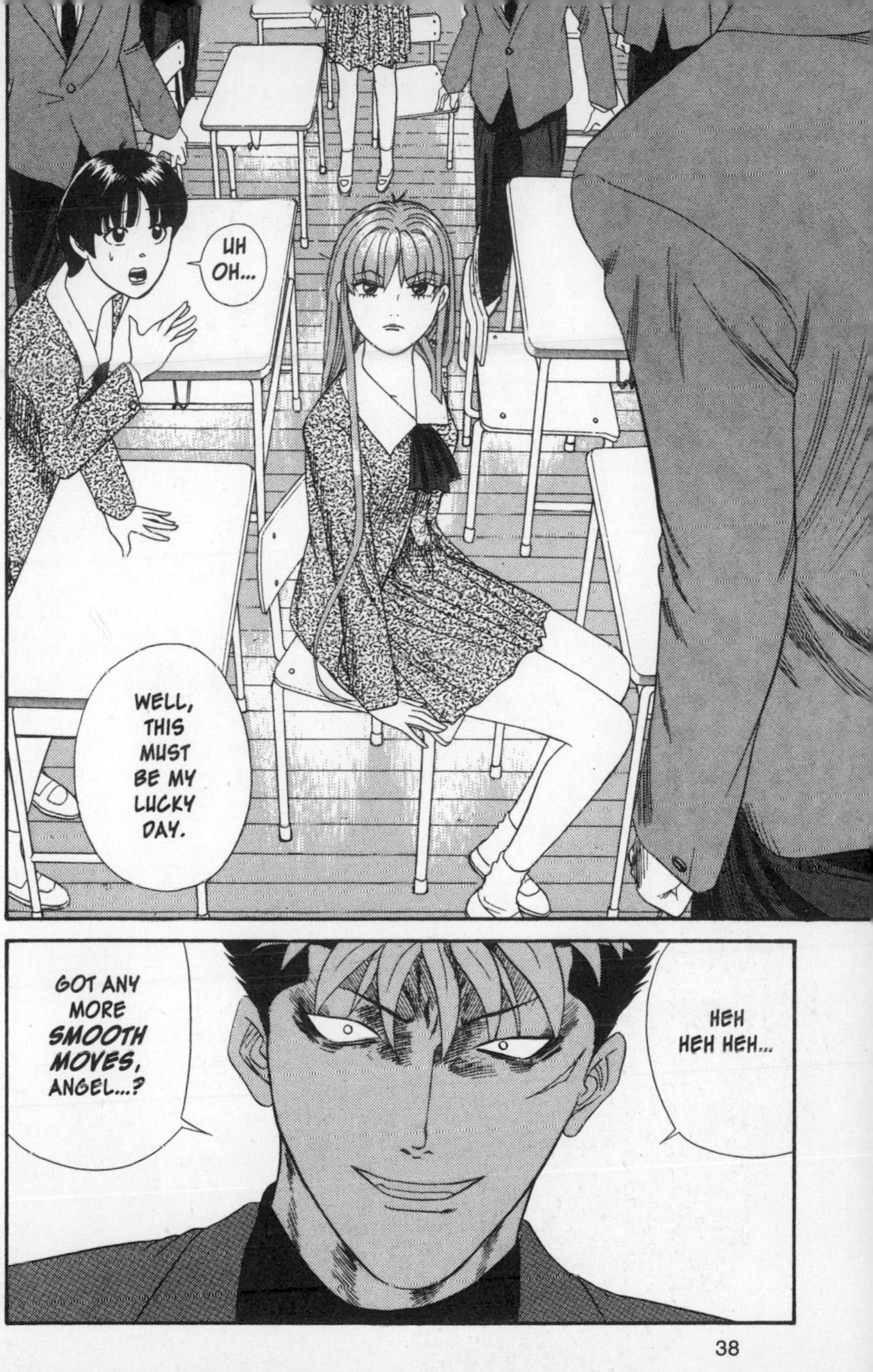
UH OH...
WELL, THIS MUST BE MY LUCKY DAY.
HEH HEH HEH...
GOT ANY MORE *SMOOTH MOVES,* ANGEL...?

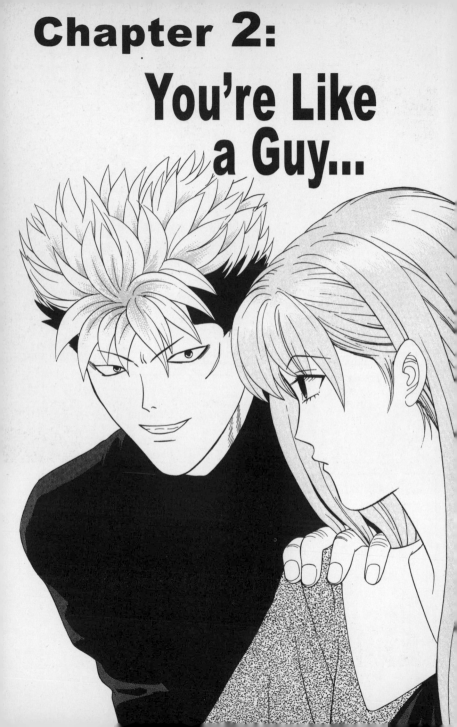

Chapter 2: You're Like a Guy...

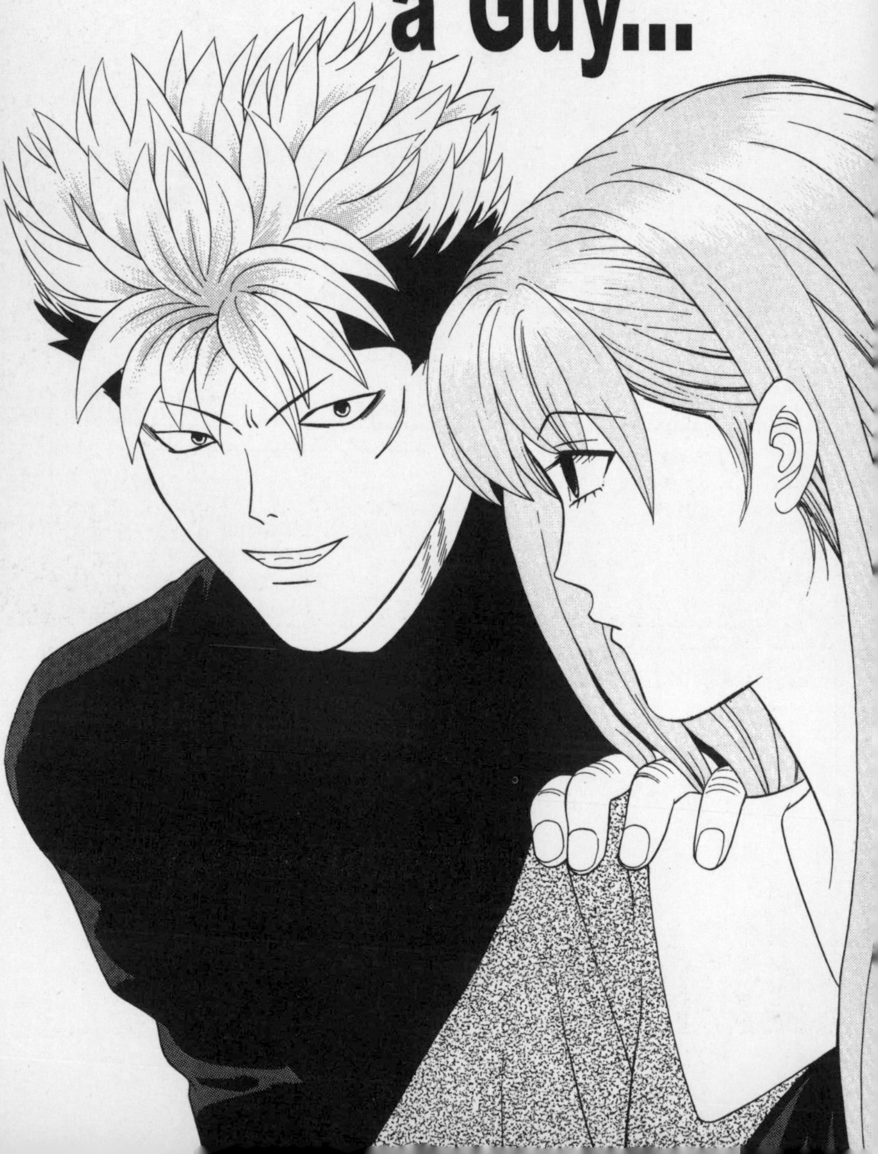

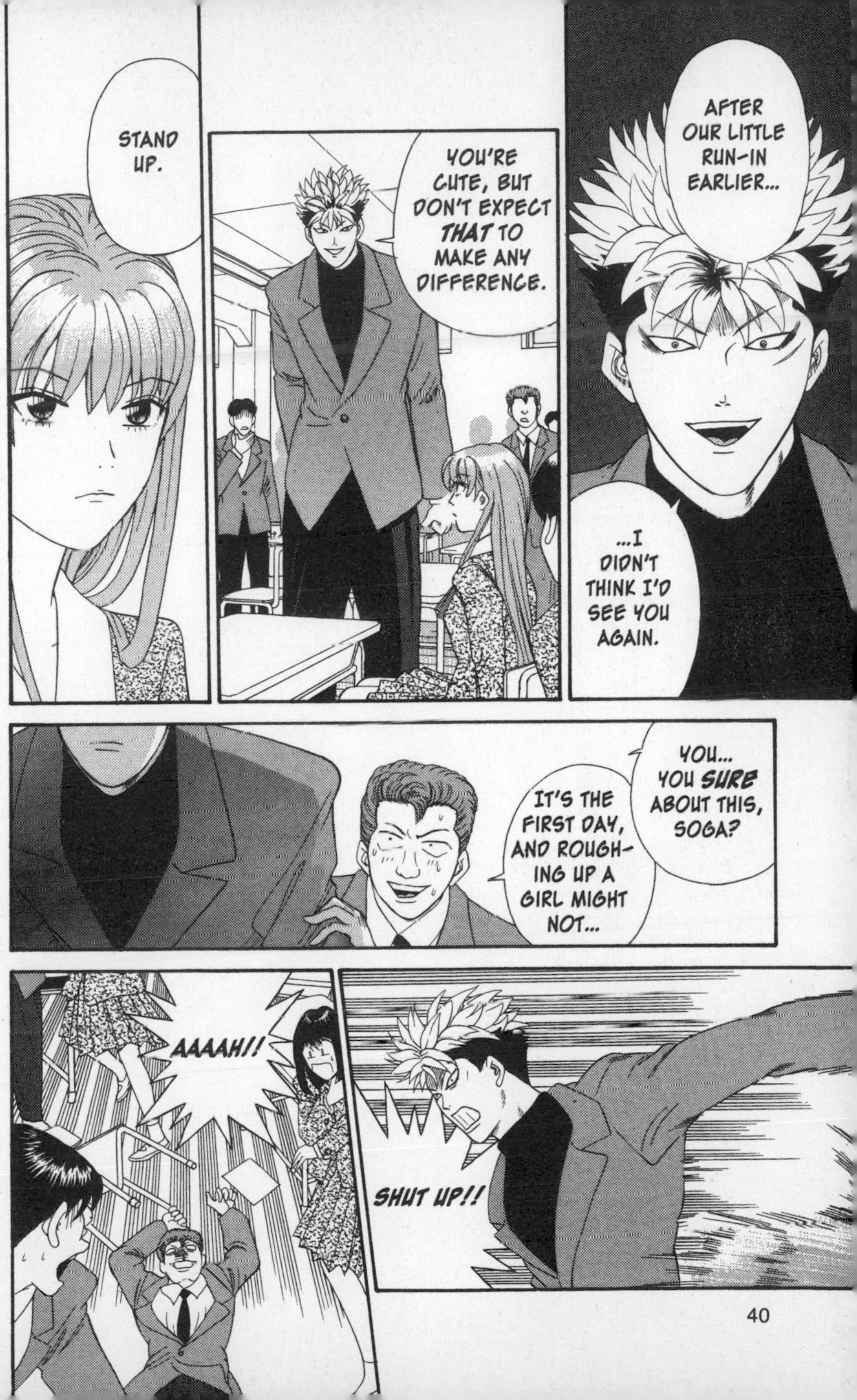
AFTER OUR LITTLE RUN-IN EARLIER...
...I DIDN'T THINK I'D SEE YOU AGAIN.
YOU'RE CUTE, BUT DON'T EXPECT THAT TO MAKE ANY DIFFERENCE.
STAND UP.
YOU... YOU SURE ABOUT THIS, SOGA?
IT'S THE FIRST DAY, AND ROUGHING UP A GIRL MIGHT NOT...
SHUT UP!!
AAAAH!!

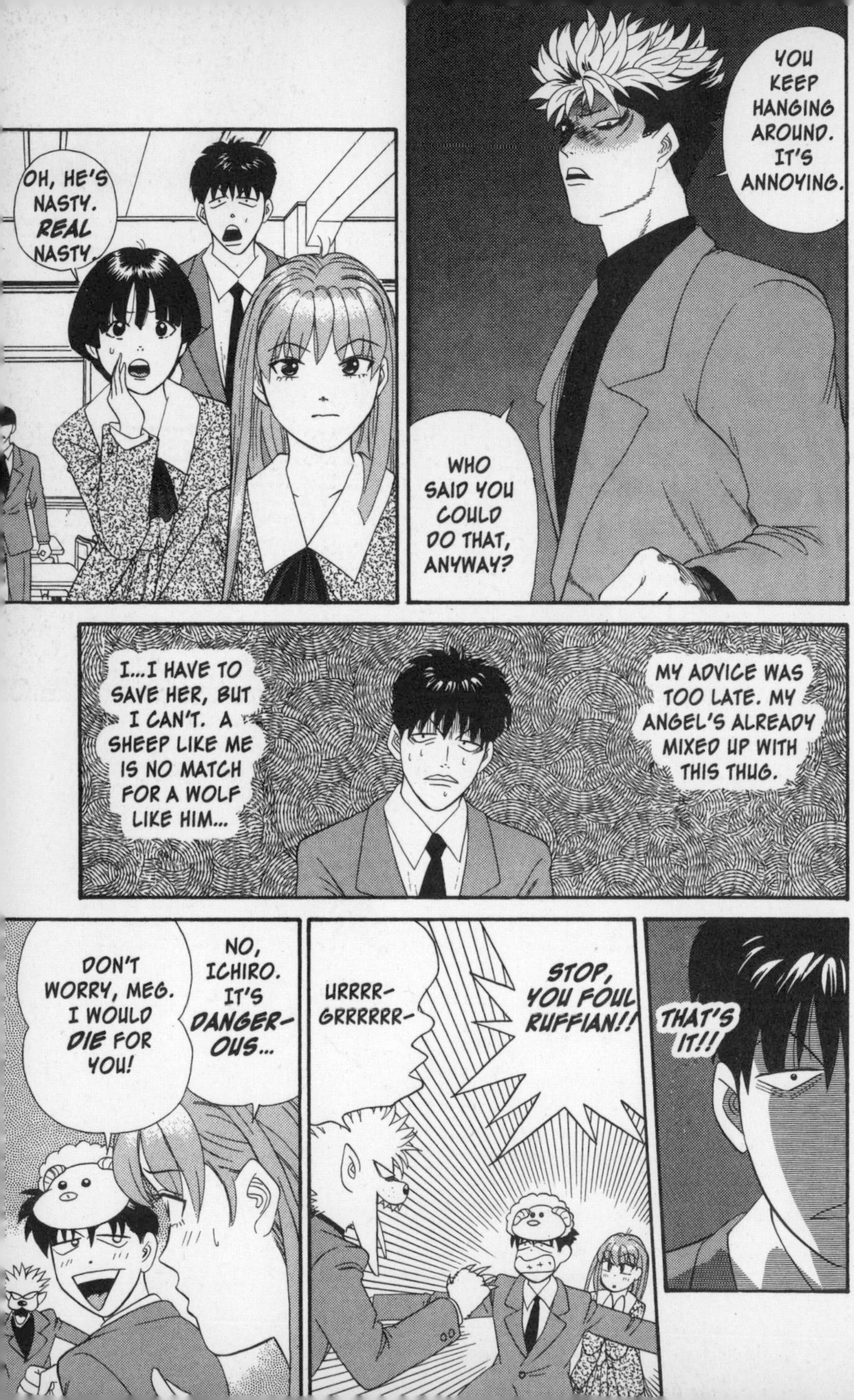
YOU KEEP HANGING AROUND. IT'S ANNOYING.
WHO SAID YOU COULD DO THAT, ANYWAY?
OH, HE'S NASTY. REAL NASTY...
MY ADVICE WAS TOO LATE. MY ANGEL'S ALREADY MIXED UP WITH THIS THUG.
I...I HAVE TO SAVE HER, BUT I CAN'T. A SHEEP LIKE ME IS NO MATCH FOR A WOLF LIKE HIM...
THAT'S IT!!
STOP, YOU FOUL RUFFIAN!!
URRRR-GRRRRRR-
NO, ICHIRO. IT'S DANGER-OUS...
DON'T WORRY, MEG. I WOULD DIE FOR YOU!

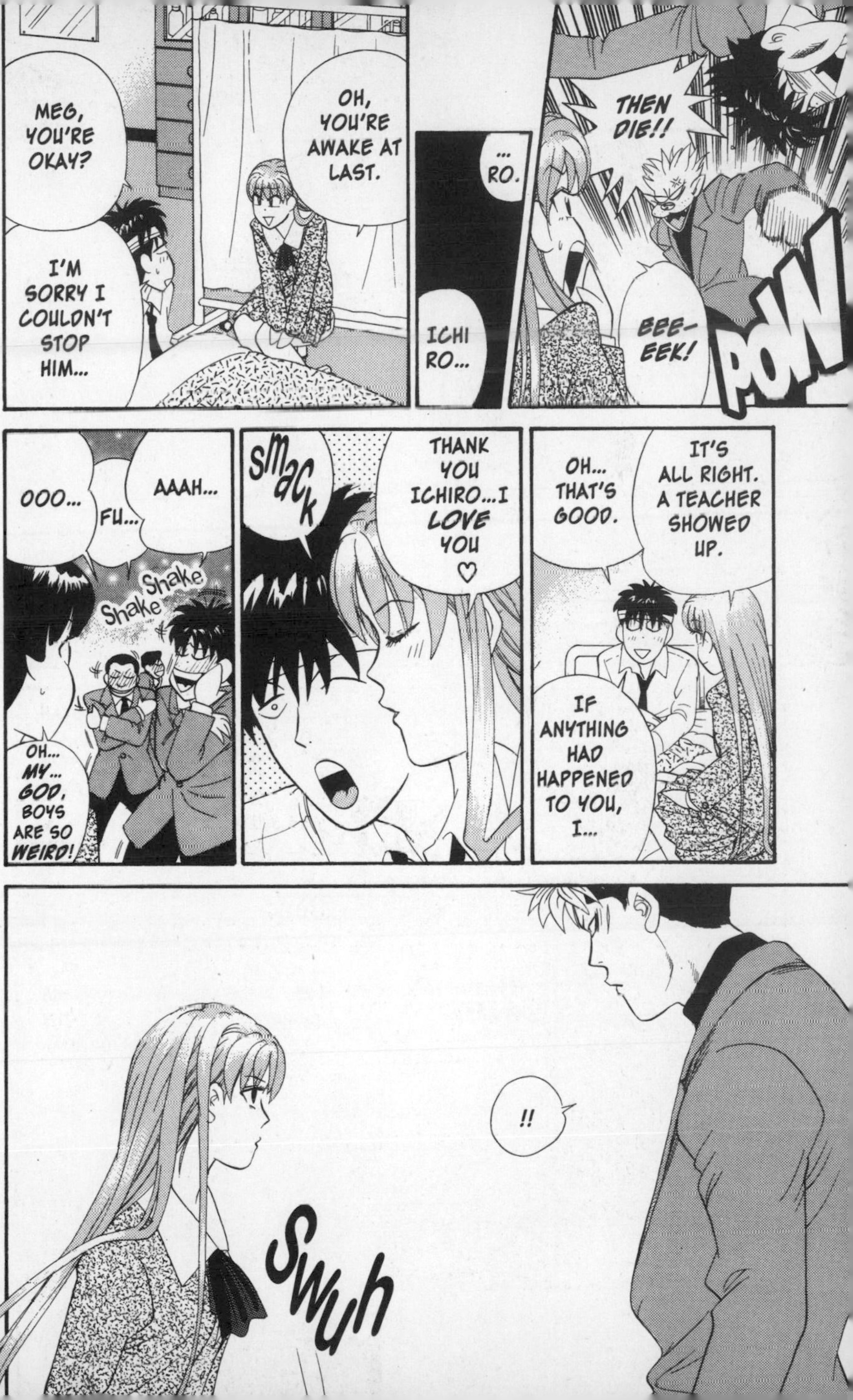
THEN DIE!!
BEEE-EEK!
POW
... RO.
ICHI RO...
OH, YOU'RE AWAKE AT LAST.
MEG, YOU'RE OKAY?
I'M SORRY I COULDN'T STOP HIM...
IT'S ALL RIGHT. A TEACHER SHOWED UP.
OH... THAT'S GOOD.
IF ANYTHING HAD HAPPENED TO YOU, I...
THANK YOU ICHIRO...I LOVE YOU ♡
smack
AAAH...
FU...
OOO...
Shake Shake
OH... MY... GOD. BOYS ARE SO WEIRD!
!!
SWUH

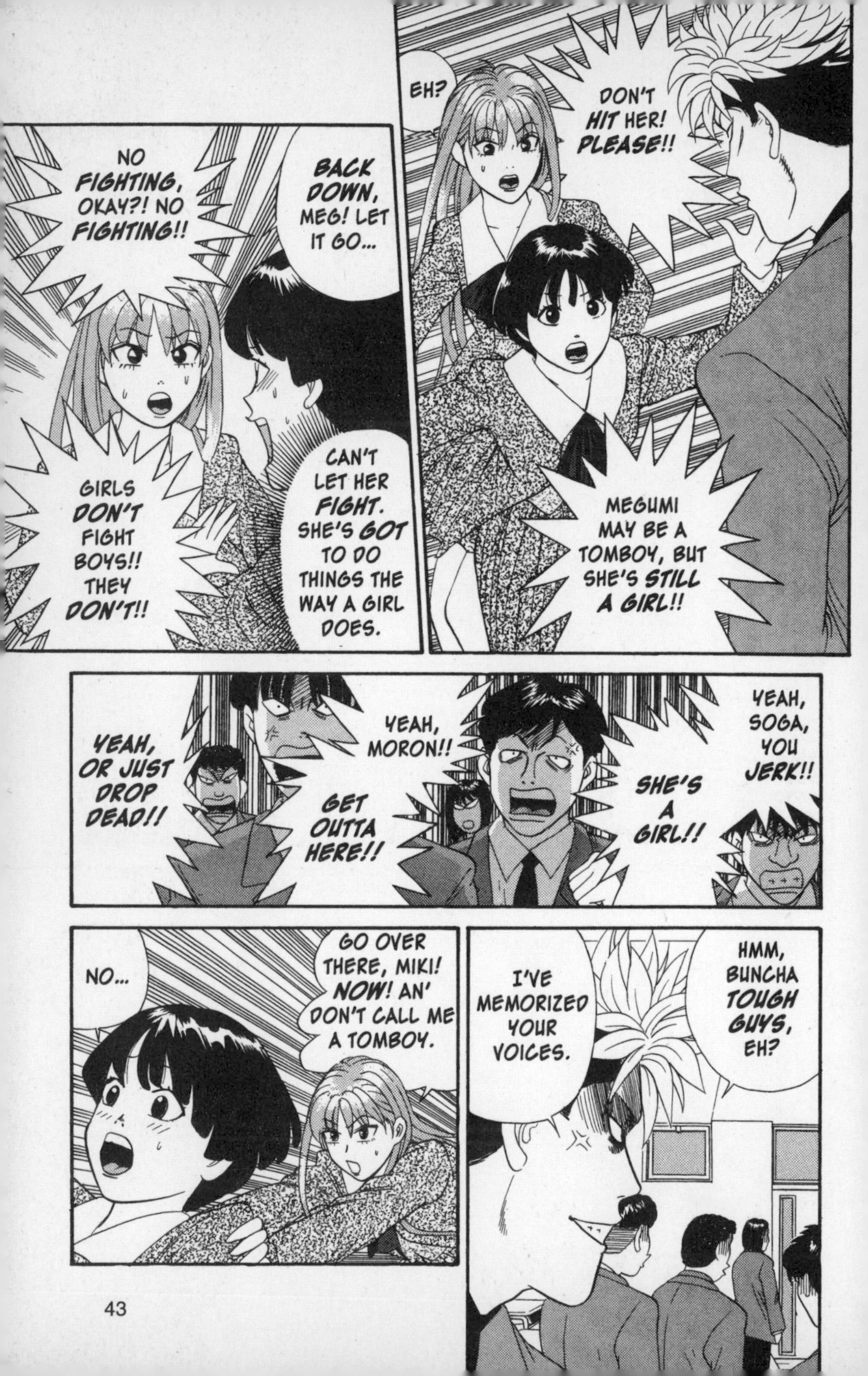
DON'T HIT HER! PLEASE!!
EH?
MEGUMI MAY BE A TOMBOY, BUT SHE'S STILL A GIRL!!
BACK DOWN, MEG! LET IT GO...
NO FIGHTING, OKAY?! NO FIGHTING!!
CAN'T LET HER FIGHT. SHE'S GOT TO DO THINGS THE WAY A GIRL DOES.
GIRLS DON'T FIGHT BOYS!! THEY DON'T!!
YEAH, SOGA, YOU JERK!!
SHE'S A GIRL!!
YEAH, MORON!!
GET OUTTA HERE!!
YEAH, OR JUST DROP DEAD!!
HMM, BUNCHA TOUGH GUYS, EH?
I'VE MEMORIZED YOUR VOICES.
GO OVER THERE, MIKI! NOW! AN' DON'T CALL ME A TOMBOY.
NO...

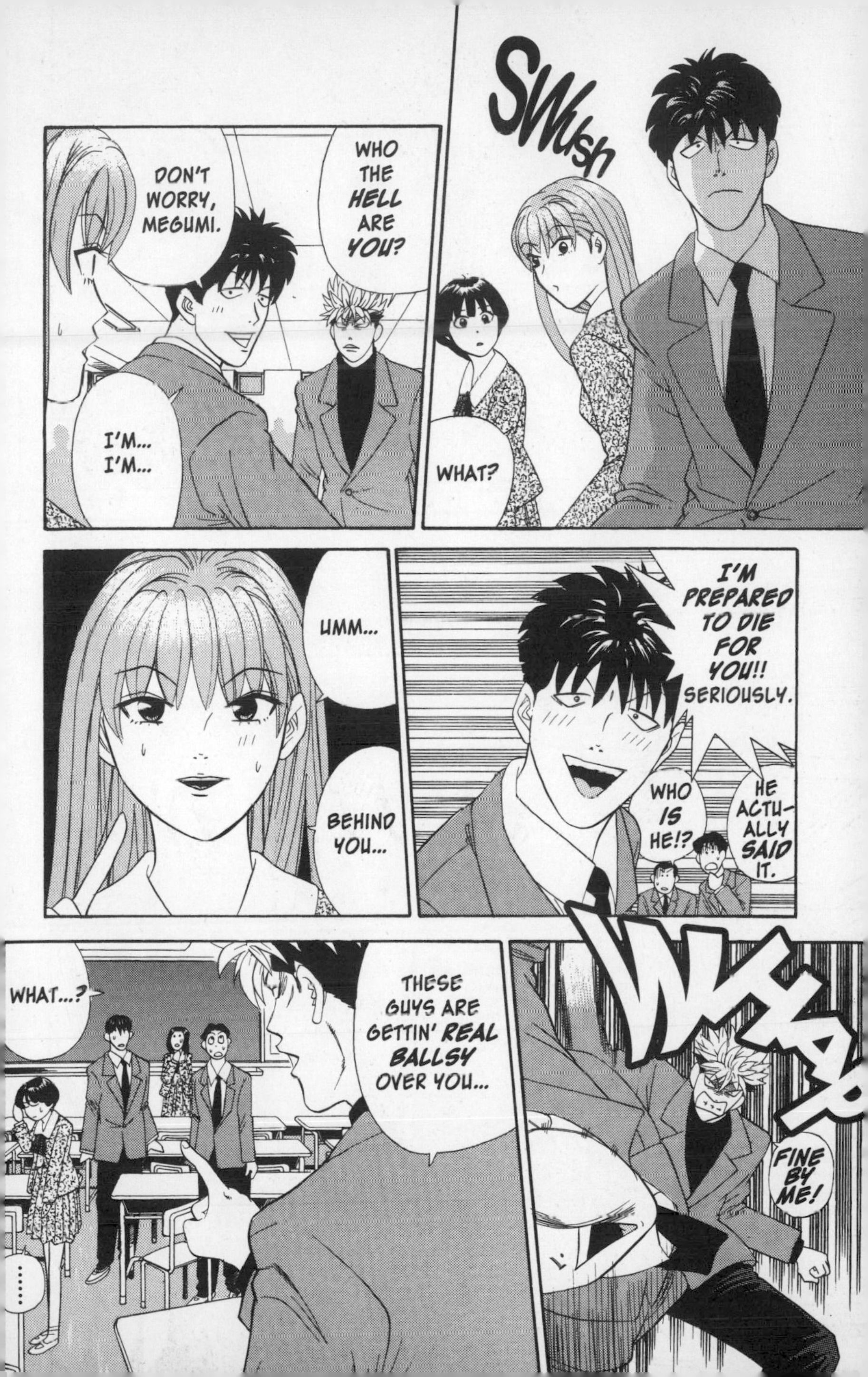
SWUSH
WHAT?
WHO THE HELL ARE YOU?
DON'T WORRY, MEGUMI.
I'M... I'M...
I'M PREPARED TO DIE FOR YOU!! SERIOUSLY.
HE ACTU-ALLY SAID IT.
WHO IS HE!?
UMM...
BEHIND YOU...
WHAP
FINE BY ME!
THESE GUYS ARE GETTIN' REAL BALLSY OVER YOU...
WHAT...?
......

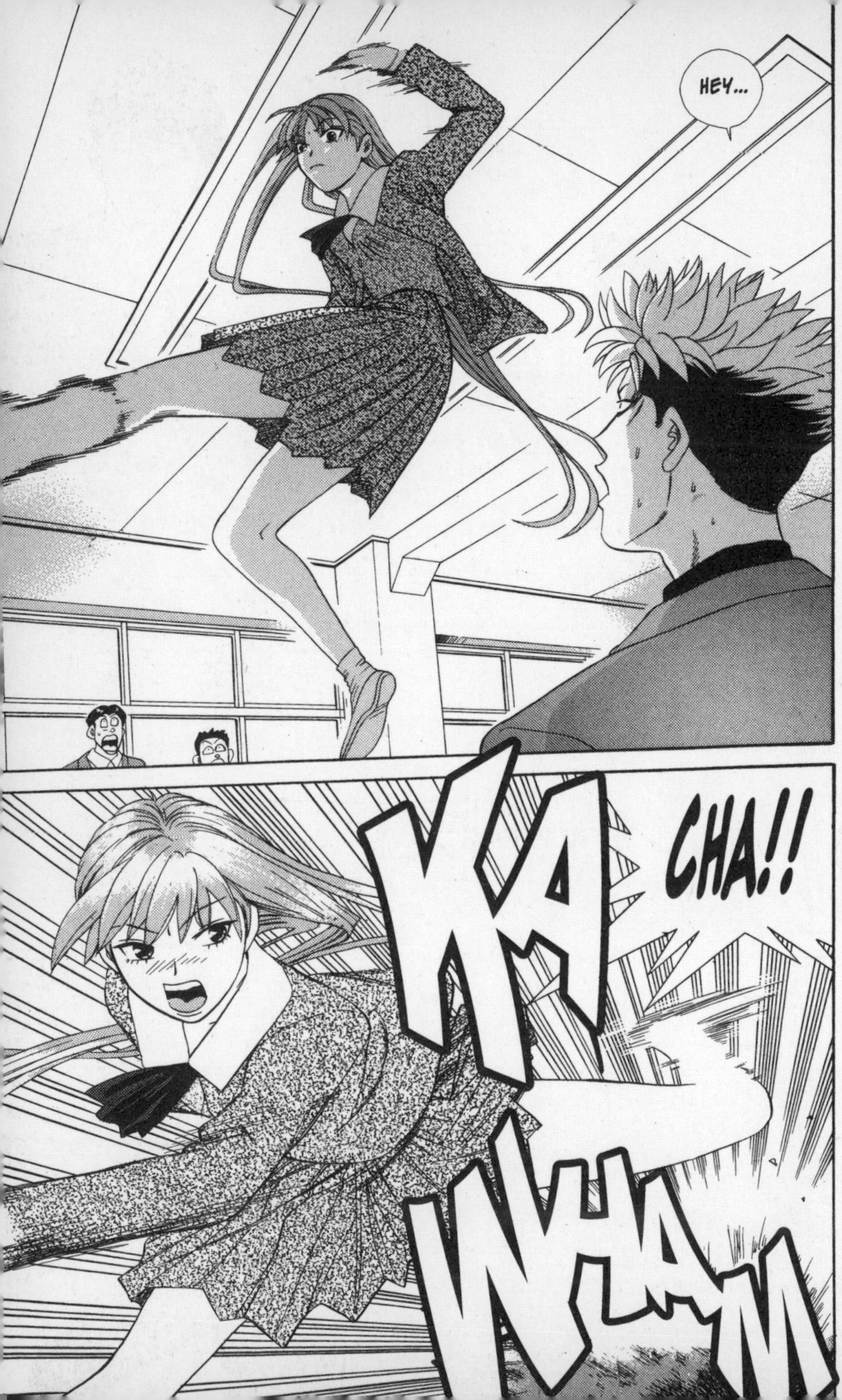
HEY...
KA
CHA!!
WHAM

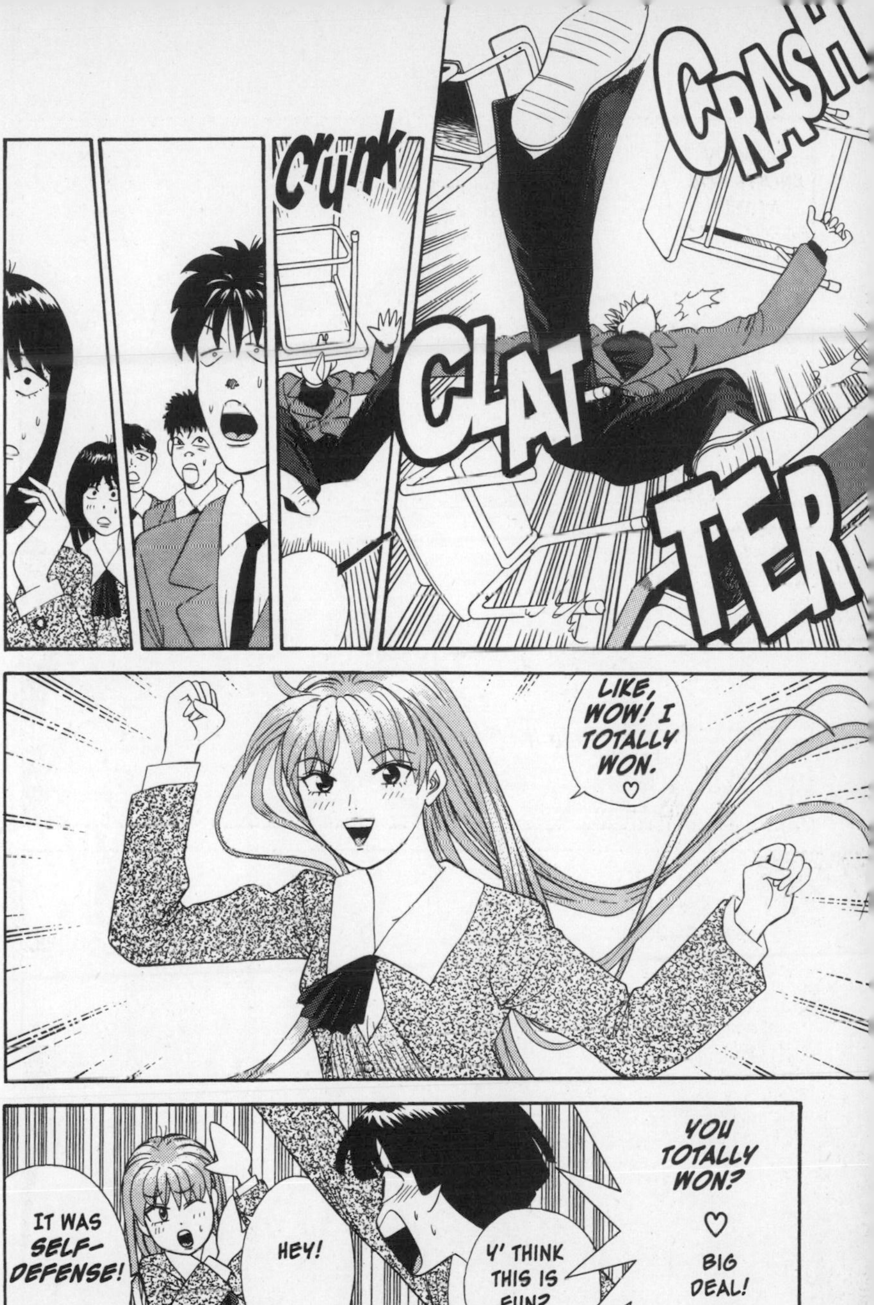
CRASH
CLAT-
TER
Crunk
LIKE, WOW! I TOTALLY WON. ♡
YOU TOTALLY WON? ♡ BIG DEAL!
Y' THINK THIS IS FUN?
HEY!
IT WAS SELF-DEFENSE!

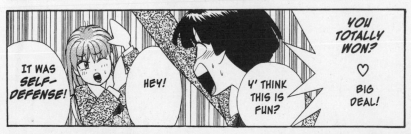

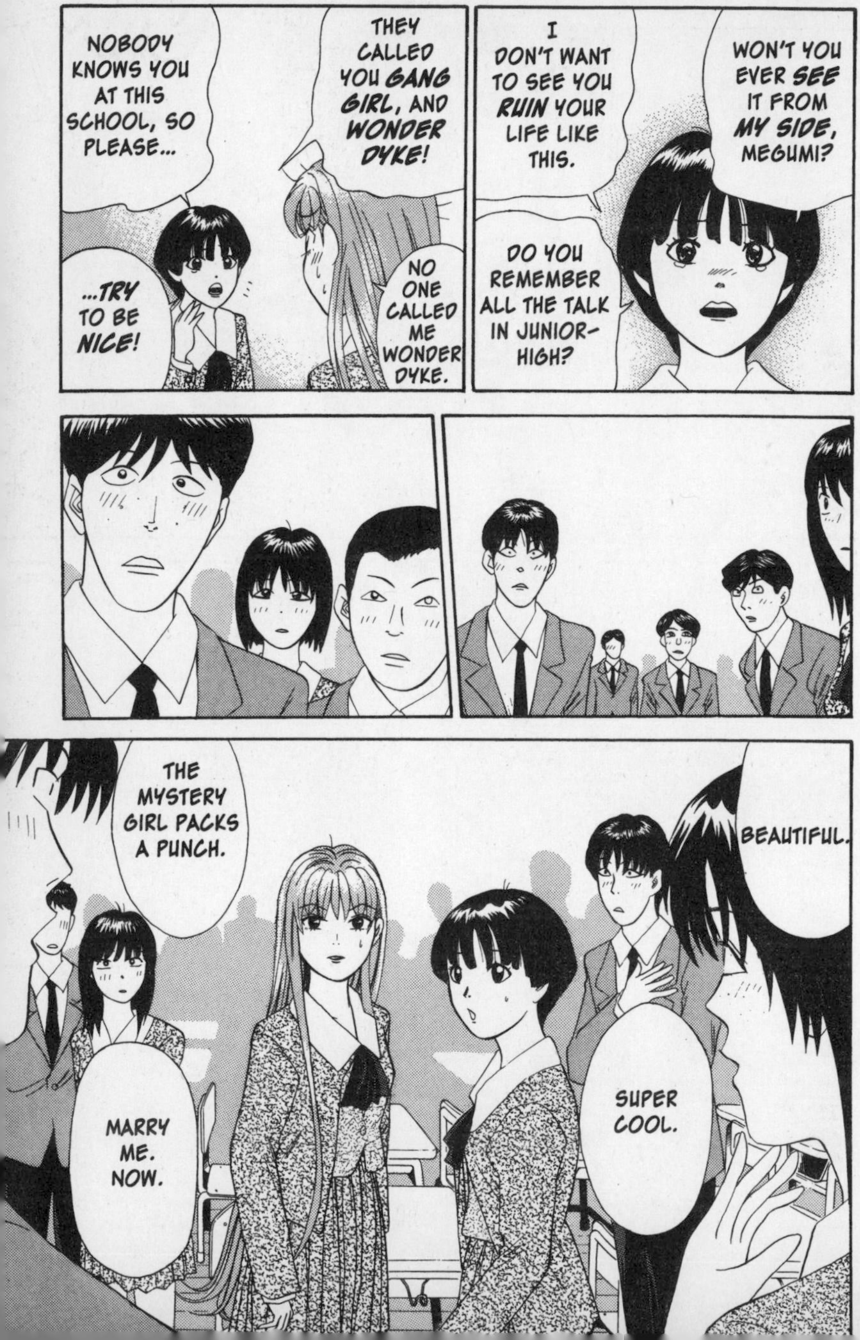
WON'T YOU EVER SEE IT FROM MY SIDE, MEGUMI?
I DON'T WANT TO SEE YOU RUIN YOUR LIFE LIKE THIS.
DO YOU REMEMBER ALL THE TALK IN JUNIOR-HIGH?
THEY CALLED YOU GANG GIRL, AND WONDER DYKE!
NOBODY KNOWS YOU AT THIS SCHOOL, SO PLEASE...
NO ONE CALLED ME WONDER DYKE.
...TRY TO BE NICE!
BEAUTIFUL.
THE MYSTERY GIRL PACKS A PUNCH.
SUPER COOL.
MARRY ME. NOW.

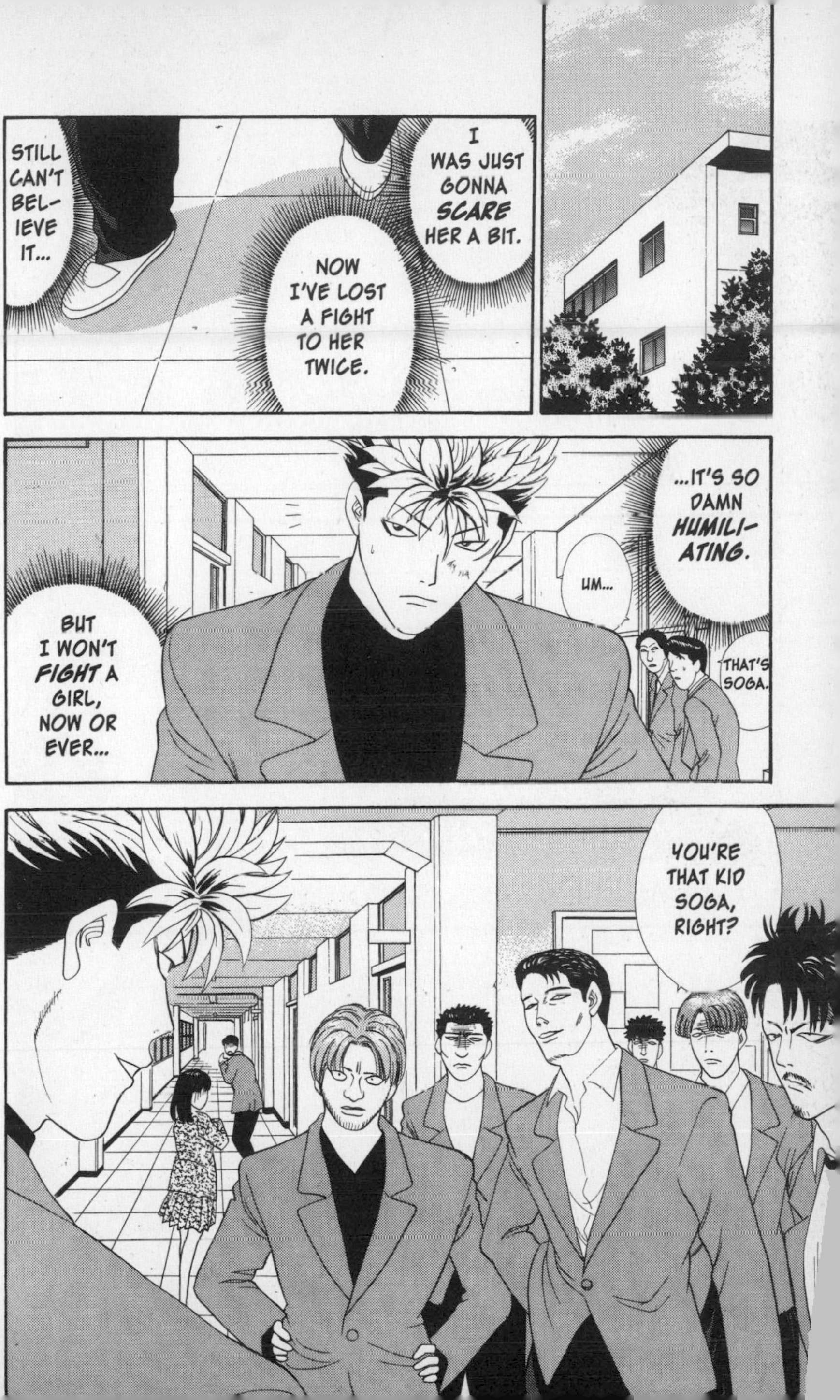
I WAS JUST GONNA SCARE HER A BIT.
NOW I'VE LOST A FIGHT TO HER TWICE.
STILL CAN'T BELIEVE IT...
...IT'S SO DAMN HUMILIATING.
THAT'S SOGA.
UM...
BUT I WON'T FIGHT A GIRL, NOW OR EVER...
YOU'RE THAT KID SOGA, RIGHT?

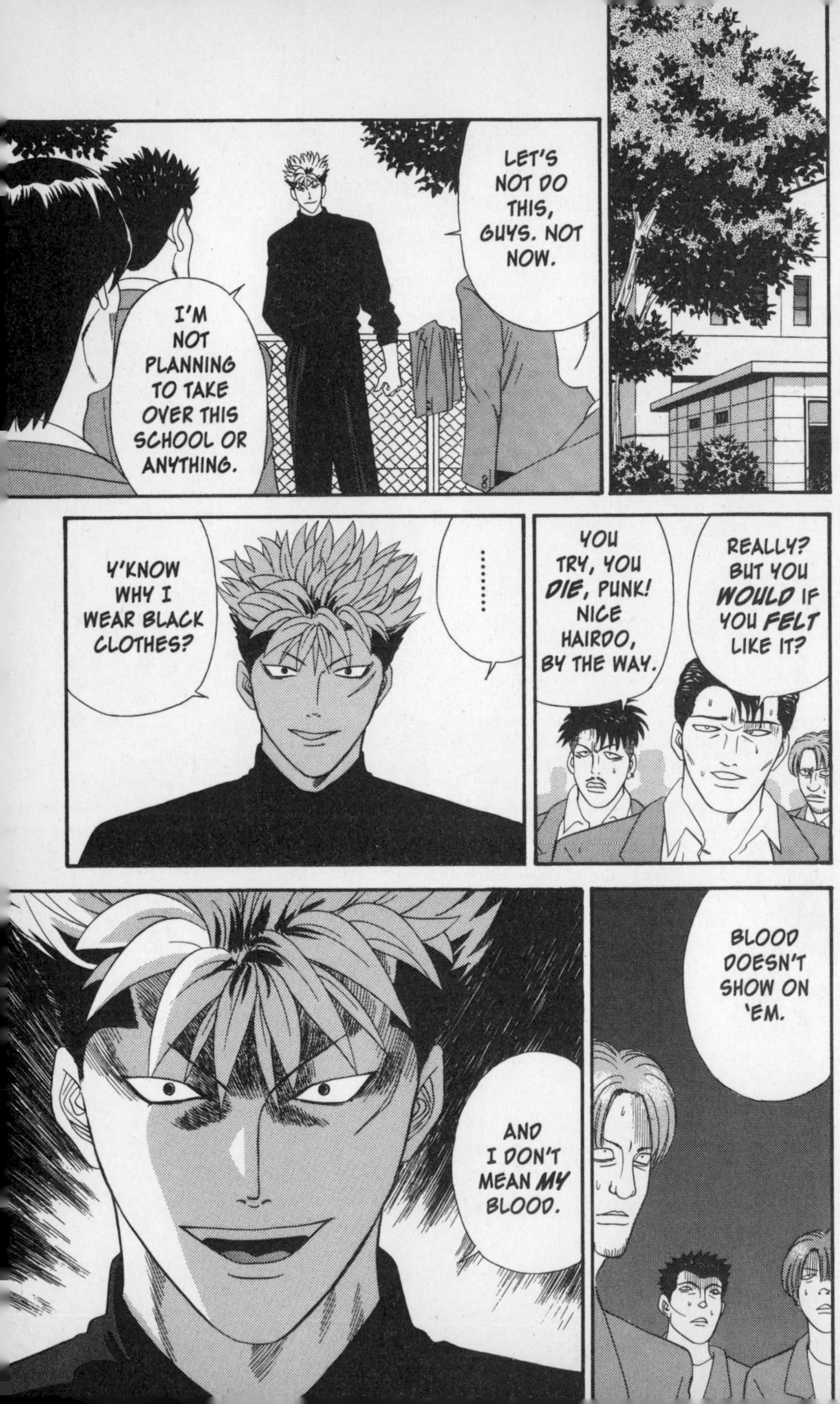
LET'S NOT DO THIS, GUYS. NOT NOW.
I'M NOT PLANNING TO TAKE OVER THIS SCHOOL OR ANYTHING.
REALLY? BUT YOU *WOULD* IF YOU *FELT* LIKE IT?
YOU TRY, YOU *DIE*, PUNK! NICE HAIRDO, BY THE WAY.
....
Y'KNOW WHY I WEAR BLACK CLOTHES?
BLOOD DOESN'T SHOW ON 'EM.
AND I DON'T MEAN *MY* BLOOD.

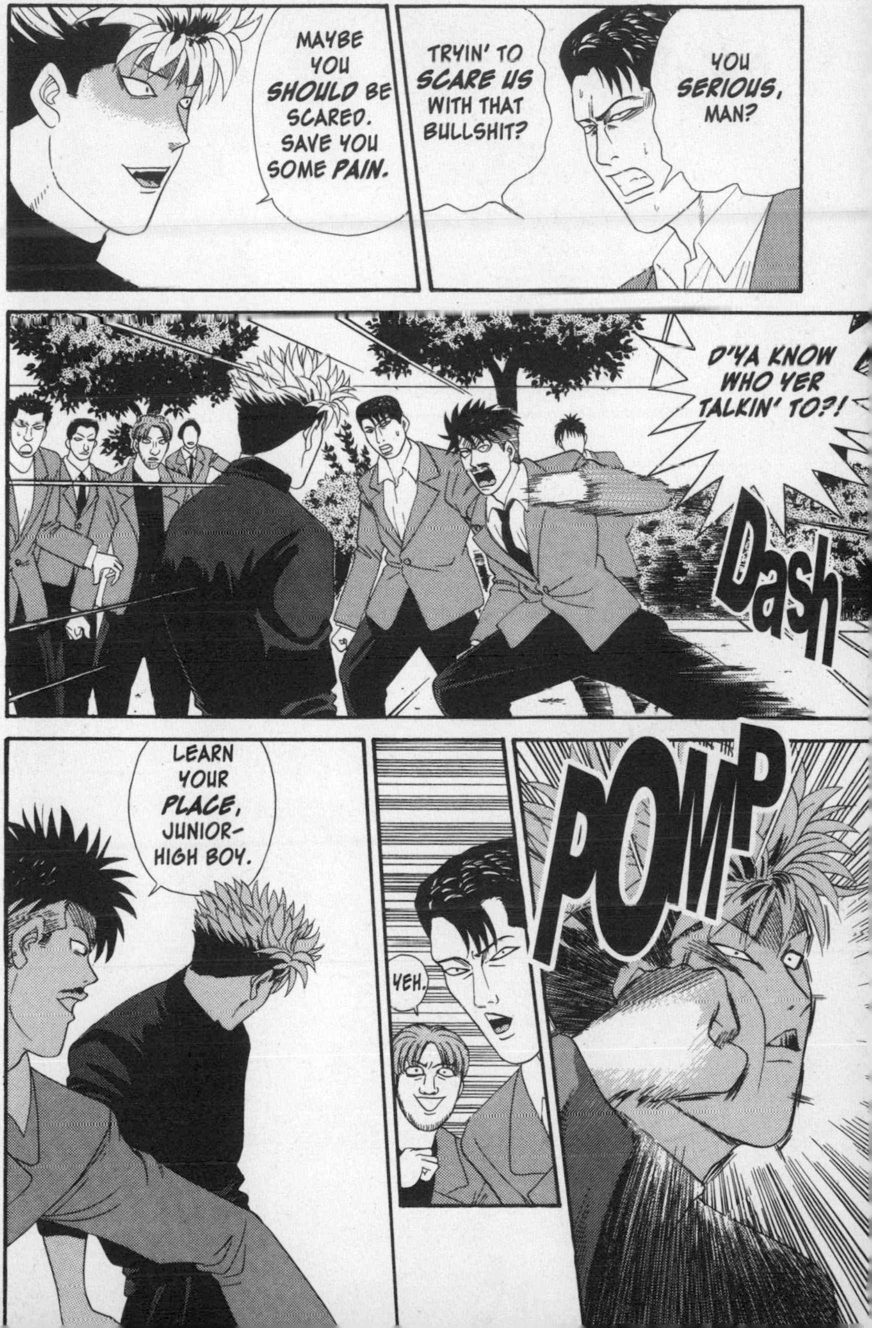
YOU SERIOUS, MAN?
TRYIN' TO SCARE US WITH THAT BULLSHIT?
MAYBE YOU SHOULD BE SCARED. SAVE YOU SOME PAIN.
D'YA KNOW WHO YER TALKIN' TO?!
Dash
POMP
YEH.
LEARN YOUR PLACE, JUNIOR-HIGH BOY.

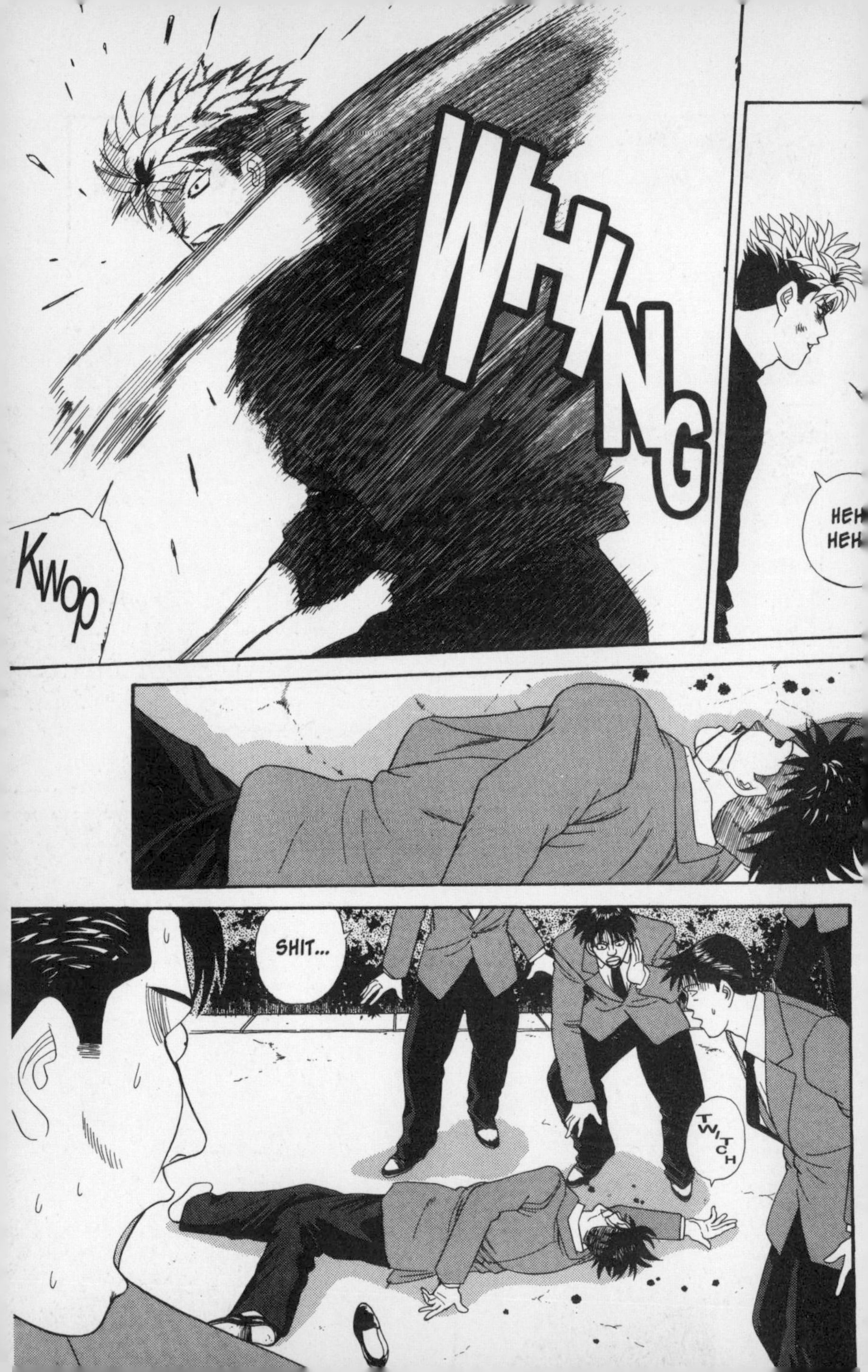
HEH HEH
WHING
Kwop
SHIT...
TWITCH

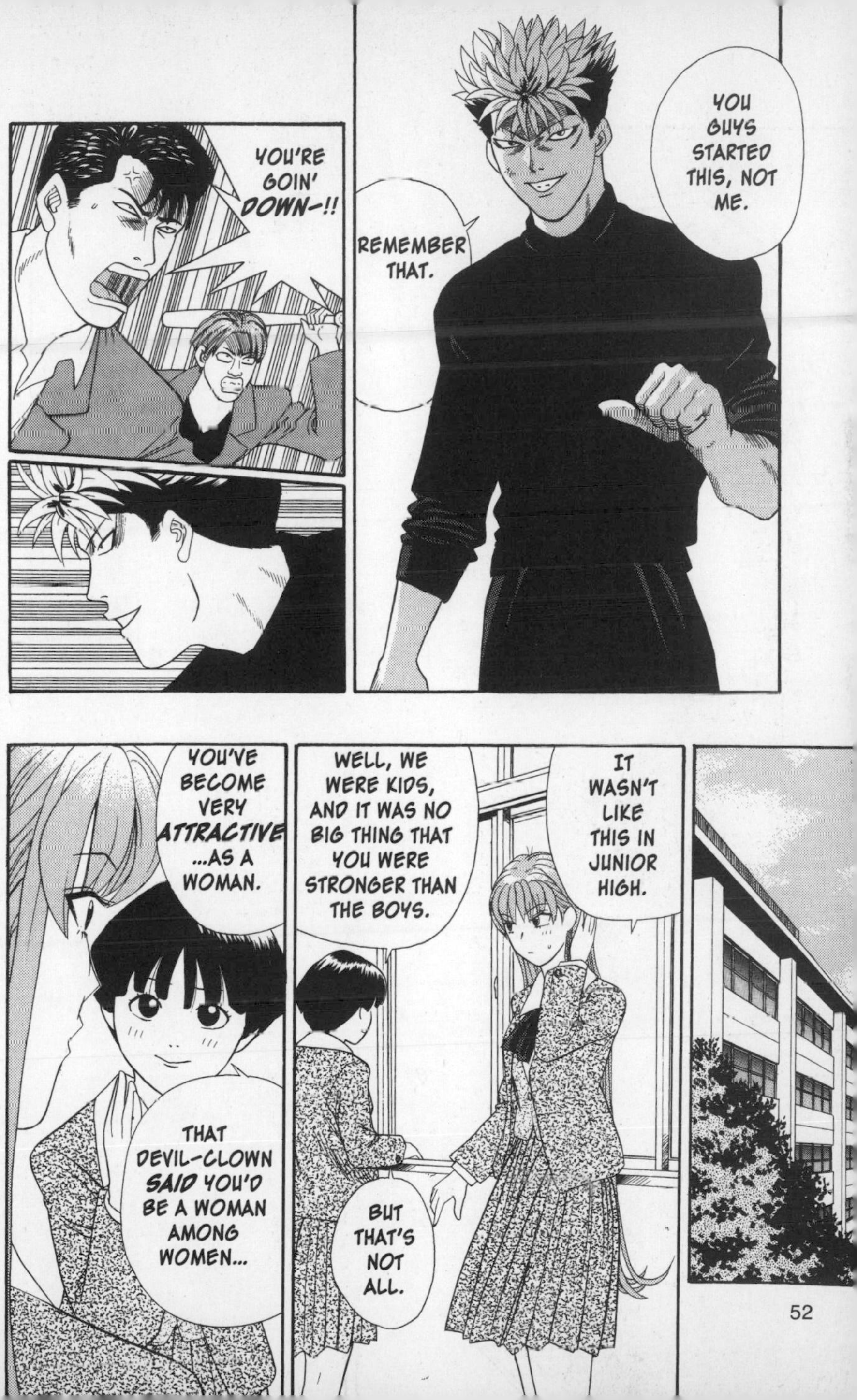
YOU GUYS STARTED THIS, NOT ME.
REMEMBER THAT.
YOU'RE GOIN' DOWN-!!
IT WASN'T LIKE THIS IN JUNIOR HIGH.
WELL, WE WERE KIDS, AND IT WAS NO BIG THING THAT YOU WERE STRONGER THAN THE BOYS.
BUT THAT'S NOT ALL.
YOU'VE BECOME VERY ATTRACTIVE ...AS A WOMAN.
THAT DEVIL-CLOWN SAID YOU'D BE A WOMAN AMONG WOMEN...

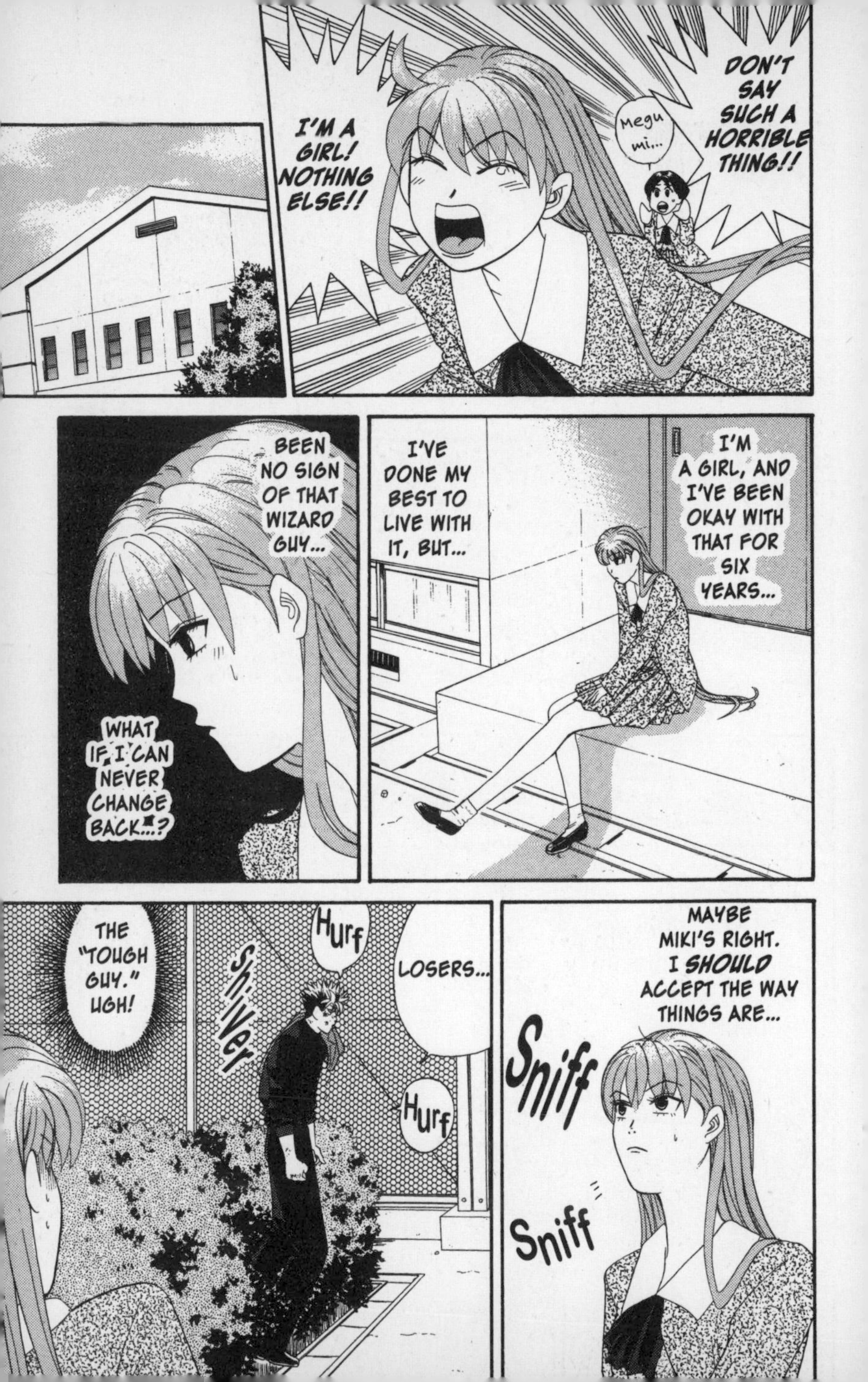
DON'T SAY SUCH A HORRIBLE THING!!
Megu mi...
I'M A GIRL! NOTHING ELSE!!
I'M A GIRL, AND I'VE BEEN OKAY WITH THAT FOR SIX YEARS...
I'VE DONE MY BEST TO LIVE WITH IT, BUT...
BEEN NO SIGN OF THAT WIZARD GUY...
WHAT IF I CAN NEVER CHANGE BACK...?
MAYBE MIKI'S RIGHT. I *SHOULD* ACCEPT THE WAY THINGS ARE...
Sniff
Sniff
LOSERS...
Hurf
Shiver
THE "TOUGH GUY." UGH!
Hurf

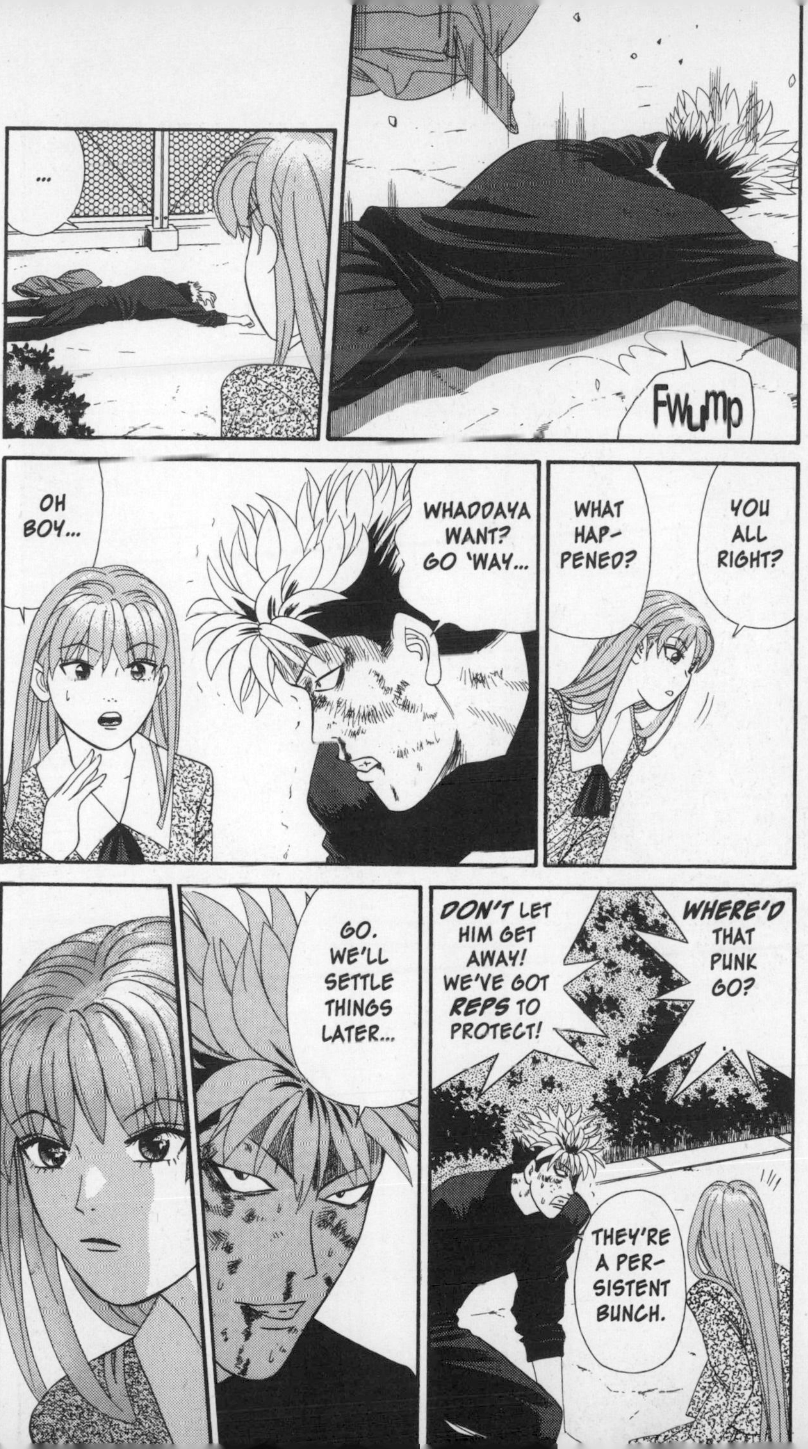
Fwump
...
YOU ALL RIGHT?
WHAT HAP-PENED?
WHADDAYA WANT? GO 'WAY...
OH BOY...
WHERE'D THAT PUNK GO?
DON'T LET HIM GET AWAY! WE'VE GOT REPS TO PROTECT!
THEY'RE A PER-SISTENT BUNCH.
GO. WE'LL SETTLE THINGS LATER...

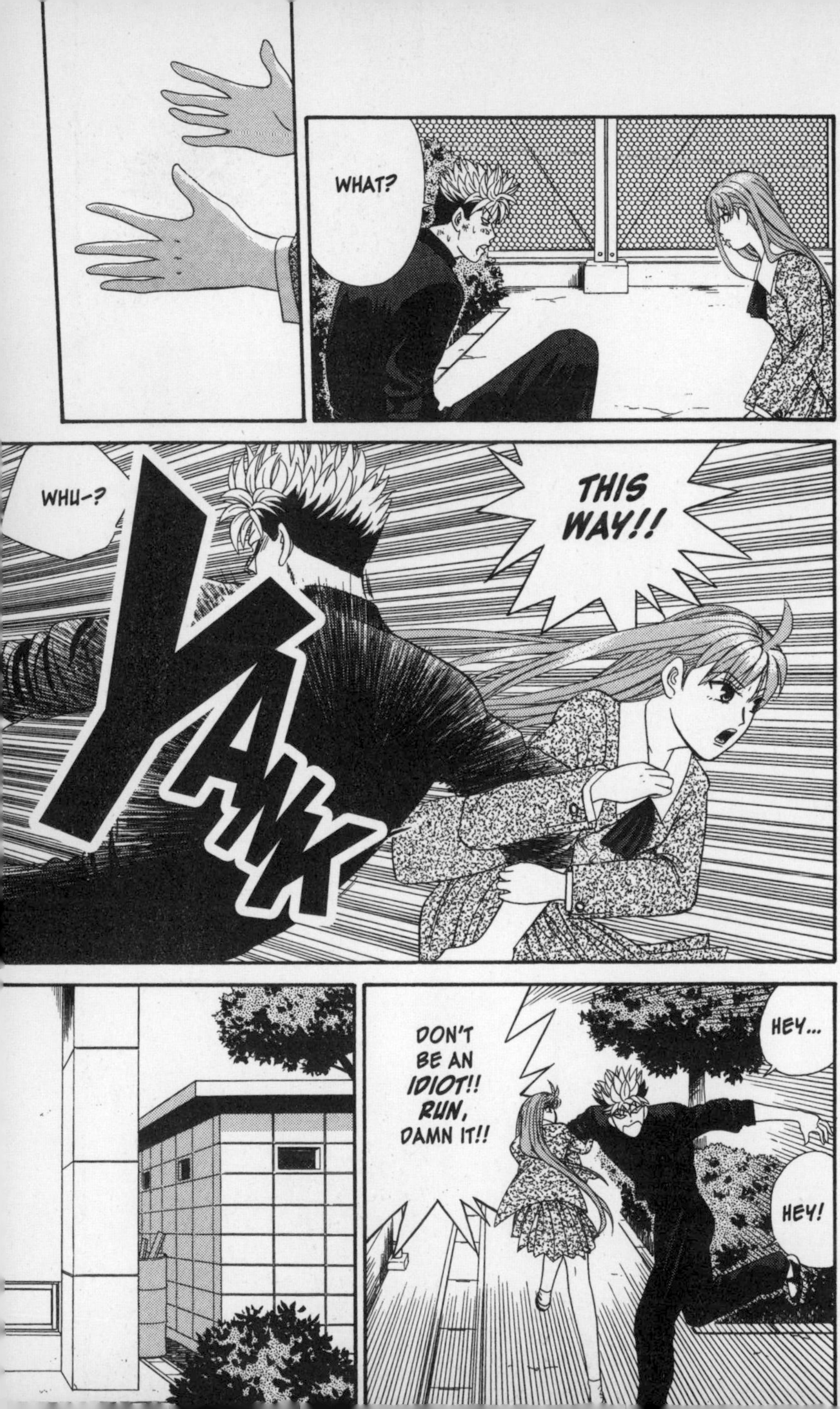
WHAT?
THIS WAY!!
WHU-?
YANK
HEY...
DON'T BE AN IDIOT!! RUN, DAMN IT!!
HEY!

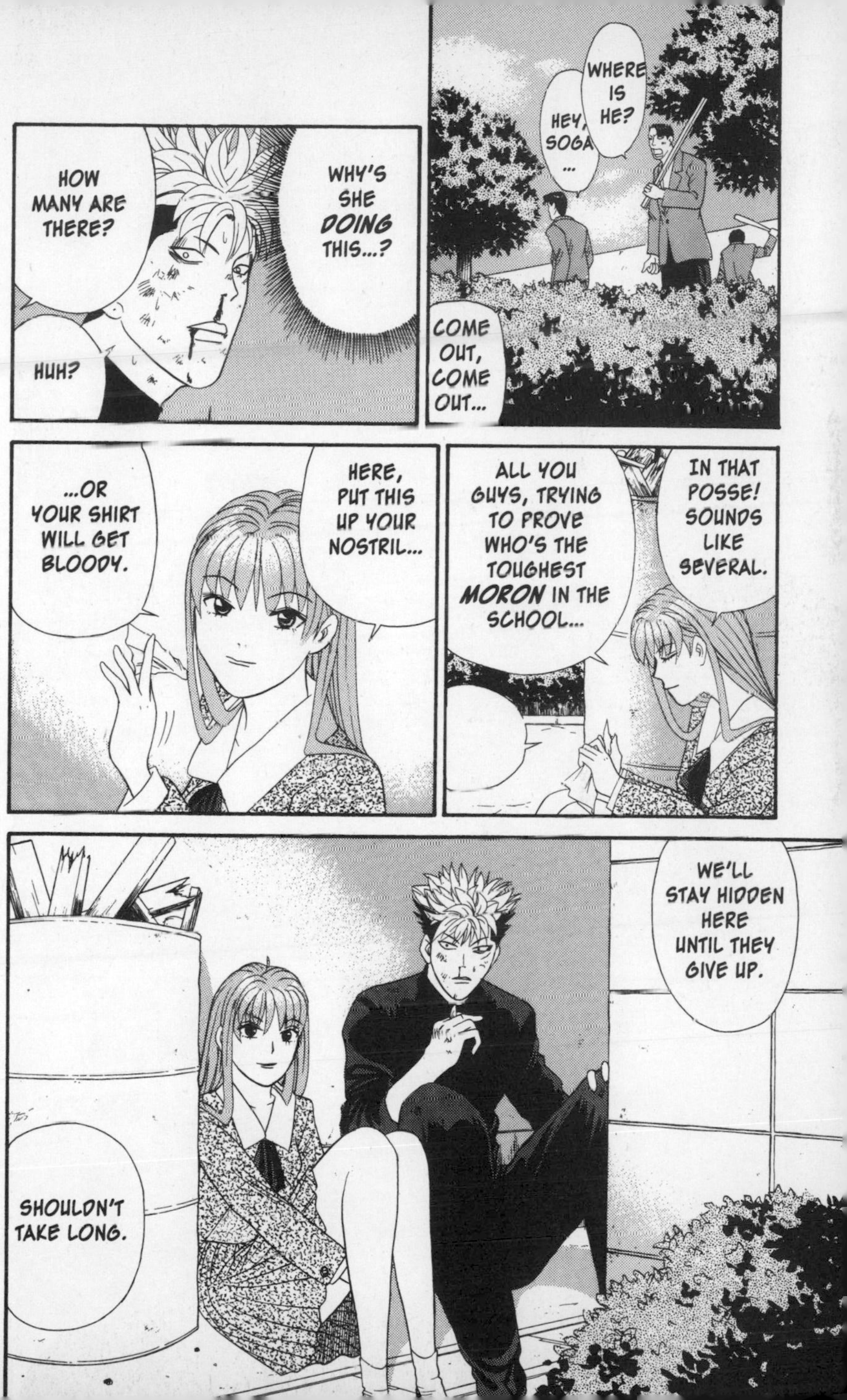
WHERE IS HE?
HEY, SOGA...
COME OUT, COME OUT...
WHY'S SHE *DOING* THIS...?
HOW MANY ARE THERE?
HUH?
IN THAT POSSE! SOUNDS LIKE SEVERAL.
ALL YOU GUYS, TRYING TO PROVE WHO'S THE TOUGHEST *MORON* IN THE SCHOOL...
HERE, PUT THIS UP YOUR NOSTRIL...
...OR YOUR SHIRT WILL GET BLOODY.
WE'LL STAY HIDDEN HERE UNTIL THEY GIVE UP.
SHOULDN'T TAKE LONG.

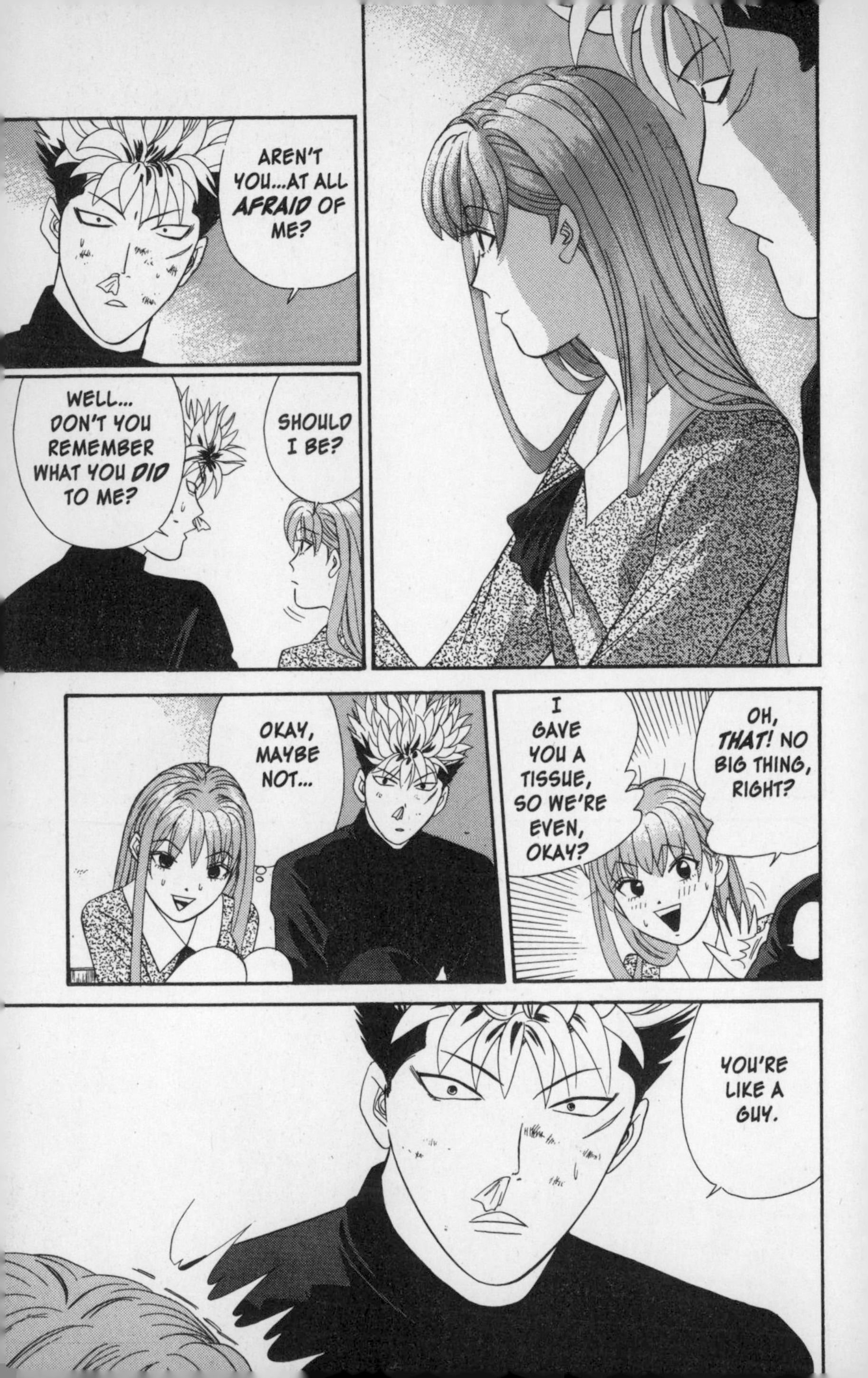
AREN'T YOU...AT ALL *AFRAID* OF ME?
SHOULD I BE?
WELL... DON'T YOU REMEMBER WHAT YOU *DID* TO ME?
OH, *THAT!* NO BIG THING, RIGHT?
I GAVE YOU A TISSUE, SO WE'RE EVEN, OKAY?
OKAY, MAYBE NOT...
YOU'RE LIKE A GUY.

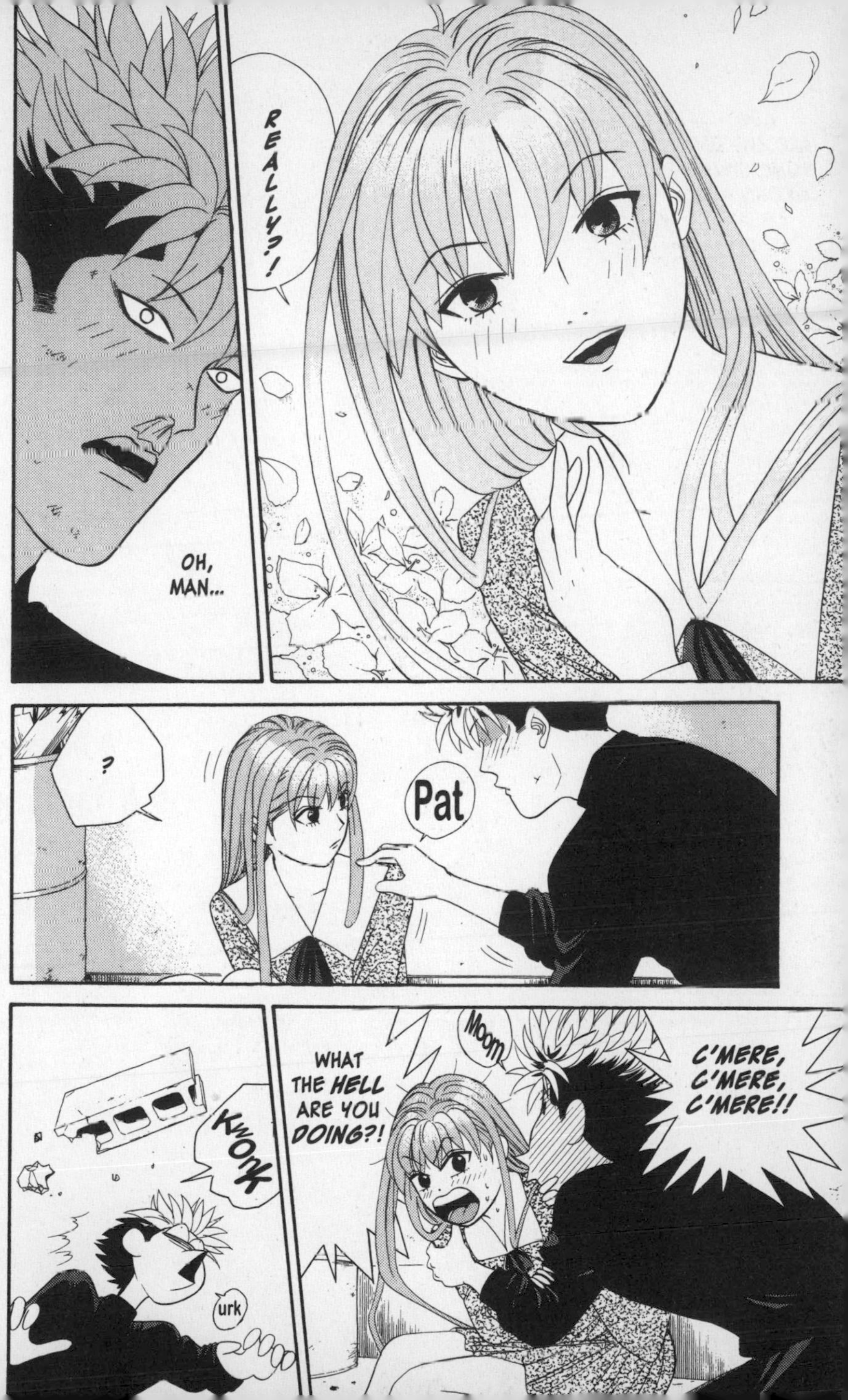
REALLY?!
OH, MAN...
Pat
?
C'MERE, C'MERE, C'MERE!!
Moom
WHAT THE HELL ARE YOU DOING?!
KWONK
urk

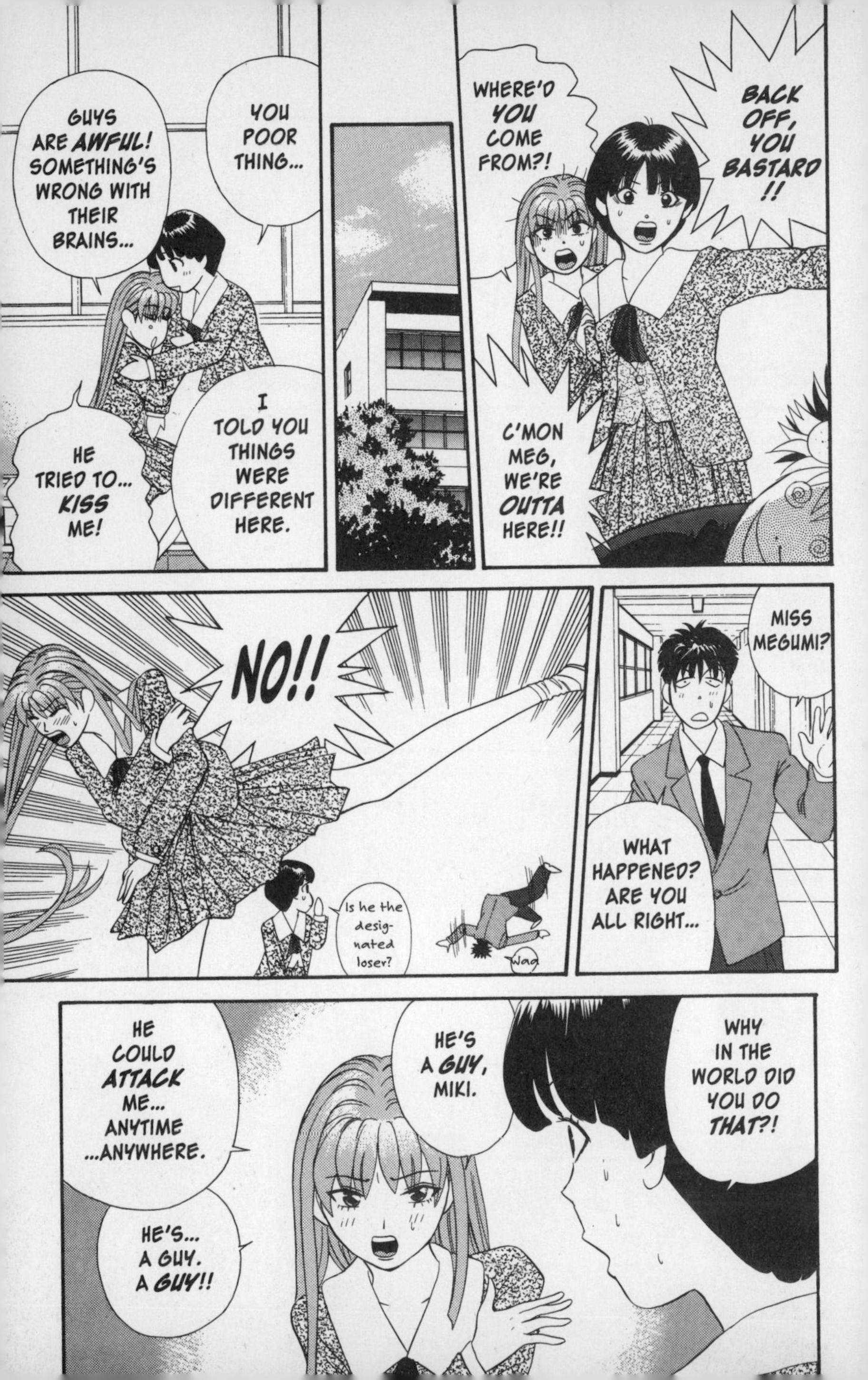

BACK OFF, YOU BASTARD!!
WHERE'D YOU COME FROM?!
C'MON MEG, WE'RE OUTTA HERE!!
YOU POOR THING...
GUYS ARE AWFUL! SOMETHING'S WRONG WITH THEIR BRAINS...
I TOLD YOU THINGS WERE DIFFERENT HERE.
HE TRIED TO... KISS ME!
MISS MEGUMI?
WHAT HAPPENED? ARE YOU ALL RIGHT...
NO!!
Wag
Is he the designated loser?
WHY IN THE WORLD DID YOU DO THAT?!
HE'S A GUY, MIKI.
HE COULD ATTACK ME... ANYTIME ...ANYWHERE.
HE'S... A GUY. A GUY!!

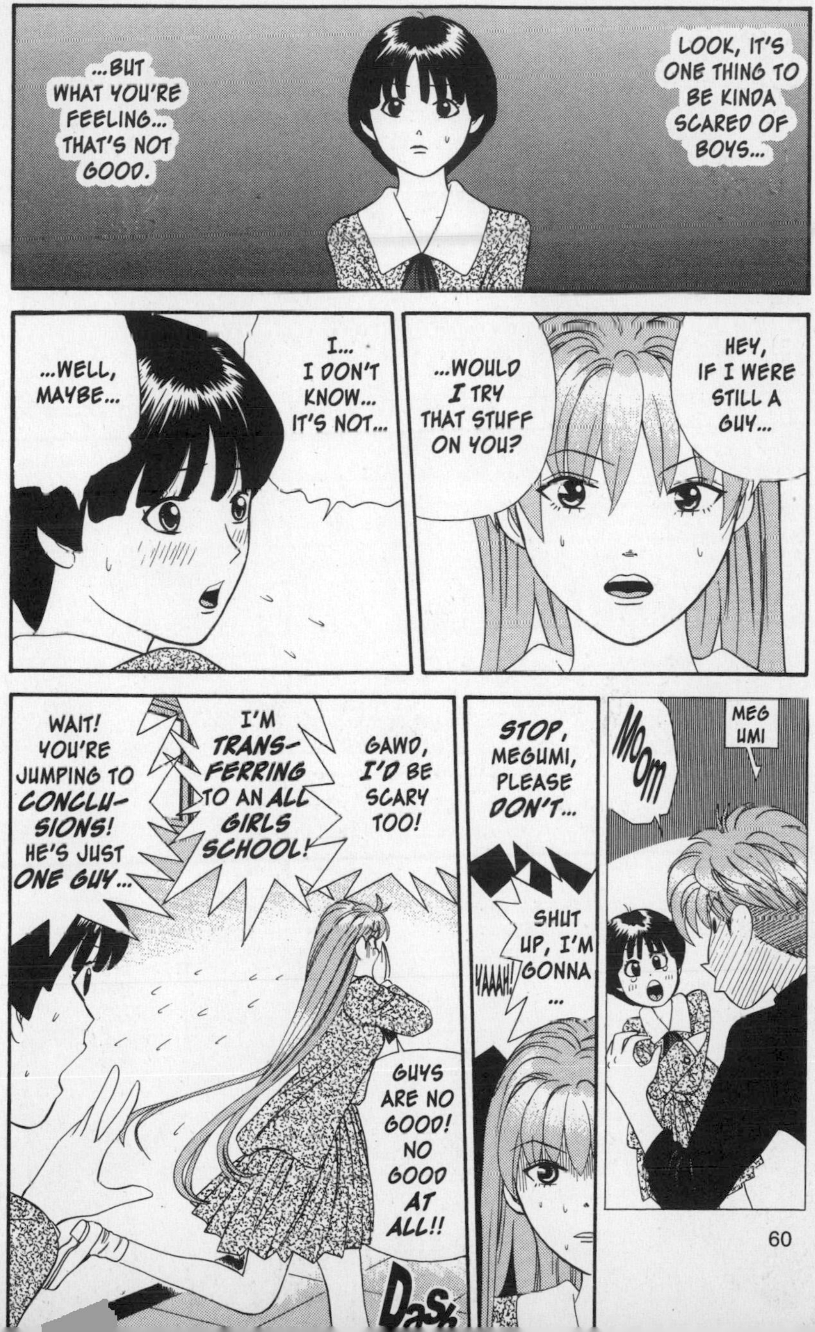
LOOK, IT'S ONE THING TO BE KINDA SCARED OF BOYS...
...BUT WHAT YOU'RE FEELING... THAT'S NOT GOOD.
HEY, IF I WERE STILL A GUY...
...WOULD I TRY THAT STUFF ON YOU?
I... I DON'T KNOW... IT'S NOT...
...WELL, MAYBE...
Moom
MEG UMI
STOP, MEGUMI, PLEASE DON'T...
SHUT UP, I'M GONNA ...
YAAAH!
GAWD, I'D BE SCARY TOO!
I'M TRANS-FERRING TO AN ALL GIRLS SCHOOL!
WAIT! YOU'RE JUMPING TO CONCLU-SIONS! HE'S JUST ONE GUY...
GUYS ARE NO GOOD! NO GOOD AT ALL!!
Dash

CHAPTER 3
THIS IS LOVE TOO...??

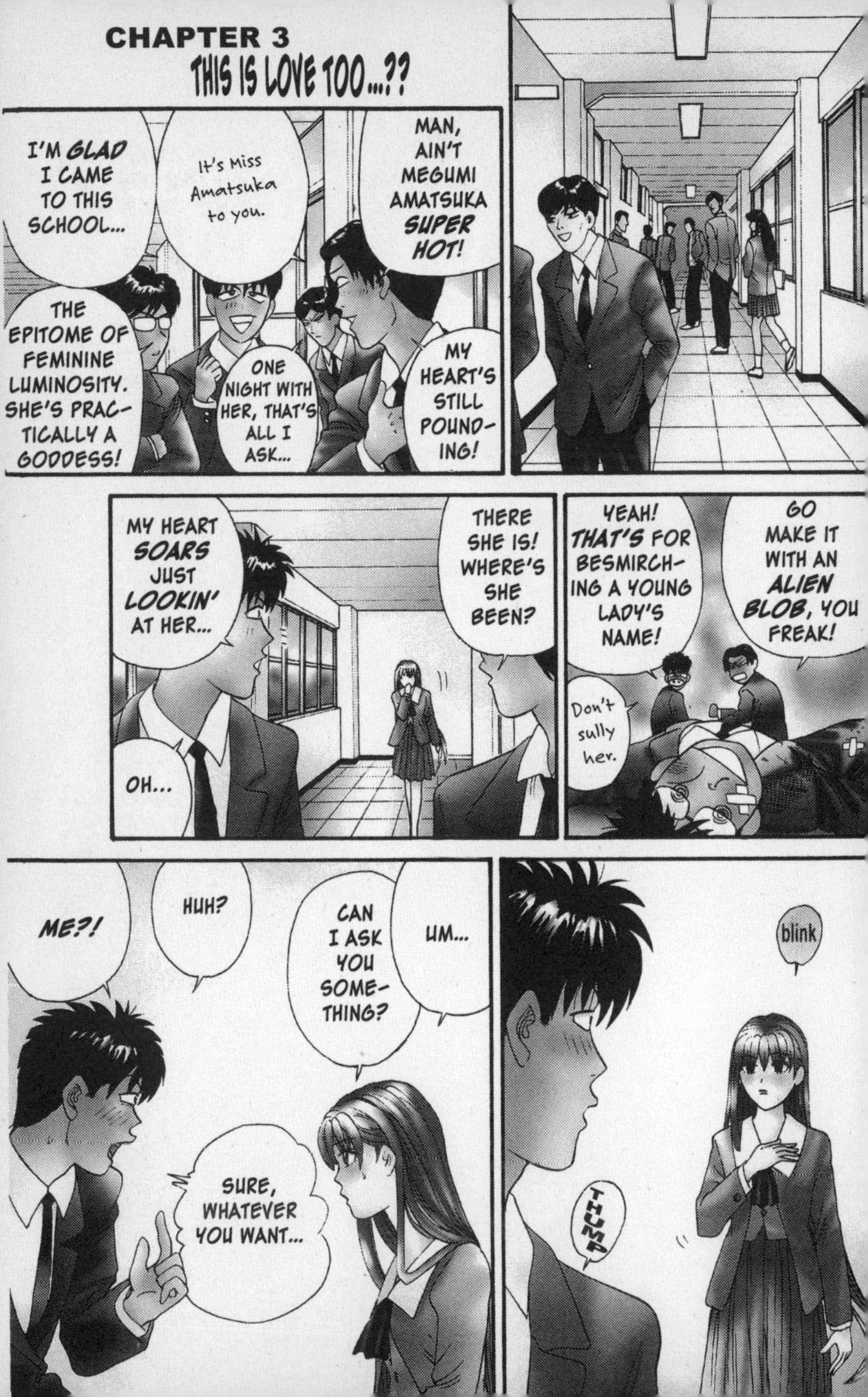
MAN, AIN'T MEGUMI AMATSUKA SUPER HOT!
It's Miss Amatsuka to you.
I'M GLAD I CAME TO THIS SCHOOL...
MY HEART'S STILL POUNDING!
ONE NIGHT WITH HER, THAT'S ALL I ASK...
THE EPITOME OF FEMININE LUMINOSITY. SHE'S PRACTICALLY A GODDESS!
GO MAKE IT WITH AN ALIEN BLOB, YOU FREAK!
YEAH! THAT'S FOR BESMIRCHING A YOUNG LADY'S NAME!
Don't sully her.
THERE SHE IS! WHERE'S SHE BEEN?
MY HEART SOARS JUST LOOKIN' AT HER...
OH...
blink
THUMP
UM...
CAN I ASK YOU SOMETHING?
HUH?
ME?!
SURE, WHATEVER YOU WANT...

Chapter 3:
This is Love Too...??

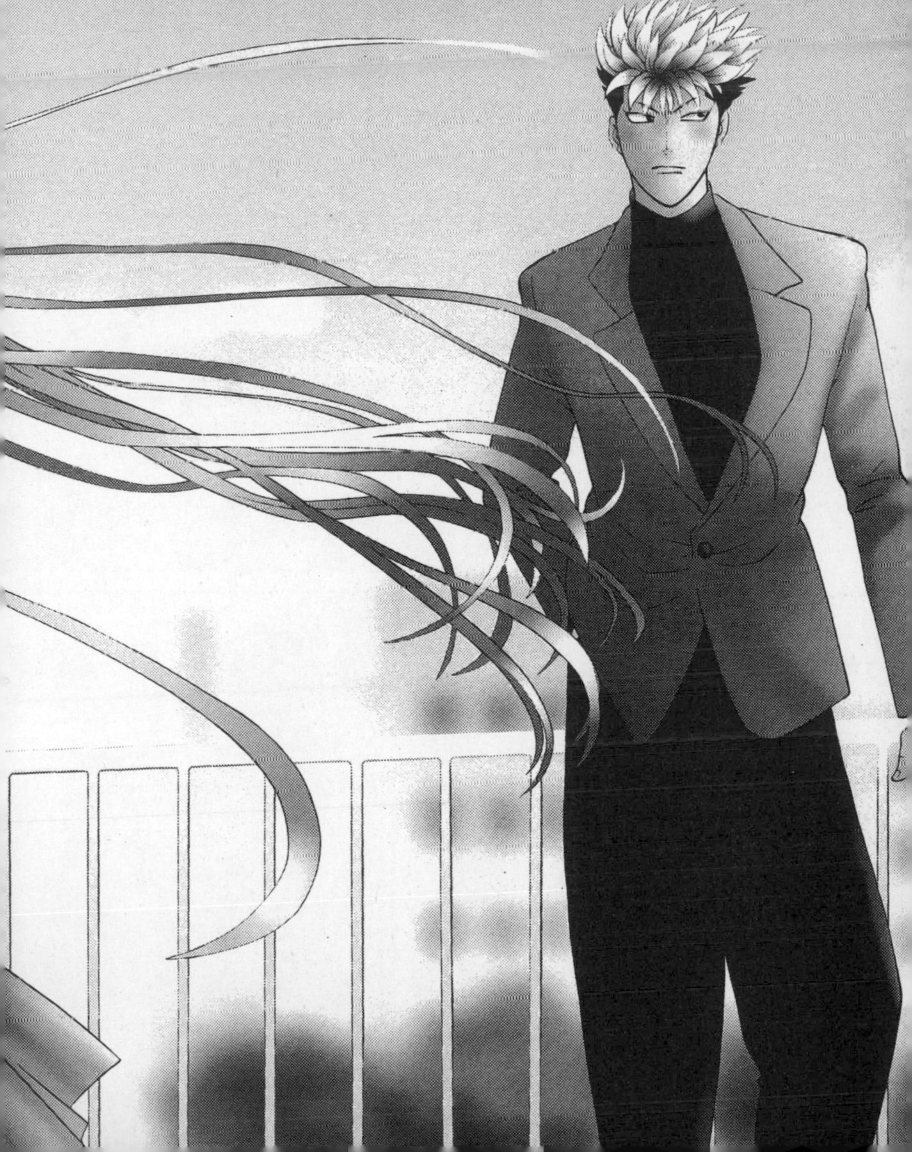

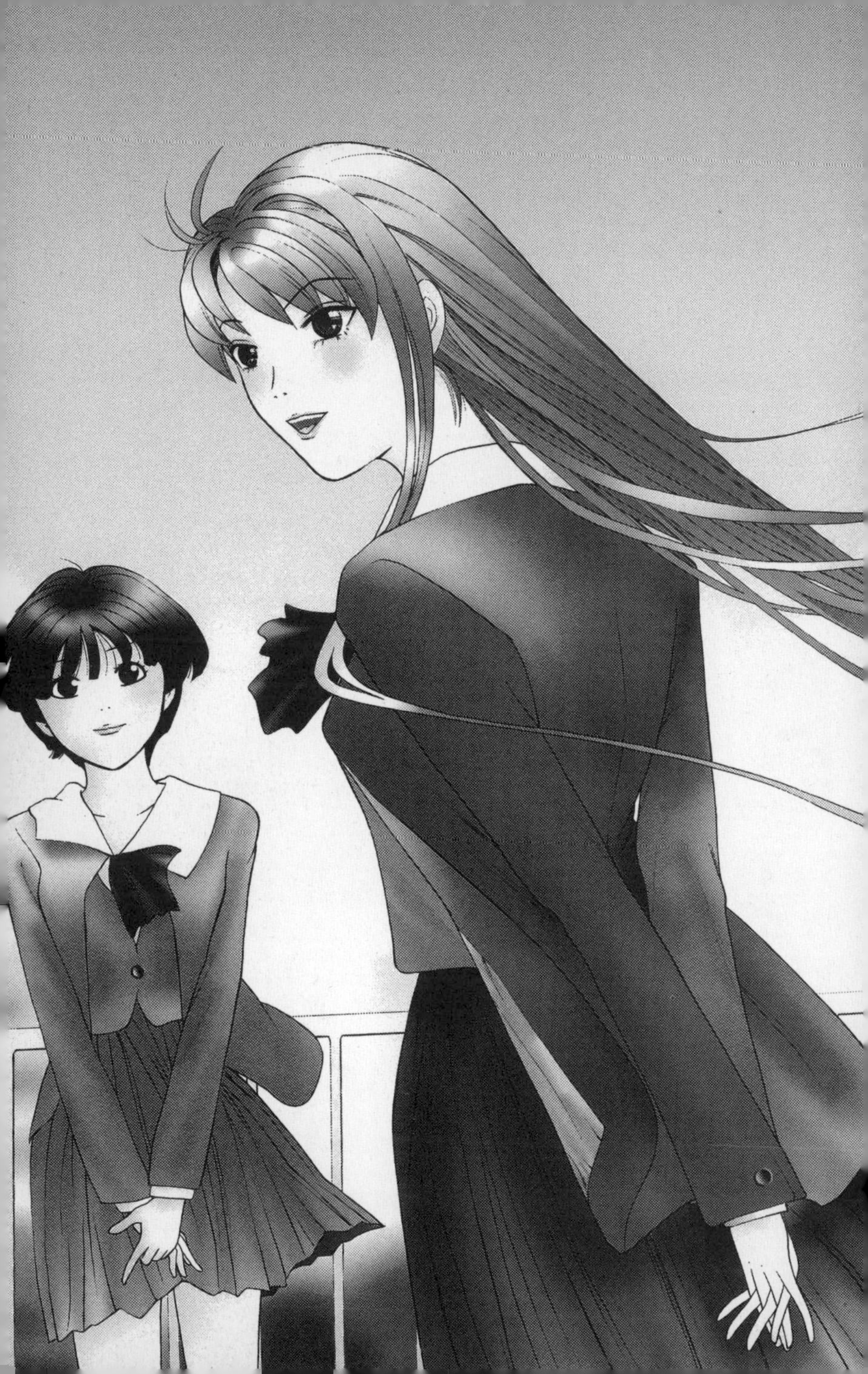

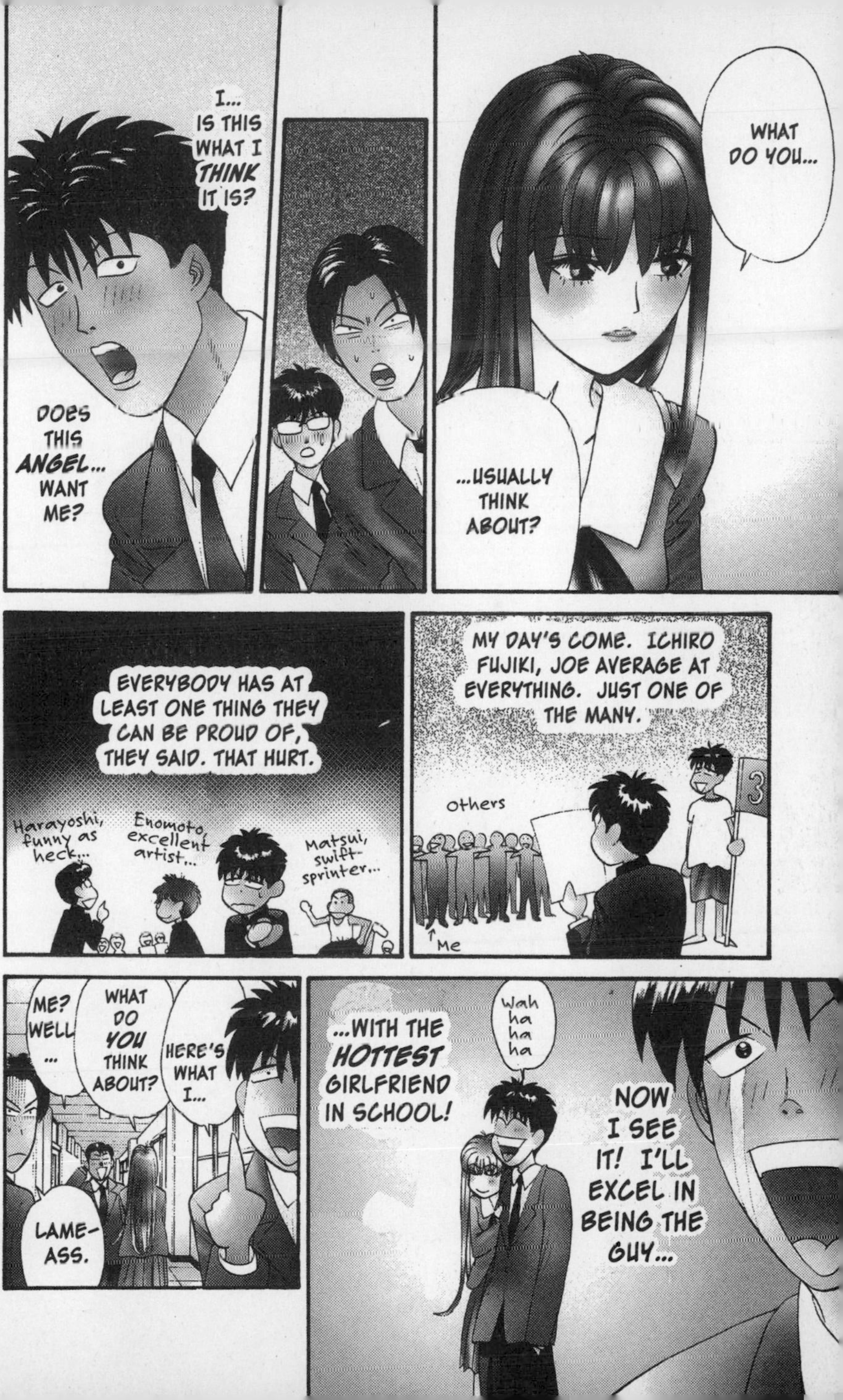
WHAT DO YOU...
...USUALLY THINK ABOUT?
I... IS THIS WHAT I THINK IT IS?
DOES THIS ANGEL... WANT ME?
MY DAY'S COME. ICHIRO FUJIKI, JOE AVERAGE AT EVERYTHING. JUST ONE OF THE MANY.
others
Me
EVERYBODY HAS AT LEAST ONE THING THEY CAN BE PROUD OF, THEY SAID. THAT HURT.
Matsui, swift sprinter...
Enomoto, excellent artist...
Harayoshi, funny as heck...
NOW I SEE IT! I'LL EXCEL IN BEING THE GUY...
...WITH THE HOTTEST GIRLFRIEND IN SCHOOL!
Wah ha ha ha
HERE'S WHAT I...
WHAT DO YOU THINK ABOUT?
ME? WELL ...
LAME-ASS.

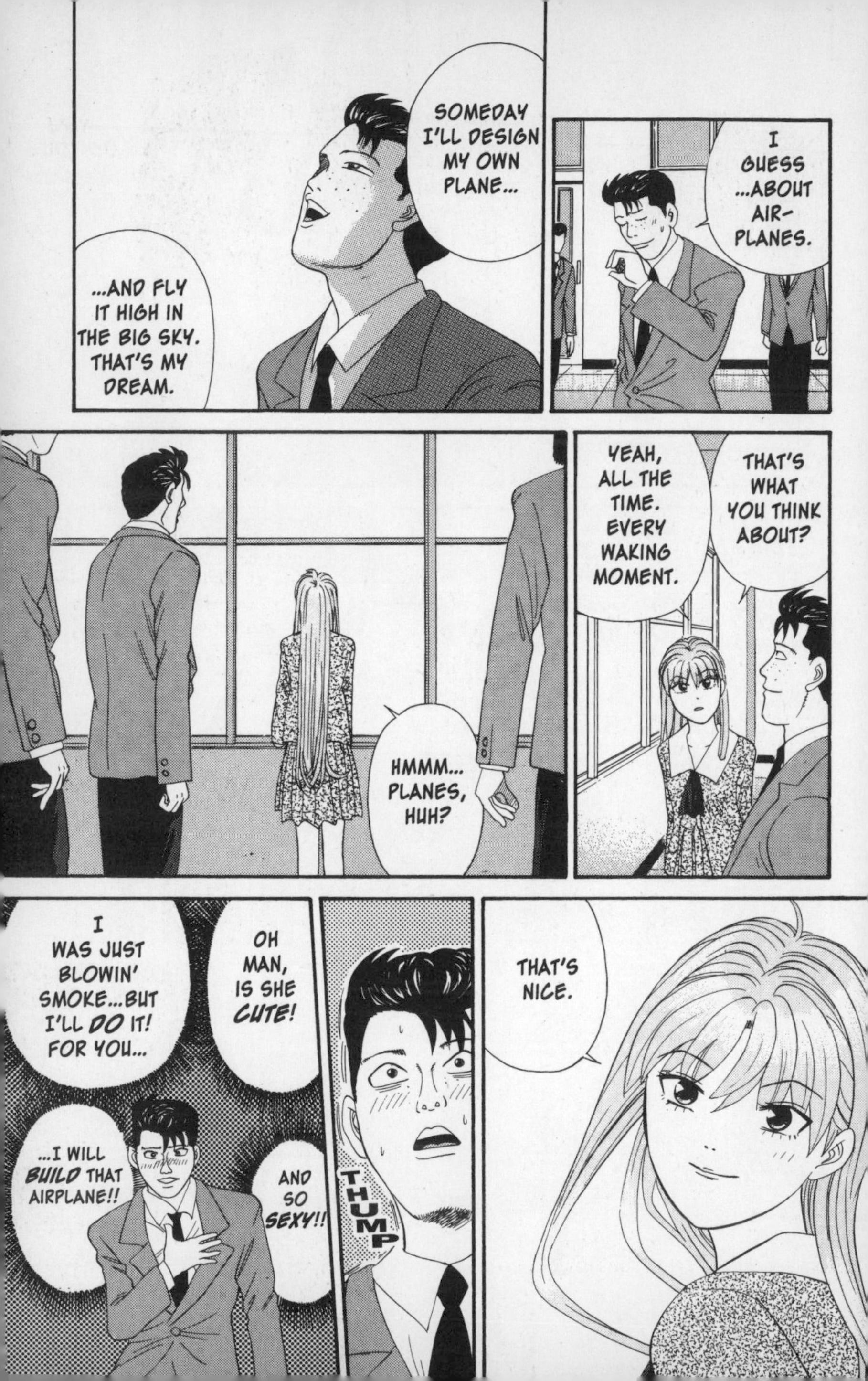
I GUESS ...ABOUT AIR-PLANES.
SOMEDAY I'LL DESIGN MY OWN PLANE...
...AND FLY IT HIGH IN THE BIG SKY. THAT'S MY DREAM.
THAT'S WHAT YOU THINK ABOUT?
YEAH, ALL THE TIME. EVERY WAKING MOMENT.
HMMM... PLANES, HUH?
THAT'S NICE.
OH MAN, IS SHE *CUTE*!
AND SO *SEXY*!!
THUMP
I WAS JUST BLOWIN' SMOKE...BUT I'LL *DO* IT! FOR YOU...
...I WILL *BUILD* THAT AIRPLANE!!

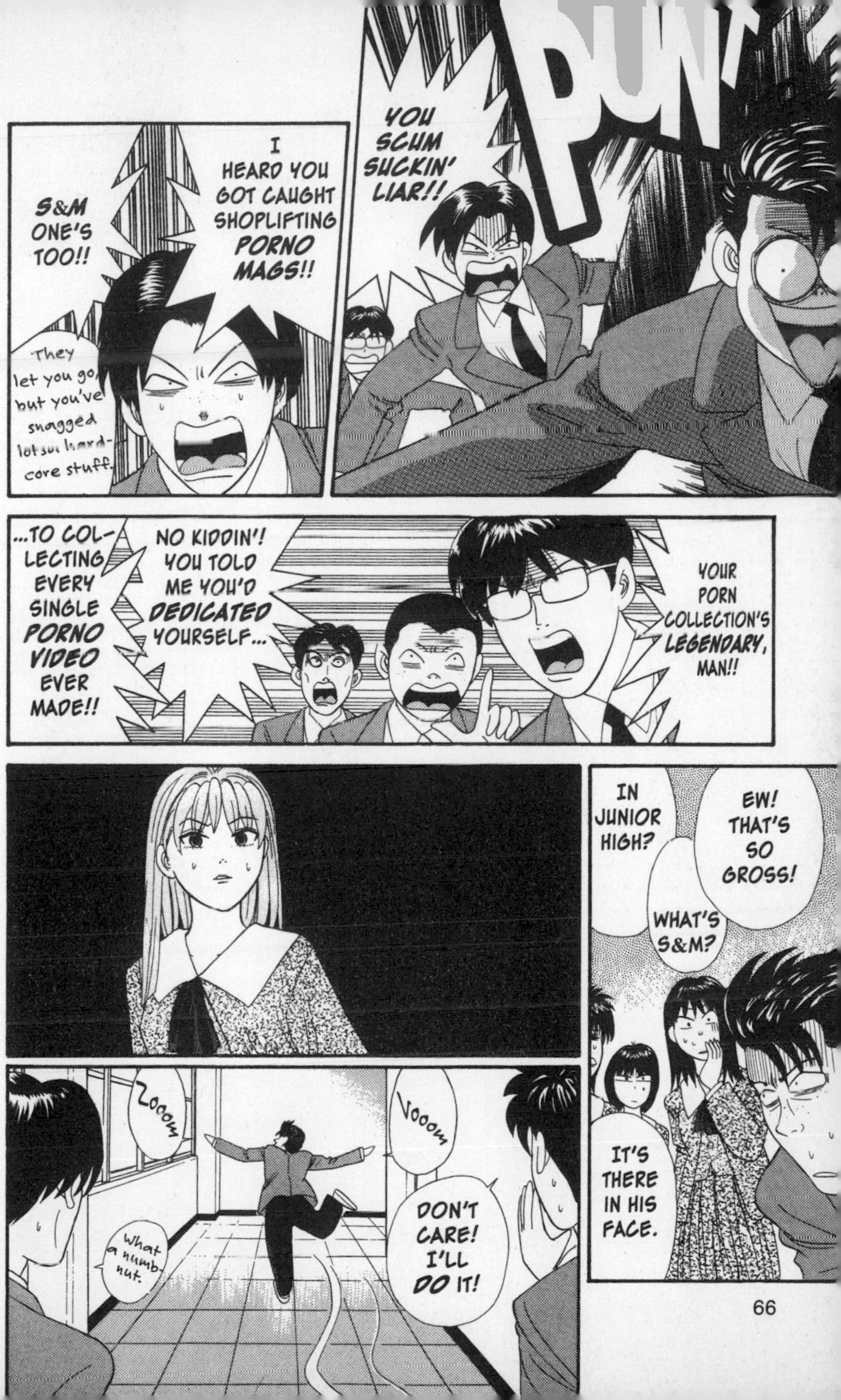
PUNT
YOU SCUM SUCKIN' LIAR!!
I HEARD YOU GOT CAUGHT SHOPLIFTING PORNO MAGS!!
S&M ONE'S TOO!!
They let you go, but you've snagged hard-core stuff.
YOUR PORN COLLECTION'S LEGENDARY, MAN!!
NO KIDDIN'! YOU TOLD ME YOU'D DEDICATED YOURSELF...
...TO COLLECTING EVERY SINGLE PORNO VIDEO EVER MADE!!
EW! THAT'S SO GROSS!
IN JUNIOR HIGH?
WHAT'S S&M?
IT'S THERE IN HIS FACE.
Vooom
DON'T CARE! I'LL DO IT!
Zocoom
What a numb-nut.

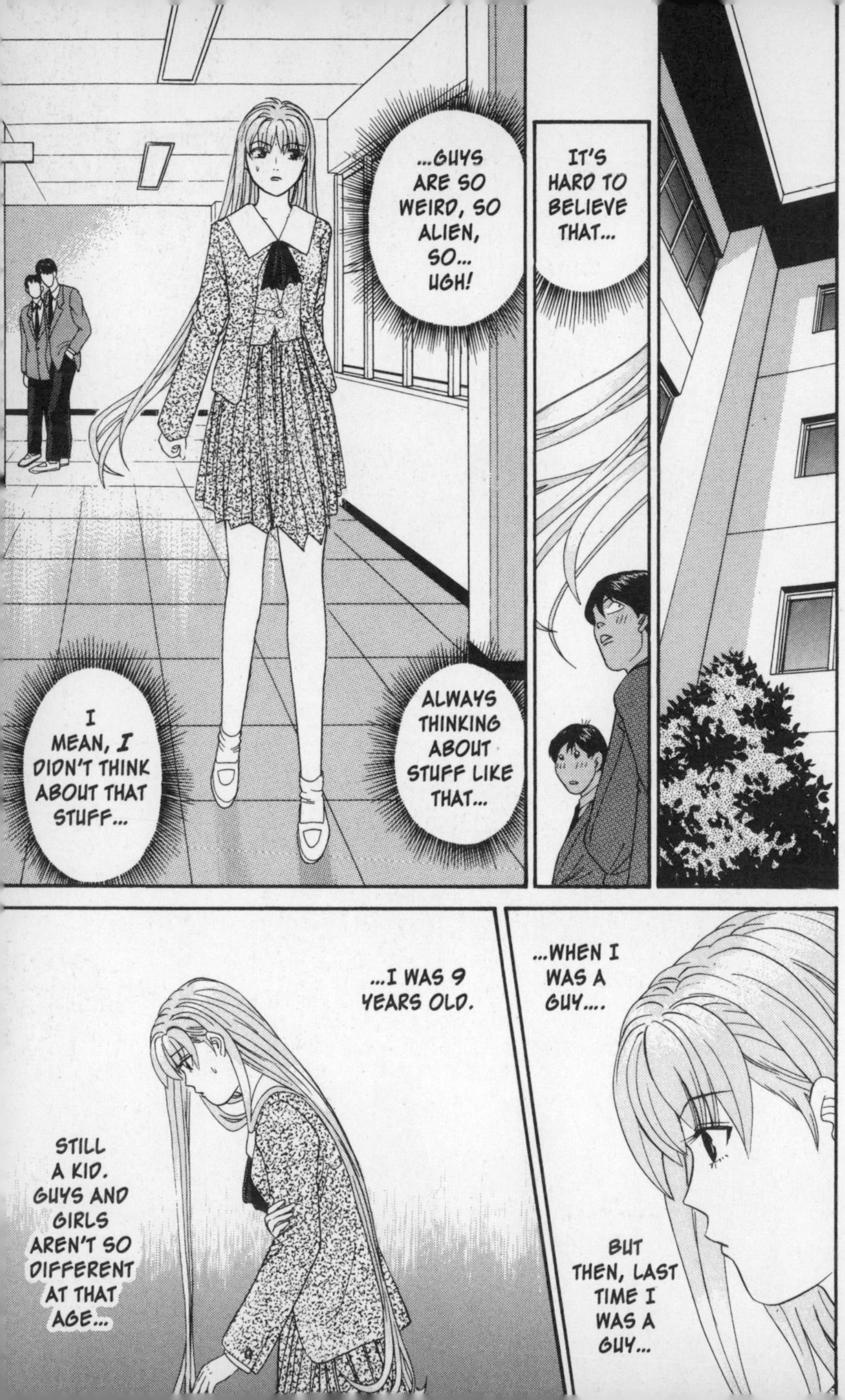
IT'S HARD TO BELIEVE THAT...
...GUYS ARE SO WEIRD, SO ALIEN, SO... UGH!
ALWAYS THINKING ABOUT STUFF LIKE THAT...
I MEAN, *I* DIDN'T THINK ABOUT THAT STUFF...
...WHEN I WAS A GUY....
BUT THEN, LAST TIME I WAS A GUY...
...I WAS 9 YEARS OLD.
STILL A KID. GUYS AND GIRLS AREN'T SO DIFFERENT AT THAT AGE...

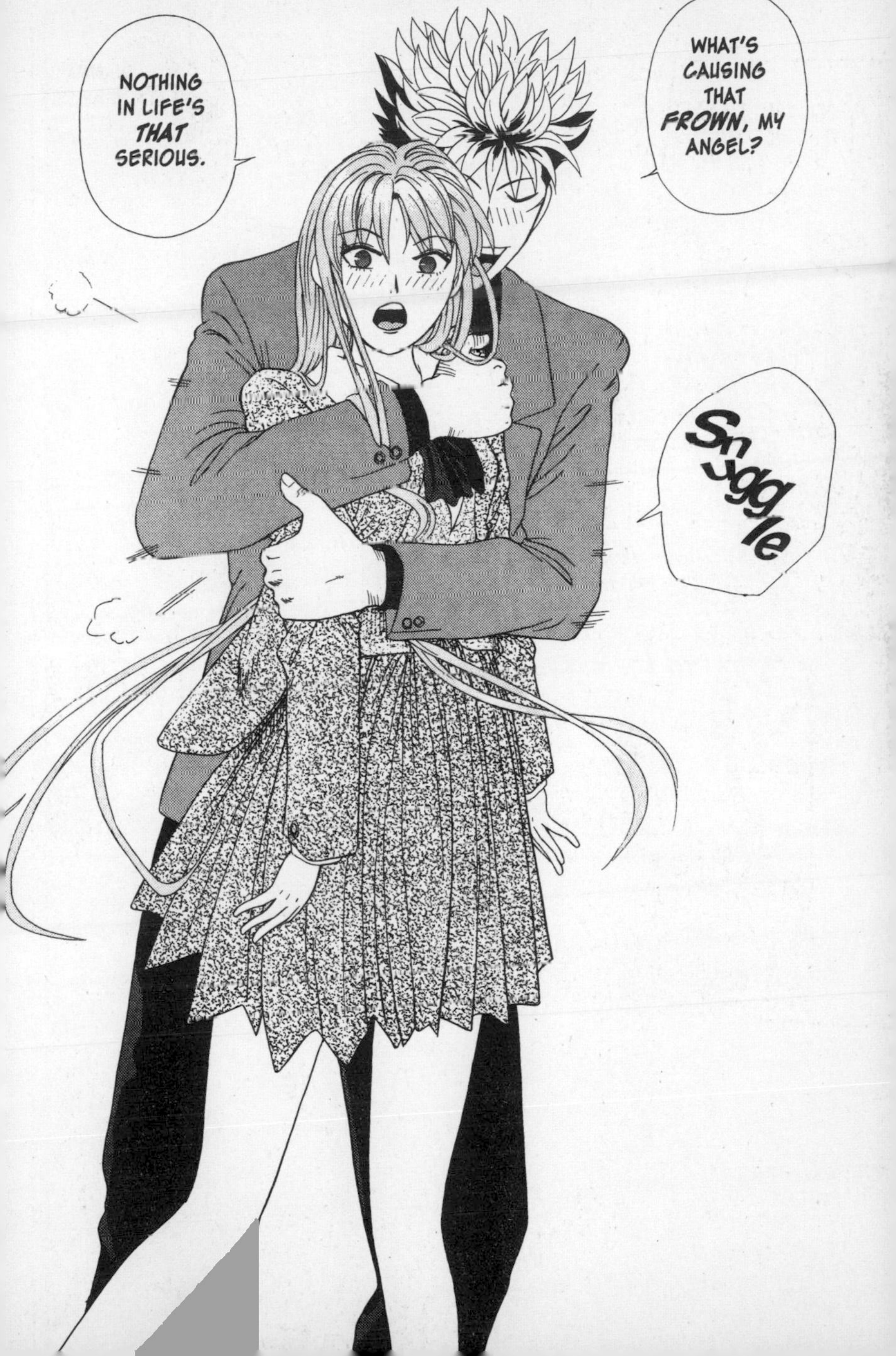
WHAT'S CAUSING THAT *FROWN*, MY ANGEL?
NOTHING IN LIFE'S *THAT* SERIOUS.
Snuggle

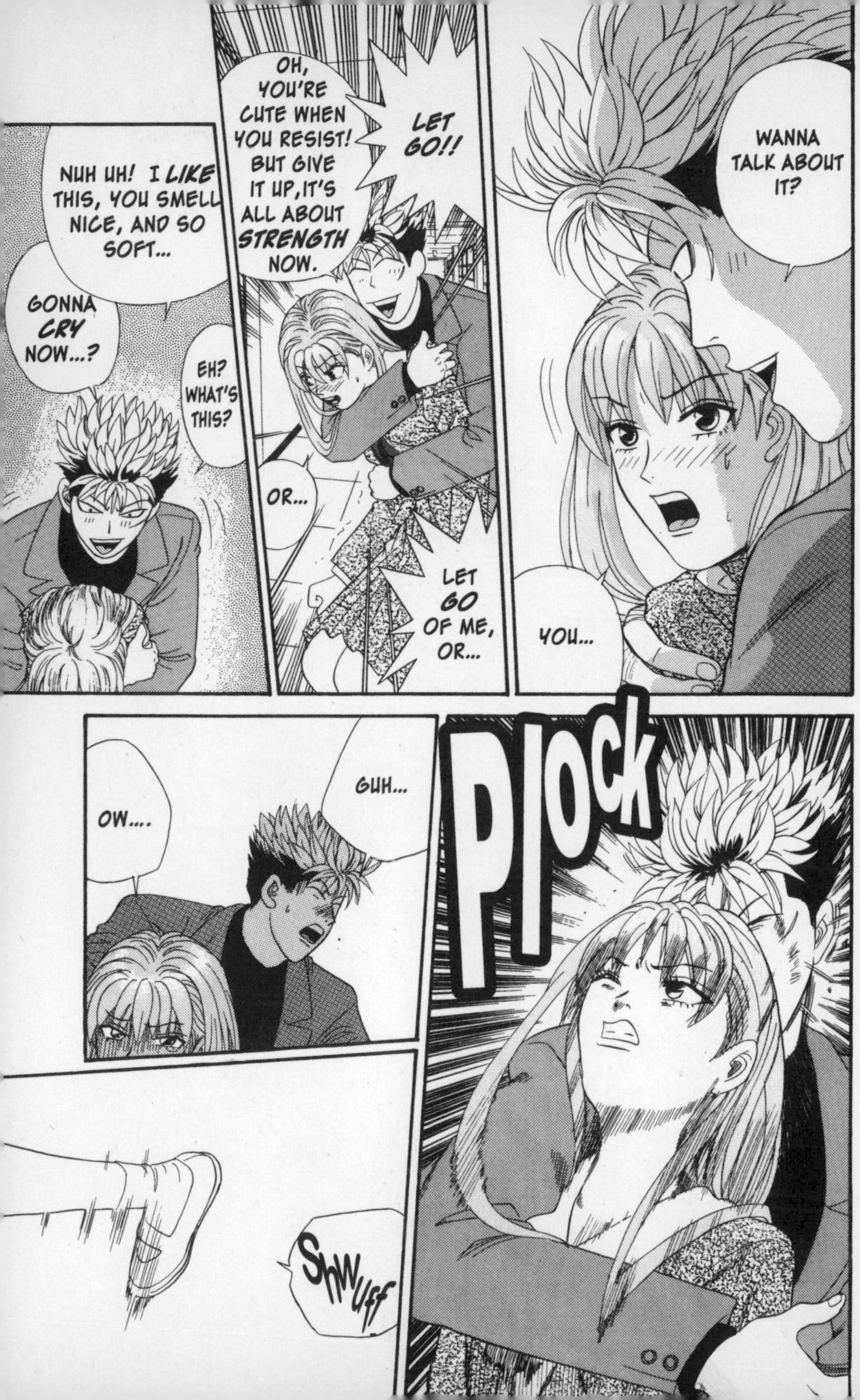
WANNA TALK ABOUT IT?
YOU...
LET GO!!
OH, YOU'RE CUTE WHEN YOU RESIST! BUT GIVE IT UP, IT'S ALL ABOUT STRENGTH NOW.
LET GO OF ME, OR...
OR...
NUH UH! I LIKE THIS, YOU SMELL NICE, AND SO SOFT...
GONNA CRY NOW...?
EH? WHAT'S THIS?
PLOCK
GUH...
OW....
SHWUFF

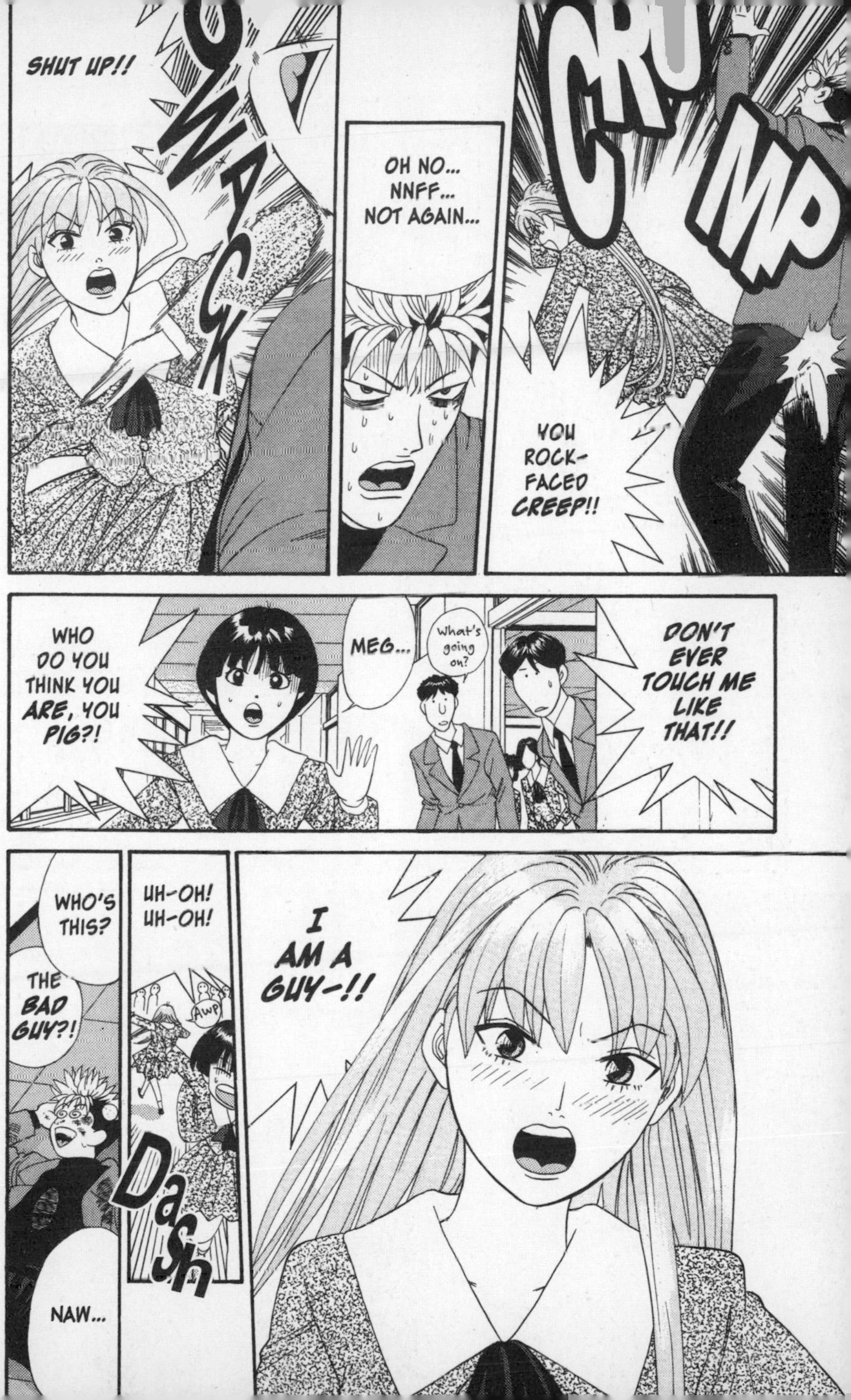
CRUMP
YOU ROCK-FACED CREEP!!
OH NO... NNFF... NOT AGAIN...
SHUT UP!!
WACK
DON'T EVER TOUCH ME LIKE THAT!!
What's going on?
MEG...
WHO DO YOU THINK YOU ARE, YOU PIG?!
I AM A GUY-!!
UH-OH! UH-OH!
Awp
DaSh
WHO'S THIS?
THE BAD GUY?!
NAW...

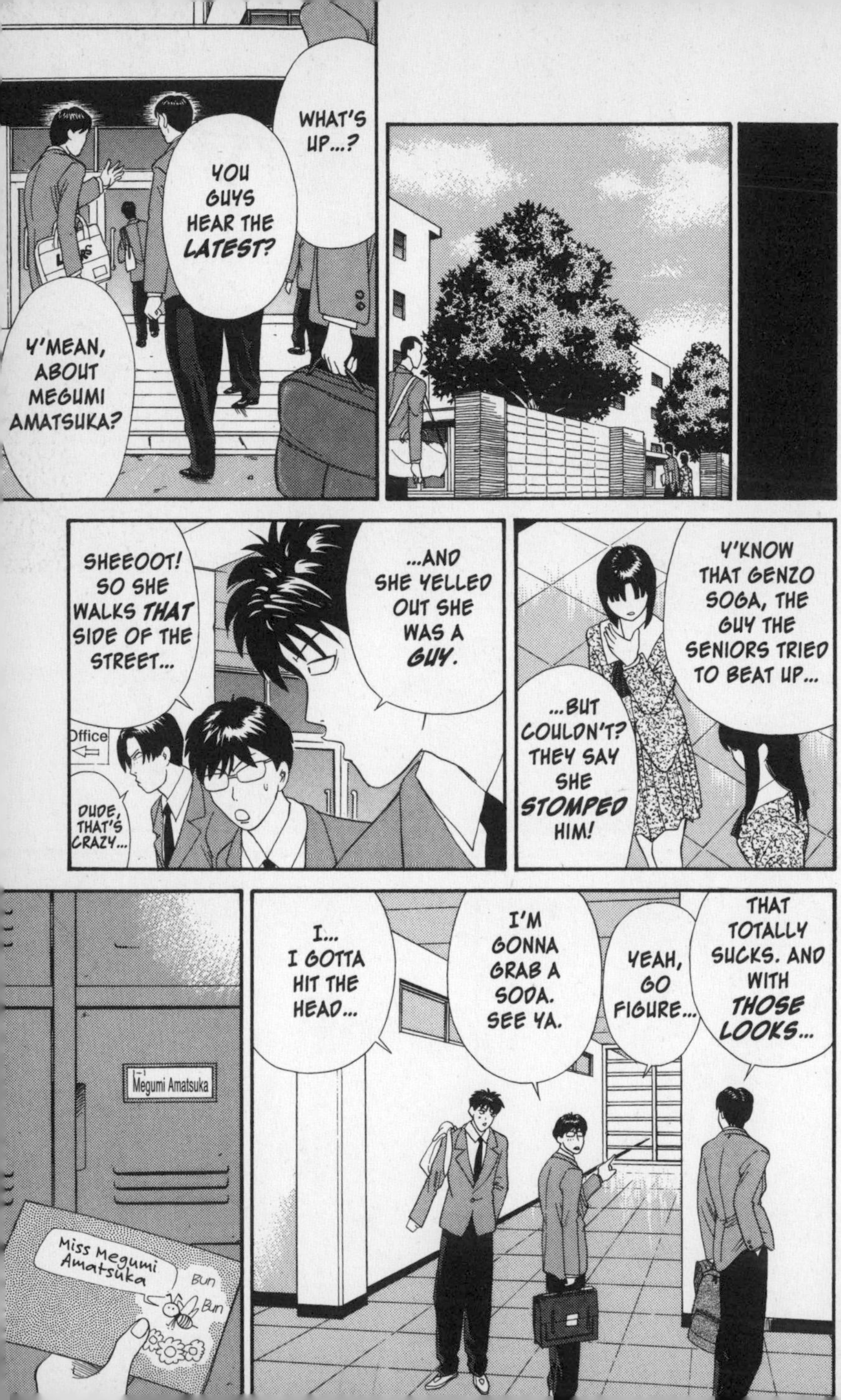
WHAT'S UP...?
YOU GUYS HEAR THE LATEST?
Y'MEAN, ABOUT MEGUMI AMATSUKA?
Y'KNOW THAT GENZO SOGA, THE GUY THE SENIORS TRIED TO BEAT UP...
...BUT COULDN'T? THEY SAY SHE STOMPED HIM!
...AND SHE YELLED OUT SHE WAS A GUY.
SHEEOOT! SO SHE WALKS THAT SIDE OF THE STREET...
Office
DUDE, THAT'S CRAZY...
THAT TOTALLY SUCKS. AND WITH THOSE LOOKS...
YEAH, GO FIGURE...
I'M GONNA GRAB A SODA. SEE YA.
I... I GOTTA HIT THE HEAD...
Megumi Amatsuka
Miss Megumi Amatsuka
Bun
Bun

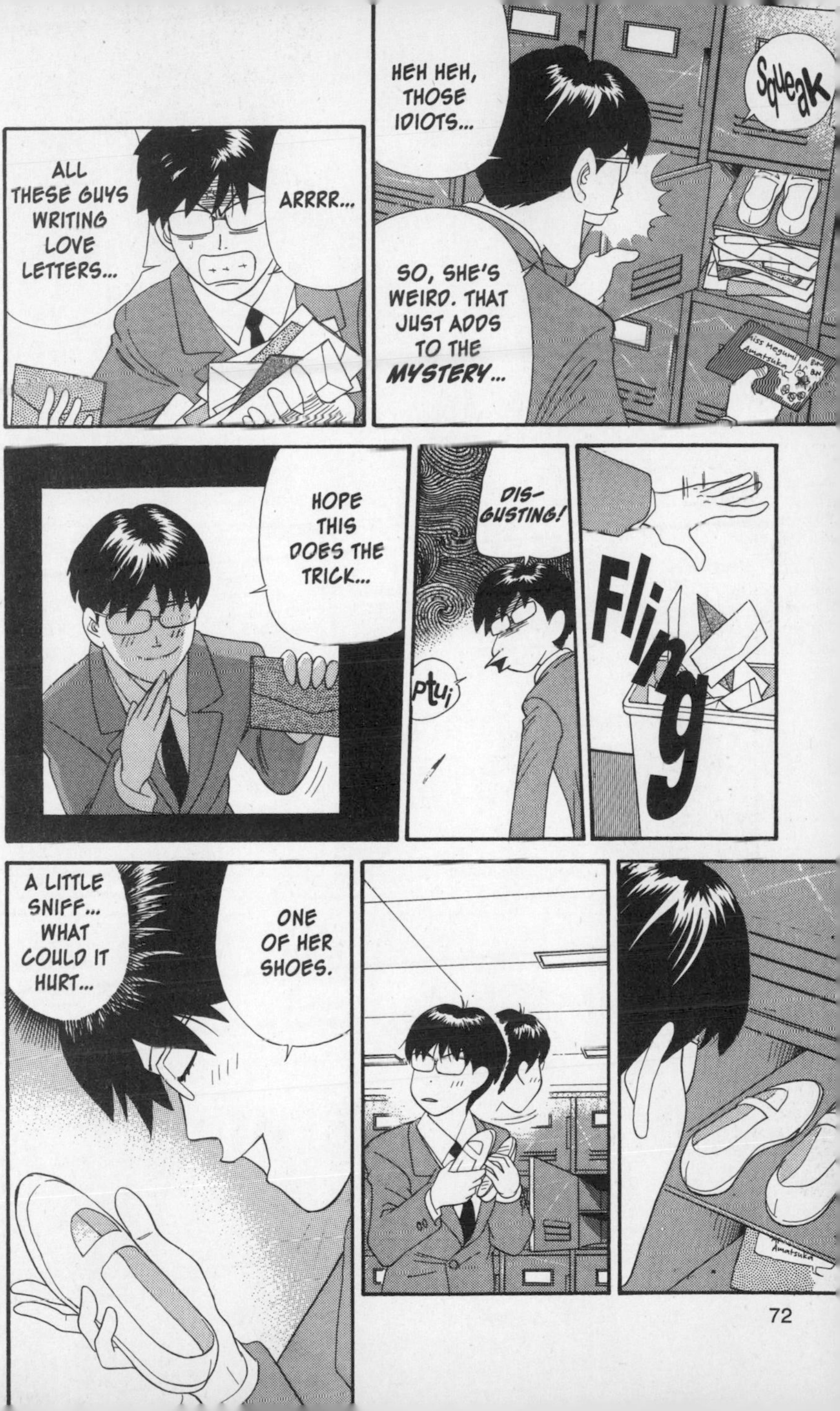

Squeak
HEH HEH, THOSE IDIOTS...
SO, SHE'S WEIRD. THAT JUST ADDS TO THE MYSTERY...
Amatsuka
ARRRR...
ALL THESE GUYS WRITING LOVE LETTERS...
Fling
DIS-GUSTING!
ptui
HOPE THIS DOES THE TRICK...
Amatsuka
ONE OF HER SHOES.
A LITTLE SNIFF... WHAT COULD IT HURT...

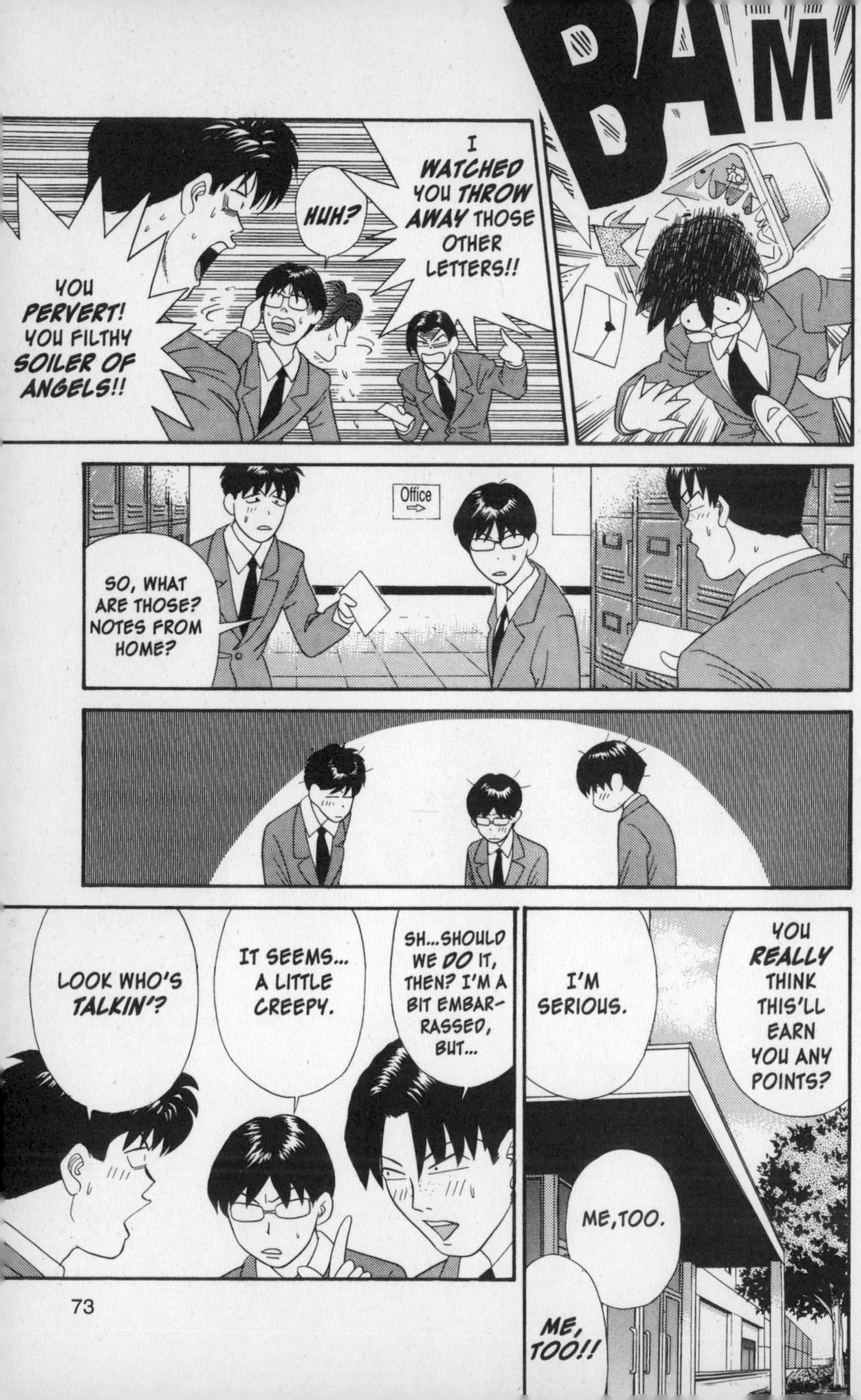
BAM
I WATCHED YOU THROW AWAY THOSE OTHER LETTERS!!
HUH?
YOU PERVERT! YOU FILTHY SOILER OF ANGELS!!
Office
SO, WHAT ARE THOSE? NOTES FROM HOME?
YOU REALLY THINK THIS'LL EARN YOU ANY POINTS?
I'M SERIOUS.
ME, TOO.
ME, TOO!!
SH...SHOULD WE DO IT, THEN? I'M A BIT EMBARRASSED, BUT...
IT SEEMS... A LITTLE CREEPY.
LOOK WHO'S TALKIN'?

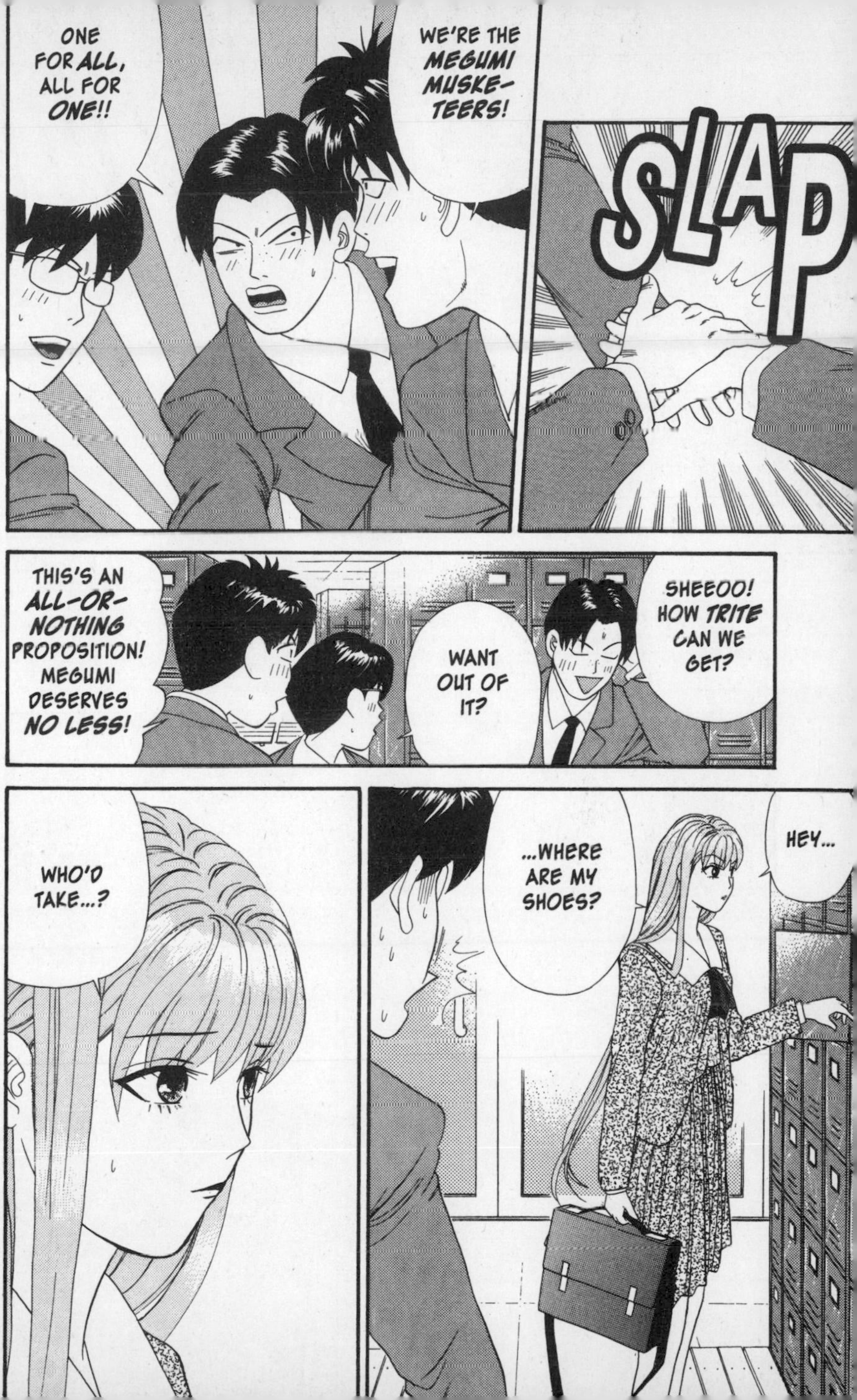
SLAP
WE'RE THE MEGUMI MUSKETEERS!
ONE FOR ALL, ALL FOR ONE!!
SHEEOO! HOW TRITE CAN WE GET?
WANT OUT OF IT?
THIS'S AN ALL-OR-NOTHING PROPOSITION! MEGUMI DESERVES NO LESS!
HEY...
...WHERE ARE MY SHOES?
WHO'D TAKE...?

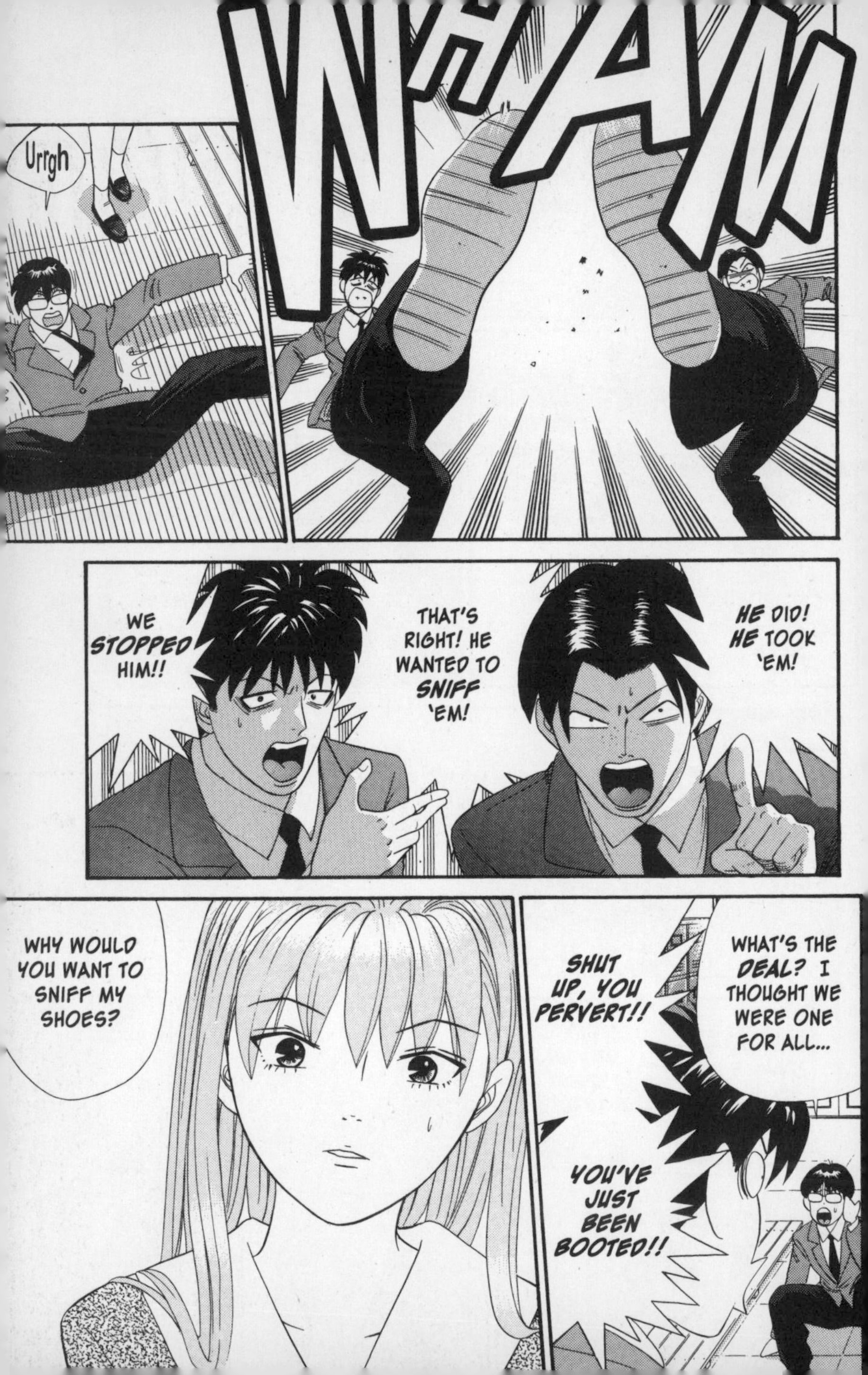
WHAM
Urrgh
HE DID! HE TOOK 'EM!
THAT'S RIGHT! HE WANTED TO SNIFF 'EM!
WE STOPPED HIM!!
WHAT'S THE DEAL? I THOUGHT WE WERE ONE FOR ALL...
SHUT UP, YOU PERVERT!!
YOU'VE JUST BEEN BOOTED!!
WHY WOULD YOU WANT TO SNIFF MY SHOES?

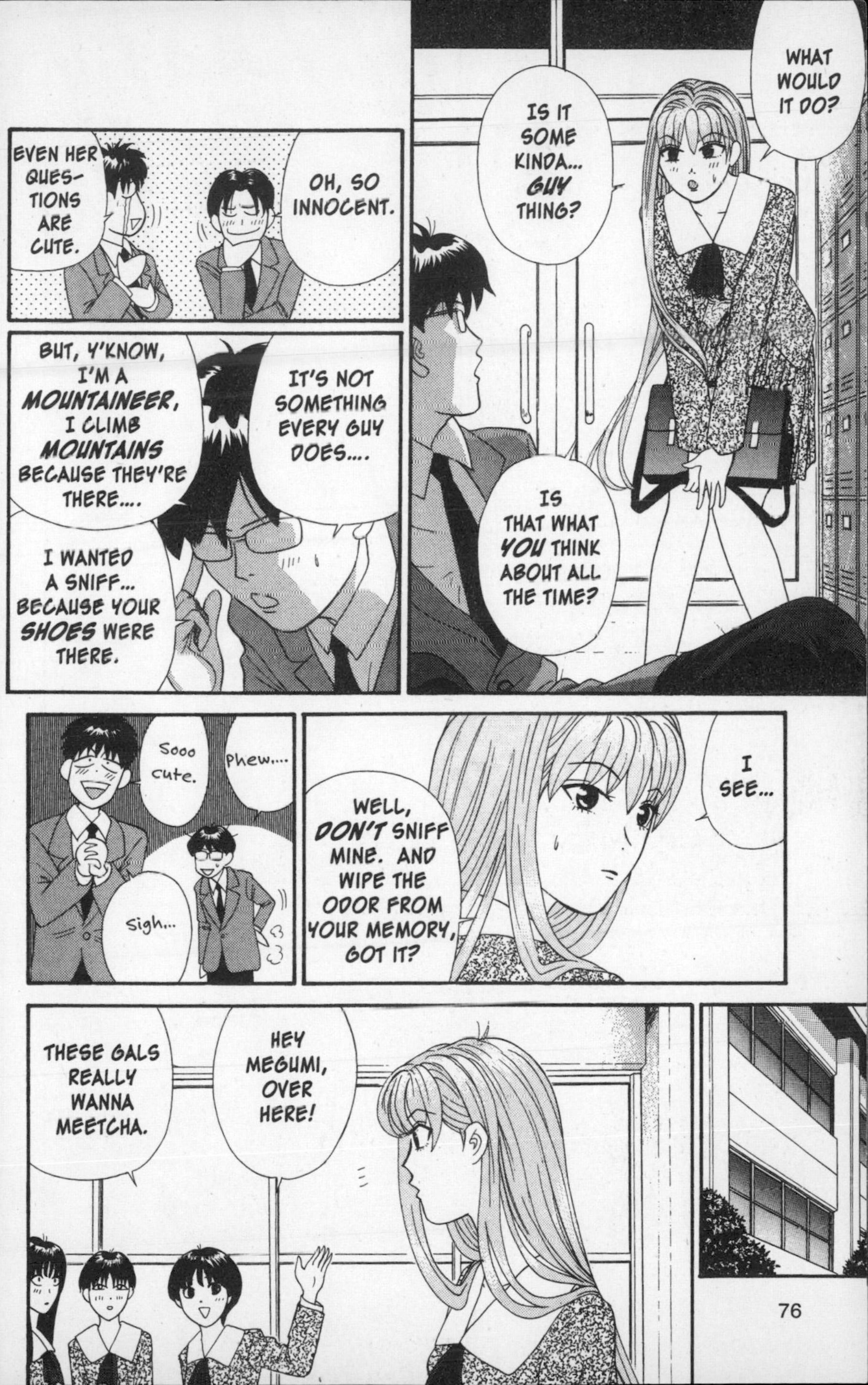
WHAT WOULD IT DO?
IS IT SOME KINDA... GUY THING?
IS THAT WHAT YOU THINK ABOUT ALL THE TIME?
OH, SO INNOCENT.
EVEN HER QUES- TIONS ARE CUTE.
IT'S NOT SOMETHING EVERY GUY DOES....
BUT, Y'KNOW, I'M A MOUNTAINEER, I CLIMB MOUNTAINS BECAUSE THEY'RE THERE....
I WANTED A SNIFF... BECAUSE YOUR SHOES WERE THERE.
I SEE...
WELL, DON'T SNIFF MINE. AND WIPE THE ODOR FROM YOUR MEMORY, GOT IT?
Phew....
Sooo cute.
Sigh...
HEY MEGUMI, OVER HERE!
THESE GALS REALLY WANNA MEETCHA.

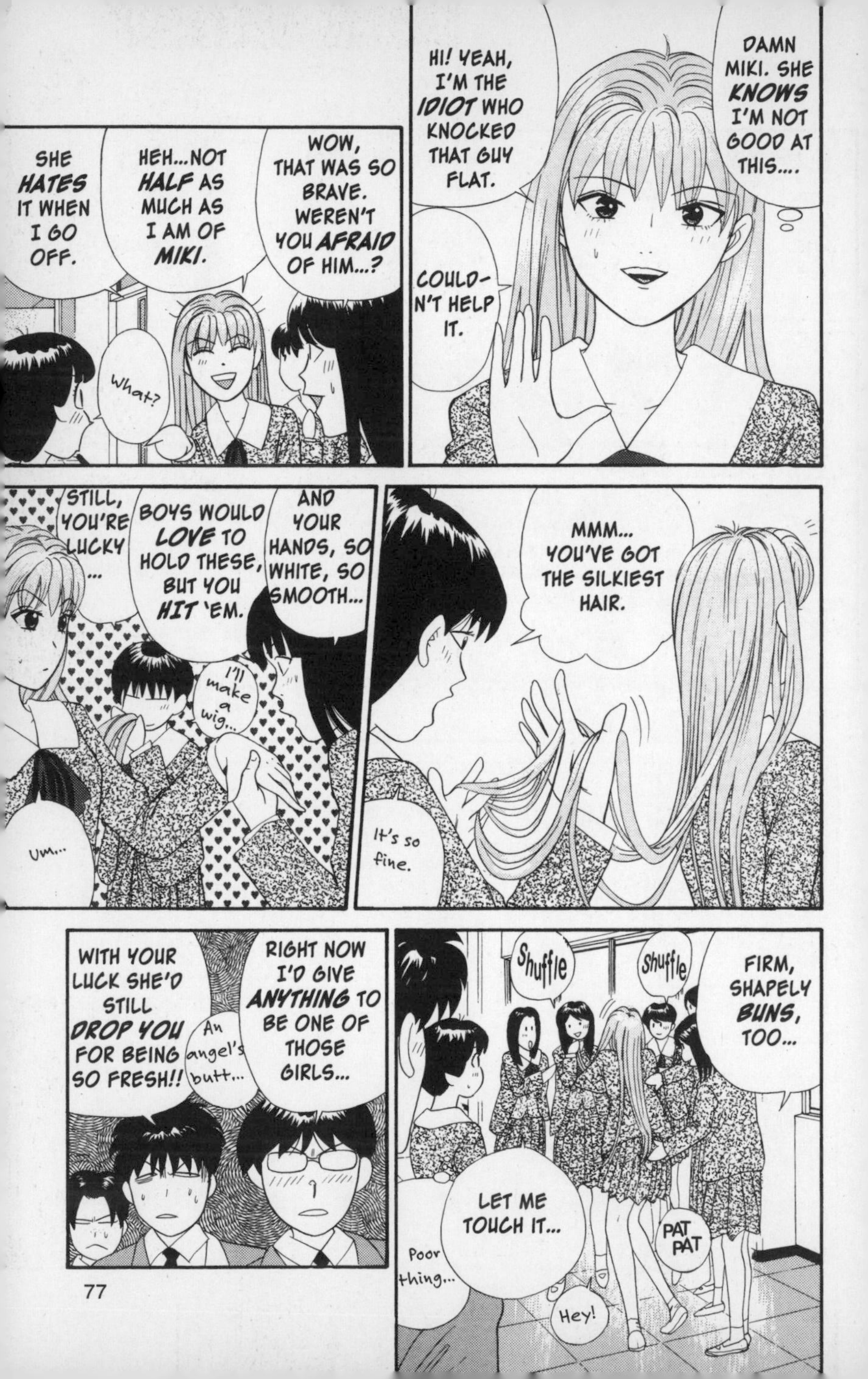
DAMN MIKI. SHE KNOWS I'M NOT GOOD AT THIS....
HI! YEAH, I'M THE IDIOT WHO KNOCKED THAT GUY FLAT.
COULDN'T HELP IT.
WOW, THAT WAS SO BRAVE. WEREN'T YOU AFRAID OF HIM...?
HEH...NOT HALF AS MUCH AS I AM OF MIKI.
SHE HATES IT WHEN I GO OFF.
What?
MMM... YOU'VE GOT THE SILKIEST HAIR.
It's so fine.
AND YOUR HANDS, SO WHITE, SO SMOOTH...
BOYS WOULD LOVE TO HOLD THESE, BUT YOU HIT 'EM.
I'll make a wig...
STILL, YOU'RE LUCKY ...
Um...
FIRM, SHAPELY BUNS, TOO...
Shuffle
Shuffle
LET ME TOUCH IT...
PAT PAT
Hey!
Poor thing...
RIGHT NOW I'D GIVE ANYTHING TO BE ONE OF THOSE GIRLS...
An angel's butt...
WITH YOUR LUCK SHE'D STILL DROP YOU FOR BEING SO FRESH!!

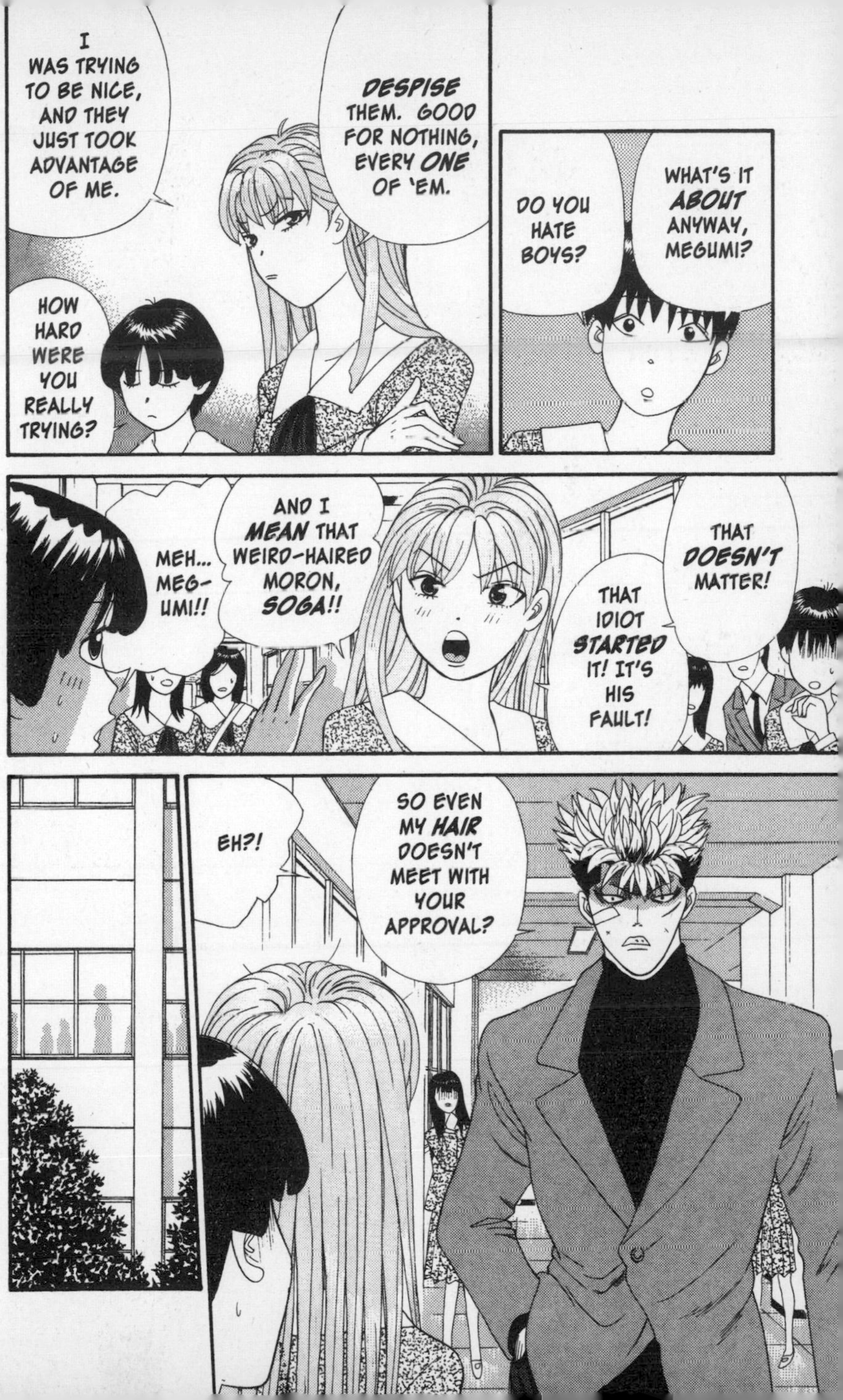
WHAT'S IT ABOUT ANYWAY, MEGUMI?
DO YOU HATE BOYS?
DESPISE THEM. GOOD FOR NOTHING, EVERY ONE OF 'EM.
I WAS TRYING TO BE NICE, AND THEY JUST TOOK ADVANTAGE OF ME.
HOW HARD WERE YOU REALLY TRYING?
THAT DOESN'T MATTER!
THAT IDIOT STARTED IT! IT'S HIS FAULT!
AND I MEAN THAT WEIRD-HAIRED MORON, SOGA!!
MEH... MEG-UMI!!
SO EVEN MY HAIR DOESN'T MEET WITH YOUR APPROVAL?
EH?!

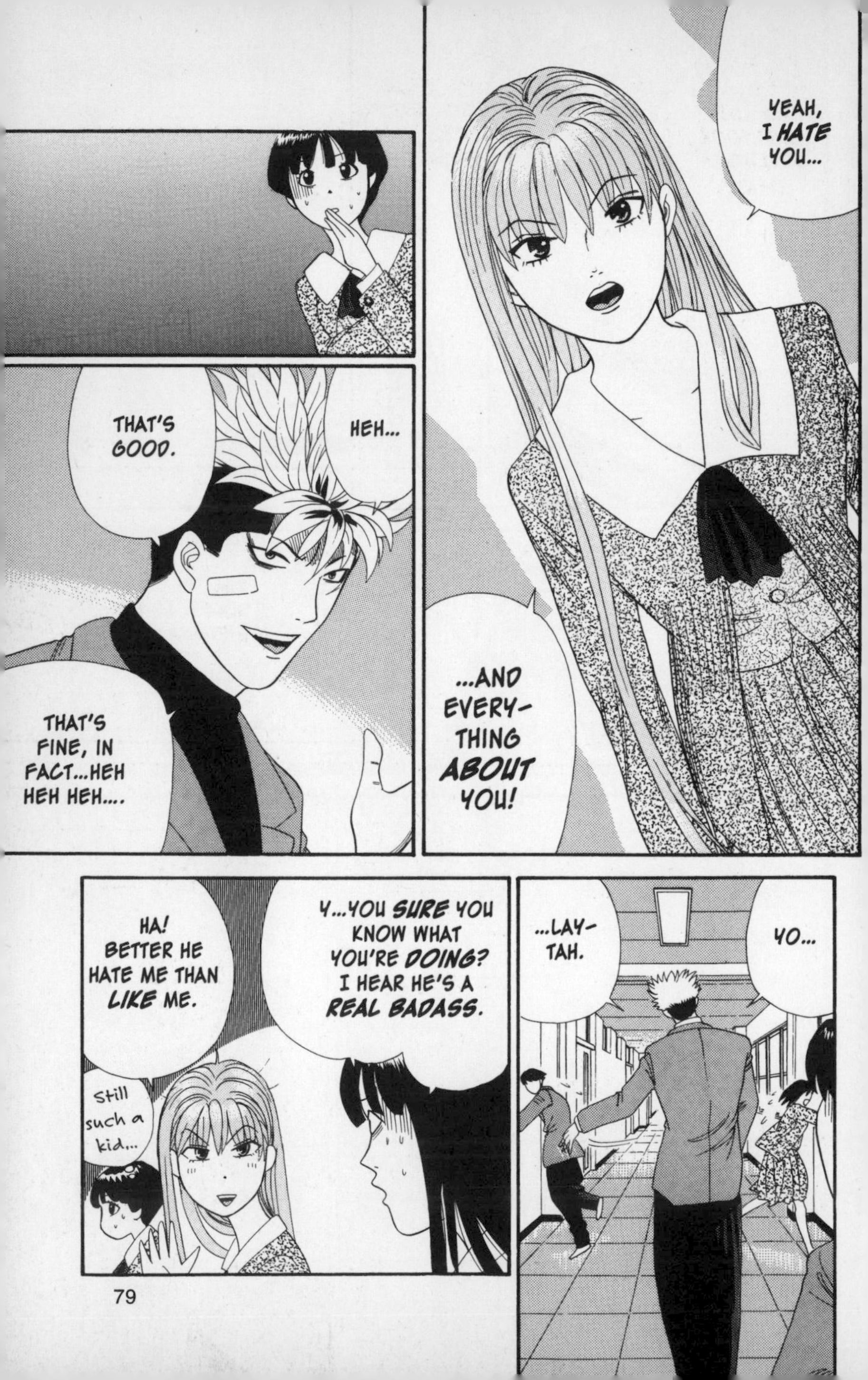
YEAH, I HATE YOU...
...AND EVERYTHING ABOUT YOU!
HEH...
THAT'S GOOD.
THAT'S FINE, IN FACT...HEH HEH HEH....
YO...
...LAY-TAH.
Y...YOU SURE YOU KNOW WHAT YOU'RE DOING? I HEAR HE'S A REAL BADASS.
HA! BETTER HE HATE ME THAN LIKE ME.
Still such a kid...

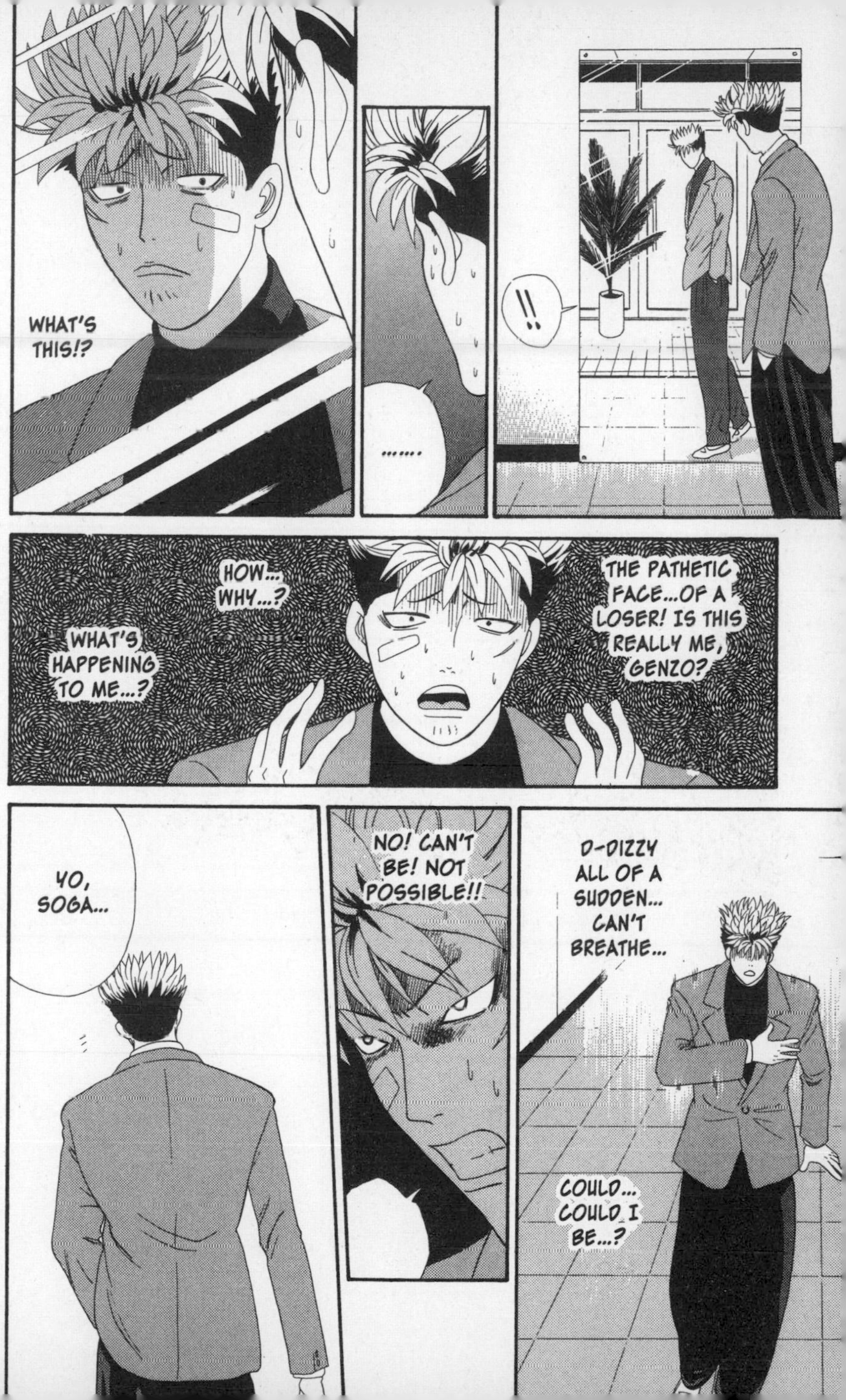
!!
....
WHAT'S THIS!?
THE PATHETIC FACE...OF A LOSER! IS THIS REALLY ME, GENZO?
HOW... WHY...?
WHAT'S HAPPENING TO ME...?
D-DIZZY ALL OF A SUDDEN... CAN'T BREATHE...
COULD... COULD I BE...?
NO! CAN'T BE! NOT POSSIBLE!!
YO, SOGA...

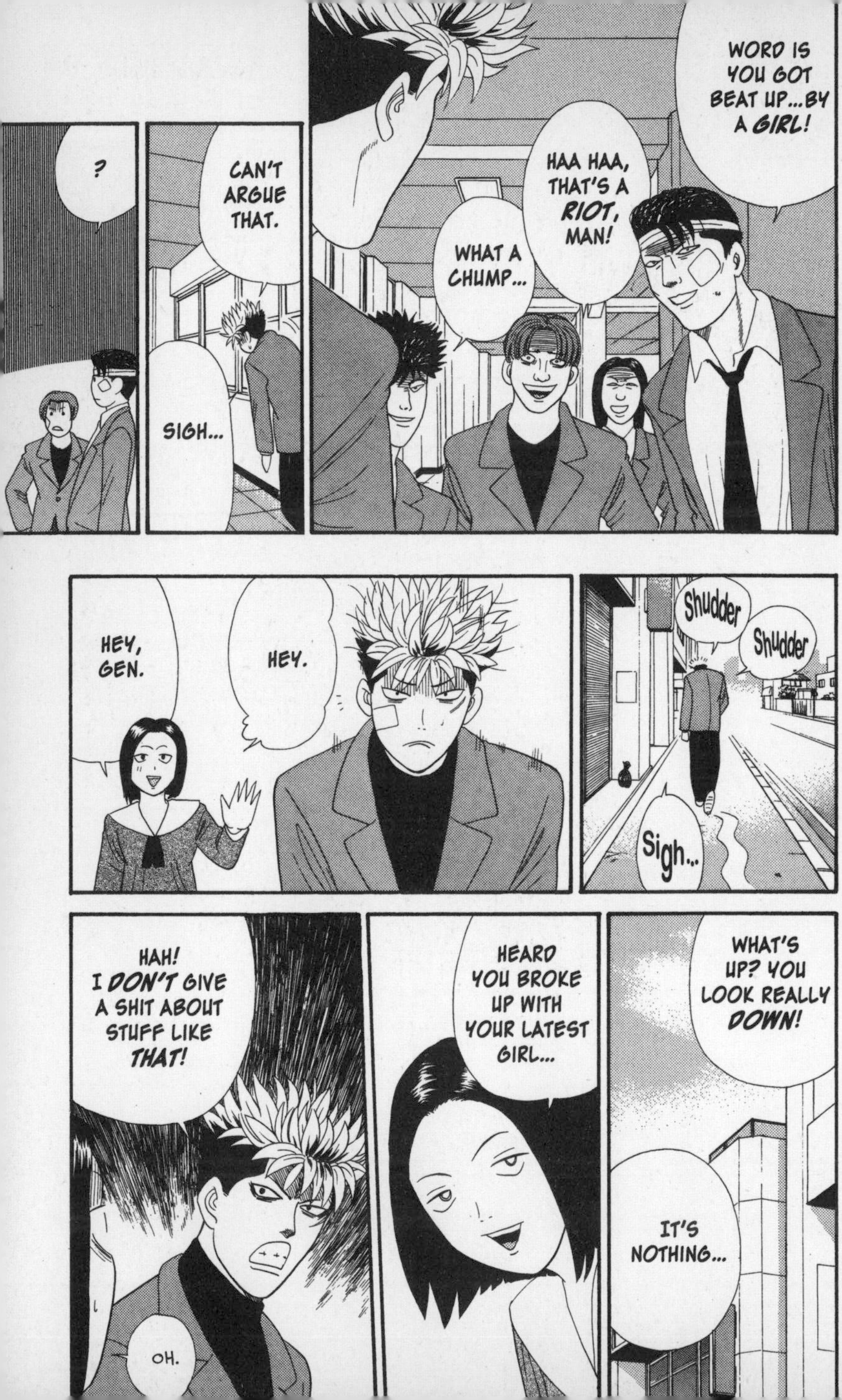
WORD IS YOU GOT BEAT UP...BY A GIRL!
HAA HAA, THAT'S A RIOT, MAN!
WHAT A CHUMP...
CAN'T ARGUE THAT.
SIGH...
?
Shudder
Shudder
Sigh...
HEY, GEN.
HEY.
WHAT'S UP? YOU LOOK REALLY DOWN!
IT'S NOTHING...
HEARD YOU BROKE UP WITH YOUR LATEST GIRL...
HAH! I DON'T GIVE A SHIT ABOUT STUFF LIKE THAT!
OH.

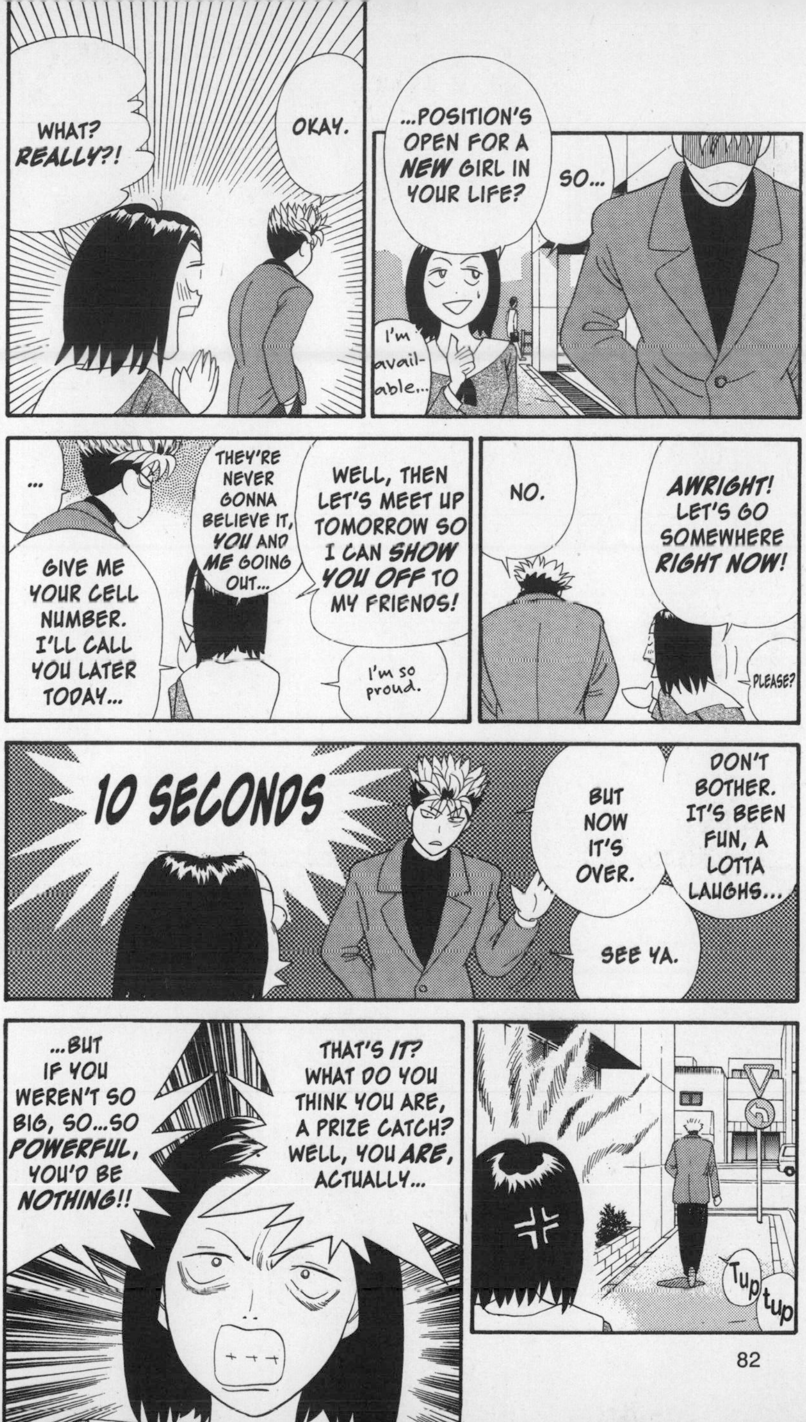
SO...
...POSITION'S OPEN FOR A NEW GIRL IN YOUR LIFE?
I'm available...
OKAY.
WHAT? REALLY?!
AWRIGHT! LET'S GO SOMEWHERE RIGHT NOW!
NO.
PLEASE?
WELL, THEN LET'S MEET UP TOMORROW SO I CAN SHOW YOU OFF TO MY FRIENDS!
THEY'RE NEVER GONNA BELIEVE IT, YOU AND ME GOING OUT...
I'm so proud.
...
GIVE ME YOUR CELL NUMBER. I'LL CALL YOU LATER TODAY...
DON'T BOTHER. IT'S BEEN FUN, A LOTTA LAUGHS...
BUT NOW IT'S OVER.
10 SECONDS
SEE YA.
Tup tup
THAT'S IT? WHAT DO YOU THINK YOU ARE, A PRIZE CATCH? WELL, YOU ARE, ACTUALLY...
...BUT IF YOU WEREN'T SO BIG, SO...SO POWERFUL, YOU'D BE NOTHING!!

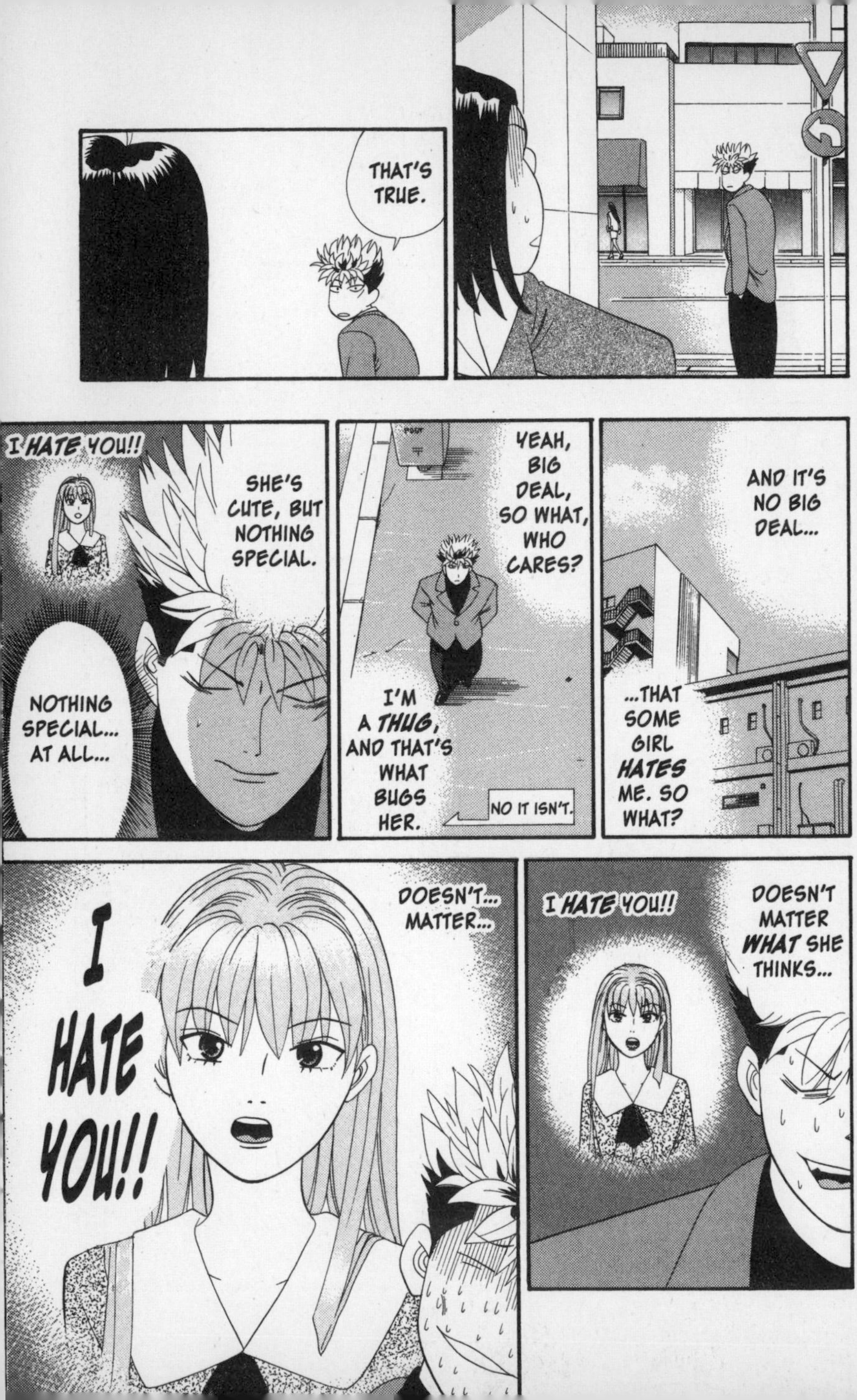
THAT'S TRUE.
AND IT'S NO BIG DEAL...
...THAT SOME GIRL HATES ME. SO WHAT?
YEAH, BIG DEAL, SO WHAT, WHO CARES?
I'M A THUG, AND THAT'S WHAT BUGS HER.
NO IT ISN'T.
I HATE YOU!!
SHE'S CUTE, BUT NOTHING SPECIAL.
NOTHING SPECIAL... AT ALL...
DOESN'T MATTER WHAT SHE THINKS...
I HATE YOU!!
DOESN'T... MATTER...
I HATE YOU!!

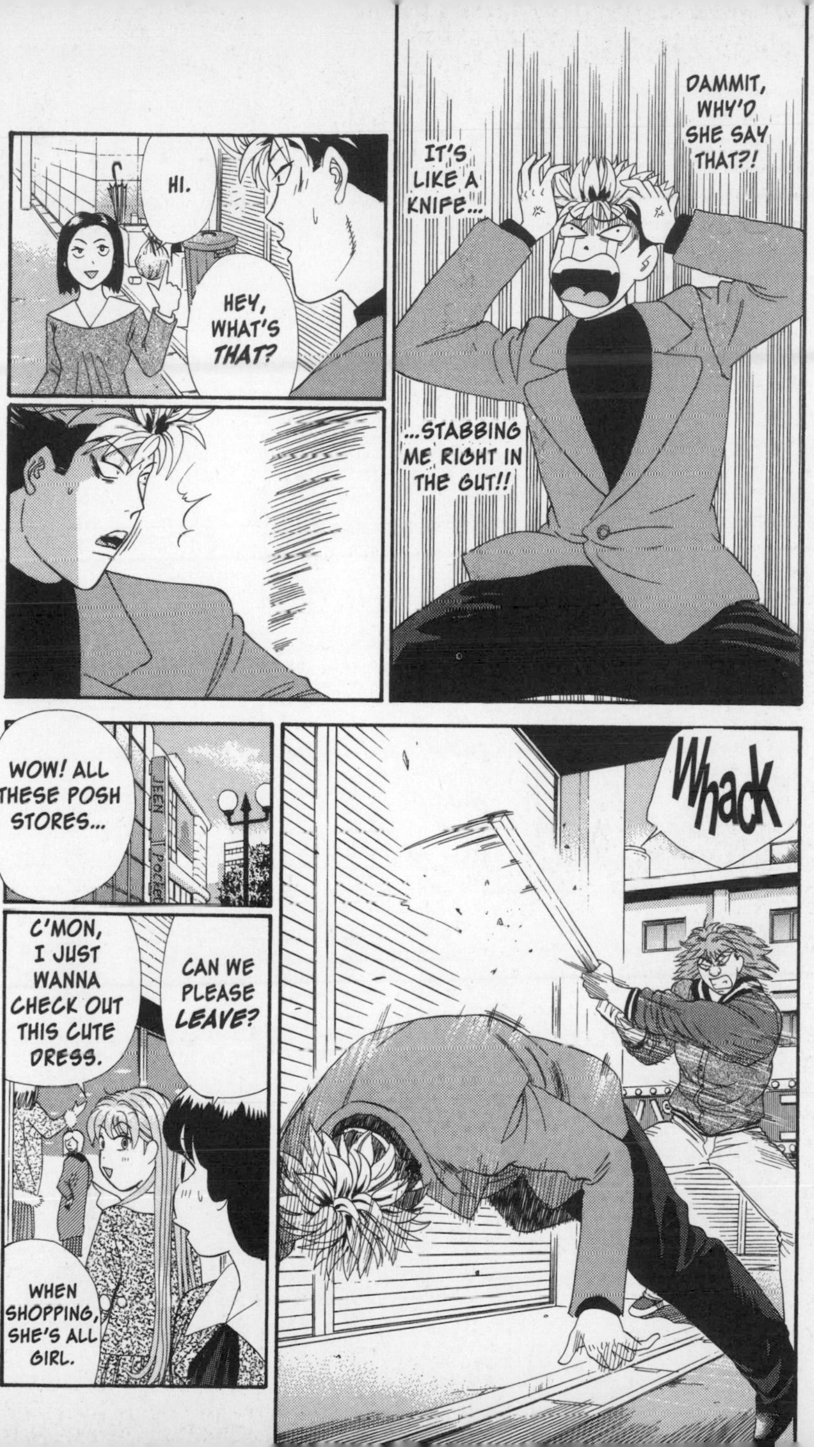
DAMMIT, WHY'D SHE SAY THAT?!
IT'S LIKE A KNIFE...
...STABBING ME RIGHT IN THE GUT!!
HI.
HEY, WHAT'S *THAT?*
Whack
WOW! ALL THESE POSH STORES...
CAN WE PLEASE *LEAVE?*
C'MON, I JUST WANNA CHECK OUT THIS CUTE DRESS.
WHEN SHOPPING, SHE'S ALL GIRL.

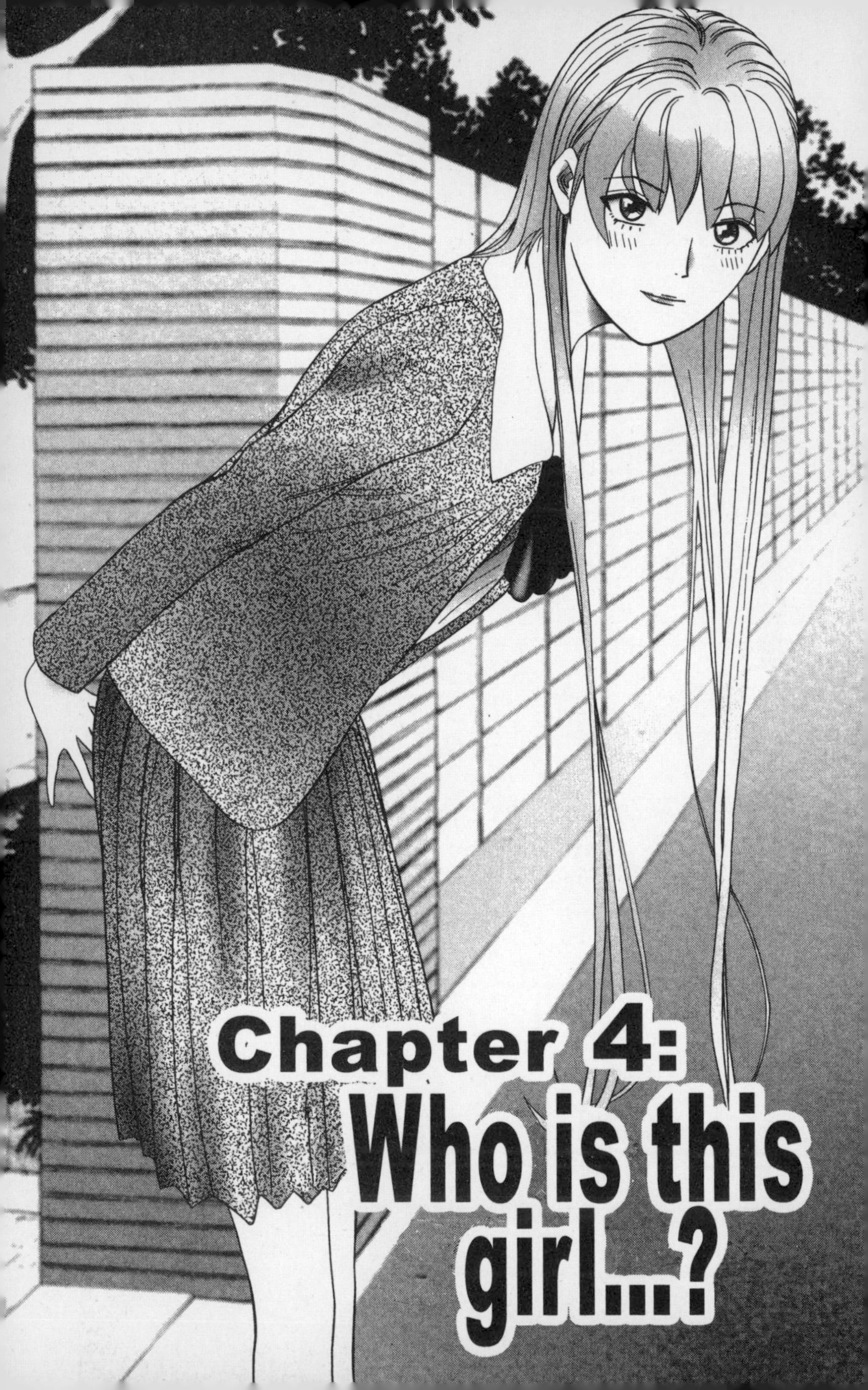
Chapter 4:
Who is this girl...?

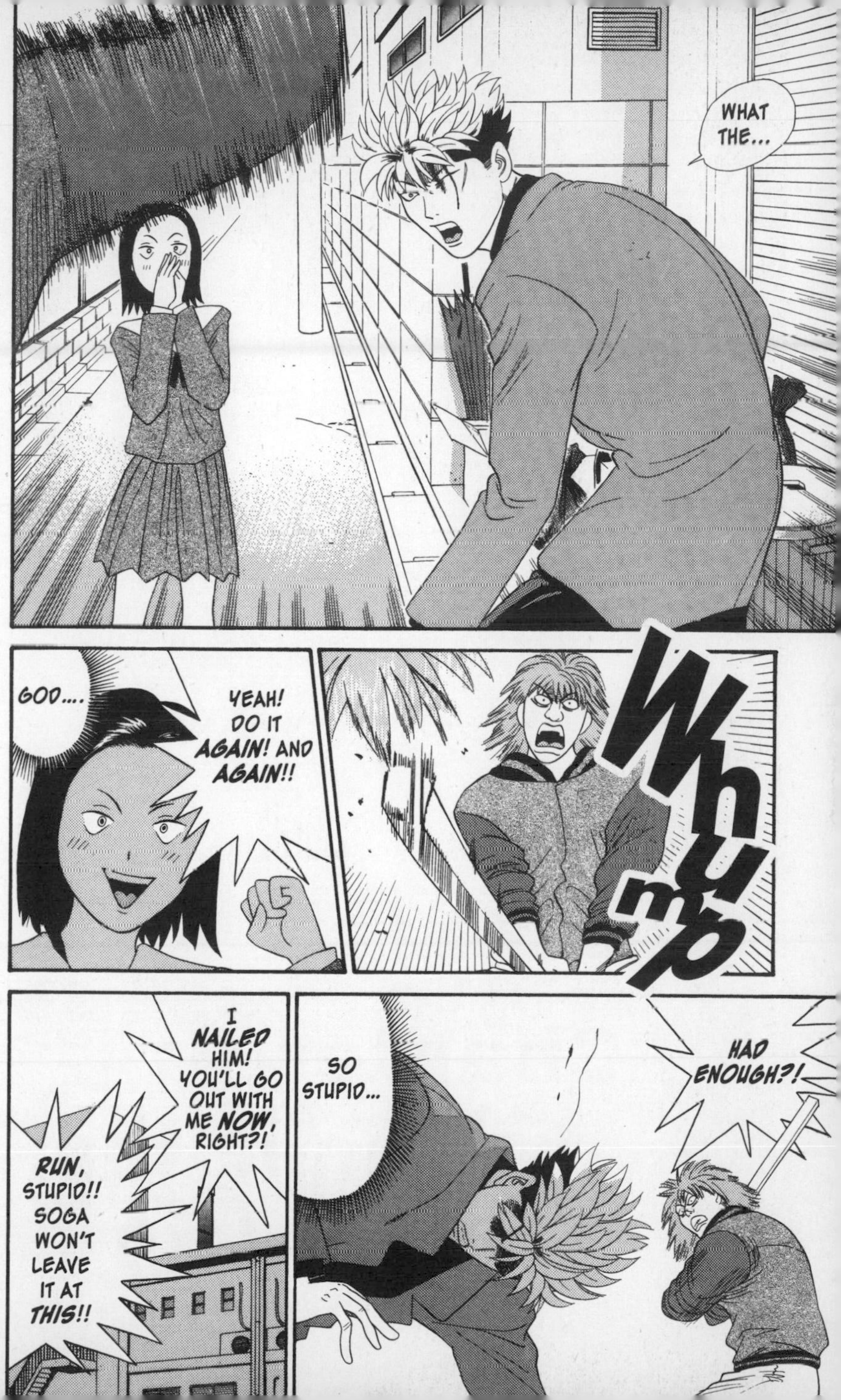
WHAT THE...
Whump
GOD....
YEAH! DO IT AGAIN! AND AGAIN!!
HAD ENOUGH?!
SO STUPID...
I NAILED HIM! YOU'LL GO OUT WITH ME NOW, RIGHT?!
RUN, STUPID!! SOGA WON'T LEAVE IT AT THIS!!

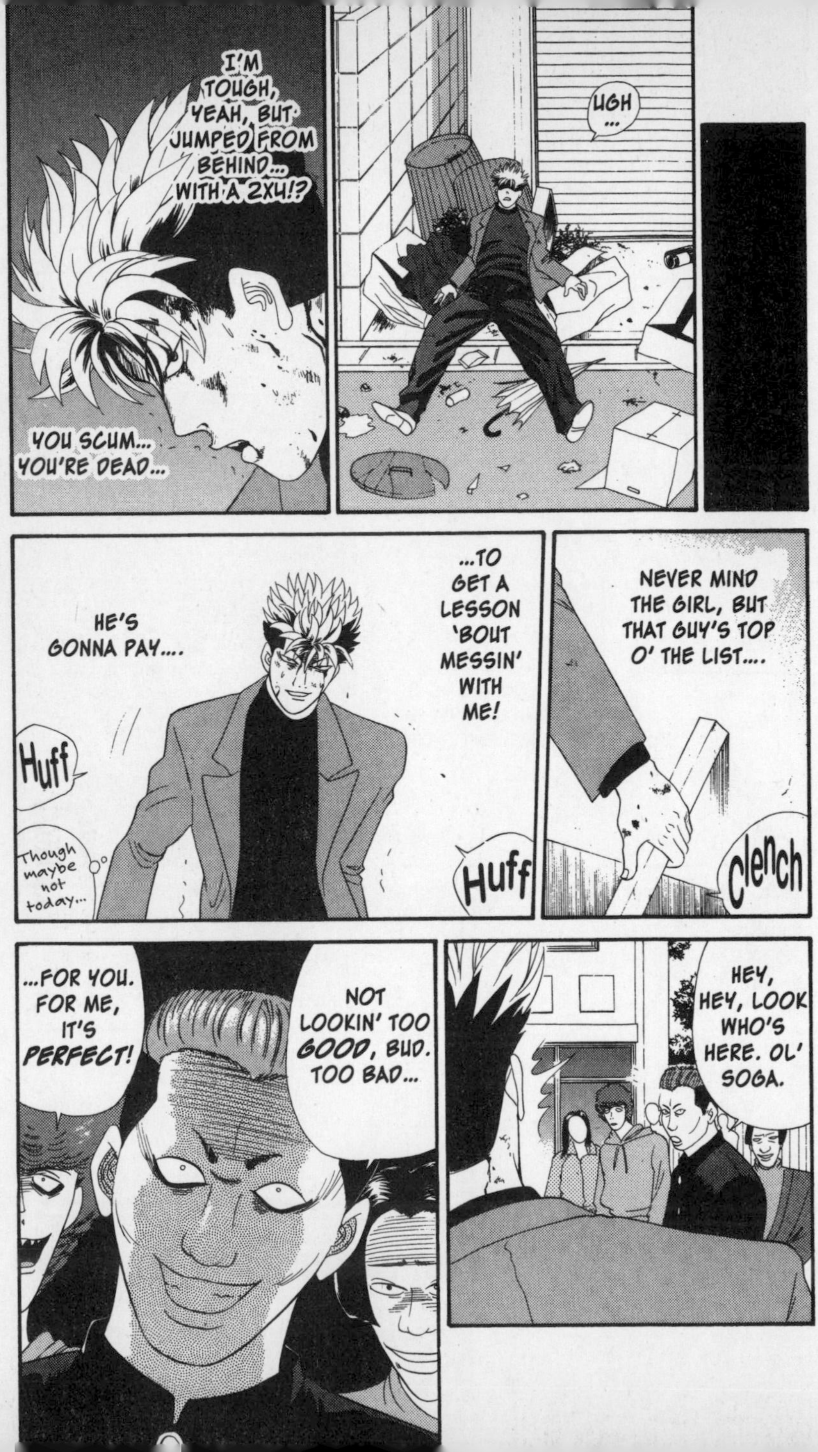
UGH ...
I'M TOUGH, YEAH, BUT JUMPED FROM BEHIND... WITH A 2X4!?
YOU SCUM... YOU'RE DEAD...
NEVER MIND THE GIRL, BUT THAT GUY'S TOP O' THE LIST....
Clench
HE'S GONNA PAY....
...TO GET A LESSON 'BOUT MESSIN' WITH ME!
Huff
Huff
Though maybe not today...
HEY, HEY, LOOK WHO'S HERE. OL' SOGA.
NOT LOOKIN' TOO GOOD, BUD. TOO BAD...
...FOR YOU. FOR ME, IT'S PERFECT!

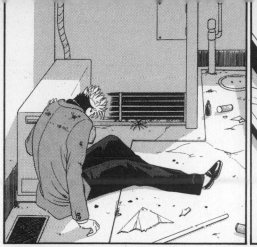

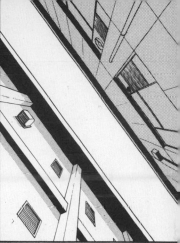

WHAT GOES
AROUND COMES
AROUND, THEY SAY...

HEH...
HA HA...

WHAT A DAY.

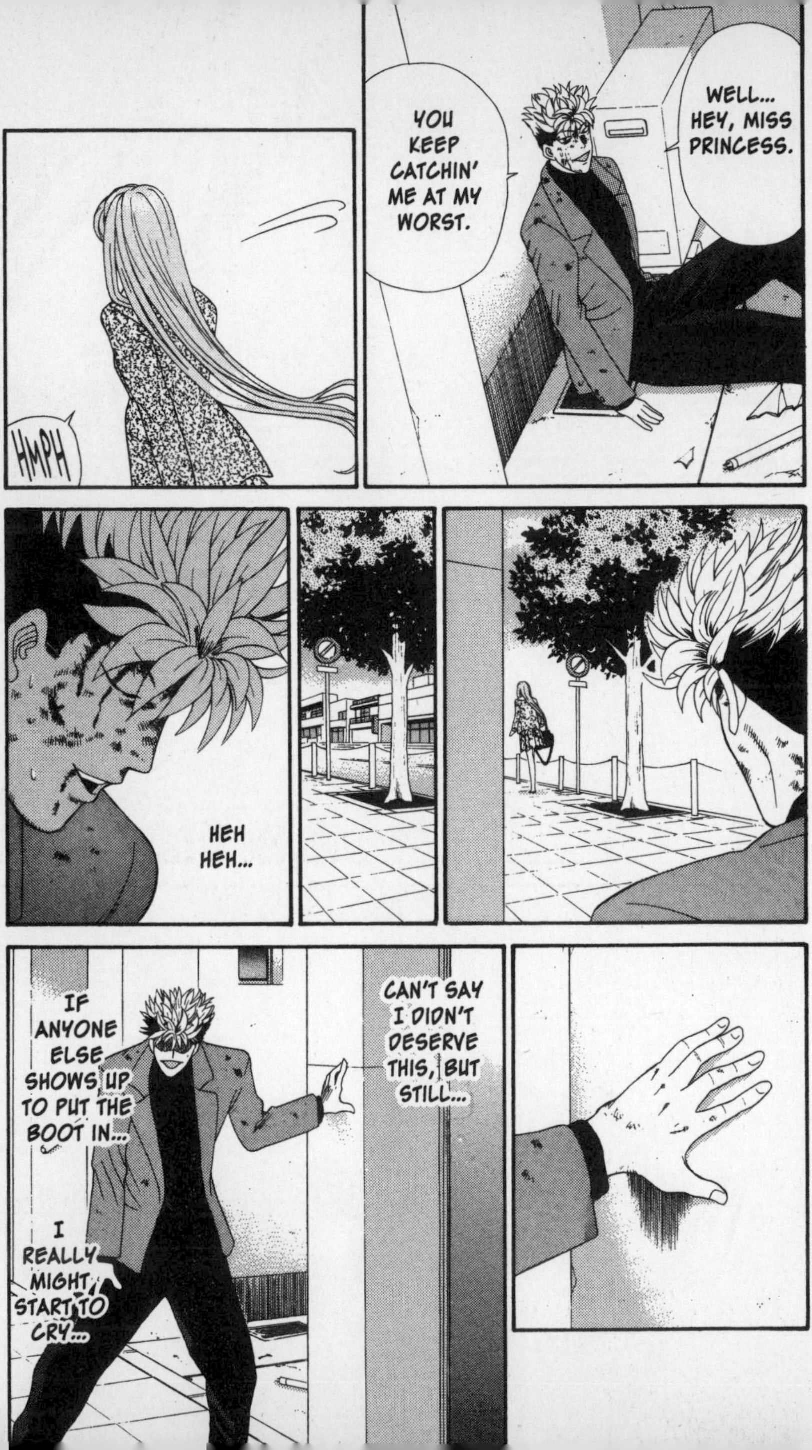
WELL... HEY, MISS PRINCESS.
YOU KEEP CATCHIN' ME AT MY WORST.
HMPH
HEH HEH...
CAN'T SAY I DIDN'T DESERVE THIS, BUT STILL...
IF ANYONE ELSE SHOWS UP TO PUT THE BOOT IN...
I REALLY MIGHT START TO CRY...

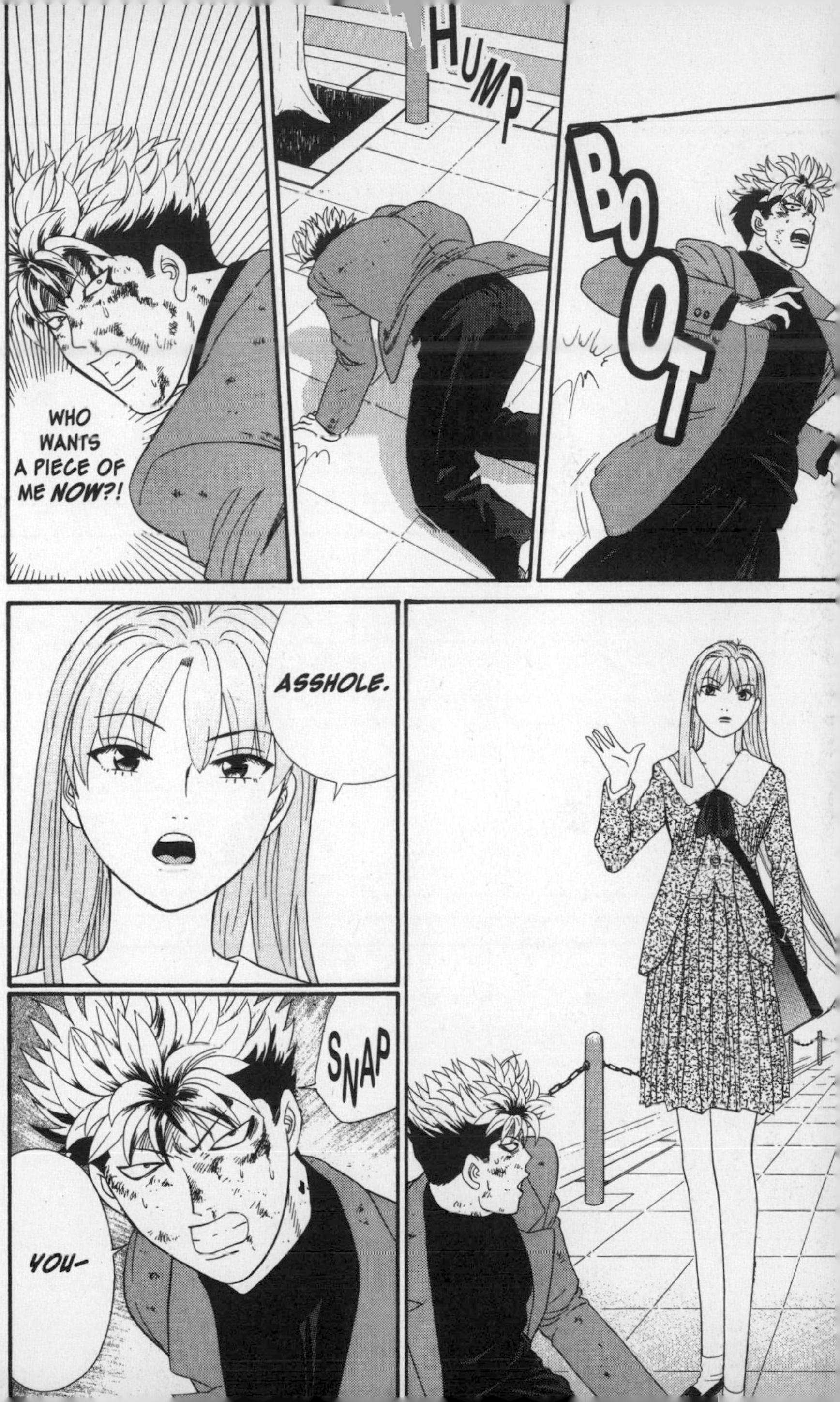
BOOT
HUMP
WHO WANTS A PIECE OF ME NOW?!
ASSHOLE.
SNAP
YOU-

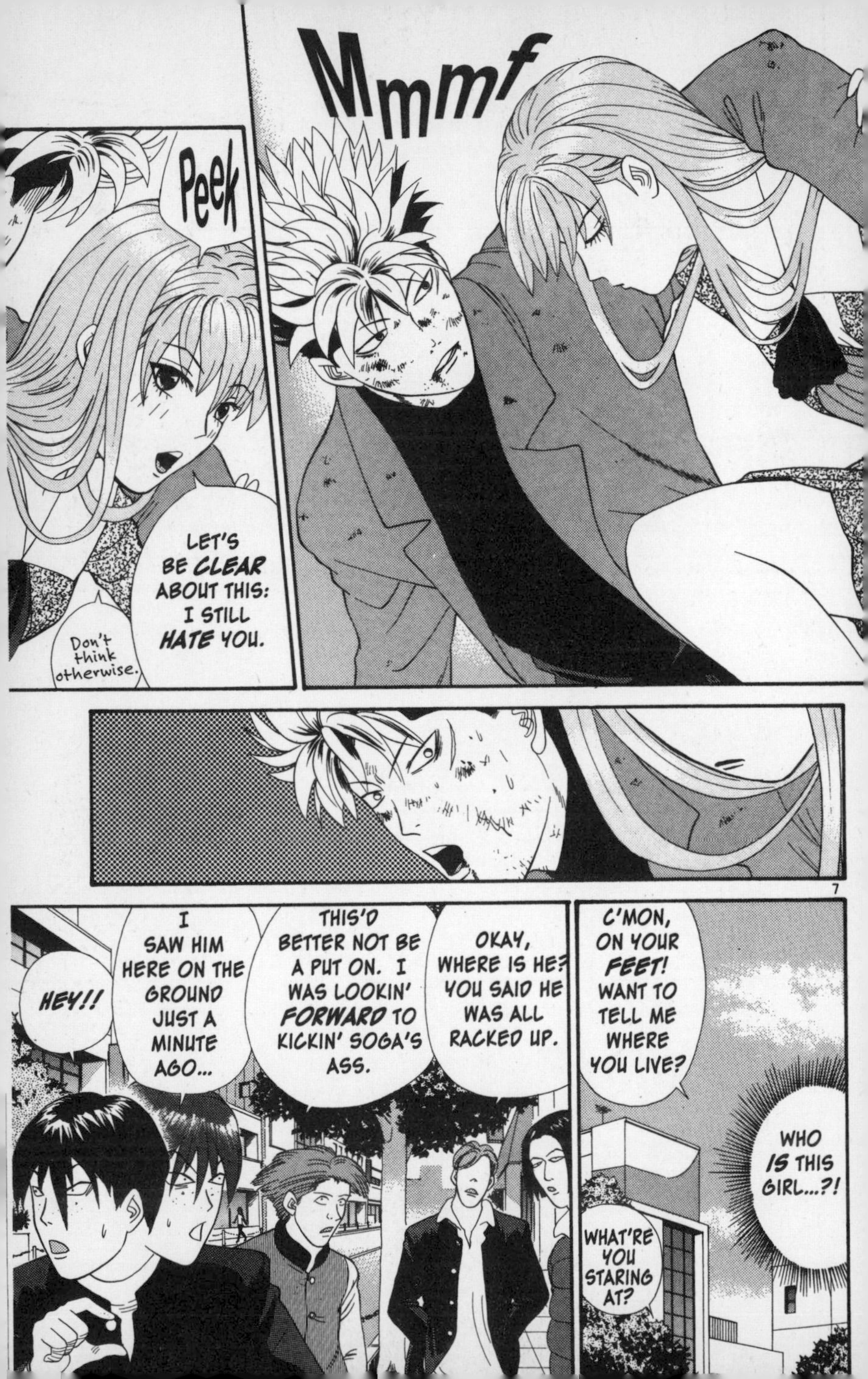
Mmmf
Peek
LET'S BE CLEAR ABOUT THIS: I STILL HATE YOU.
Don't think otherwise.
C'MON, ON YOUR FEET! WANT TO TELL ME WHERE YOU LIVE?
WHO IS THIS GIRL...?!
WHAT'RE YOU STARING AT?
OKAY, WHERE IS HE? YOU SAID HE WAS ALL RACKED UP.
THIS'D BETTER NOT BE A PUT ON. I WAS LOOKIN' FORWARD TO KICKIN' SOGA'S ASS.
I SAW HIM HERE ON THE GROUND JUST A MINUTE AGO...
HEY!!

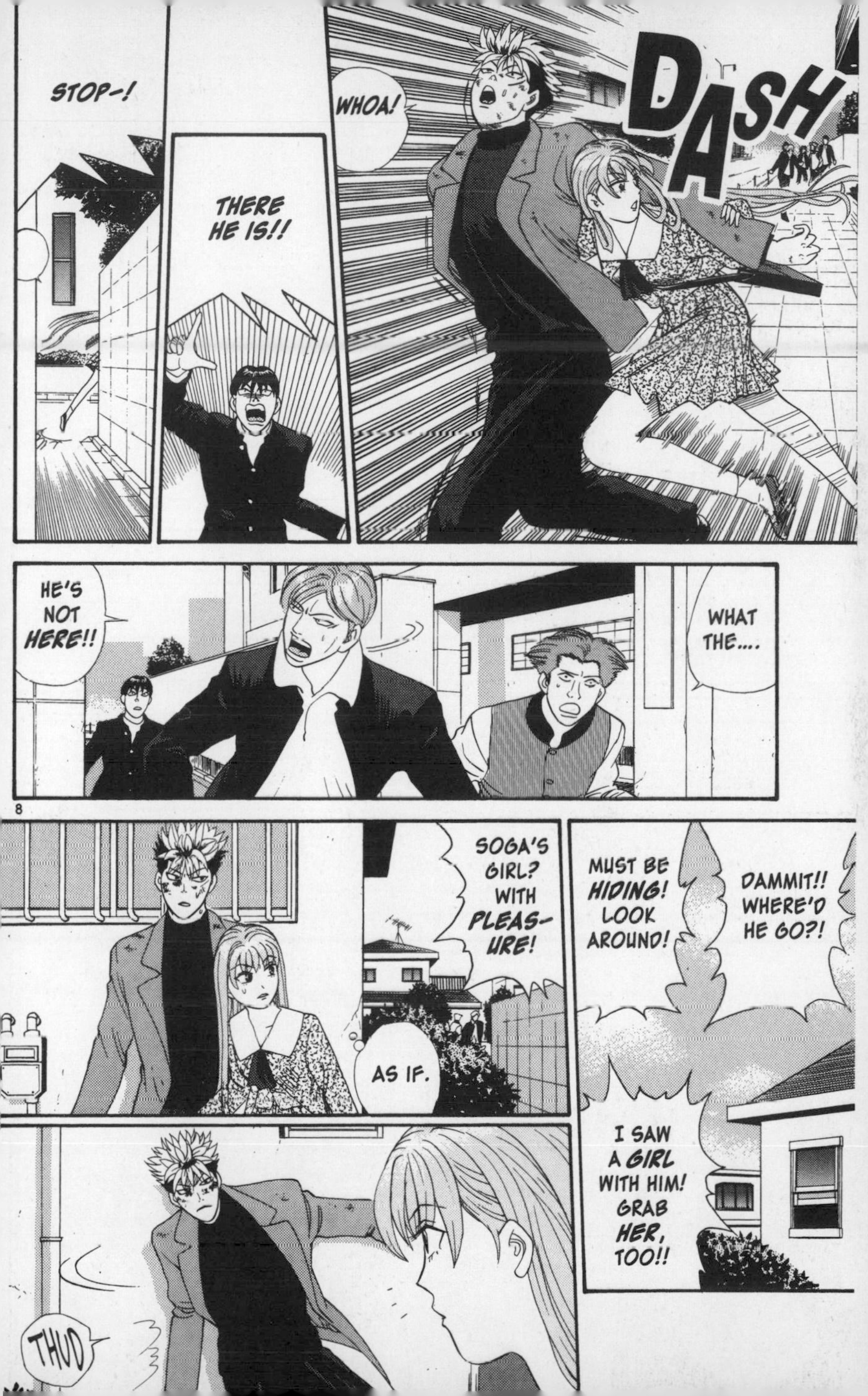
DASH
WHOA!
THERE HE IS!!
STOP-!
WHAT THE....
HE'S NOT HERE!!
DAMMIT!! WHERE'D HE GO?!
MUST BE HIDING! LOOK AROUND!
I SAW A GIRL WITH HIM! GRAB HER, TOO!!
SOGA'S GIRL? WITH PLEASURE!
AS IF.
THUD

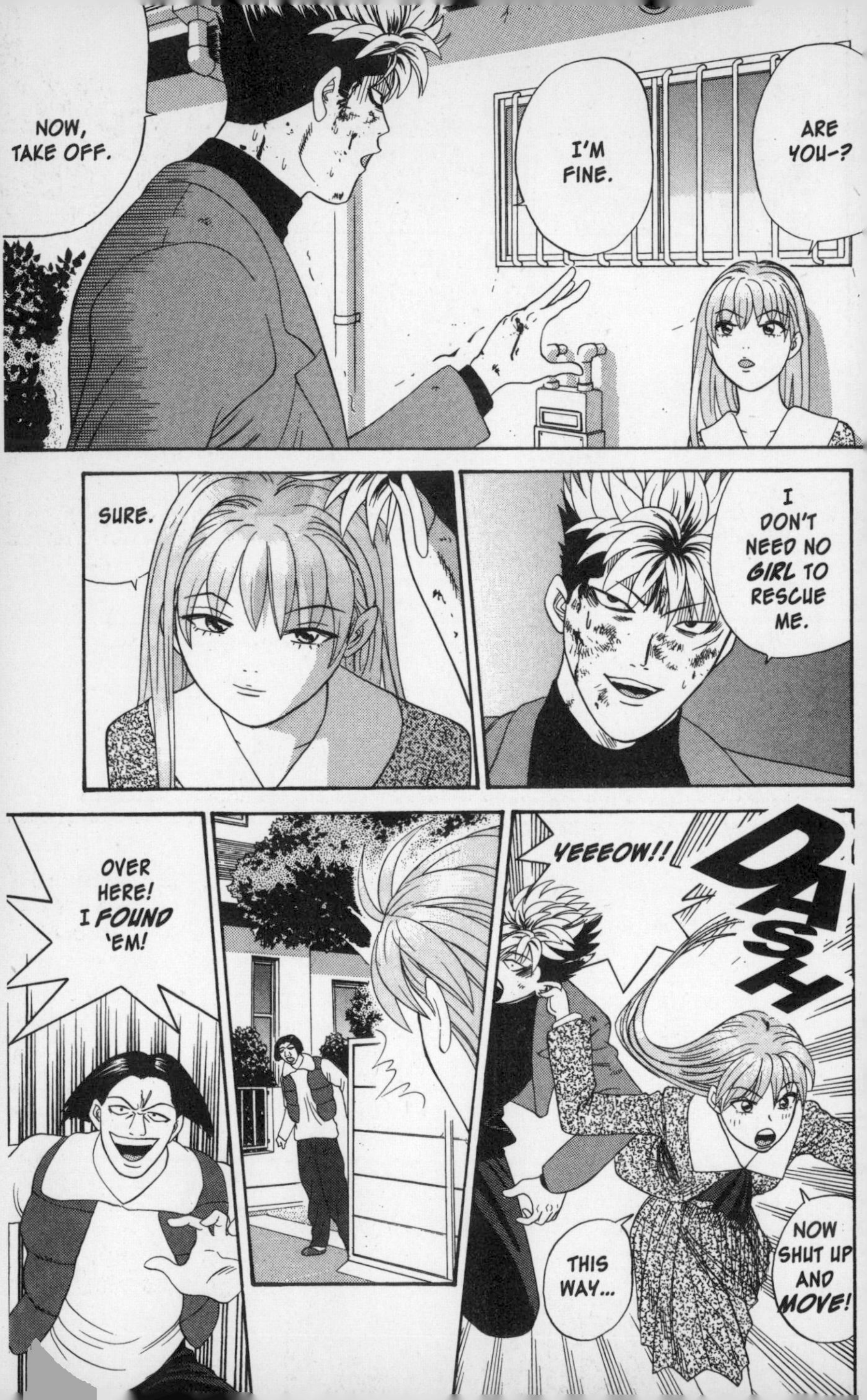
ARE YOU-?
I'M FINE.
NOW, TAKE OFF.
I DON'T NEED NO GIRL TO RESCUE ME.
SURE.
YEEEOW!!
DASH
NOW SHUT UP AND MOVE!
THIS WAY...
OVER HERE! I FOUND 'EM!

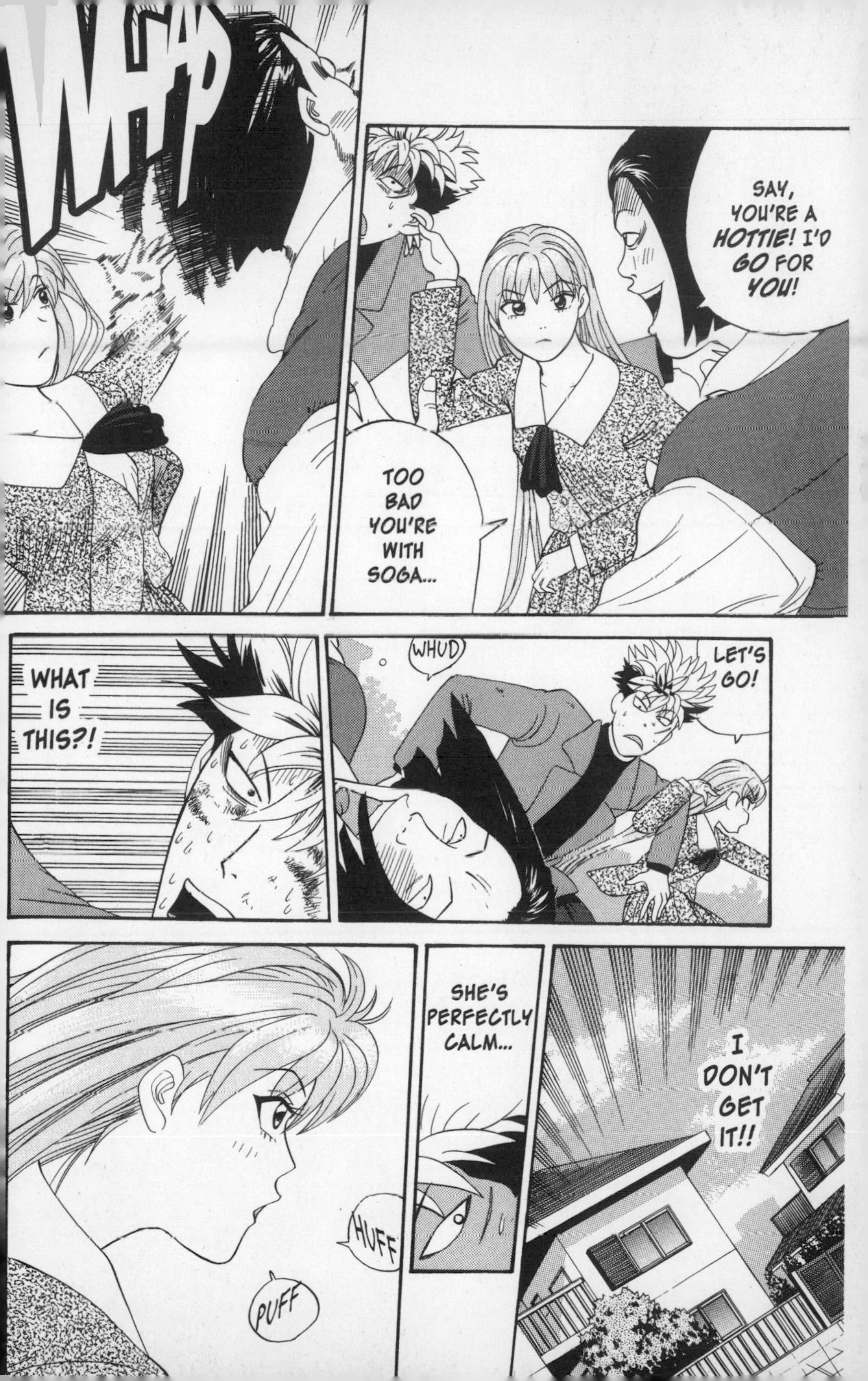
SAY, YOU'RE A HOTTIE! I'D GO FOR YOU!
TOO BAD YOU'RE WITH SOGA...
WHAP
WHUD
LET'S GO!
WHAT IS THIS?!
I DON'T GET IT!!
SHE'S PERFECTLY CALM...
HUFF
PUFF

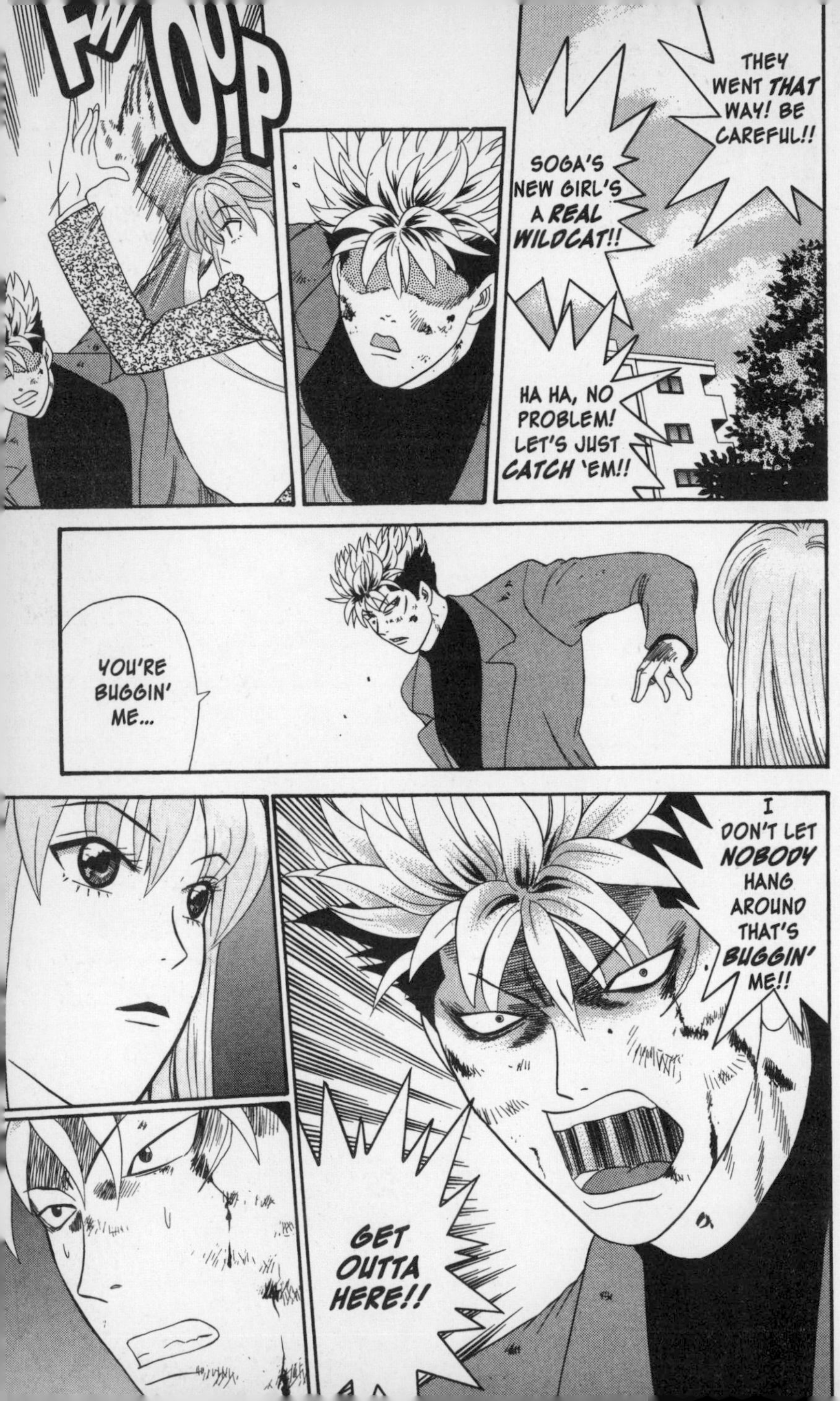
THEY WENT THAT WAY! BE CAREFUL!!
SOGA'S NEW GIRL'S A REAL WILDCAT!!
HA HA, NO PROBLEM! LET'S JUST CATCH 'EM!!
FWOUP
YOU'RE BUGGIN' ME...
I DON'T LET NOBODY HANG AROUND THAT'S BUGGIN' ME!!
GET OUTTA HERE!!

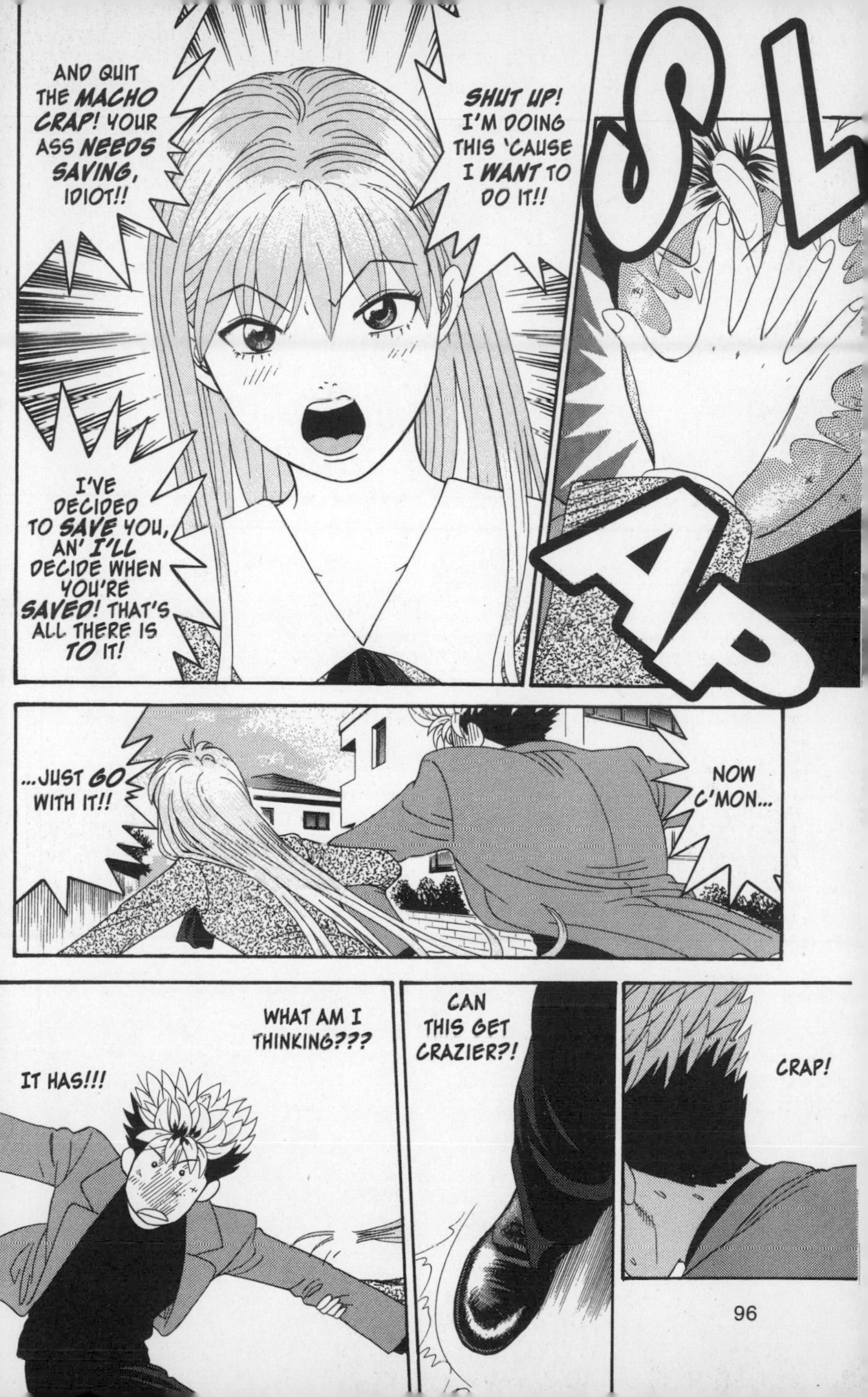
SLAP
SHUT UP! I'M DOING THIS 'CAUSE I WANT TO DO IT!!
AND QUIT THE MACHO CRAP! YOUR ASS NEEDS SAVING, IDIOT!!
I'VE DECIDED TO SAVE YOU, AN' I'LL DECIDE WHEN YOU'RE SAVED! THAT'S ALL THERE IS TO IT!
NOW C'MON...
...JUST GO WITH IT!!
CRAP!
CAN THIS GET CRAZIER?!
WHAT AM I THINKING???
IT HAS!!!

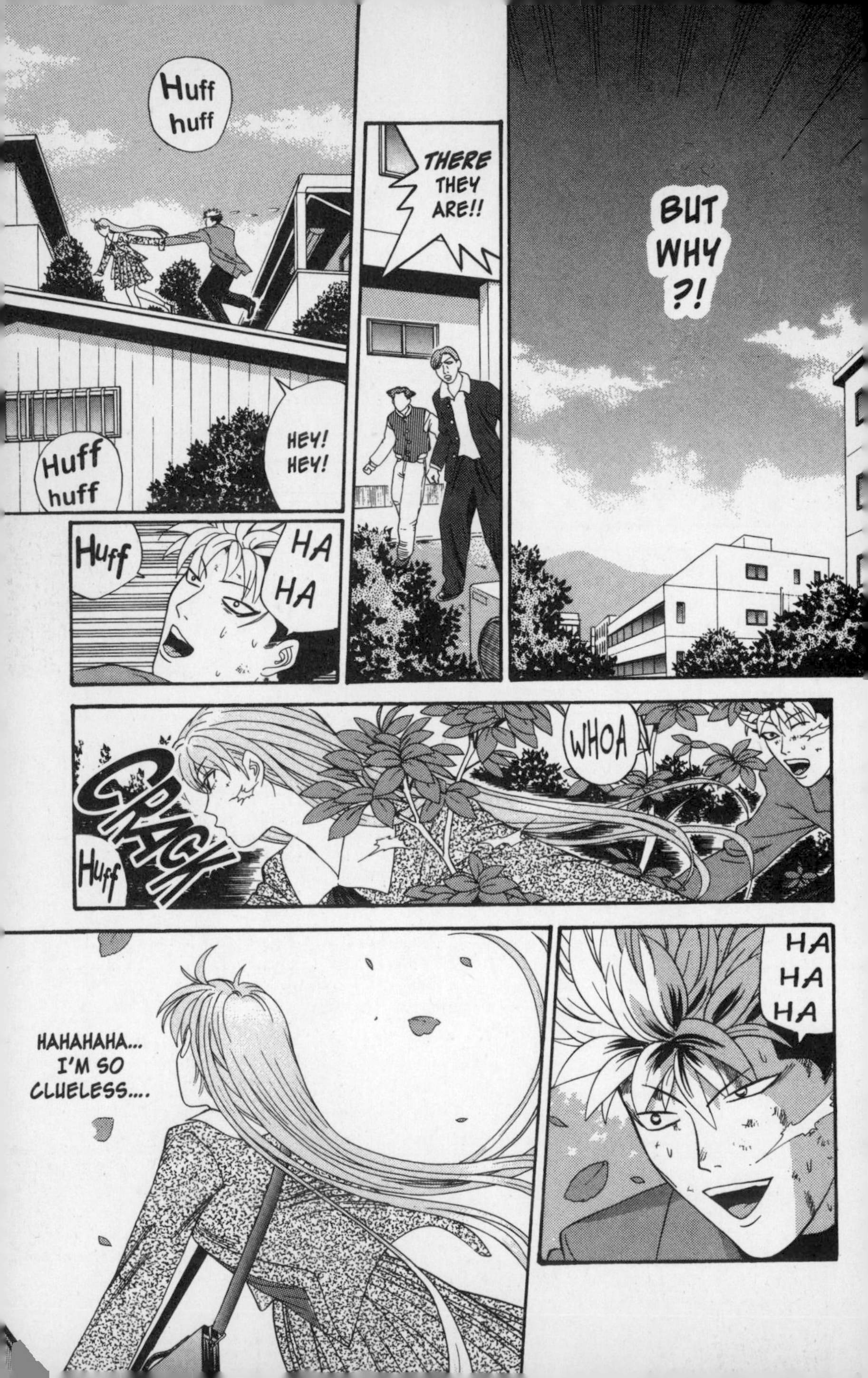
BUT WHY ?!
THERE THEY ARE!!
Huff huff
HEY! HEY!
Huff huff
HA HA
Huff
WHOA
CRACK
Huff
HA HA HA
HAHAHAHA... I'M SO CLUELESS....

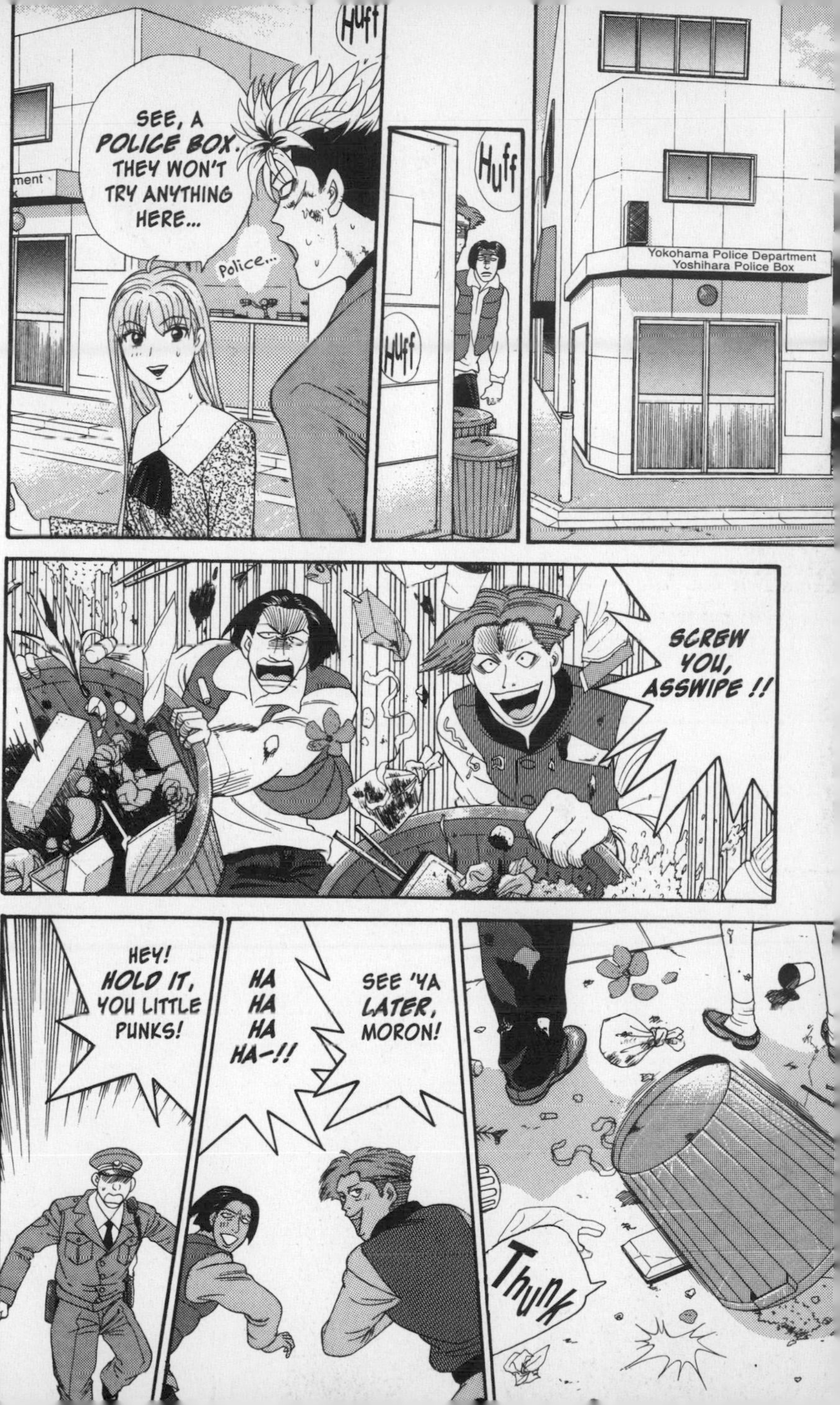
Yokohama Police Department
Yoshihara Police Box
Huff
Huff
Huff
SEE, A POLICE BOX. THEY WON'T TRY ANYTHING HERE...
Police...
SCREW YOU, ASSWIPE !!
Thunk
SEE 'YA LATER, MORON!
HA HA HA HA-!!
HEY! HOLD IT, YOU LITTLE PUNKS!

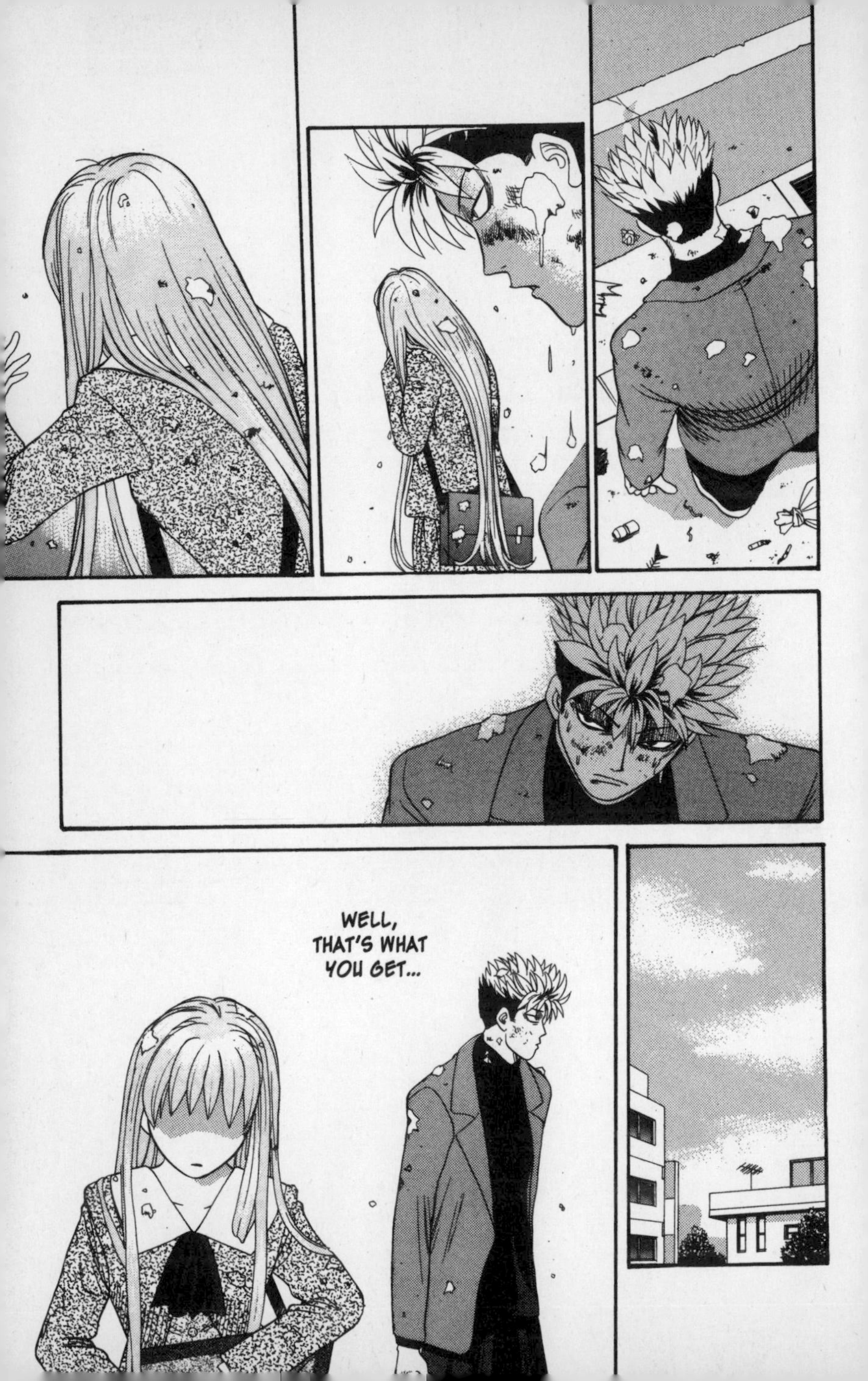
WELL, THAT'S WHAT YOU GET...

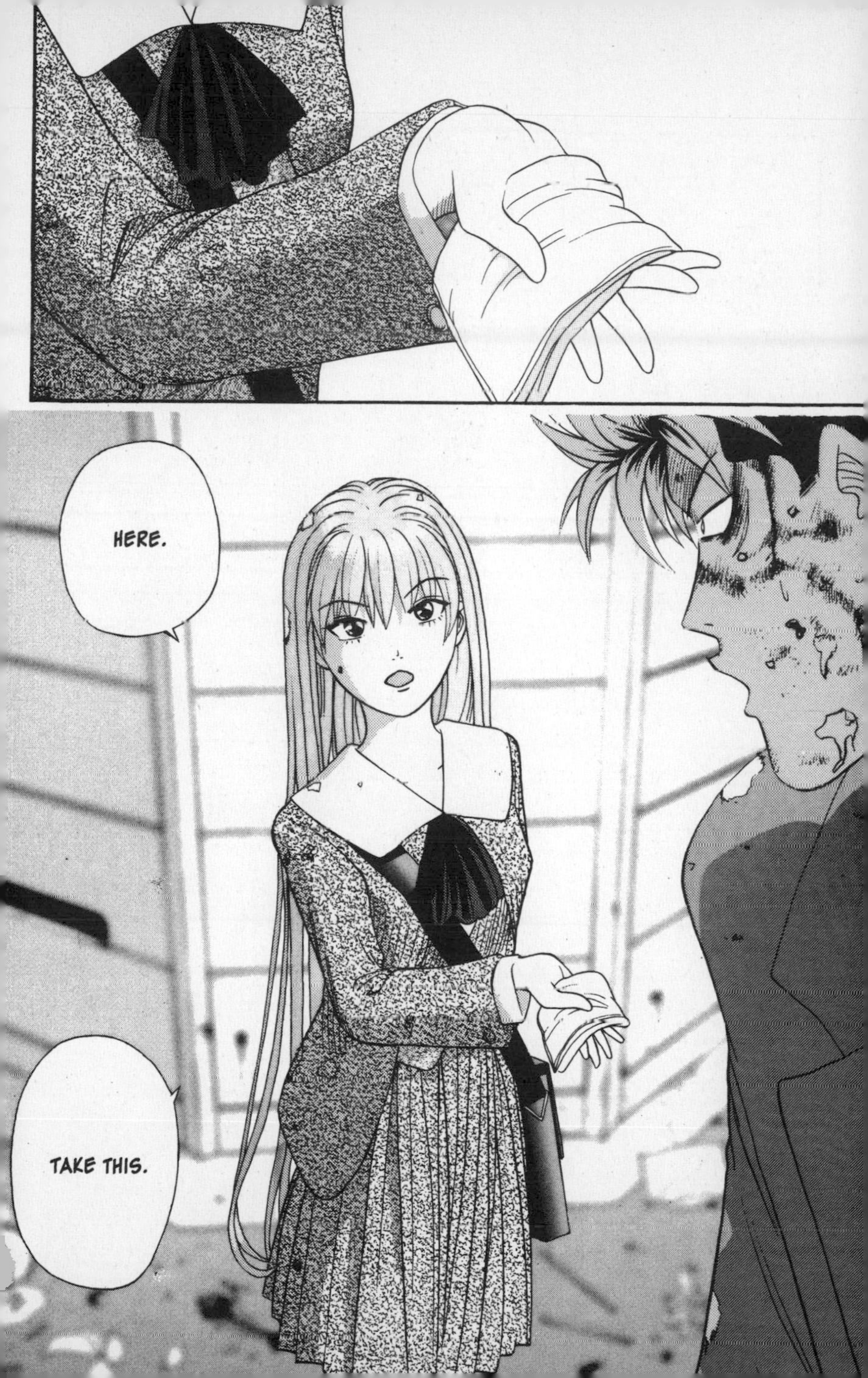
HERE.
TAKE THIS.

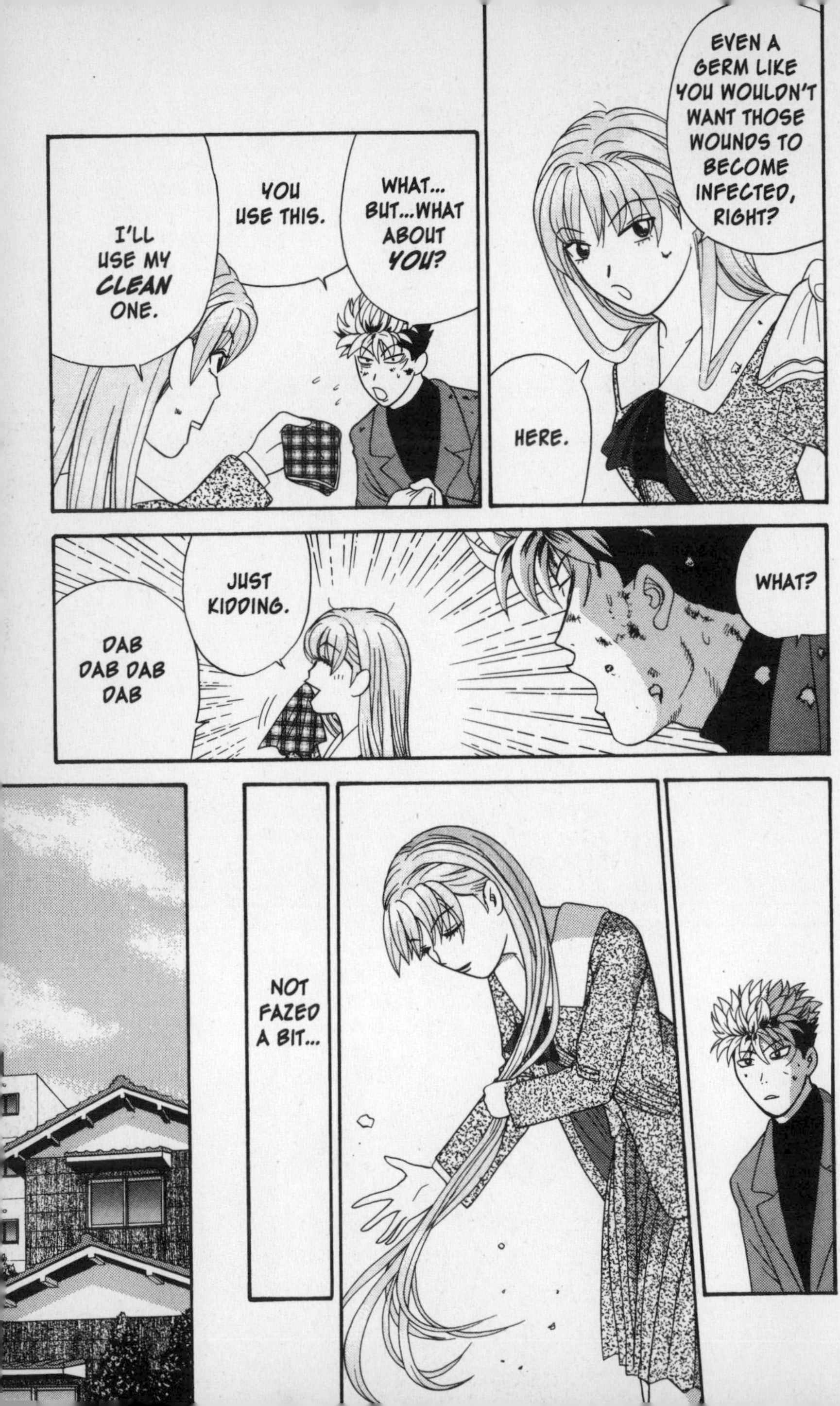
EVEN A GERM LIKE YOU WOULDN'T WANT THOSE WOUNDS TO BECOME INFECTED, RIGHT?
HERE.
WHAT... BUT...WHAT ABOUT *YOU?*
YOU USE THIS.
I'LL USE MY *CLEAN* ONE.
WHAT?
JUST KIDDING.
DAB DAB DAB DAB
NOT FAZED A BIT...

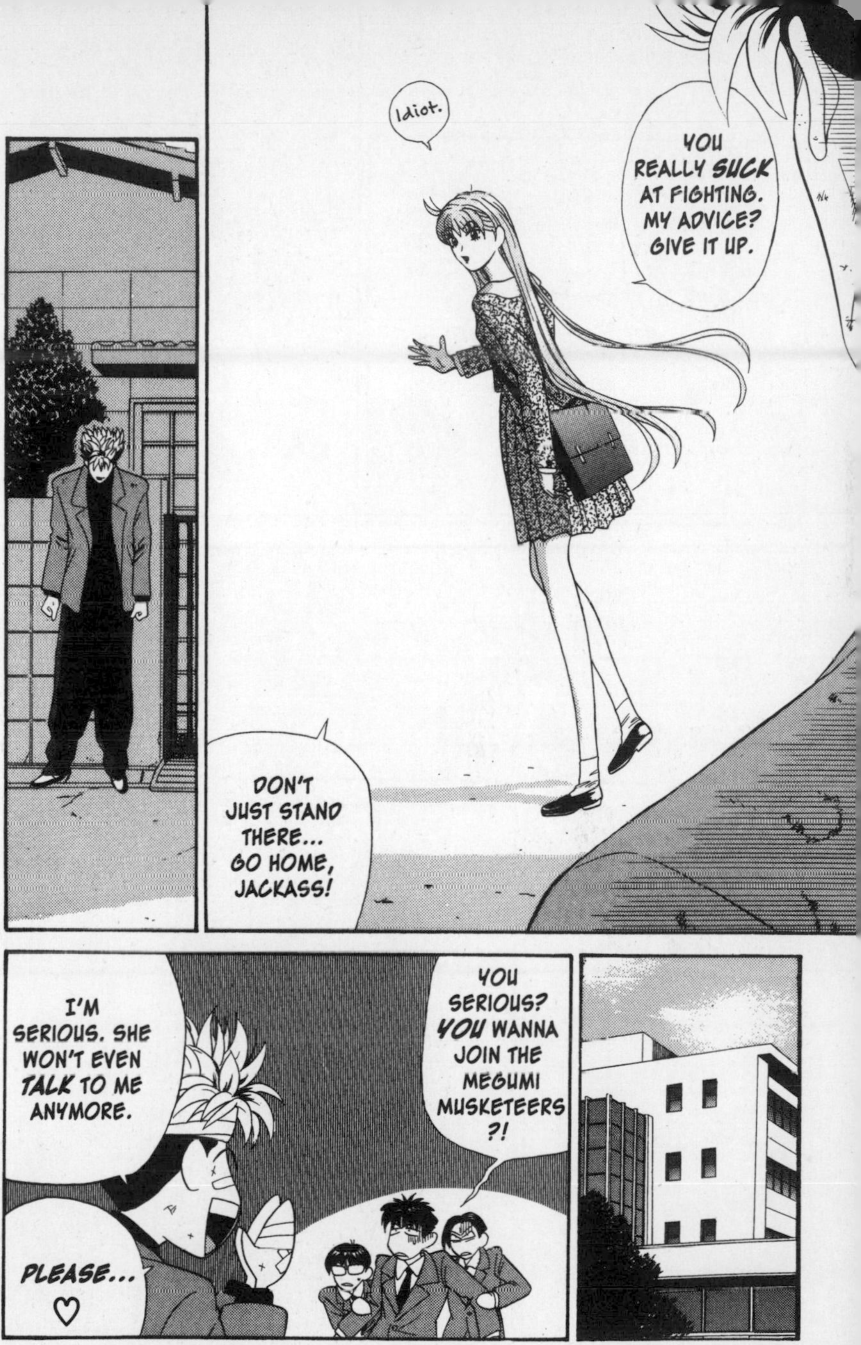
YOU REALLY SUCK AT FIGHTING. MY ADVICE? GIVE IT UP.
Idiot.
DON'T JUST STAND THERE... GO HOME, JACKASS!
YOU SERIOUS? YOU WANNA JOIN THE MEGUMI MUSKETEERS ?!
I'M SERIOUS. SHE WON'T EVEN TALK TO ME ANYMORE.
PLEASE... ♡

Chapter 5: I Like You...

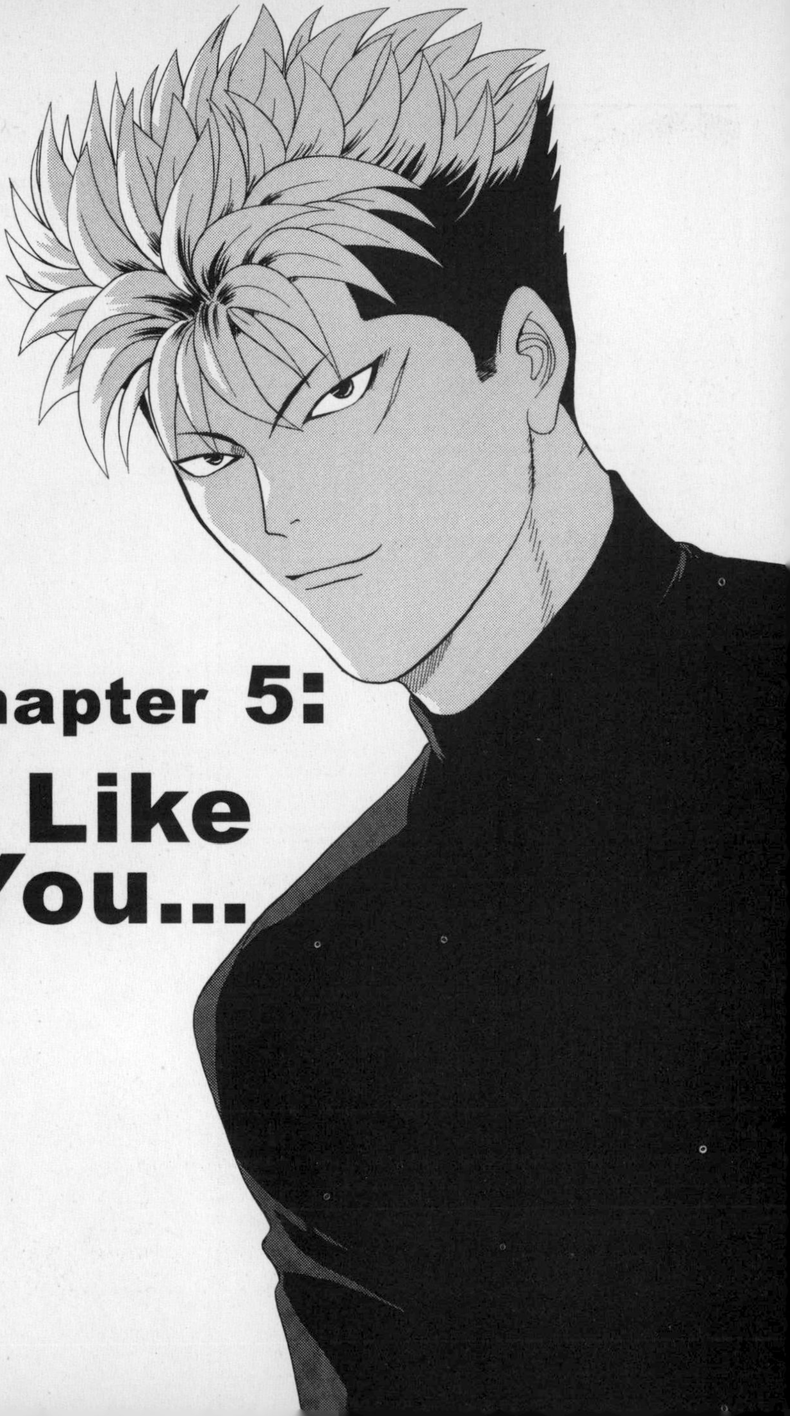

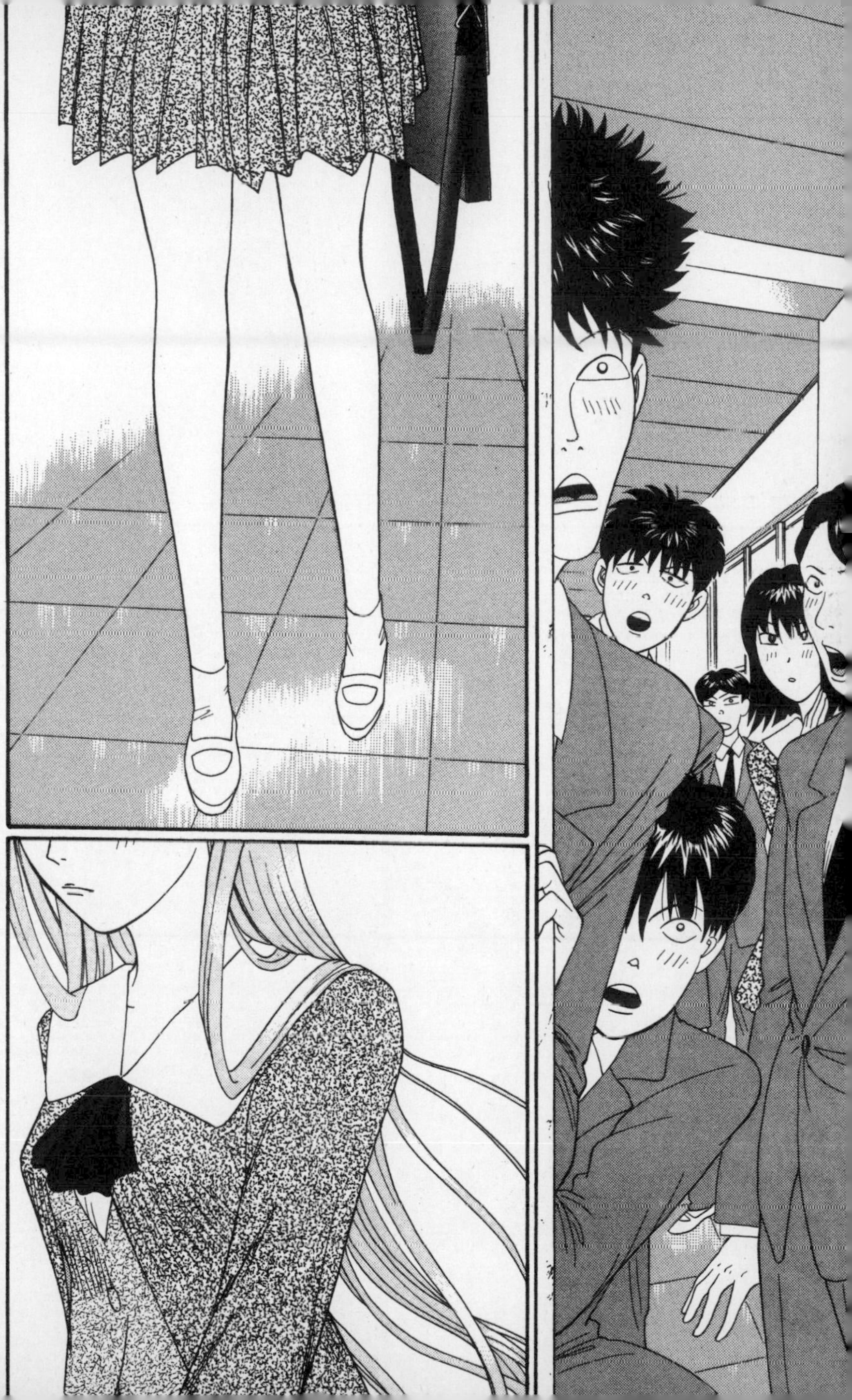

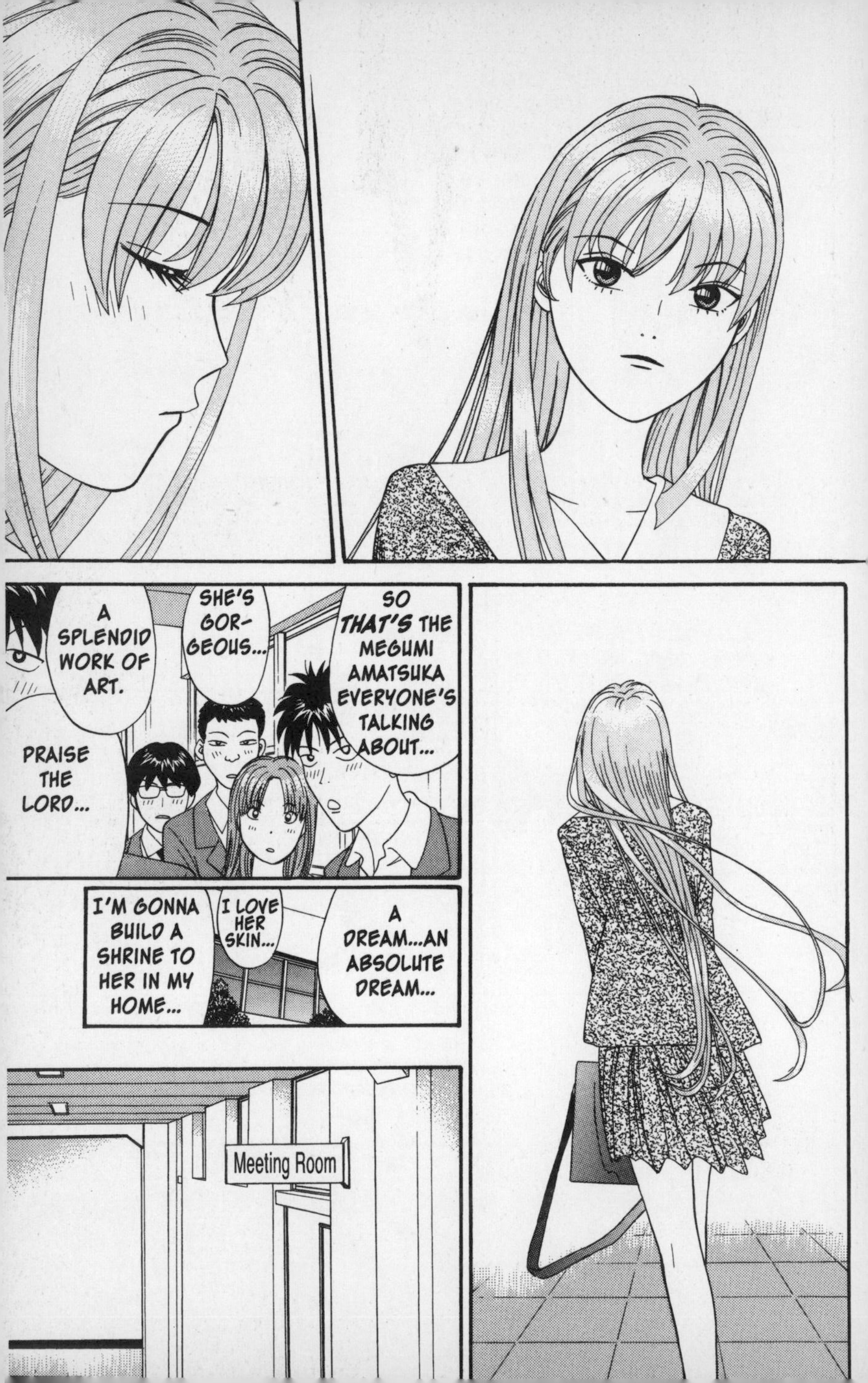
SO THAT'S THE MEGUMI AMATSUKA EVERYONE'S TALKING ABOUT...
SHE'S GOR-GEOUS...
A SPLENDID WORK OF ART.
PRAISE THE LORD...
A DREAM...AN ABSOLUTE DREAM...
I LOVE HER SKIN...
I'M GONNA BUILD A SHRINE TO HER IN MY HOME...
Meeting Room

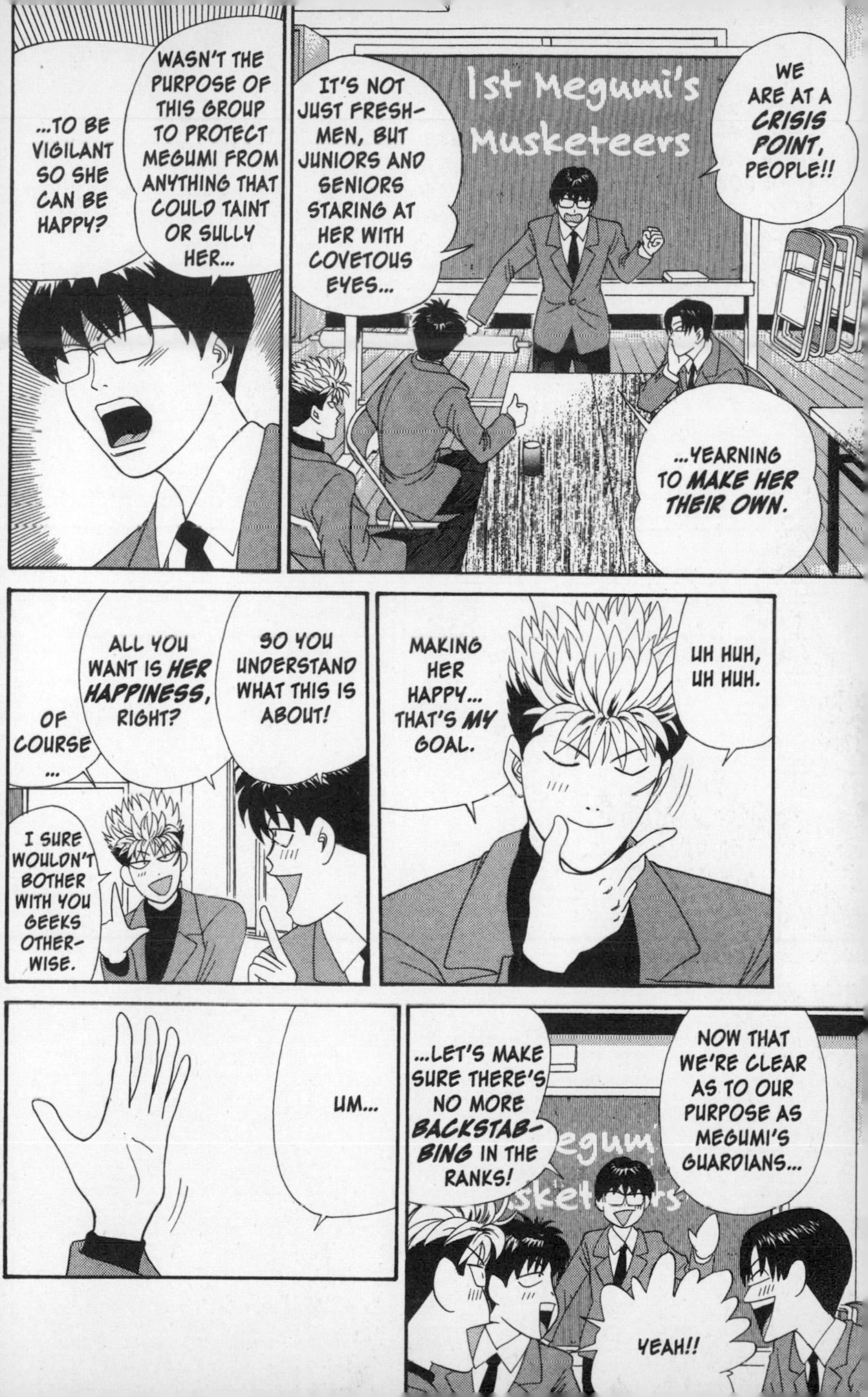
1st Megumi's Musketeers
WE ARE AT A *CRISIS POINT*, PEOPLE!!
IT'S NOT JUST FRESHMEN, BUT JUNIORS AND SENIORS STARING AT HER WITH COVETOUS EYES...
...YEARNING TO *MAKE HER THEIR OWN*.
WASN'T THE PURPOSE OF THIS GROUP TO PROTECT MEGUMI FROM ANYTHING THAT COULD TAINT OR SULLY HER...
...TO BE VIGILANT SO SHE CAN BE HAPPY?
UH HUH, UH HUH.
MAKING HER HAPPY... THAT'S *MY* GOAL.
SO YOU UNDERSTAND WHAT THIS IS ABOUT!
ALL YOU WANT IS *HER HAPPINESS*, RIGHT?
OF COURSE...
I SURE WOULDN'T BOTHER WITH YOU GEEKS OTHERWISE.
NOW THAT WE'RE CLEAR AS TO OUR PURPOSE AS MEGUMI'S GUARDIANS...
...LET'S MAKE SURE THERE'S NO MORE *BACKSTABBING* IN THE RANKS!
YEAH!!
UM...

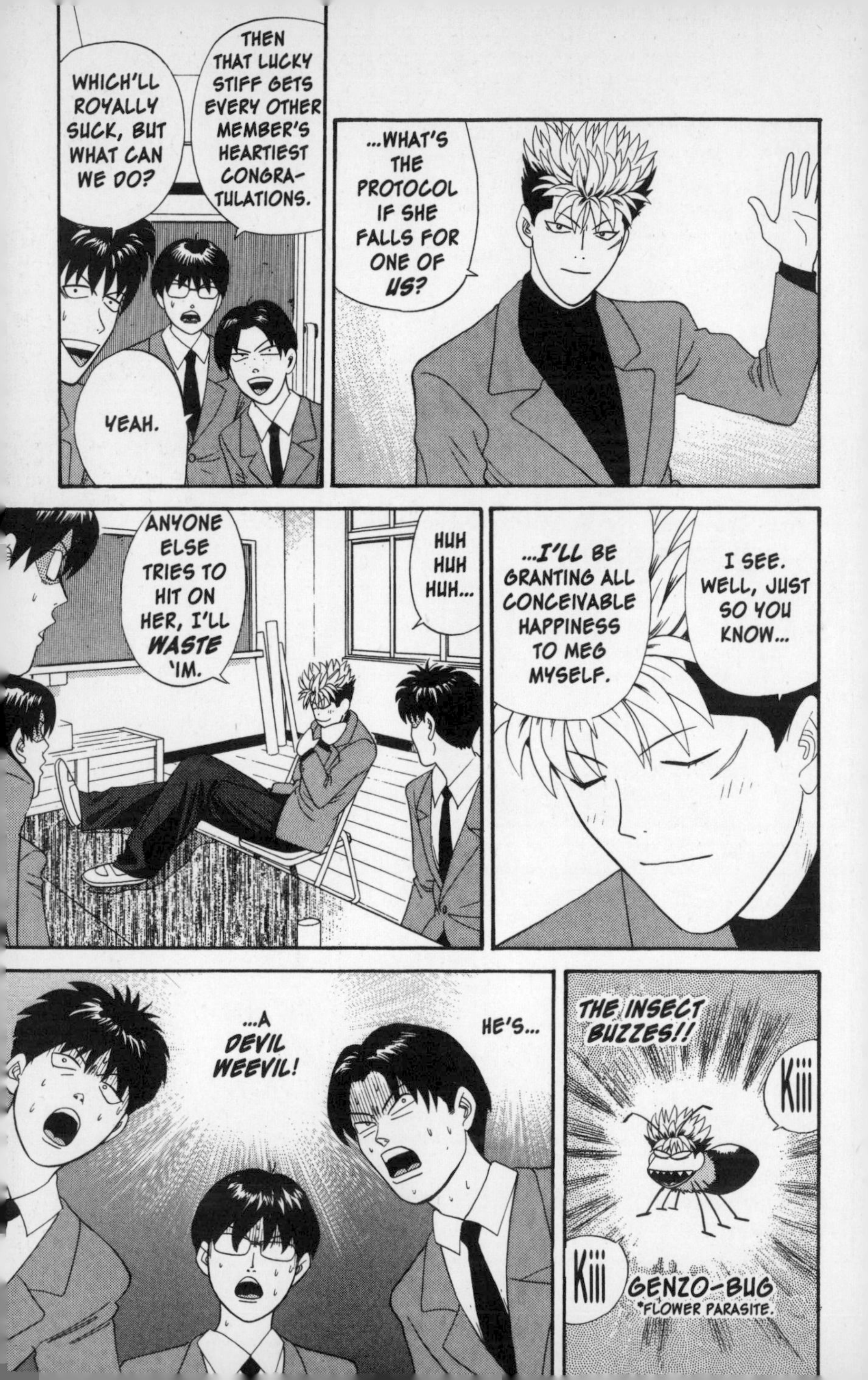
...WHAT'S THE PROTOCOL IF SHE FALLS FOR ONE OF *US*?
THEN THAT LUCKY STIFF GETS EVERY OTHER MEMBER'S HEARTIEST CONGRATULATIONS.
WHICH'LL ROYALLY SUCK, BUT WHAT CAN WE DO?
YEAH.
I SEE. WELL, JUST SO YOU KNOW...
...*I'LL* BE GRANTING ALL CONCEIVABLE HAPPINESS TO MEG MYSELF.
HUH HUH HUH...
ANYONE ELSE TRIES TO HIT ON HER, I'LL *WASTE* 'IM.
THE INSECT BUZZES!!
Kiii
Kiii
GENZO-BUG
*FLOWER PARASITE.
HE'S...
...A DEVIL WEEVIL!

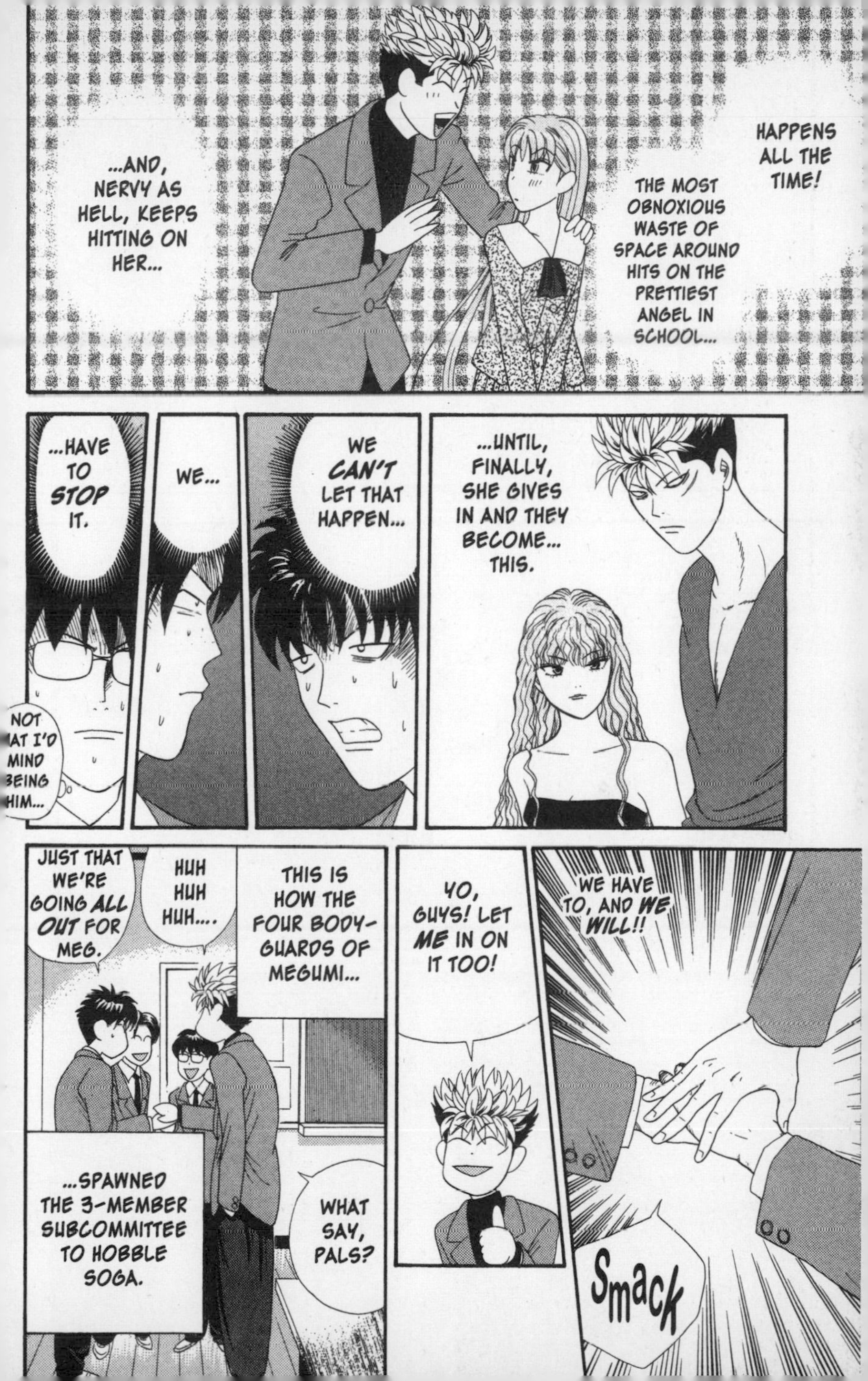
HAPPENS ALL THE TIME!
THE MOST OBNOXIOUS WASTE OF SPACE AROUND HITS ON THE PRETTIEST ANGEL IN SCHOOL...
...AND, NERVY AS HELL, KEEPS HITTING ON HER...
...UNTIL, FINALLY, SHE GIVES IN AND THEY BECOME... THIS.
WE *CAN'T* LET THAT HAPPEN...
WE...
...HAVE TO *STOP* IT.
NOT AT I'D MIND EING HIM...
WE HAVE TO, AND *WE WILL*!!
Smack
YO, GUYS! LET *ME* IN ON IT TOO!
WHAT SAY, PALS?
THIS IS HOW THE FOUR BODY-GUARDS OF MEGUMI...
HUH HUH HUH....
JUST THAT WE'RE GOING *ALL OUT* FOR MEG.
...SPAWNED THE 3-MEMBER SUBCOMMITTEE TO HOBBLE SOGA.

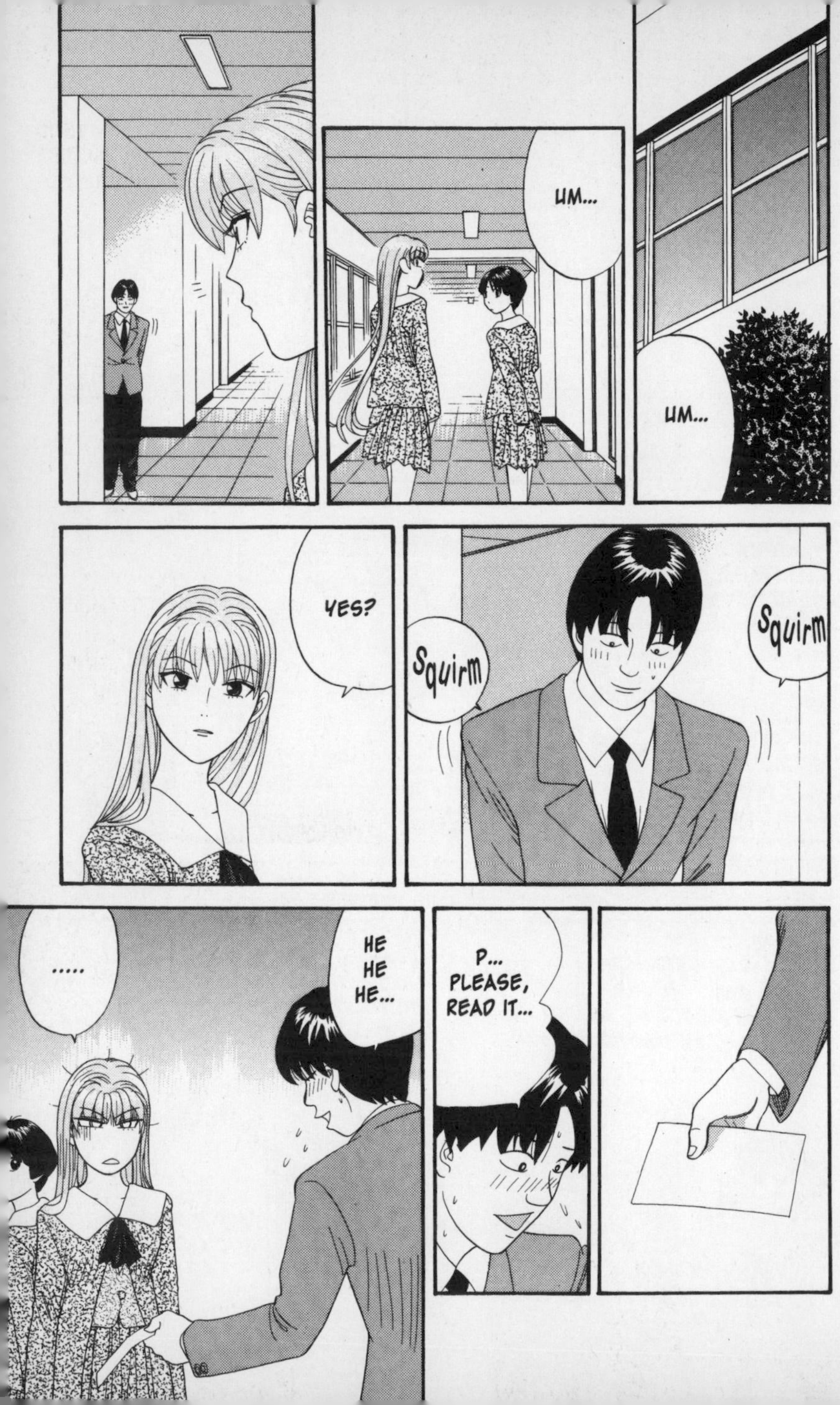
UM...
UM...
Squirm
Squirm
YES?
P... PLEASE, READ IT...
HE HE HE...
.....

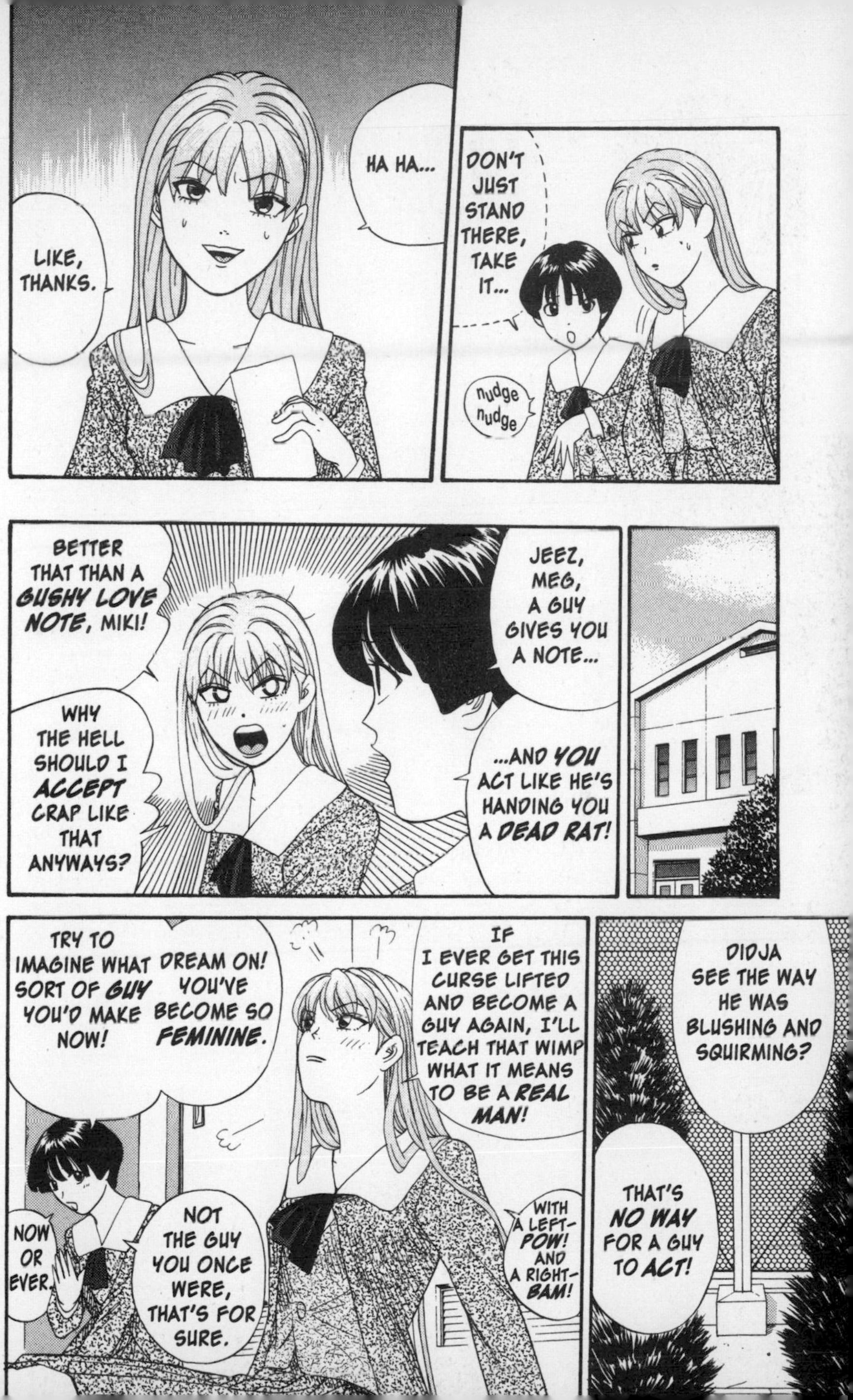
DON'T JUST STAND THERE, TAKE IT...
nudge nudge
HA HA...
LIKE, THANKS.
JEEZ, MEG, A GUY GIVES YOU A NOTE...
...AND YOU ACT LIKE HE'S HANDING YOU A DEAD RAT!
BETTER THAT THAN A GUSHY LOVE NOTE, MIKI!
WHY THE HELL SHOULD I ACCEPT CRAP LIKE THAT ANYWAYS?
DIDJA SEE THE WAY HE WAS BLUSHING AND SQUIRMING?
THAT'S NO WAY FOR A GUY TO ACT!
IF I EVER GET THIS CURSE LIFTED AND BECOME A GUY AGAIN, I'LL TEACH THAT WIMP WHAT IT MEANS TO BE A REAL MAN!
WITH A LEFT-POW! AND A RIGHT-BAM!
DREAM ON! YOU'VE BECOME SO FEMININE.
TRY TO IMAGINE WHAT SORT OF GUY YOU'D MAKE NOW!
NOT THE GUY YOU ONCE WERE, THAT'S FOR SURE.
NOW OR EVER.

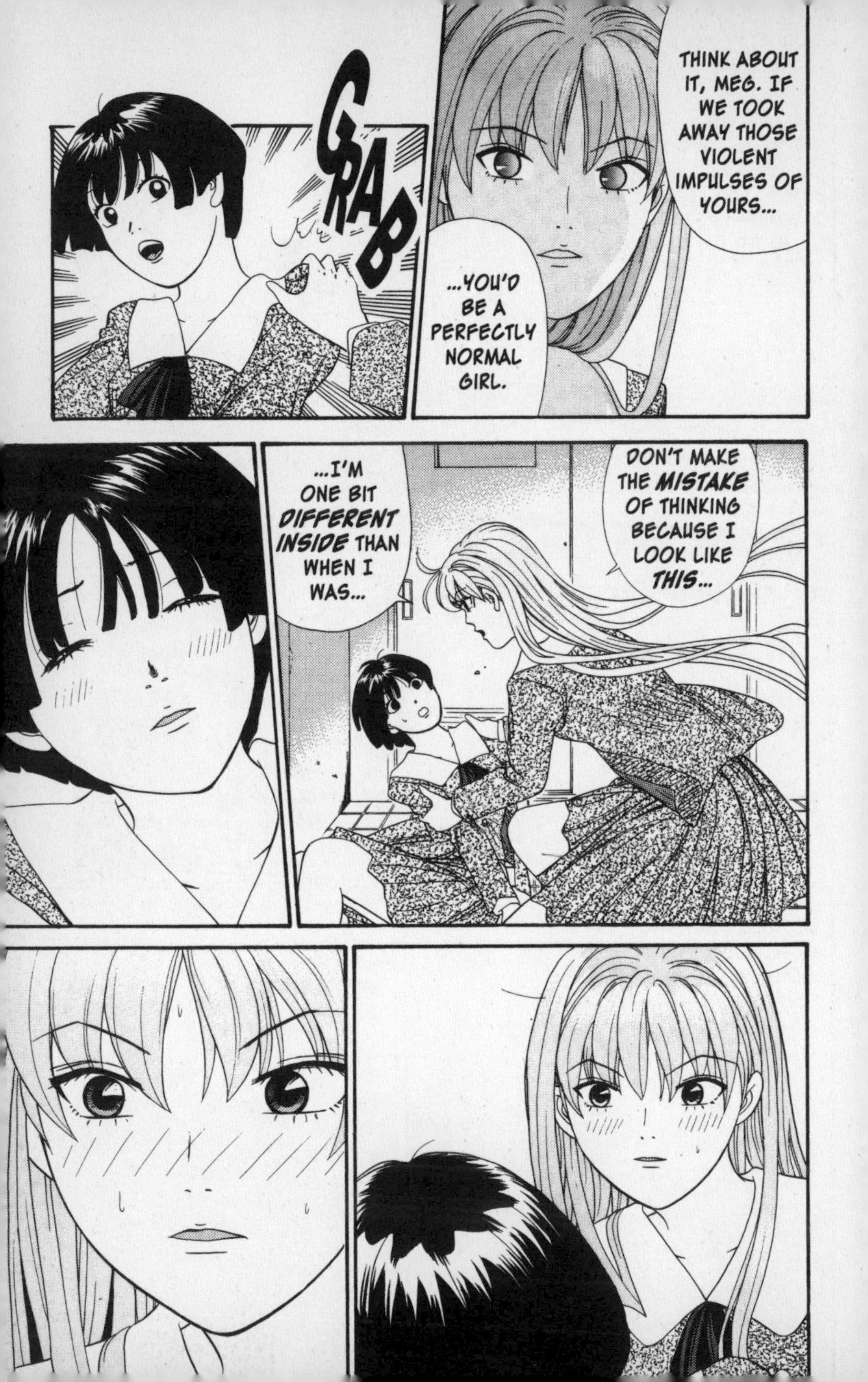

THINK ABOUT IT, MEG. IF WE TOOK AWAY THOSE VIOLENT IMPULSES OF YOURS...
...YOU'D BE A PERFECTLY NORMAL GIRL.
GRAB
DON'T MAKE THE *MISTAKE* OF THINKING BECAUSE I LOOK LIKE *THIS*...
...I'M ONE BIT *DIFFERENT INSIDE* THAN WHEN I WAS...

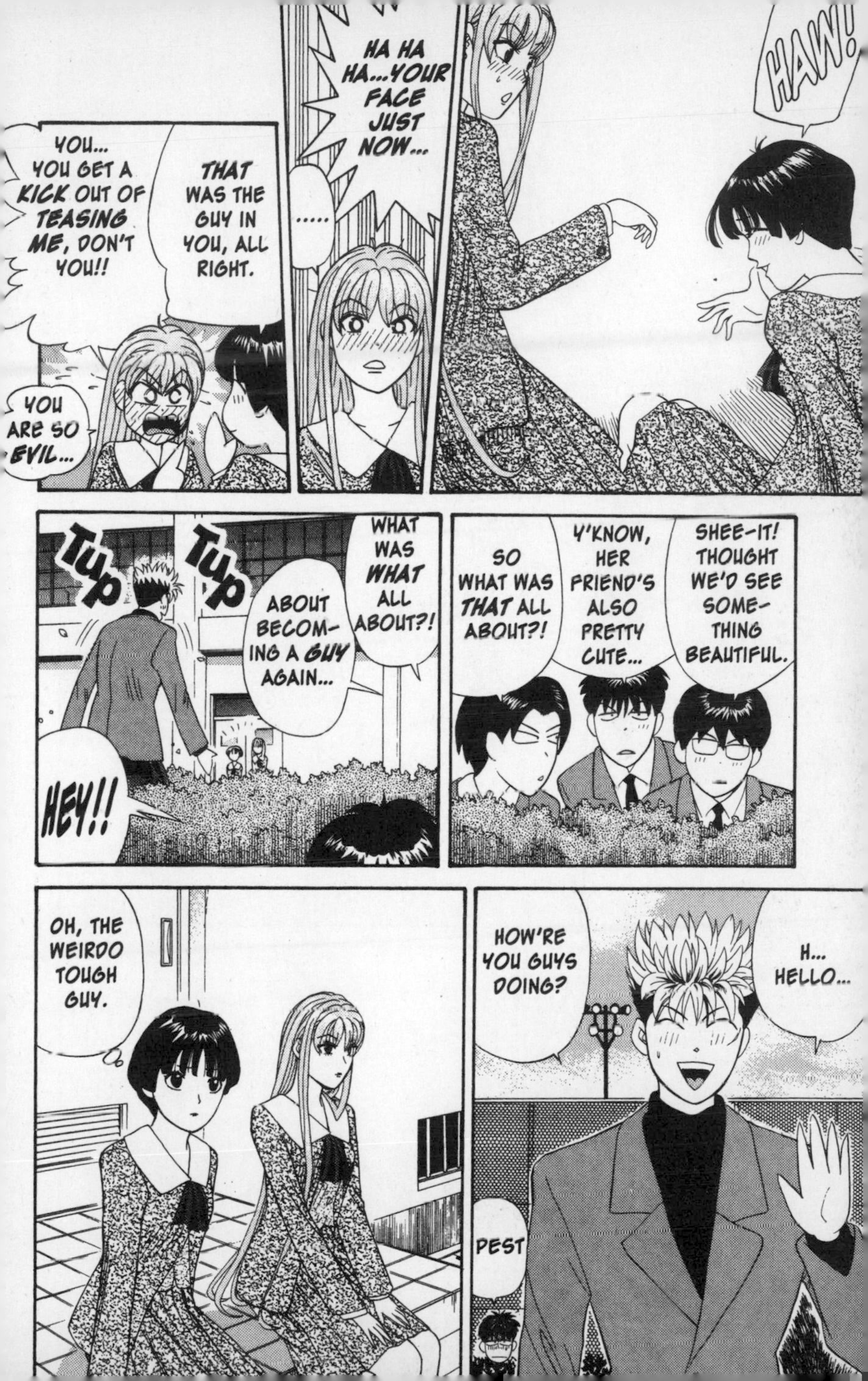
HAW!
HA HA HA...YOUR FACE JUST NOW...
......
THAT WAS THE GUY IN YOU, ALL RIGHT.
YOU... YOU GET A KICK OUT OF TEASING ME, DON'T YOU!!
YOU ARE SO EVIL...
SHEE-IT! THOUGHT WE'D SEE SOME-THING BEAUTIFUL.
Y'KNOW, HER FRIEND'S ALSO PRETTY CUTE...
SO WHAT WAS THAT ALL ABOUT?!
Tup
Tup
WHAT WAS WHAT ALL ABOUT?!
ABOUT BECOM-ING A GUY AGAIN...
HEY!!
H... HELLO...
HOW'RE YOU GUYS DOING?
PEST
OH, THE WEIRDO TOUGH GUY.

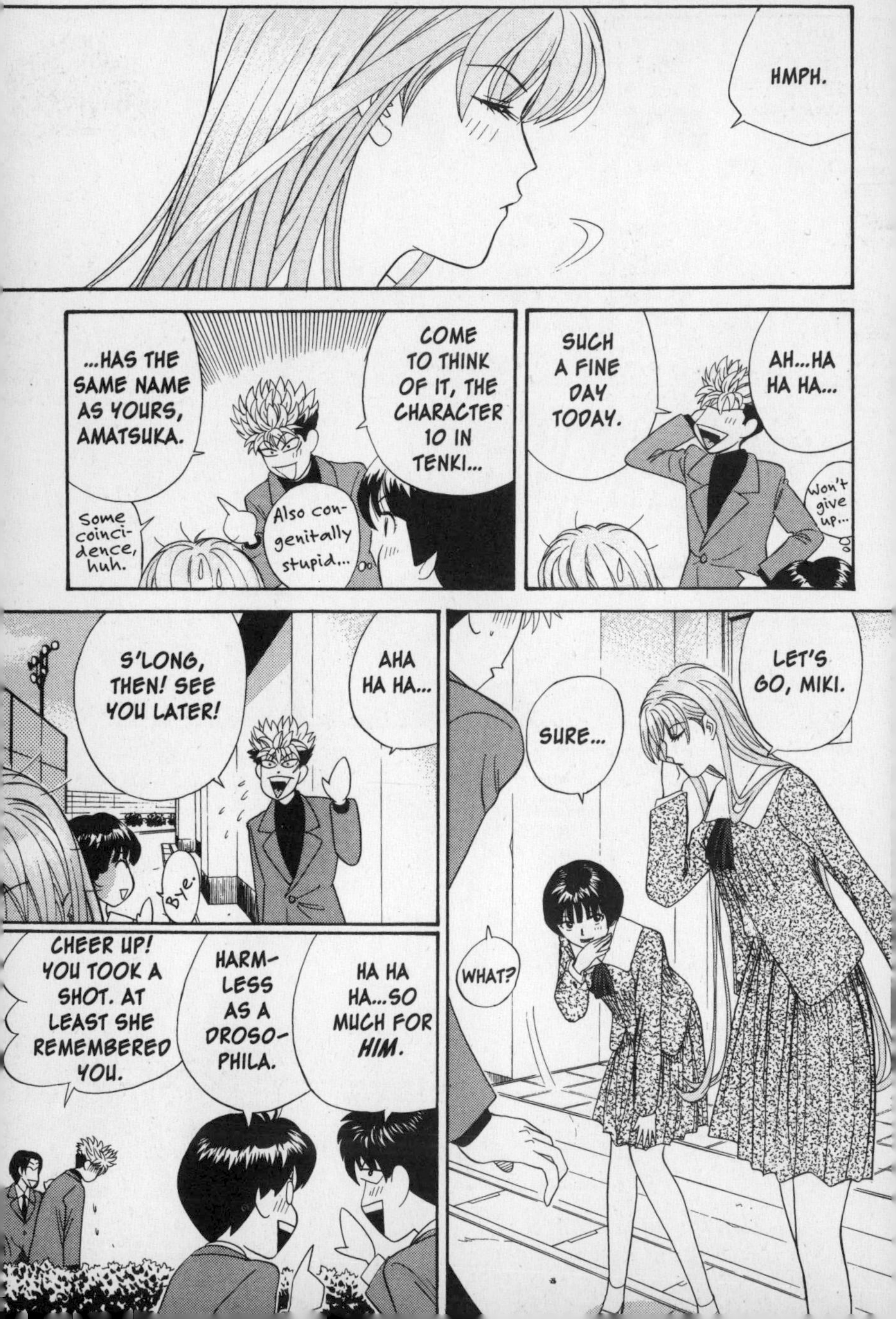
HMPH.
AH...HA HA HA...
SUCH A FINE DAY TODAY.
Won't give up...
COME TO THINK OF IT, THE CHARACTER 10 IN TENKI...
...HAS THE SAME NAME AS YOURS, AMATSUKA.
Also congenitally stupid...
Some coincidence, huh.
LET'S GO, MIKI.
SURE...
WHAT?
AHA HA HA...
S'LONG, THEN! SEE YOU LATER!
Bye.
HA HA HA...SO MUCH FOR *HIM*.
HARMLESS AS A DROSOPHILA.
CHEER UP! YOU TOOK A SHOT. AT LEAST SHE REMEMBERED YOU.

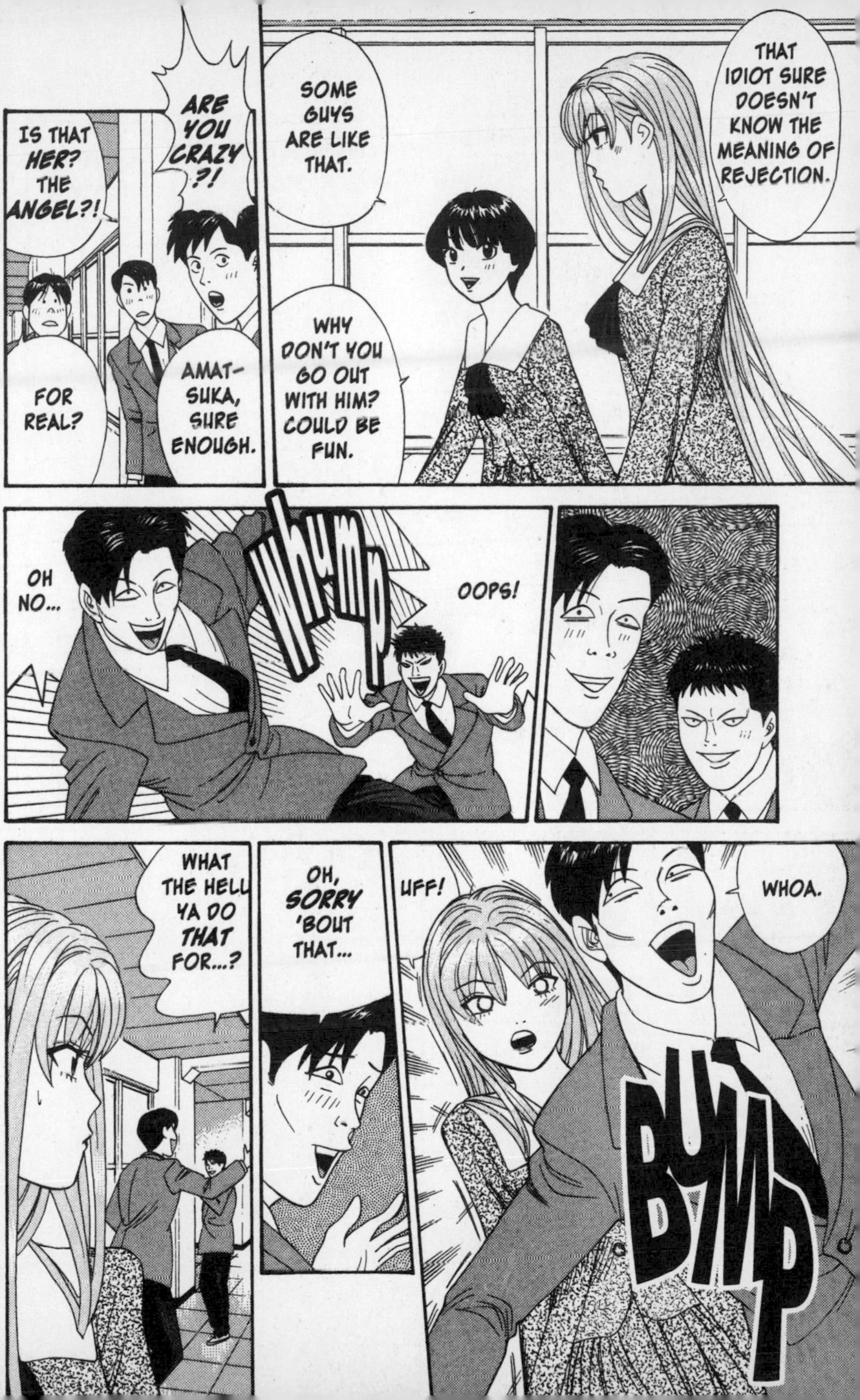
THAT IDIOT SURE DOESN'T KNOW THE MEANING OF REJECTION.
SOME GUYS ARE LIKE THAT.
WHY DON'T YOU GO OUT WITH HIM? COULD BE FUN.
ARE YOU CRAZY?!
IS THAT HER? THE ANGEL?!
AMAT-SUKA, SURE ENOUGH.
FOR REAL?
OOPS!
WHUMP
OH NO...
WHOA.
UFF!
BUMP
OH, SORRY 'BOUT THAT...
WHAT THE HELL YA DO THAT FOR...?

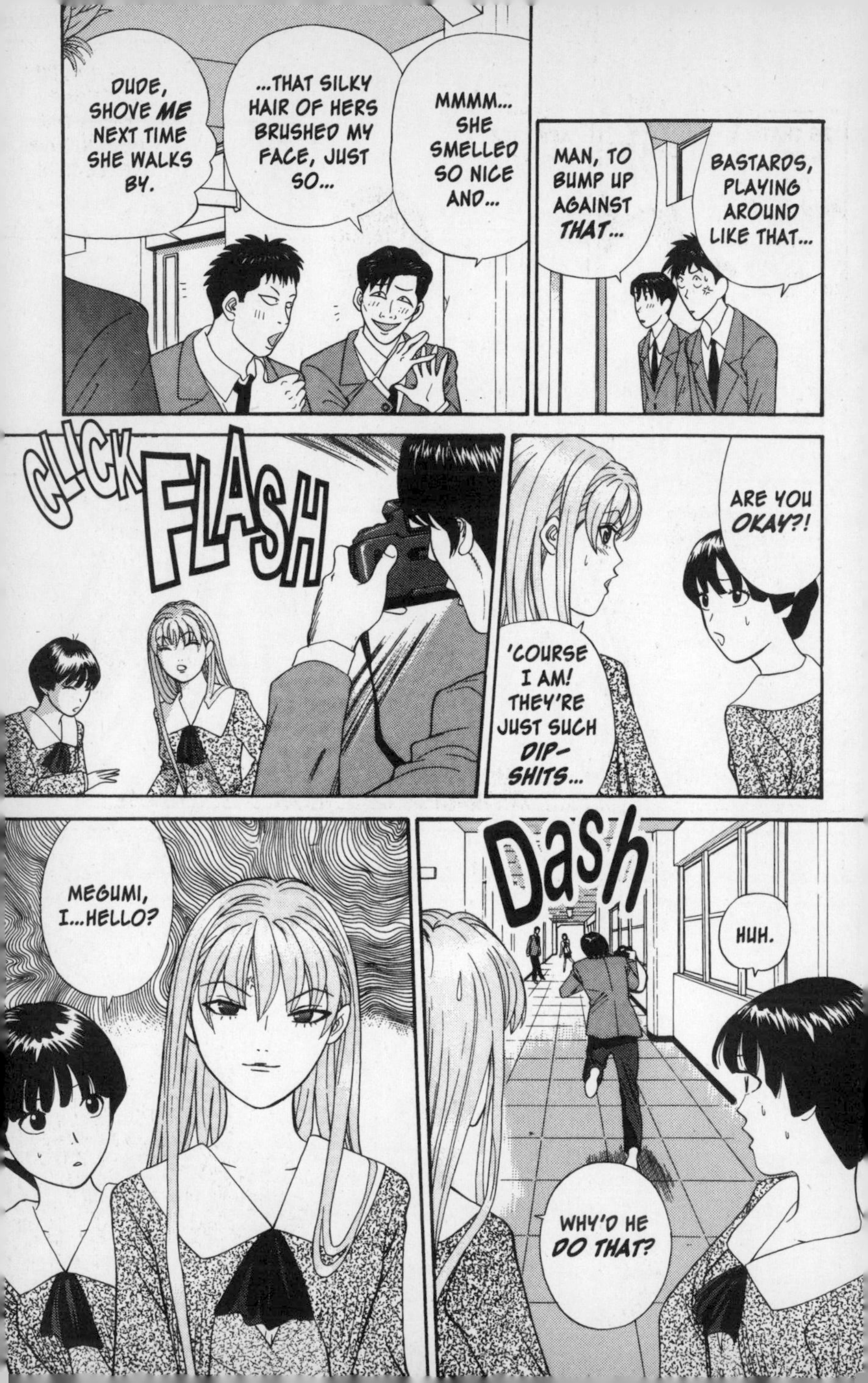
BASTARDS, PLAYING AROUND LIKE THAT...
MAN, TO BUMP UP AGAINST *THAT*...
MMMM... SHE SMELLED SO NICE AND...
...THAT SILKY HAIR OF HERS BRUSHED MY FACE, JUST SO...
DUDE, SHOVE *ME* NEXT TIME SHE WALKS BY.
ARE YOU *OKAY?!*
'COURSE I AM! THEY'RE JUST SUCH *DIP-SHITS*...
CLICK
FLASH
Dash
HUH.
WHY'D HE *DO THAT?*
MEGUMI, I...HELLO?

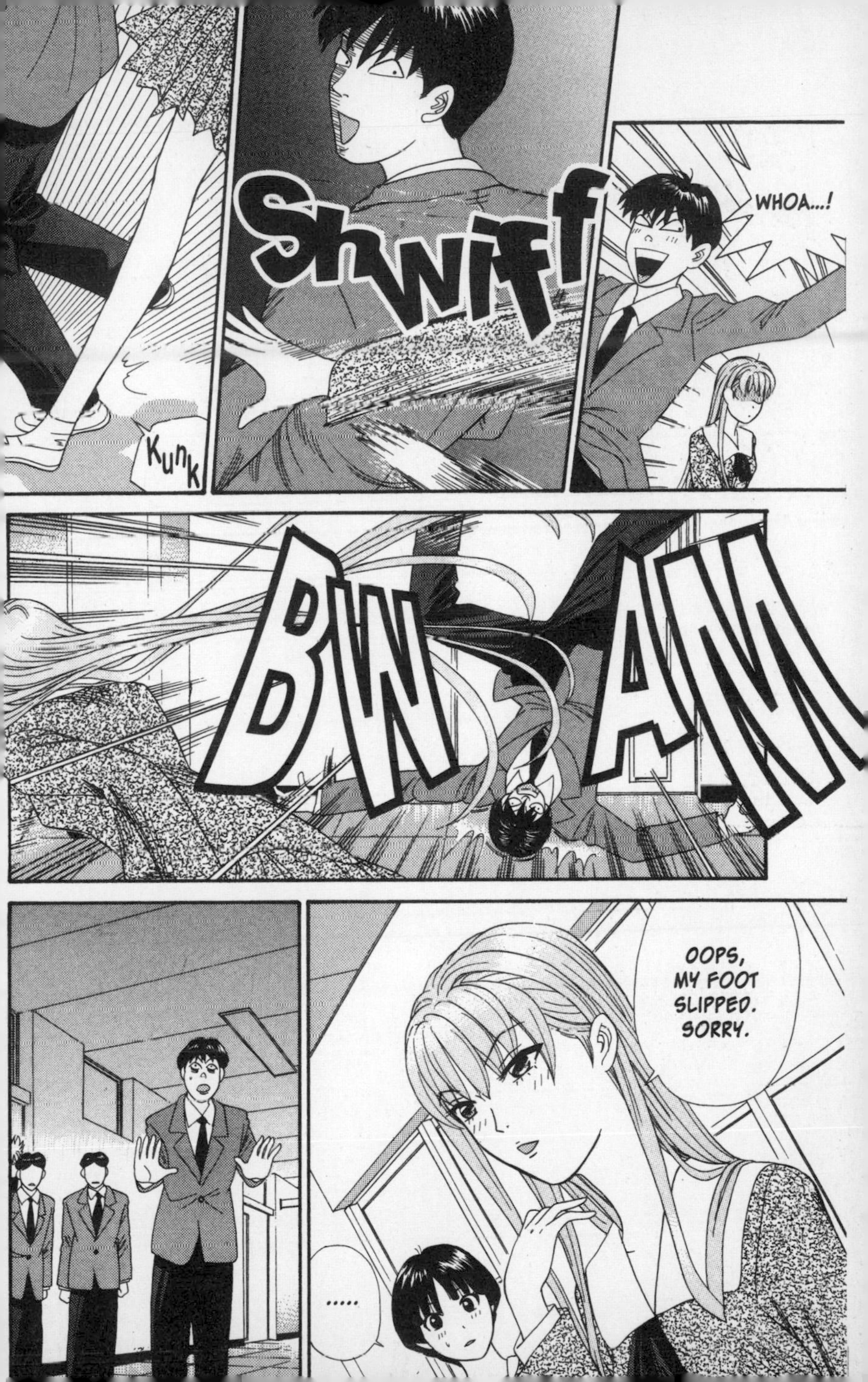
WHOA...!
Shwiff
Kunk
BWAM
OOPS, MY FOOT SLIPPED. SORRY.
......

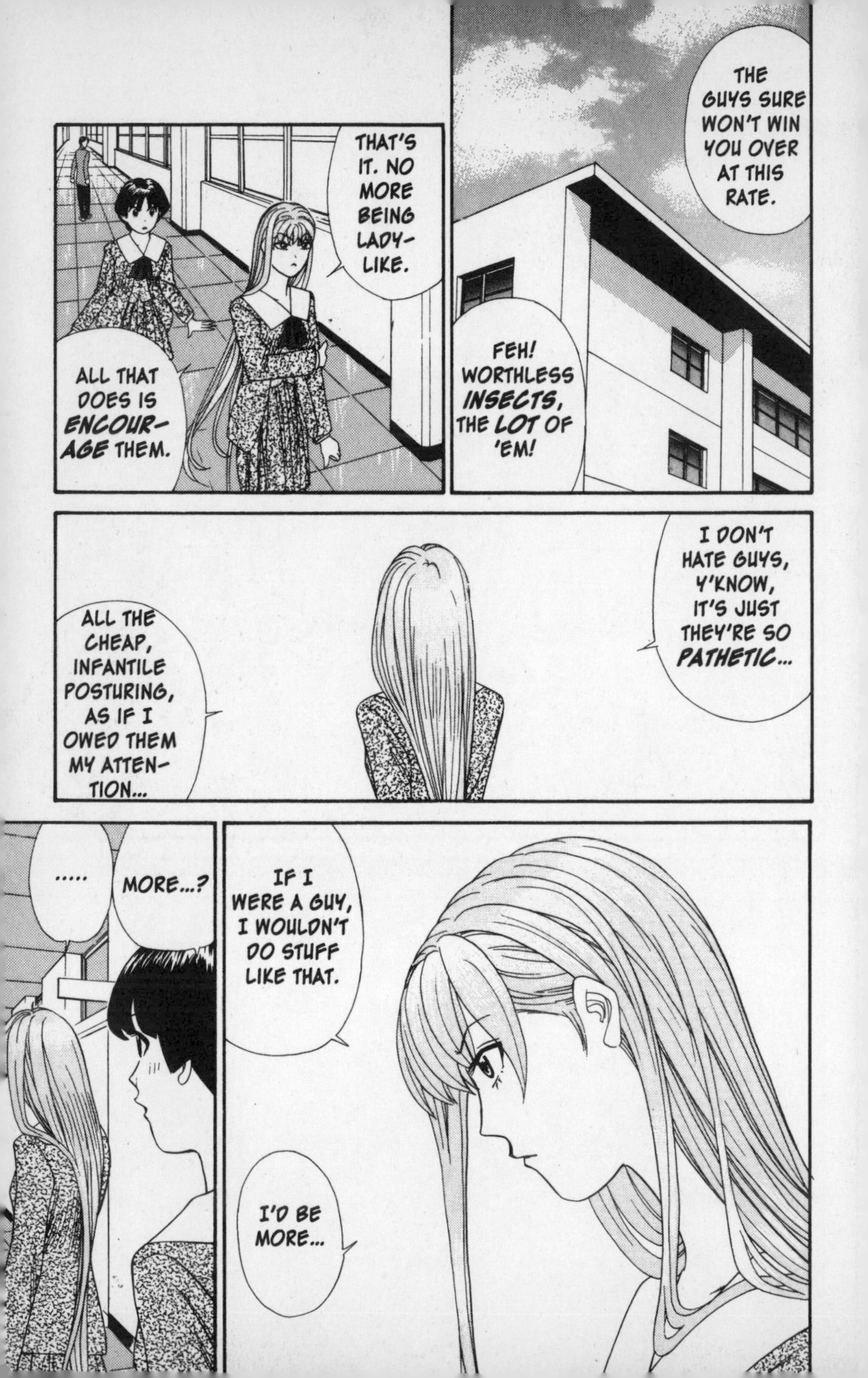
THE GUYS SURE WON'T WIN YOU OVER AT THIS RATE.
FEH! WORTHLESS *INSECTS*, THE *LOT* OF 'EM!
THAT'S IT. NO MORE BEING LADY-LIKE.
ALL THAT DOES IS *ENCOURAGE* THEM.
I DON'T HATE GUYS, Y'KNOW, IT'S JUST THEY'RE SO *PATHETIC*...
ALL THE CHEAP, INFANTILE POSTURING, AS IF I OWED THEM MY ATTENTION...
IF I WERE A GUY, I WOULDN'T DO STUFF LIKE THAT.
I'D BE MORE...
MORE...?
.....

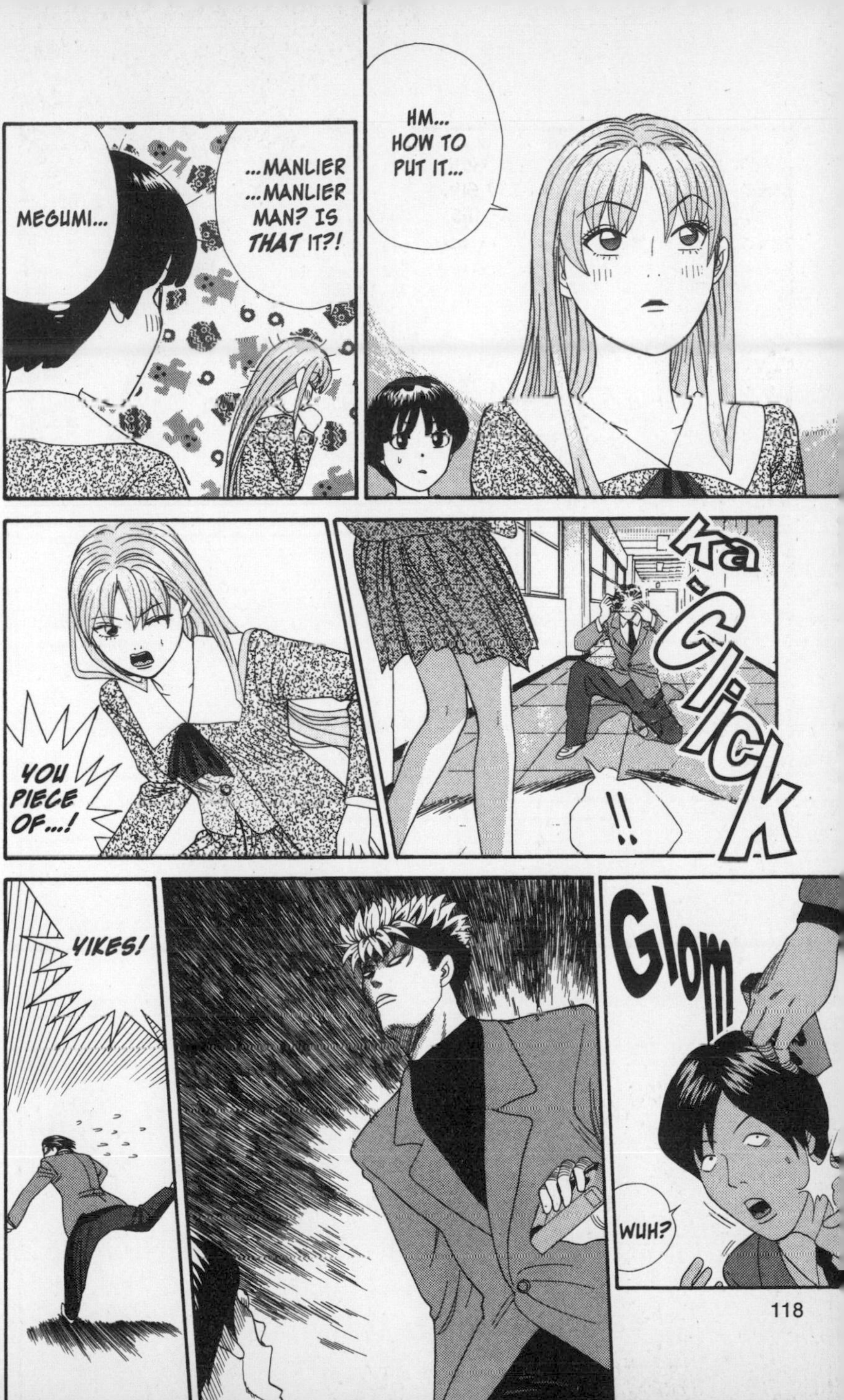
HM... HOW TO PUT IT...
...MANLIER ...MANLIER MAN? IS THAT IT?!
MEGUMI...
ka Click
!!
YOU PIECE OF...!
Glom
WUH?
YIKES!

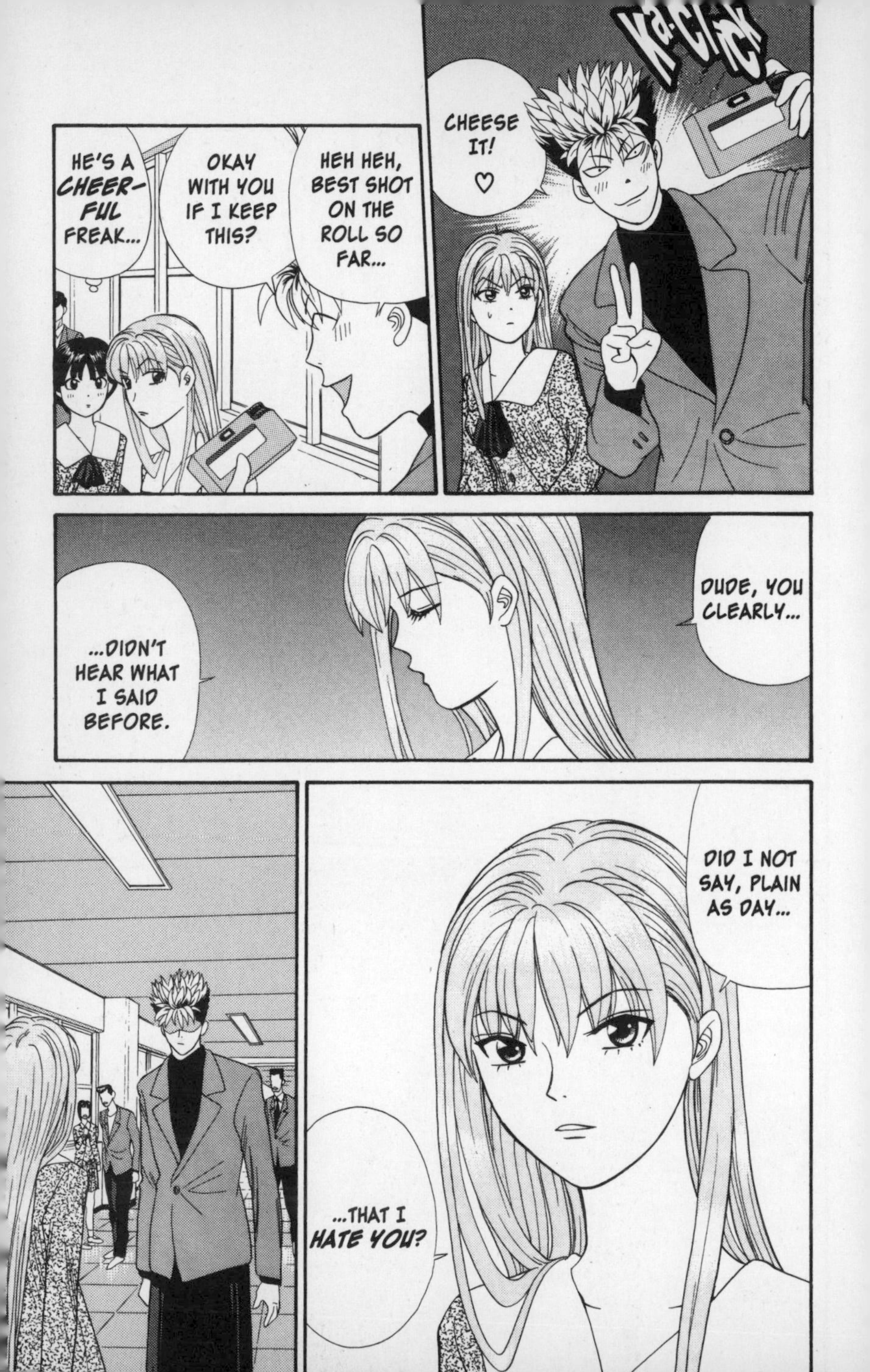
KA-CLACK
CHEESE IT! ♡
HEH HEH, BEST SHOT ON THE ROLL SO FAR...
OKAY WITH YOU IF I KEEP THIS?
HE'S A *CHEERFUL* FREAK...
DUDE, YOU CLEARLY...
...DIDN'T HEAR WHAT I SAID BEFORE.
DID I NOT SAY, PLAIN AS DAY...
...THAT I *HATE YOU*?

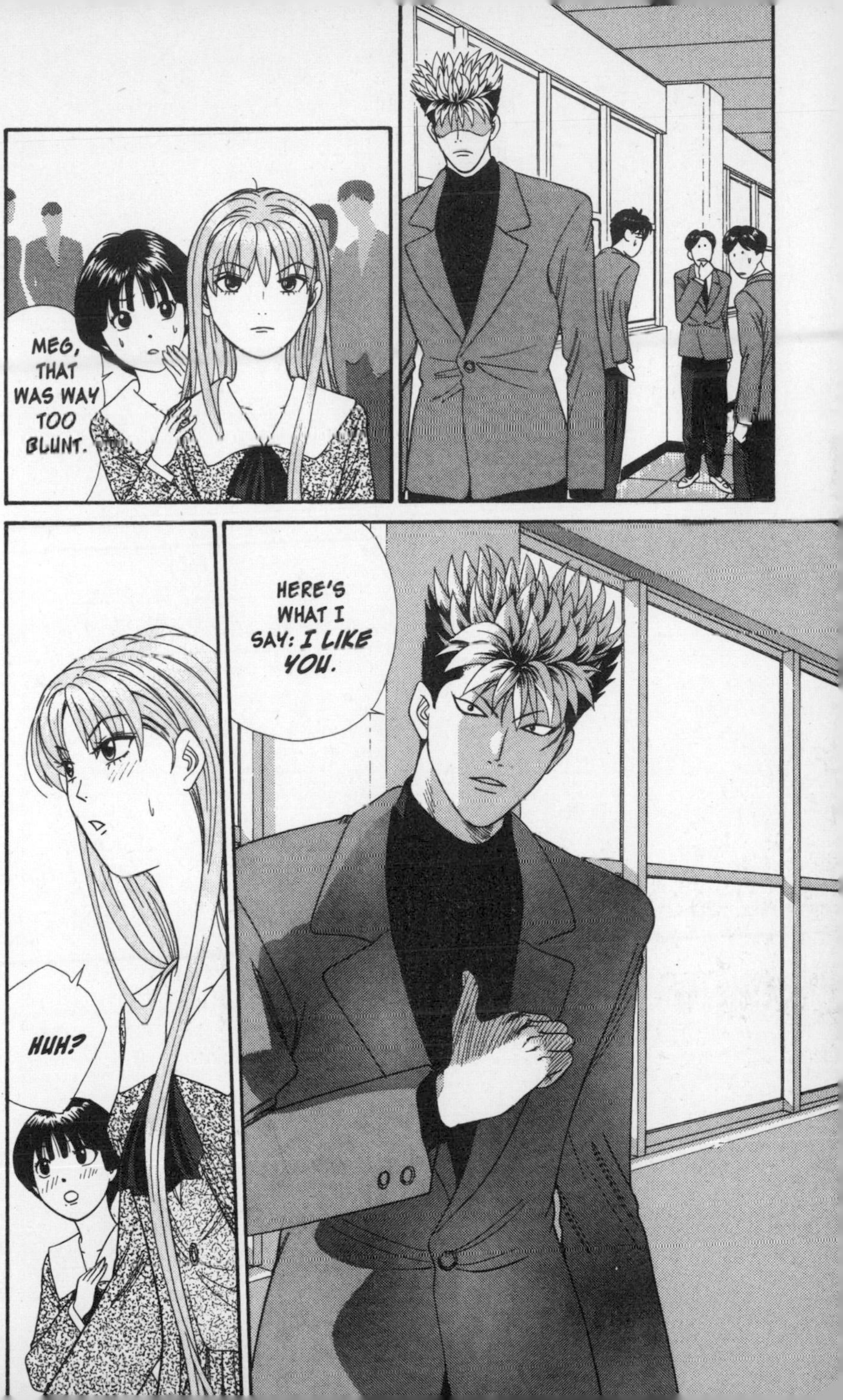
MEG, THAT WAS WAY TOO BLUNT.
HERE'S WHAT I SAY: I LIKE YOU.
HUH?

Chapter 6: Feelings For a Man...

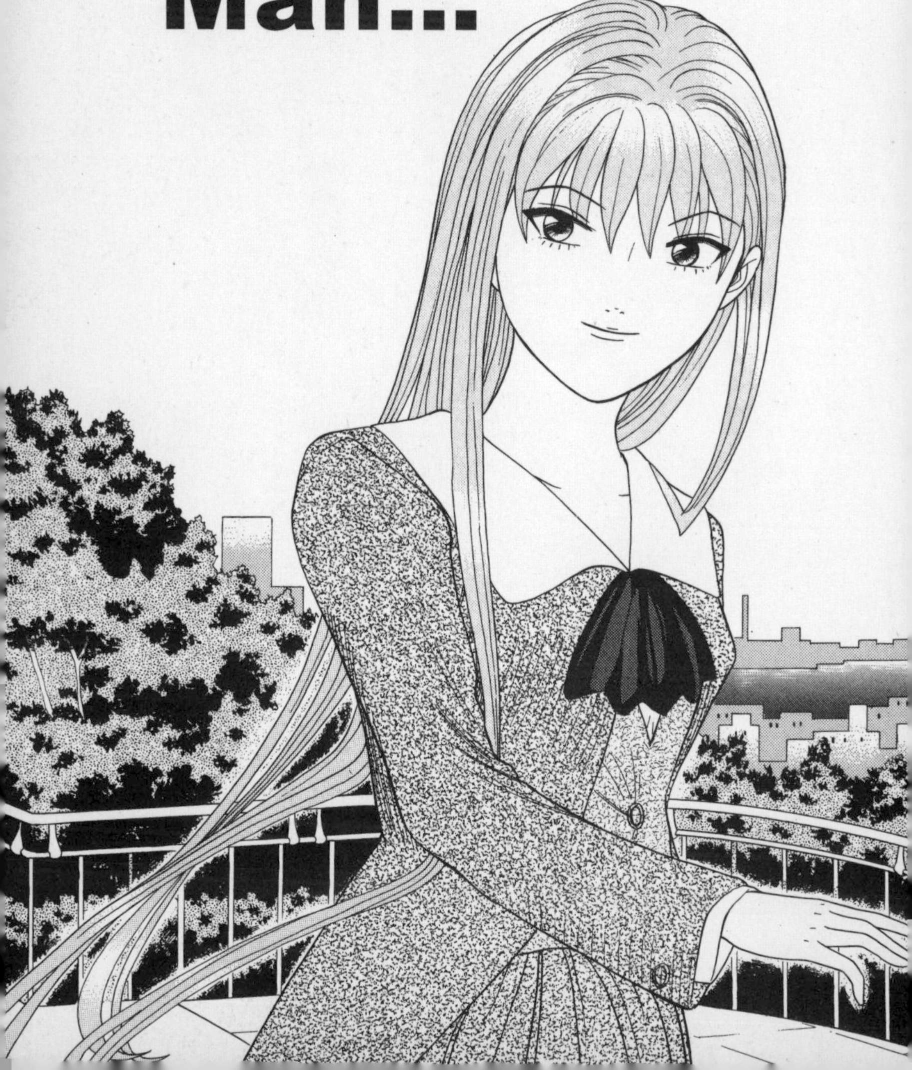

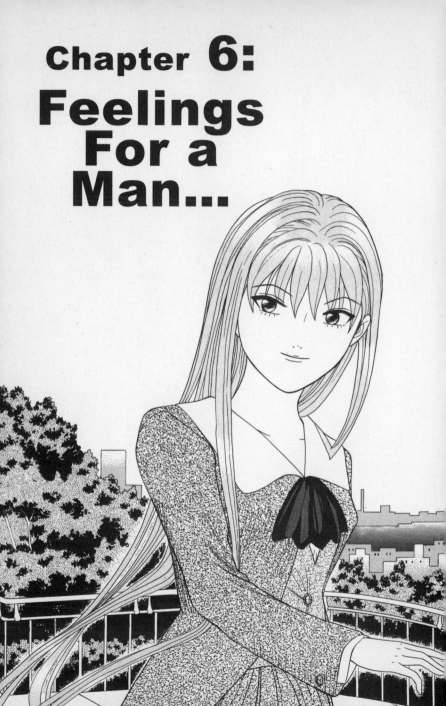

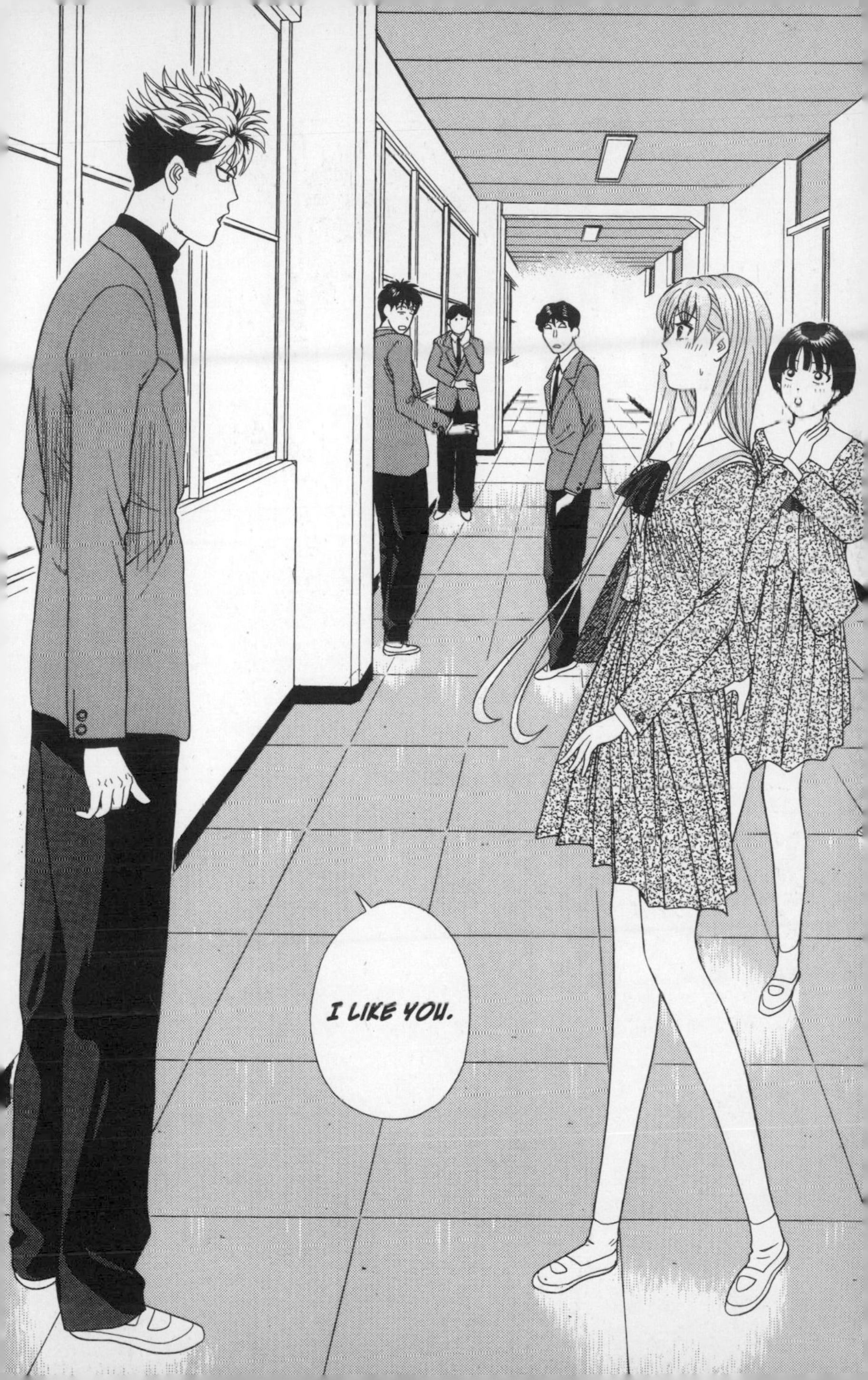
I LIKE YOU.

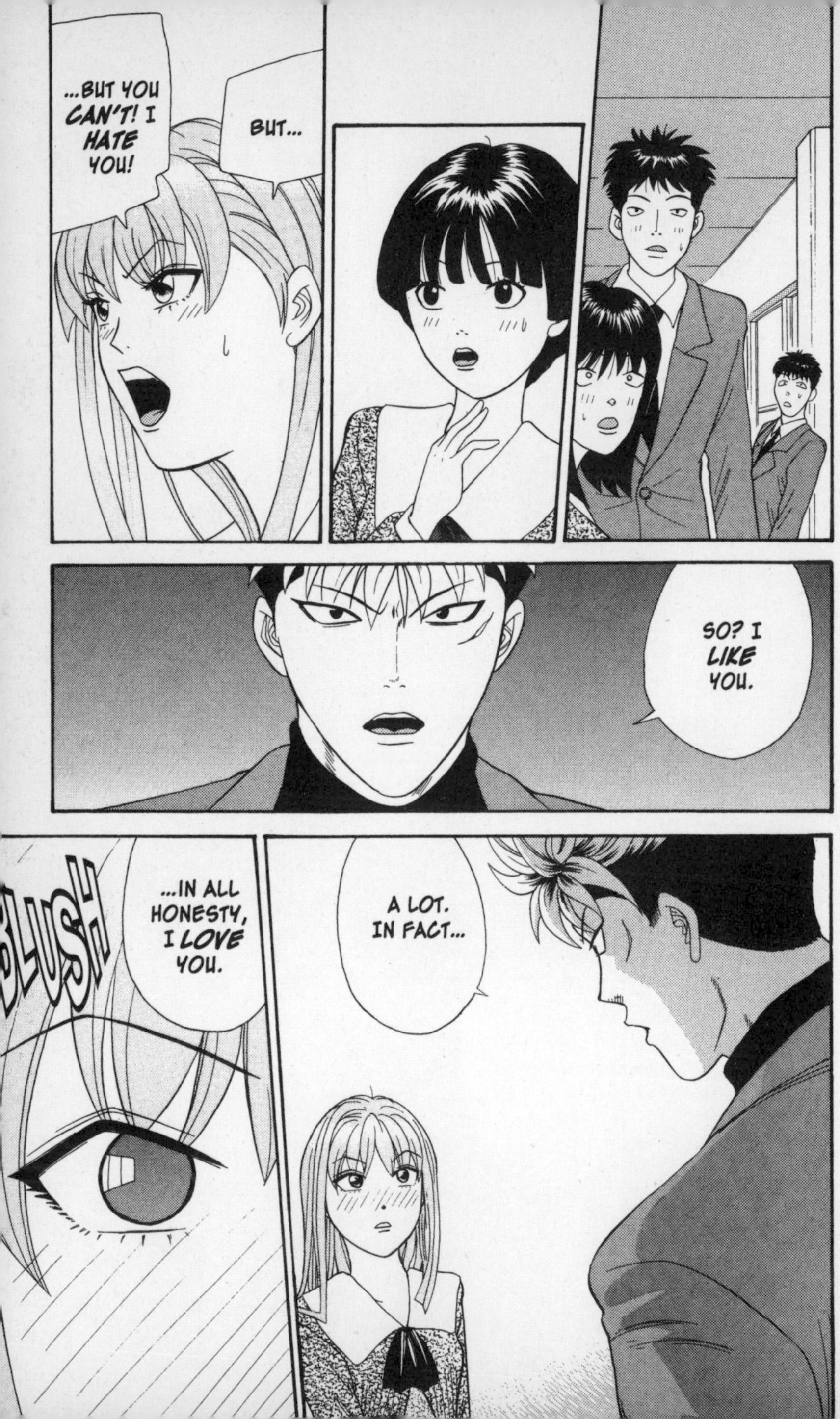

BUT...
...BUT YOU *CAN'T*! I *HATE* YOU!
SO? I *LIKE* YOU.
A LOT. IN FACT...
...IN ALL HONESTY, I *LOVE* YOU.
BLUSH

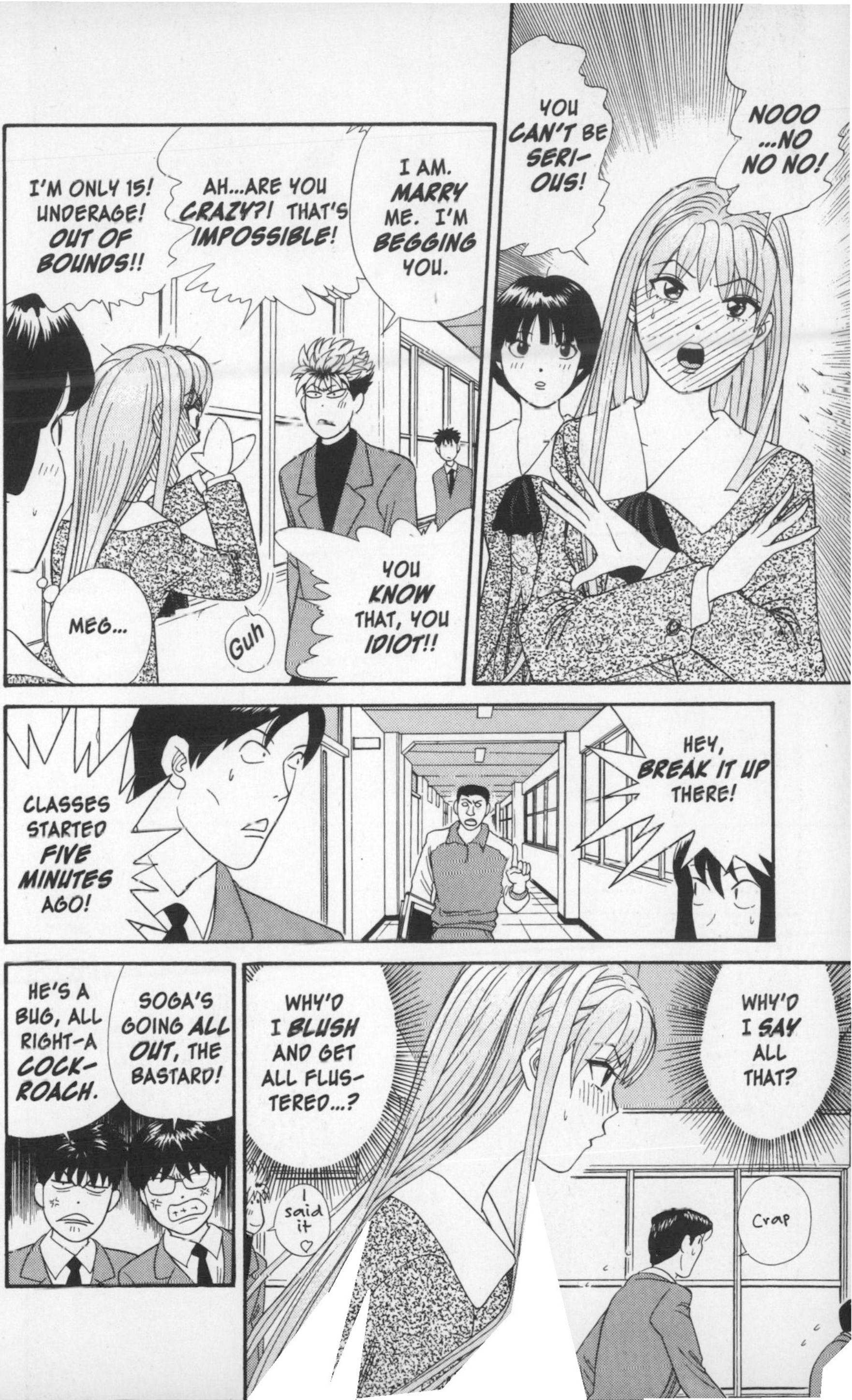
NOOO ...NO NO NO!
YOU CAN'T BE SERI-OUS!
I AM. MARRY ME. I'M BEGGING YOU.
AH...ARE YOU CRAZY?! THAT'S IMPOSSIBLE!
I'M ONLY 15! UNDERAGE! OUT OF BOUNDS!!
YOU KNOW THAT, YOU IDIOT!!
Guh
MEG...
HEY, BREAK IT UP THERE!
CLASSES STARTED FIVE MINUTES AGO!
WHY'D I SAY ALL THAT?
Crap
WHY'D I BLUSH AND GET ALL FLUS-TERED...?
I said it ♡
SOGA'S GOING ALL OUT, THE BASTARD!
HE'S A BUG, ALL RIGHT-A COCK-ROACH.

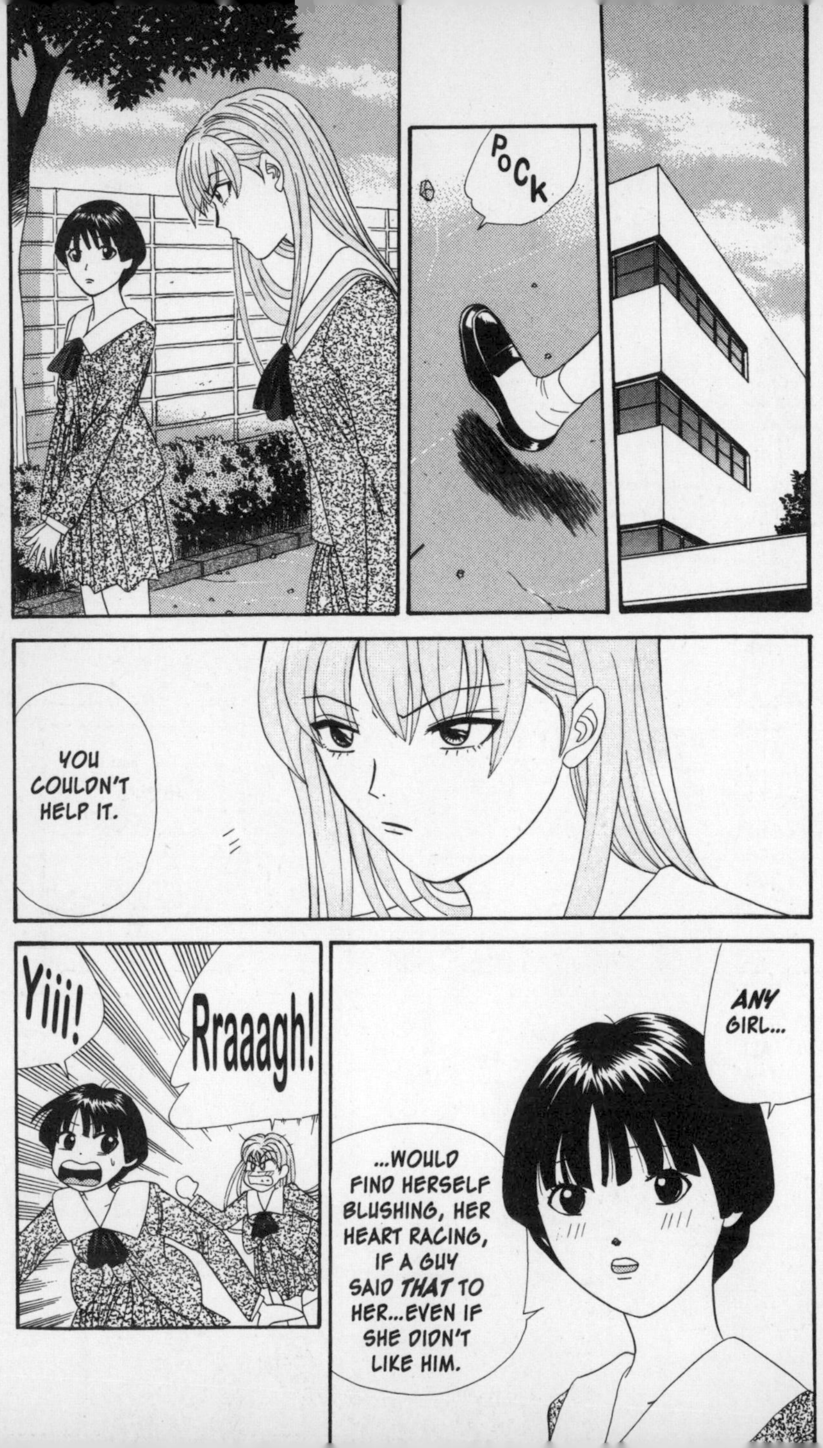
POCK
YOU COULDN'T HELP IT.
ANY GIRL...
...WOULD FIND HERSELF BLUSHING, HER HEART RACING, IF A GUY SAID *THAT* TO HER...EVEN IF SHE DIDN'T LIKE HIM.
Rraaagh!
Yiii!

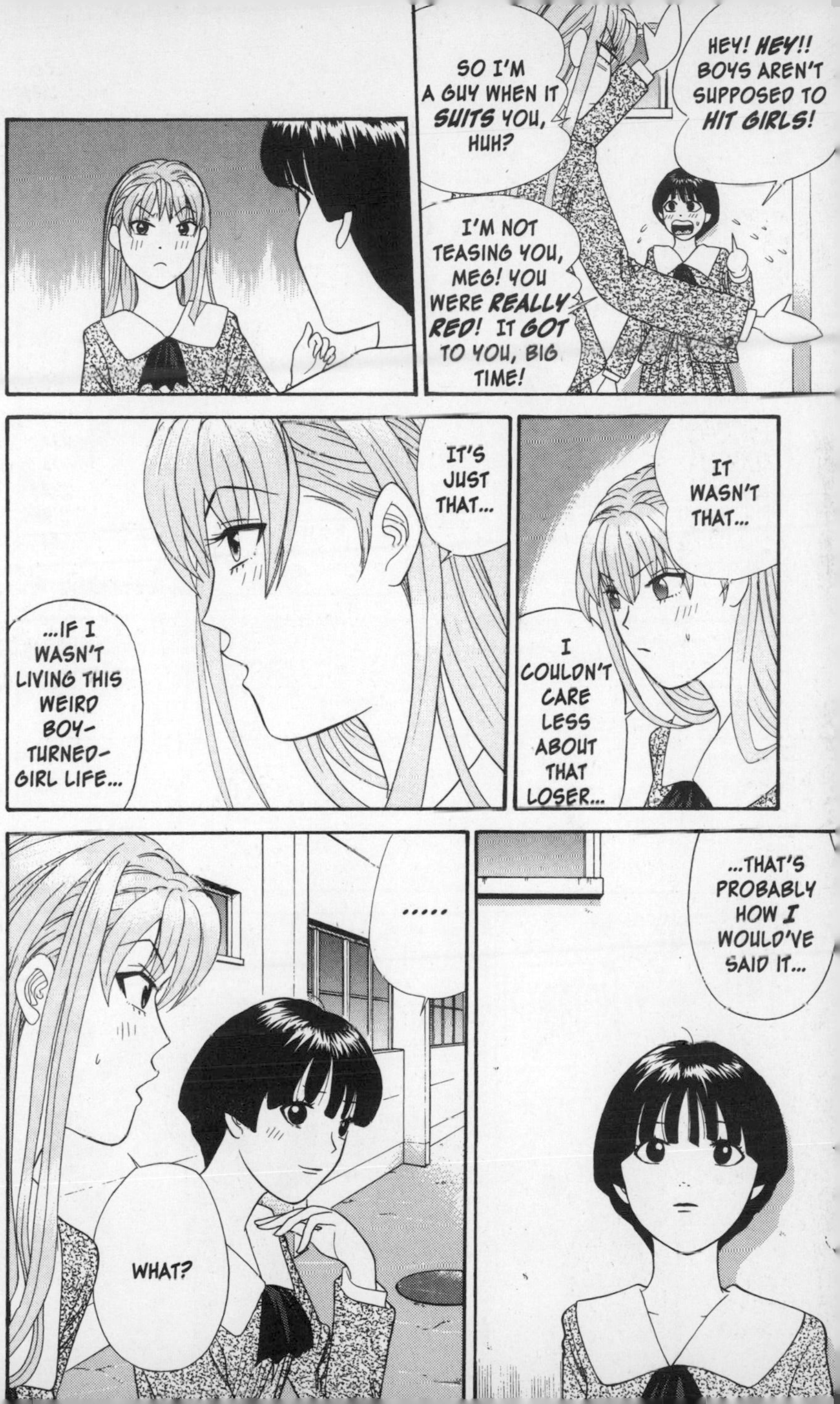
I'M NOT TEASING YOU, MEG! YOU WERE *REALLY RED!* IT *GOT* TO YOU, BIG TIME!
HEY! *HEY!!* BOYS AREN'T SUPPOSED TO *HIT GIRLS!*
SO I'M A GUY WHEN IT *SUITS* YOU, HUH?
IT WASN'T THAT...
I COULDN'T CARE LESS ABOUT THAT LOSER...
IT'S JUST THAT...
...IF I WASN'T LIVING THIS WEIRD BOY-TURNED-GIRL LIFE...
...THAT'S PROBABLY HOW *I* WOULD'VE SAID IT...
.....
WHAT?

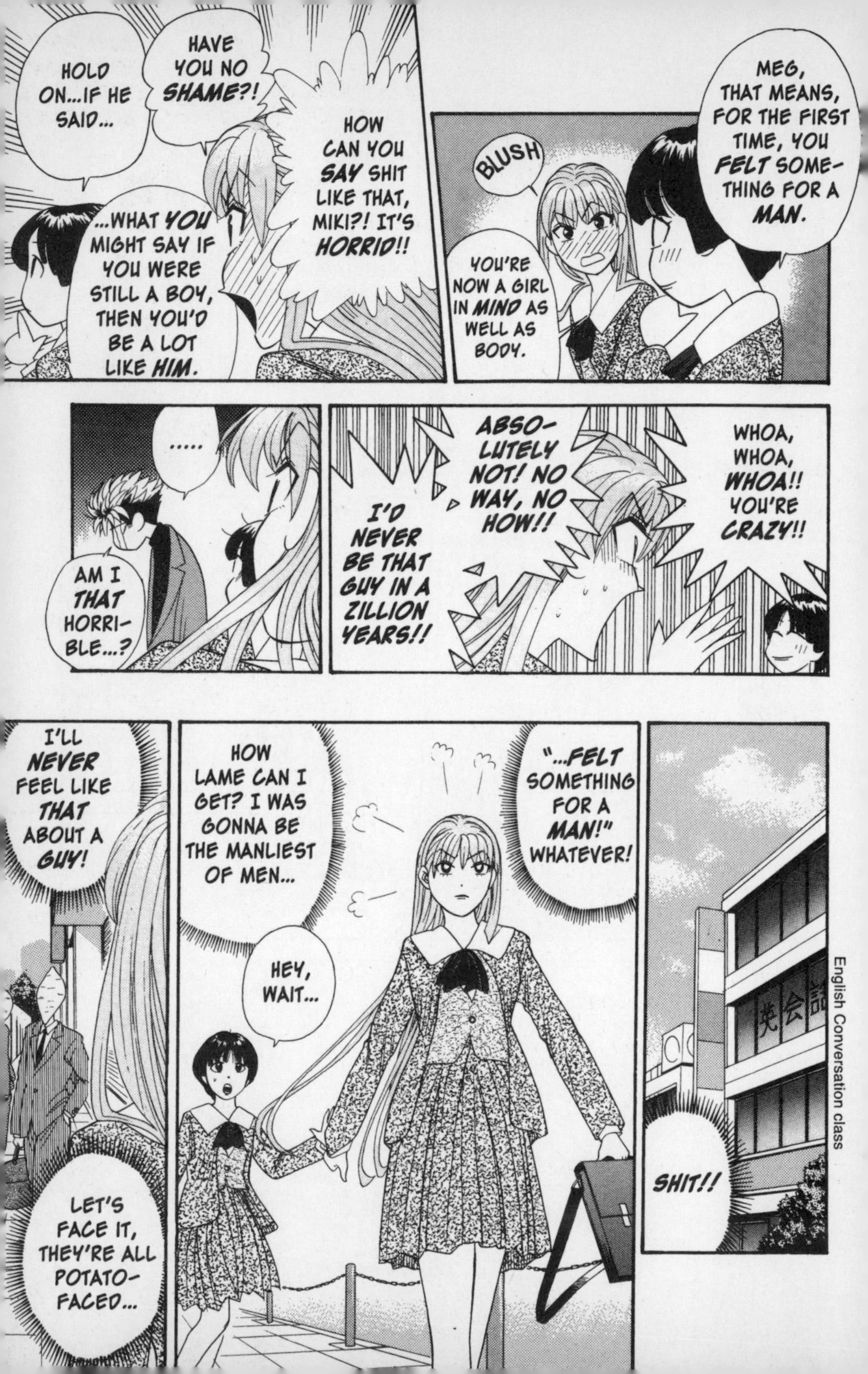
MEG, THAT MEANS, FOR THE FIRST TIME, YOU FELT SOME-THING FOR A MAN.
BLUSH
YOU'RE NOW A GIRL IN MIND AS WELL AS BODY.
HAVE YOU NO SHAME?!
HOW CAN YOU SAY SHIT LIKE THAT, MIKI?! IT'S HORRID!!
HOLD ON...IF HE SAID...
...WHAT YOU MIGHT SAY IF YOU WERE STILL A BOY, THEN YOU'D BE A LOT LIKE HIM.
WHOA, WHOA, WHOA!! YOU'RE CRAZY!!
ABSO-LUTELY NOT! NO WAY, NO HOW!!
I'D NEVER BE THAT GUY IN A ZILLION YEARS!!
.....
AM I THAT HORRI-BLE...?
English Conversation class
SHIT!!
"...FELT SOMETHING FOR A MAN!" WHATEVER!
HOW LAME CAN I GET? I WAS GONNA BE THE MANLIEST OF MEN...
HEY, WAIT...
I'LL NEVER FEEL LIKE THAT ABOUT A GUY!
LET'S FACE IT, THEY'RE ALL POTATO-FACED...

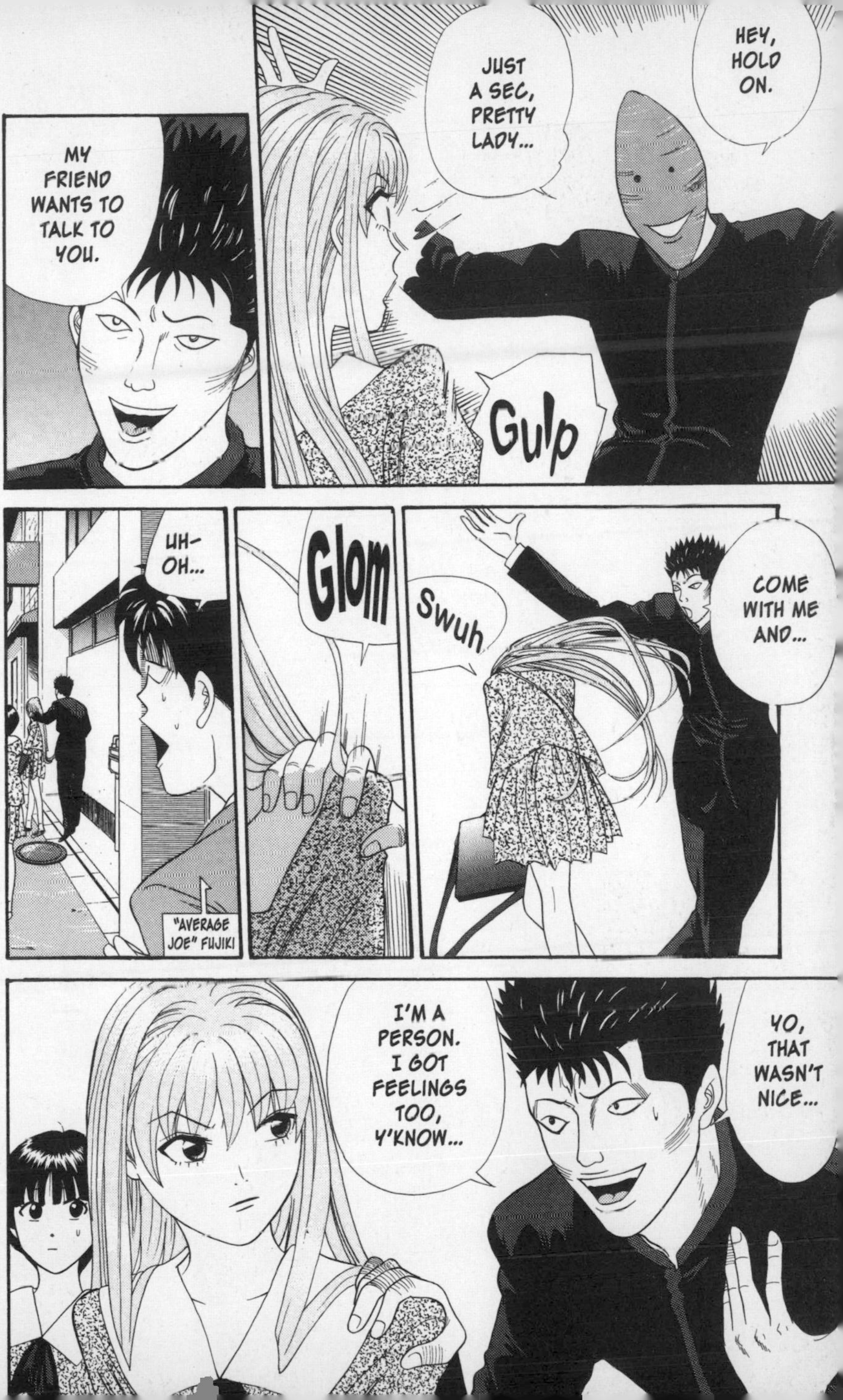
HEY, HOLD ON.
JUST A SEC, PRETTY LADY...
Gulp
MY FRIEND WANTS TO TALK TO YOU.
COME WITH ME AND...
Swuh
Glom
UH-OH...
"AVERAGE JOE" FUJIKI
YO, THAT WASN'T NICE...
I'M A PERSON. I GOT FEELINGS TOO, Y'KNOW...

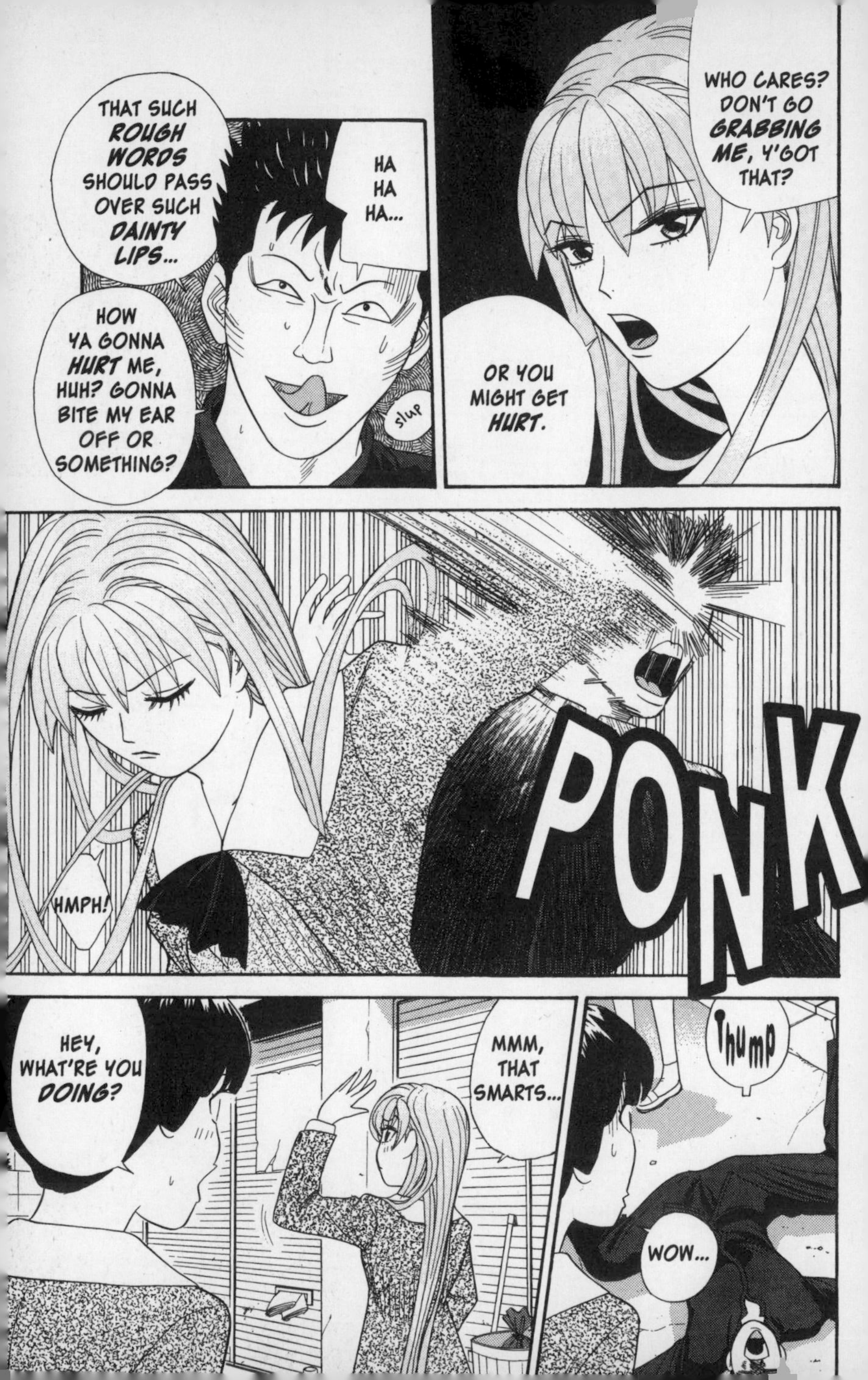
WHO CARES? DON'T GO GRABBING ME, Y'GOT THAT?
OR YOU MIGHT GET HURT.
THAT SUCH ROUGH WORDS SHOULD PASS OVER SUCH DAINTY LIPS...
HA HA HA...
HOW YA GONNA HURT ME, HUH? GONNA BITE MY EAR OFF OR SOMETHING?
slup
PONK
HMPH!
Thump
WOW...
MMM, THAT SMARTS...
HEY, WHAT'RE YOU DOING?

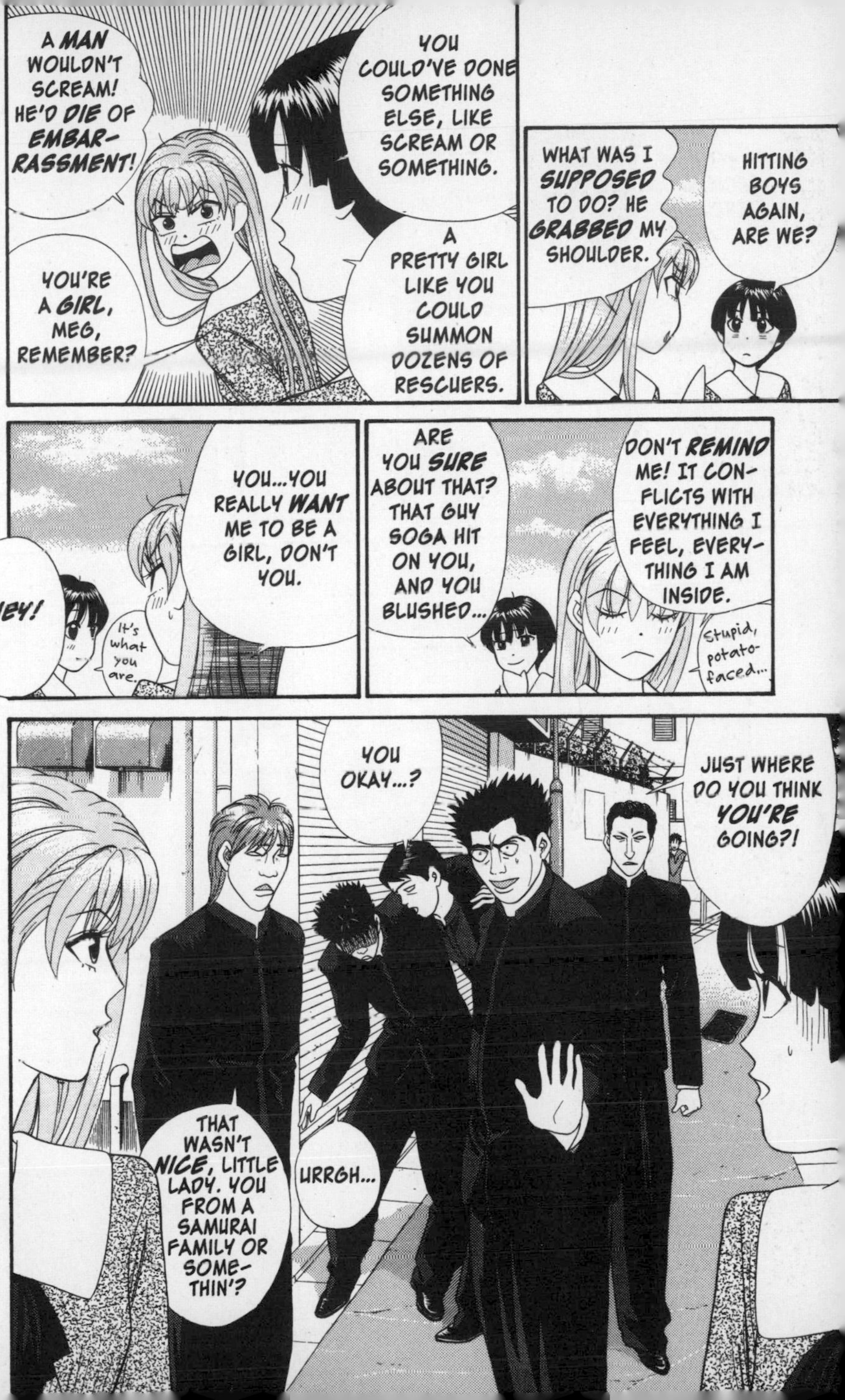
HITTING BOYS AGAIN, ARE WE?
WHAT WAS I SUPPOSED TO DO? HE GRABBED MY SHOULDER.
YOU COULD'VE DONE SOMETHING ELSE, LIKE SCREAM OR SOMETHING.
A PRETTY GIRL LIKE YOU COULD SUMMON DOZENS OF RESCUERS.
A MAN WOULDN'T SCREAM! HE'D DIE OF EMBAR-RASSMENT!
YOU'RE A GIRL, MEG, REMEMBER?
DON'T REMIND ME! IT CON-FLICTS WITH EVERYTHING I FEEL, EVERY-THING I AM INSIDE.
ARE YOU SURE ABOUT THAT? THAT GUY SOGA HIT ON YOU, AND YOU BLUSHED...
Stupid, potato-faced...
YOU...YOU REALLY WANT ME TO BE A GIRL, DON'T YOU.
It's what you are.
HEY!
JUST WHERE DO YOU THINK YOU'RE GOING?!
YOU OKAY...?
URRGH...
THAT WASN'T NICE, LITTLE LADY. YOU FROM A SAMURAI FAMILY OR SOME-THIN'?

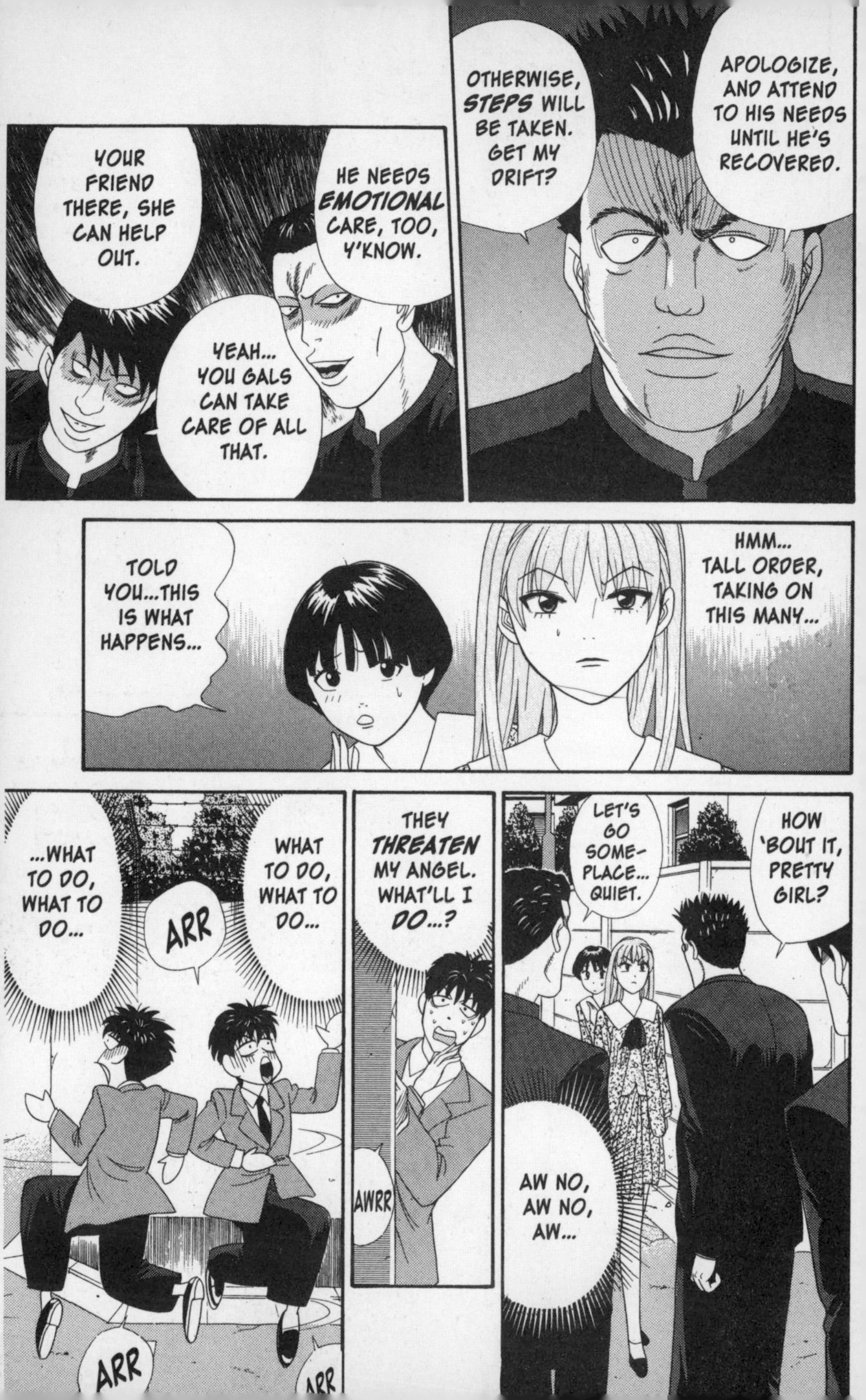
APOLOGIZE, AND ATTEND TO HIS NEEDS UNTIL HE'S RECOVERED.
OTHERWISE, STEPS WILL BE TAKEN. GET MY DRIFT?
HE NEEDS EMOTIONAL CARE, TOO, Y'KNOW.
YOUR FRIEND THERE, SHE CAN HELP OUT.
YEAH... YOU GALS CAN TAKE CARE OF ALL THAT.
HMM... TALL ORDER, TAKING ON THIS MANY...
TOLD YOU...THIS IS WHAT HAPPENS...
HOW 'BOUT IT, PRETTY GIRL?
LET'S GO SOME-PLACE... QUIET.
AW NO, AW NO, AW...
THEY THREATEN MY ANGEL. WHAT'LL I DO...?
AWRR
WHAT TO DO, WHAT TO DO...
ARR
...WHAT TO DO, WHAT TO DO...
ARR
ARR

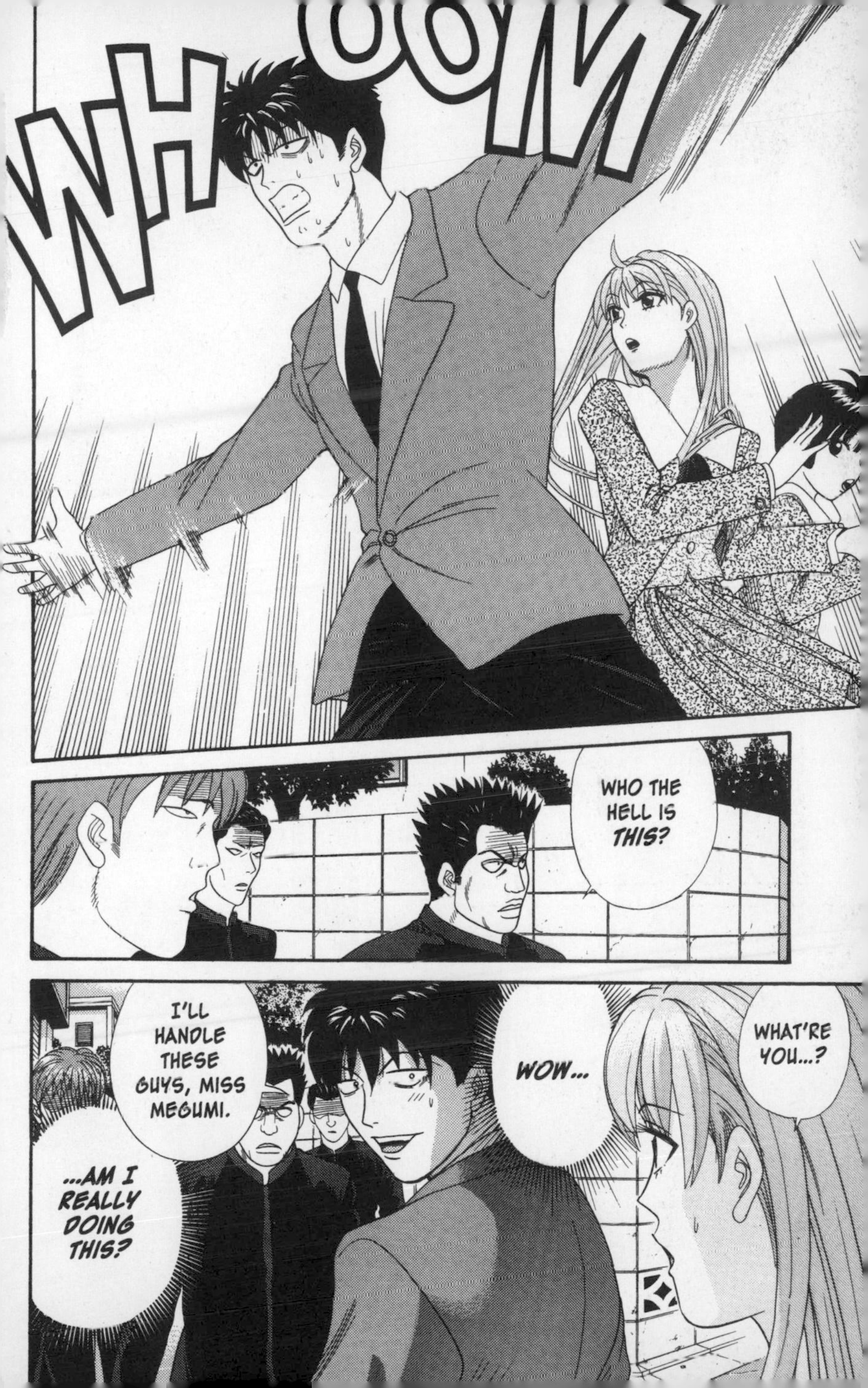
WHOOM
WHO THE HELL IS *THIS?*
WHAT'RE YOU...?
WOW...
I'LL HANDLE THESE GUYS, MISS MEGUMI.
...AM I REALLY DOING THIS?

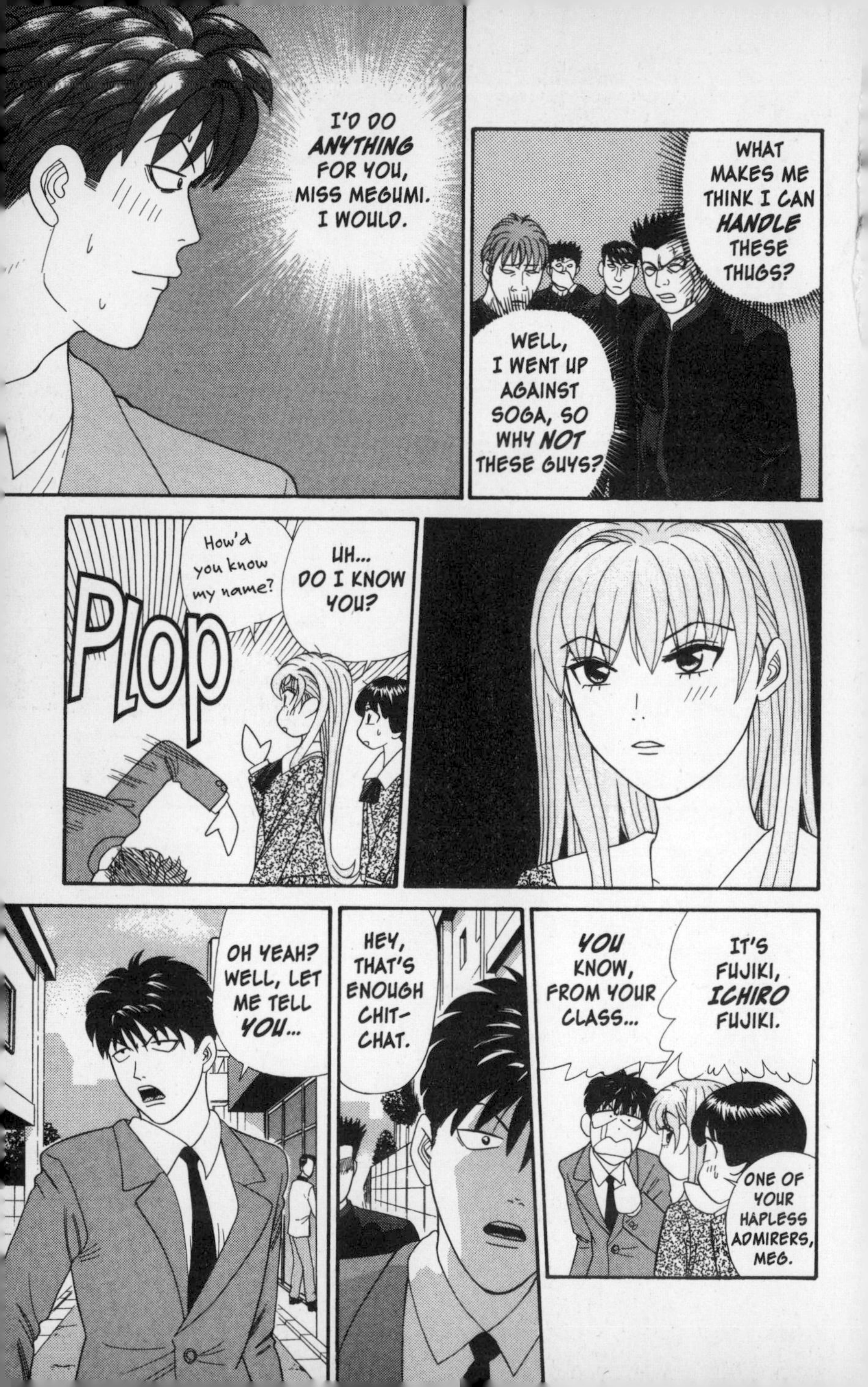
WHAT MAKES ME THINK I CAN HANDLE THESE THUGS?
WELL, I WENT UP AGAINST SOGA, SO WHY NOT THESE GUYS?
I'D DO ANYTHING FOR YOU, MISS MEGUMI. I WOULD.
UH... DO I KNOW YOU?
How'd you know my name?
Plop
IT'S FUJIKI, ICHIRO FUJIKI.
YOU KNOW, FROM YOUR CLASS...
ONE OF YOUR HAPLESS ADMIRERS, MEG.
HEY, THAT'S ENOUGH CHIT-CHAT.
OH YEAH? WELL, LET ME TELL YOU...

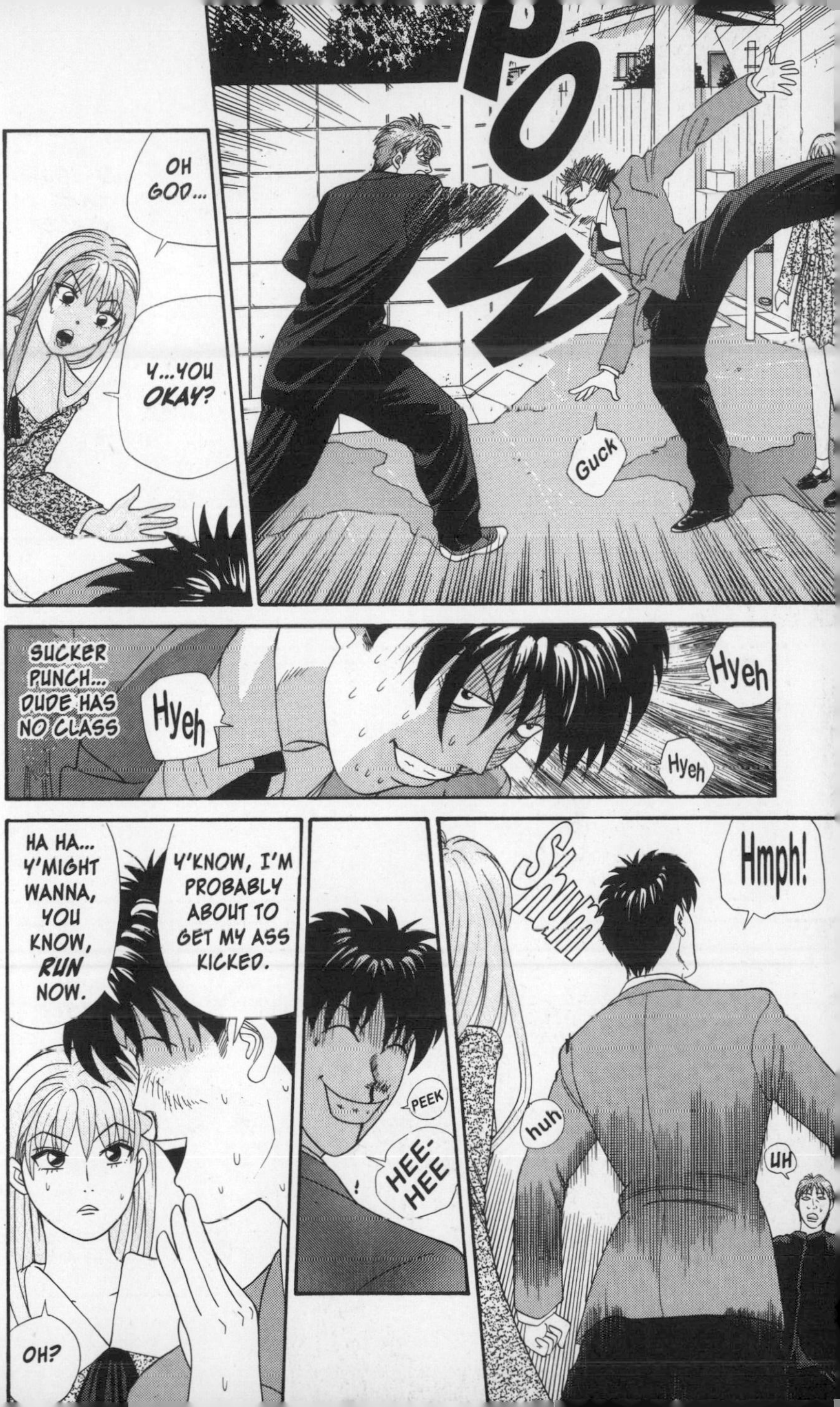
POW
Guck
OH GOD...
Y...YOU OKAY?
Hyeh
Hyeh
Hyeh
SUCKER PUNCH... DUDE HAS NO CLASS
Hmph!
Shum
huh
uh
PEEK
HEE-HEE
Y'KNOW, I'M PROBABLY ABOUT TO GET MY ASS KICKED.
HA HA... Y'MIGHT WANNA, YOU KNOW, RUN NOW.
OH?

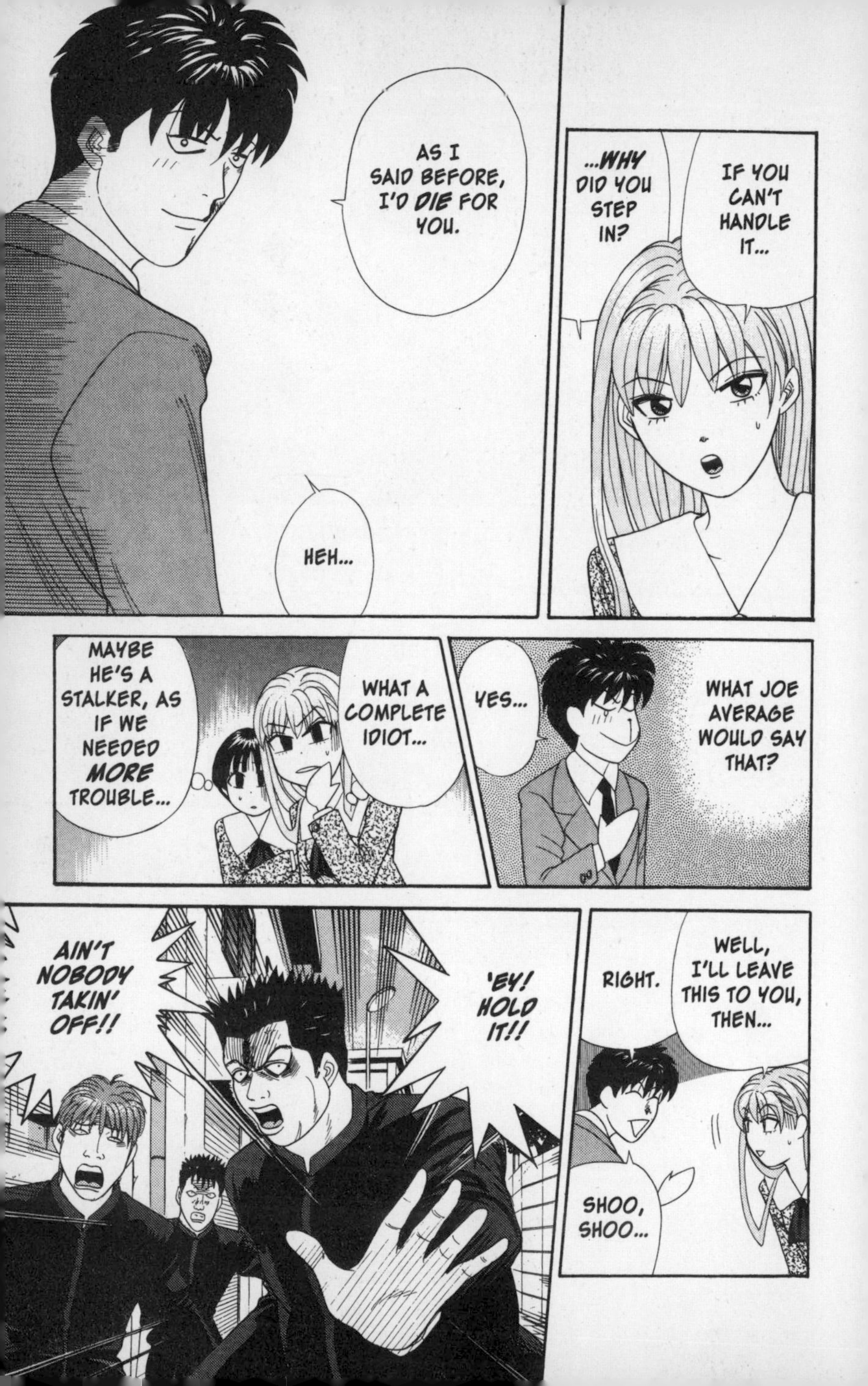
IF YOU CAN'T HANDLE IT...
...WHY DID YOU STEP IN?
AS I SAID BEFORE, I'D DIE FOR YOU.
HEH...
WHAT JOE AVERAGE WOULD SAY THAT?
YES...
WHAT A COMPLETE IDIOT...
MAYBE HE'S A STALKER, AS IF WE NEEDED MORE TROUBLE...
WELL, I'LL LEAVE THIS TO YOU, THEN...
RIGHT.
SHOO, SHOO...
'EY! HOLD IT!!
AIN'T NOBODY TAKIN' OFF!!

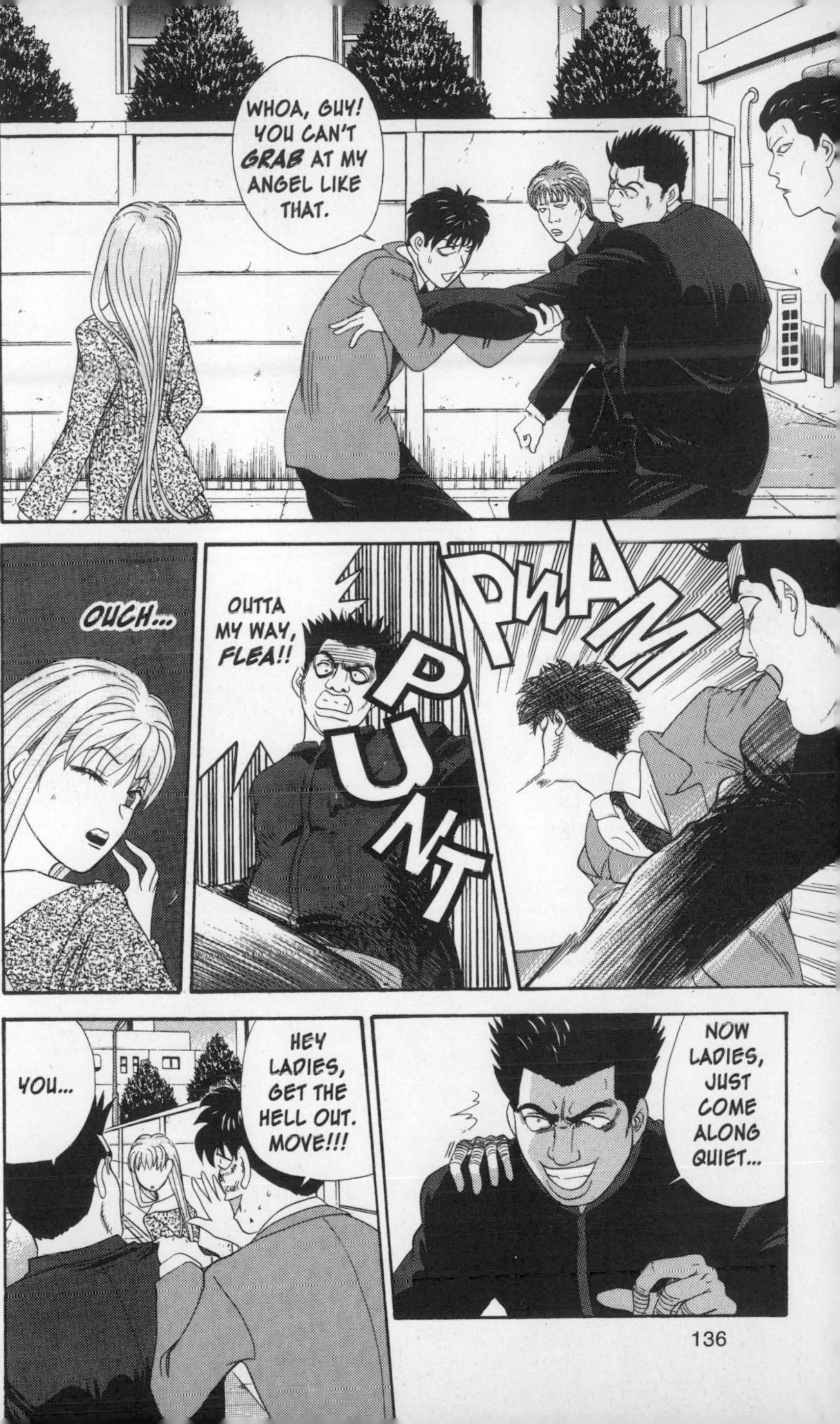
WHOA, GUY! YOU CAN'T GRAB AT MY ANGEL LIKE THAT.
PWAM
OUTTA MY WAY, FLEA!!
PUNT
OUCH...
NOW LADIES, JUST COME ALONG QUIET...
HEY LADIES, GET THE HELL OUT. MOVE!!!
YOU...

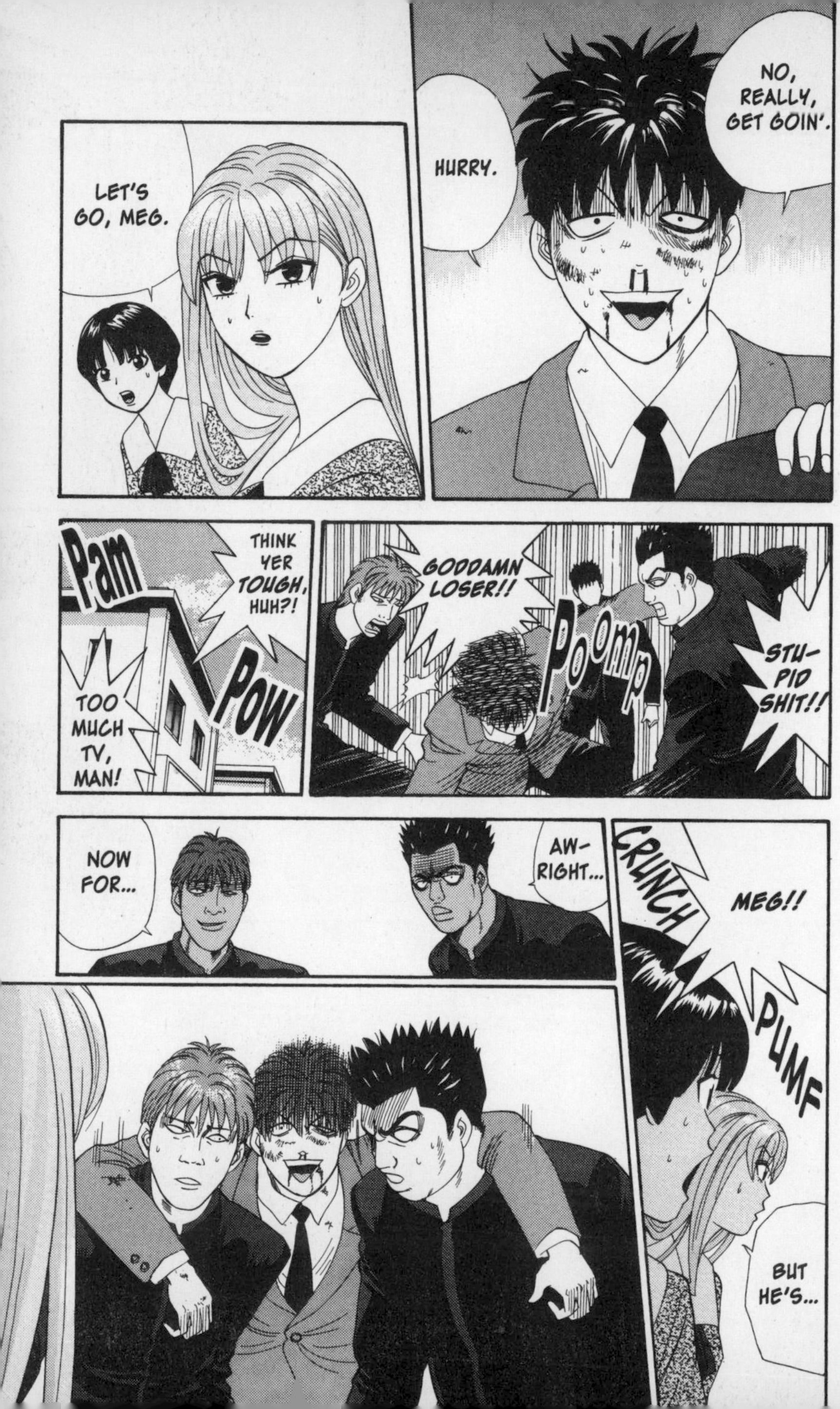
NO, REALLY, GET GOIN'.
HURRY.
LET'S GO, MEG.
GODDAMN LOSER!!
STU-PID SHIT!!
Poomp
THINK YER TOUGH, HUH?!
Pam
Pow
TOO MUCH TV, MAN!
CRUNCH
MEG!!
PUMF
BUT HE'S...
AW-RIGHT...
NOW FOR...

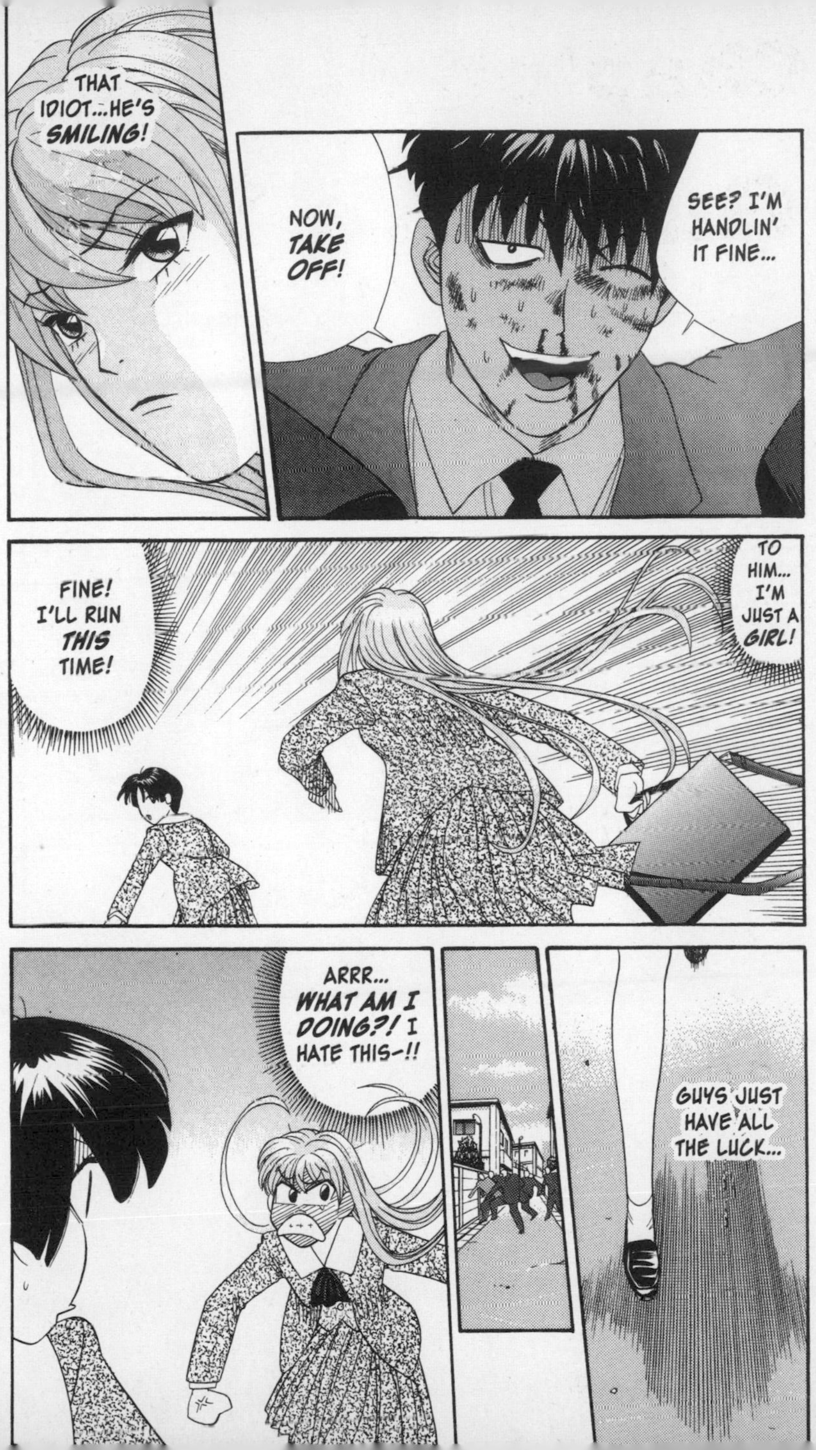
SEE? I'M HANDLIN' IT FINE...
NOW, TAKE OFF!
THAT IDIOT...HE'S SMILING!
TO HIM... I'M JUST A GIRL!
FINE! I'LL RUN THIS TIME!
GUYS JUST HAVE ALL THE LUCK...
ARRR... WHAT AM I DOING?! I HATE THIS-!!

Chapter 7:

Guys Are So Lucky...

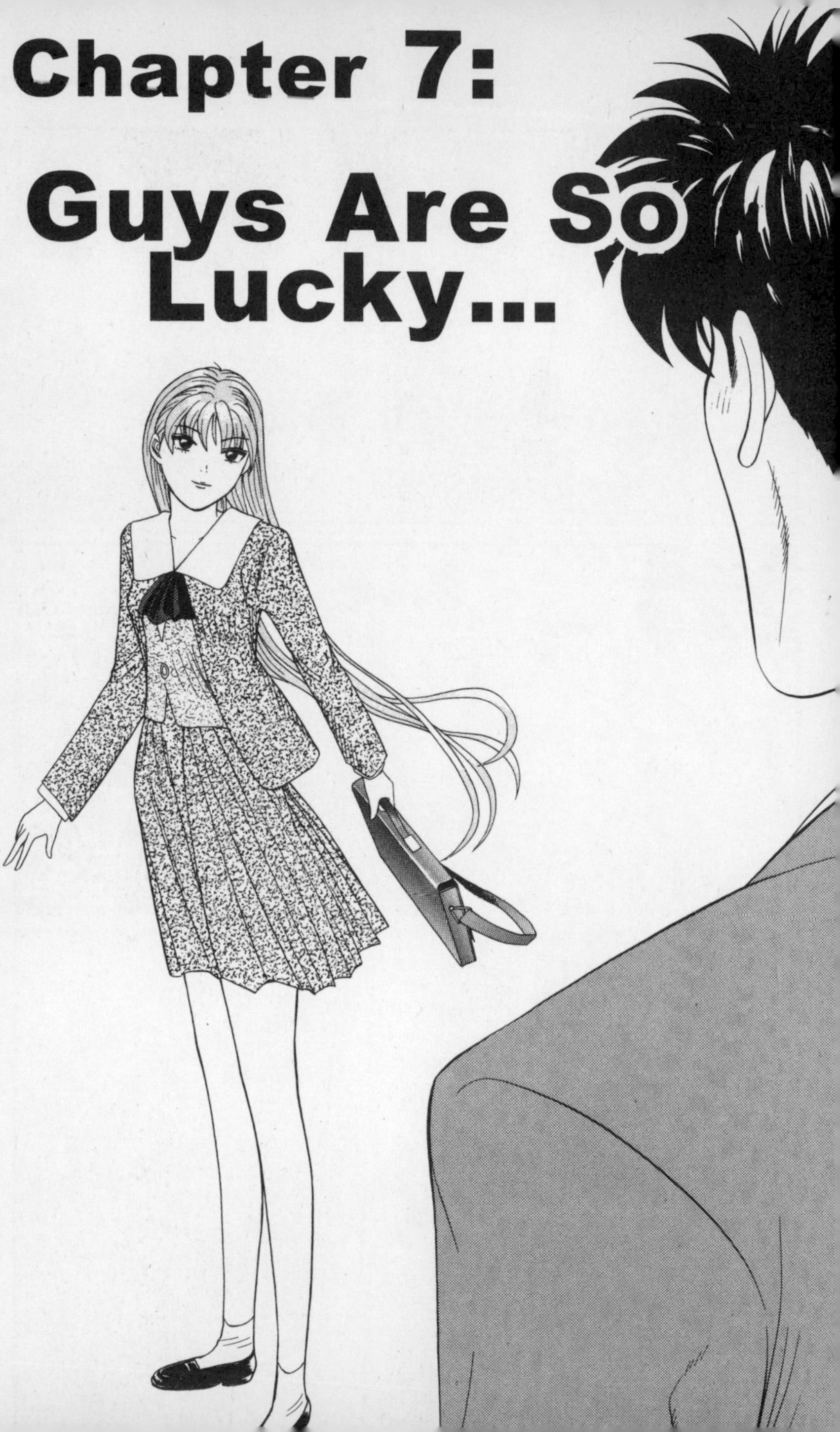

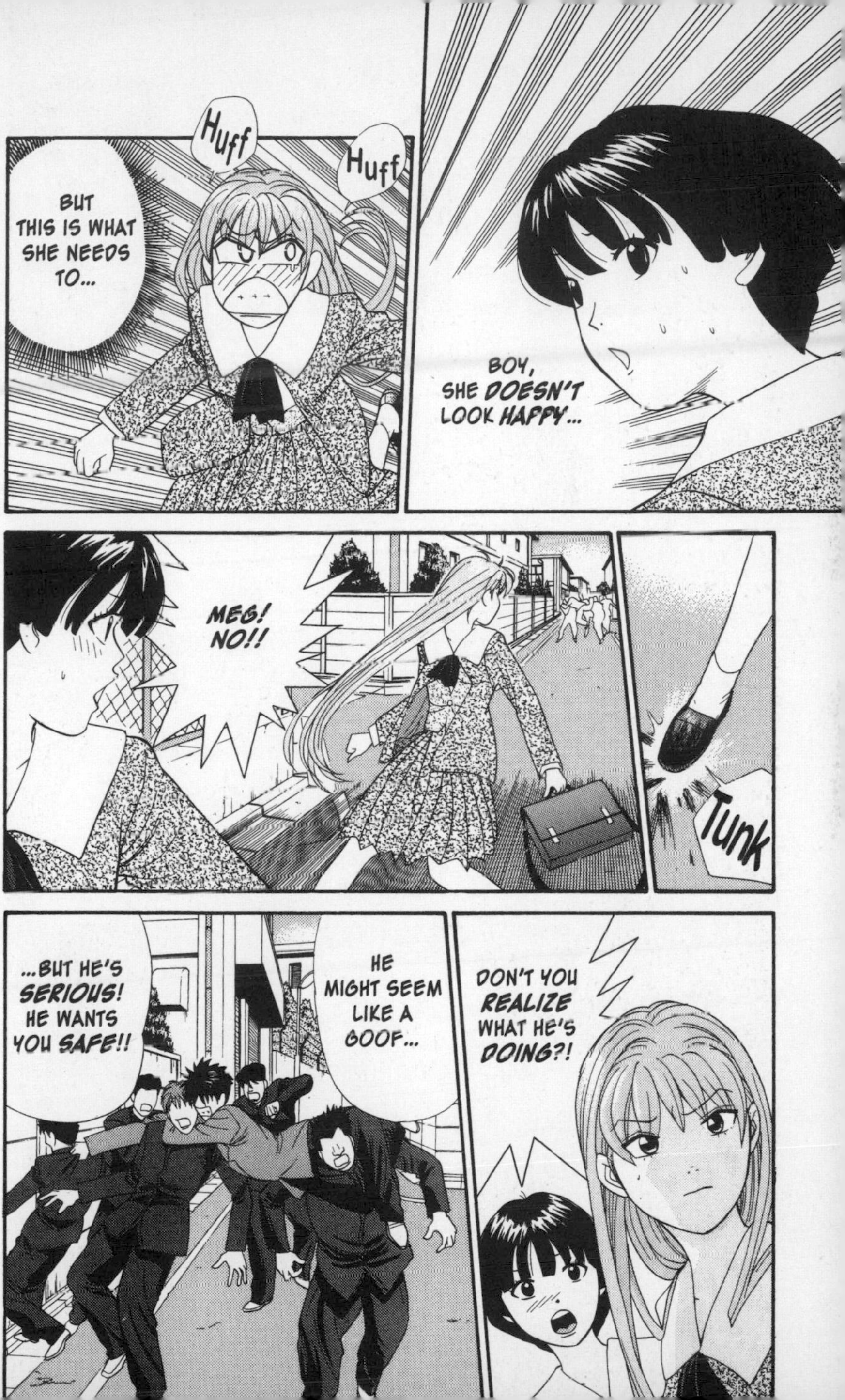
BOY, SHE DOESN'T LOOK HAPPY...
Huff
Huff
BUT THIS IS WHAT SHE NEEDS TO...
Tunk
MEG! NO!!
DON'T YOU REALIZE WHAT HE'S DOING?!
HE MIGHT SEEM LIKE A GOOF...
...BUT HE'S SERIOUS! HE WANTS YOU SAFE!!

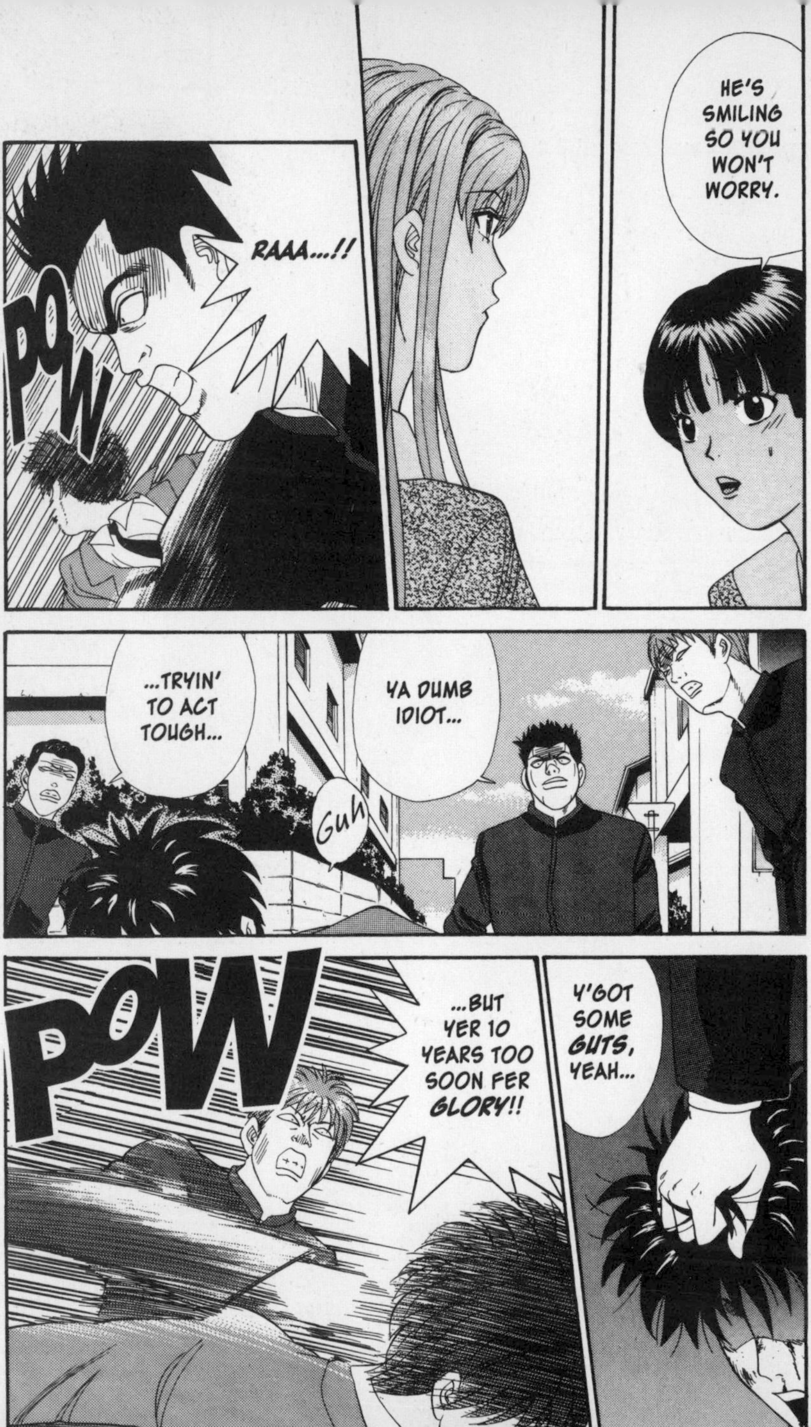
HE'S SMILING SO YOU WON'T WORRY.
RAAA...!!
POW
YA DUMB IDIOT...
Guh
...TRYIN' TO ACT TOUGH...
Y'GOT SOME GUTS, YEAH...
...BUT YER 10 YEARS TOO SOON FER GLORY!!
POW

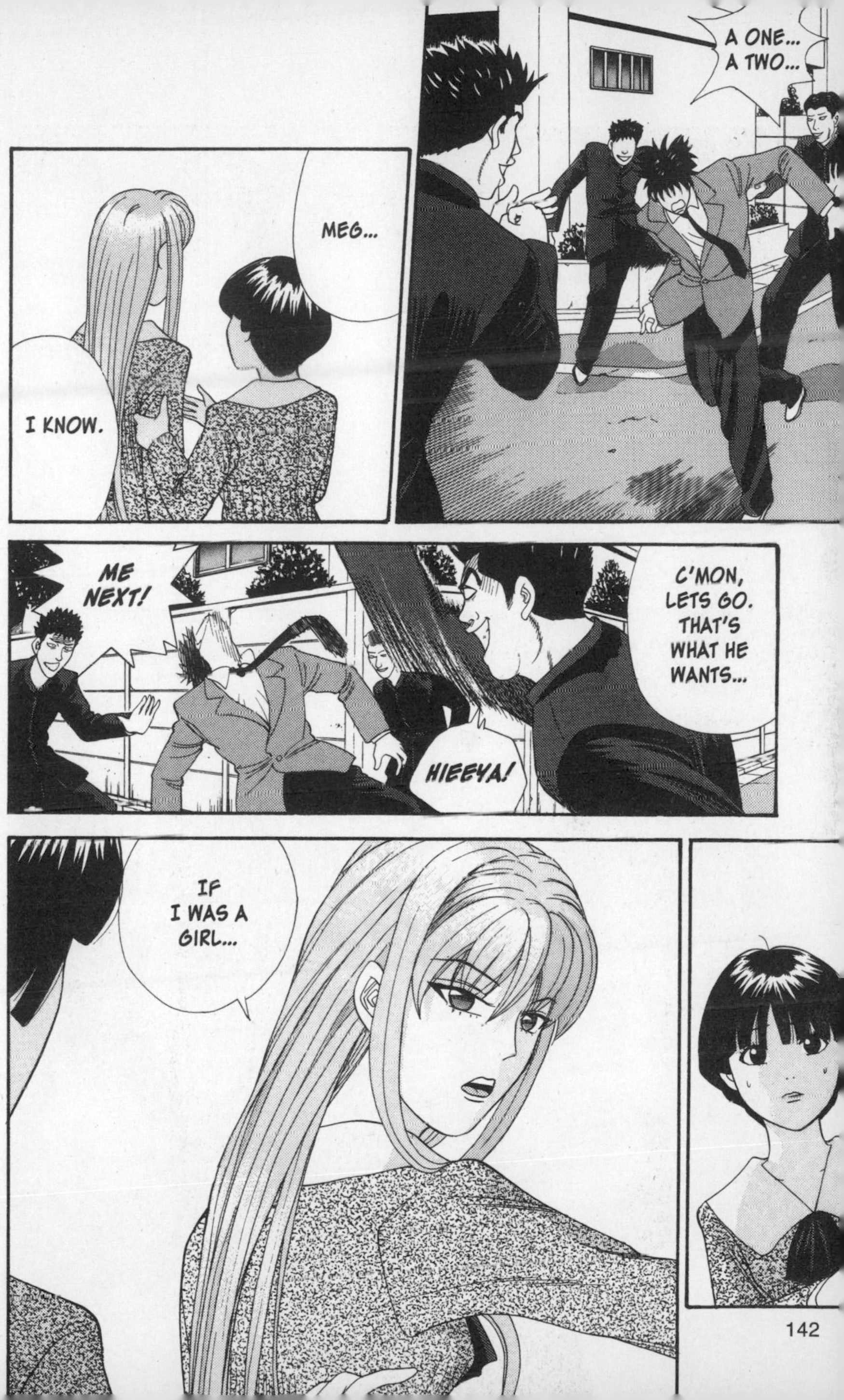
A ONE... A TWO...
MEG...
I KNOW.
C'MON, LETS GO. THAT'S WHAT HE WANTS...
HIEEYA!
ME NEXT!
IF I WAS A GIRL...

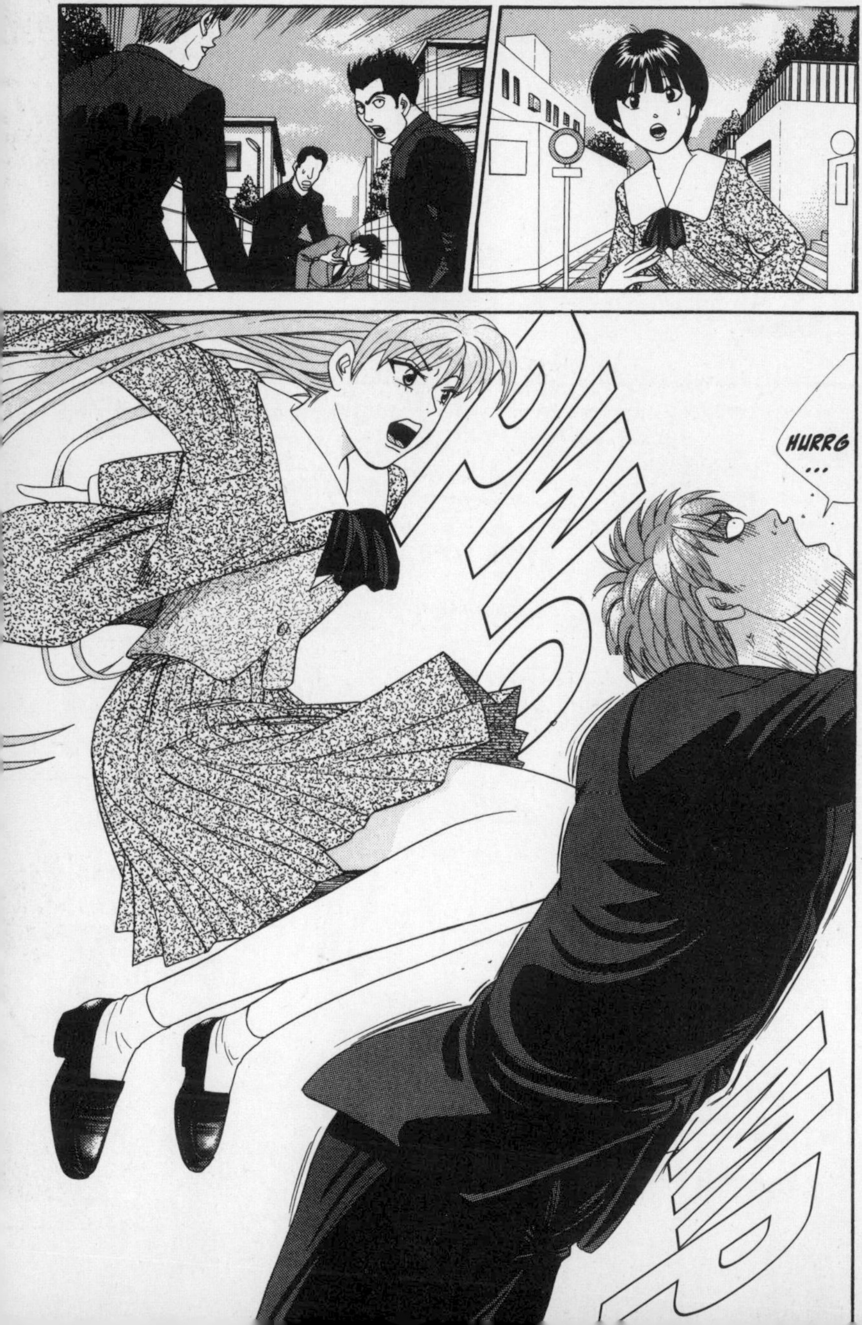
HURRG …

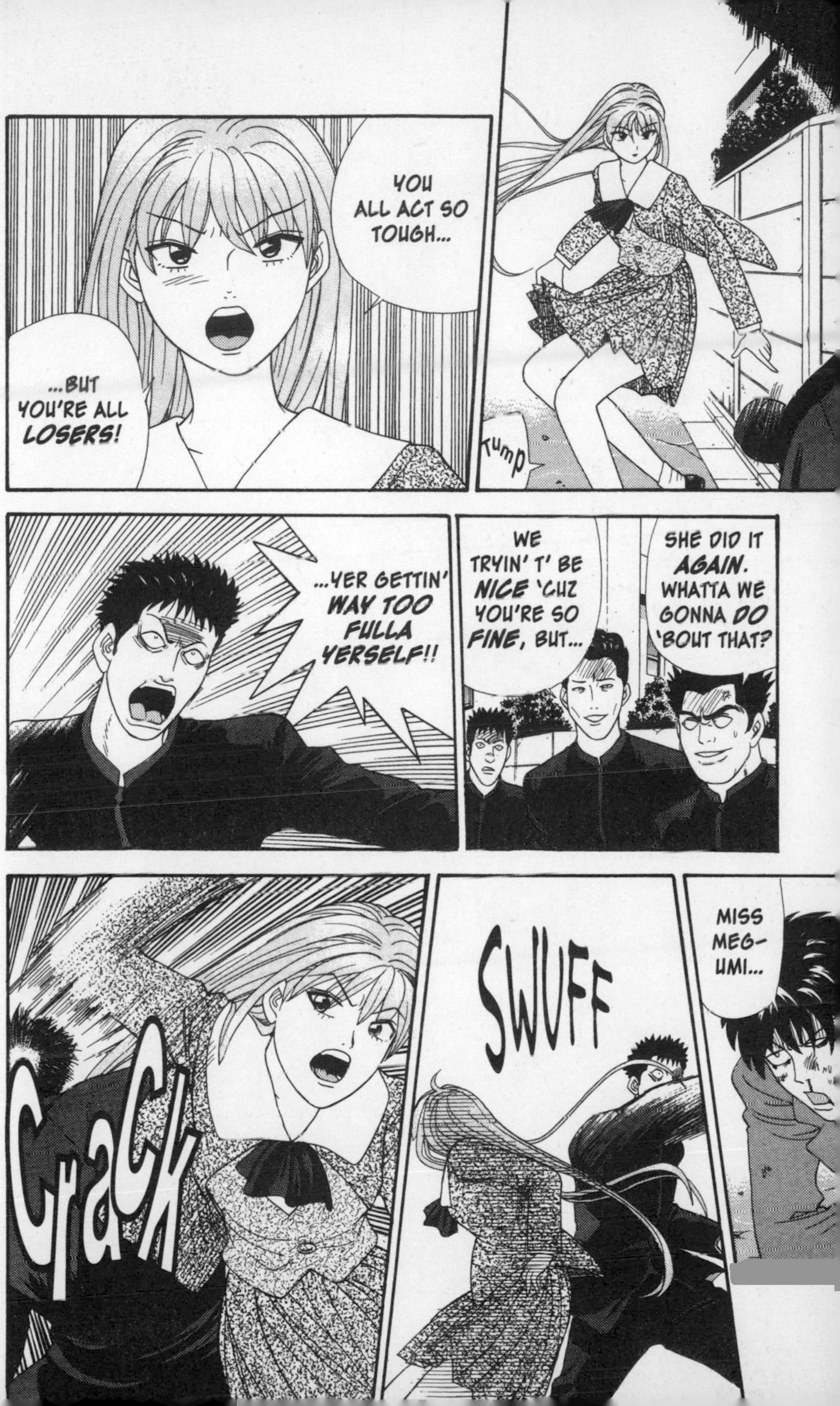
Tump
YOU ALL ACT SO TOUGH...
...BUT YOU'RE ALL **LOSERS!**
SHE DID IT **AGAIN**. WHATTA WE GONNA **DO** 'BOUT THAT?
WE TRYIN' T' BE **NICE** 'CUZ YOU'RE SO **FINE**, BUT...
...YER GETTIN' **WAY TOO FULLA YERSELF!!**
MISS MEG-UMI...
SWUFF
CRACK

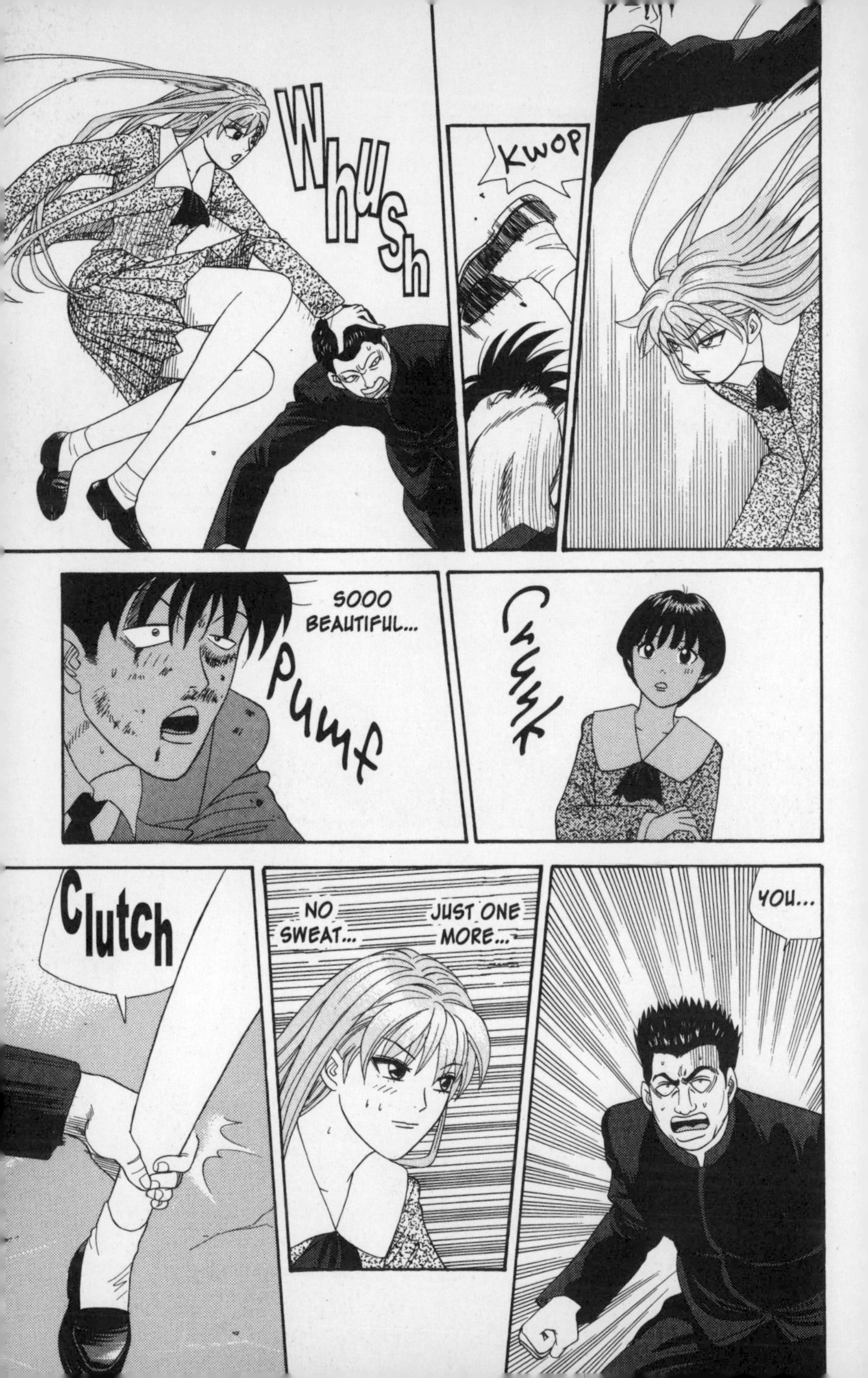
KWOP
Whush
Crunk
SOOO BEAUTIFUL...
Pumf
YOU...
JUST ONE MORE...
NO SWEAT...
Clutch

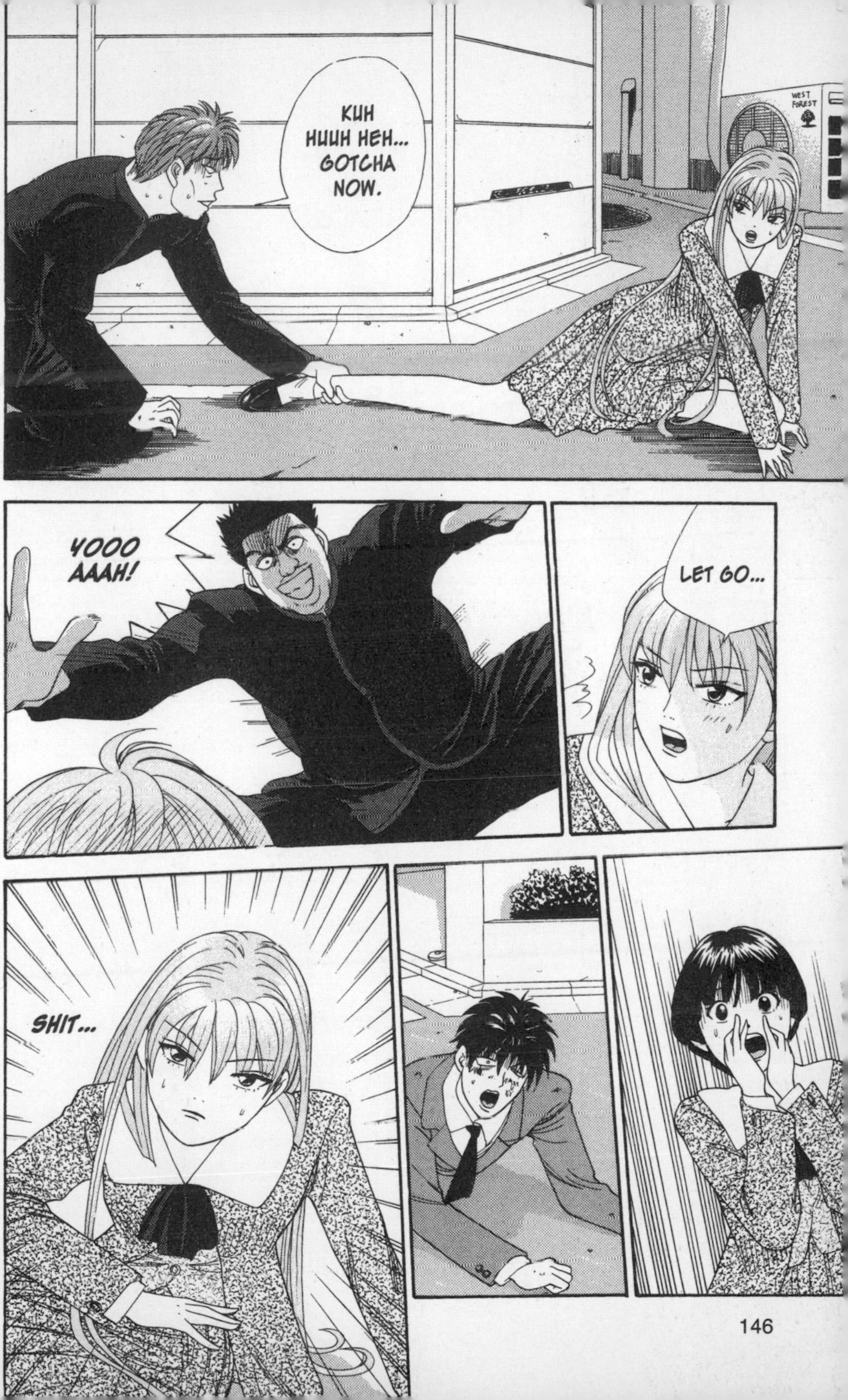
KUH HUUH HEH... GOTCHA NOW.
WEST FOREST
LET GO...
YOOO AAAH!
SHIT...

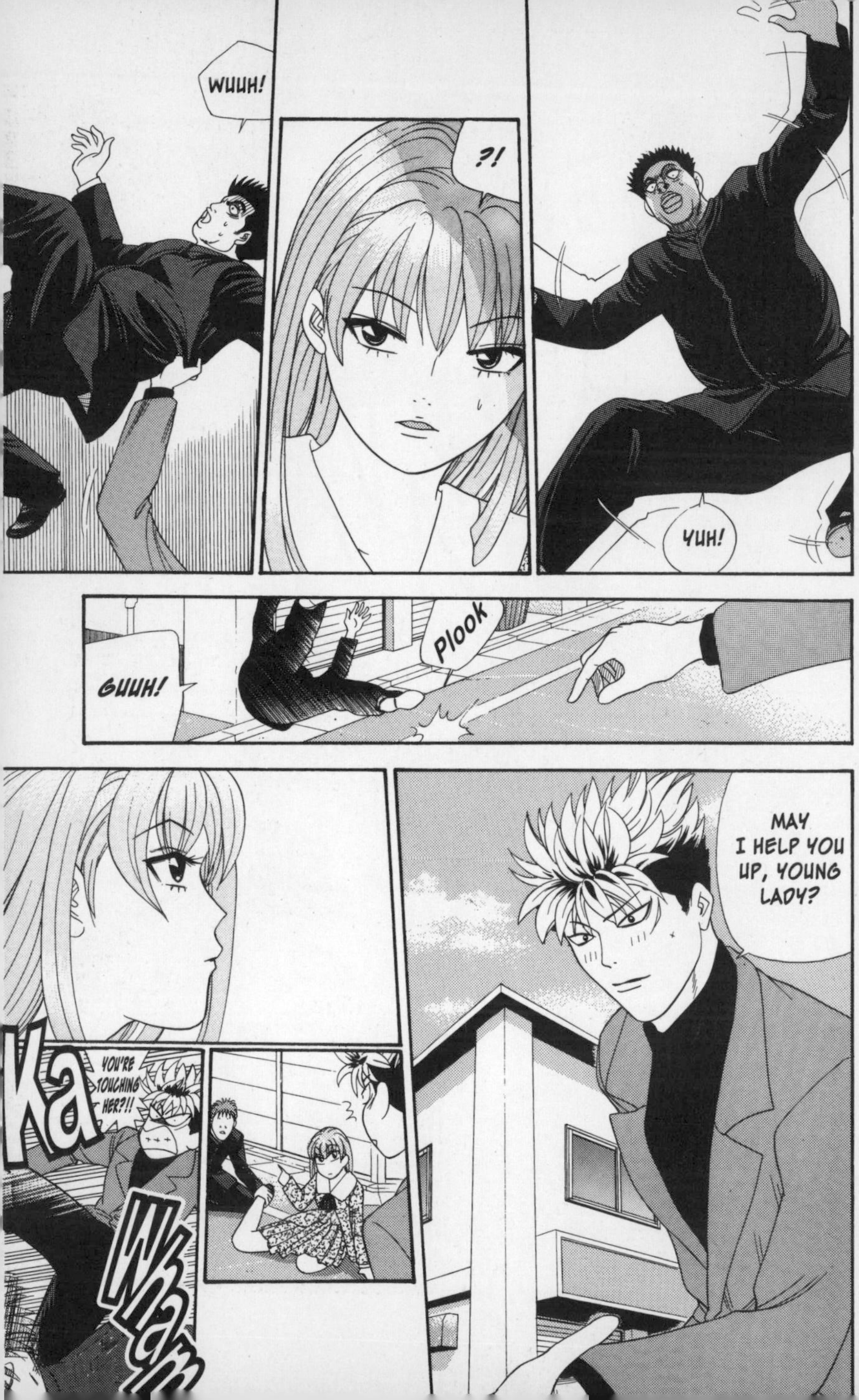
YUH!
?!
WUUH!
Plook
GUUH!
MAY I HELP YOU UP, YOUNG LADY?
YOU'RE TOUCHING HER?!!
Ka
Wham

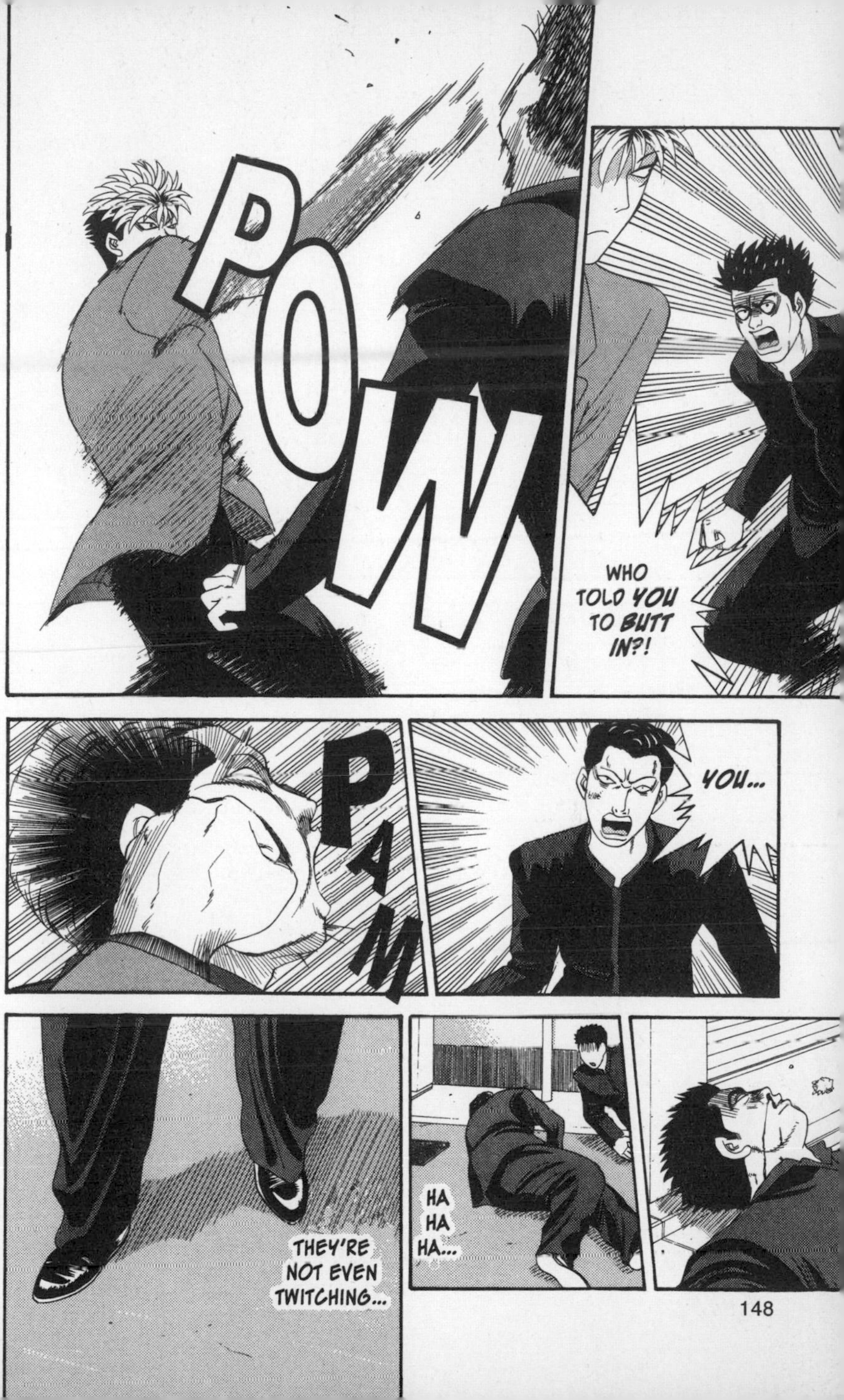
WHO TOLD YOU TO BUTT IN?!
POW
YOU...
PAM
HA HA HA...
THEY'RE NOT EVEN TWITCHING...

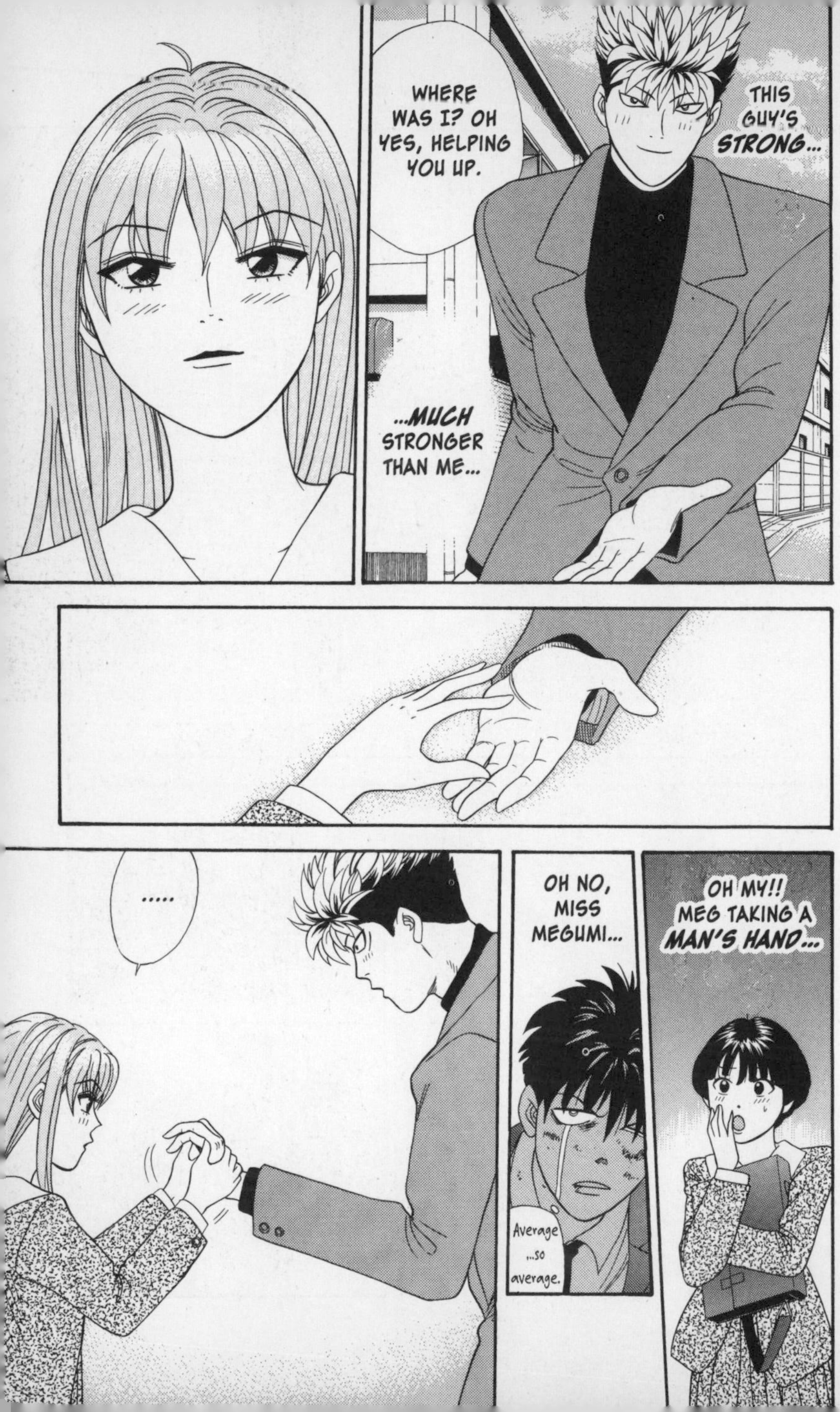
THIS GUY'S **STRONG...**
WHERE WAS I? OH YES, HELPING YOU UP.
...MUCH STRONGER THAN ME...
OH MY!! MEG TAKING A **MAN'S HAND...**
OH NO, MISS MEGUMI...
Average ...so average.
.....

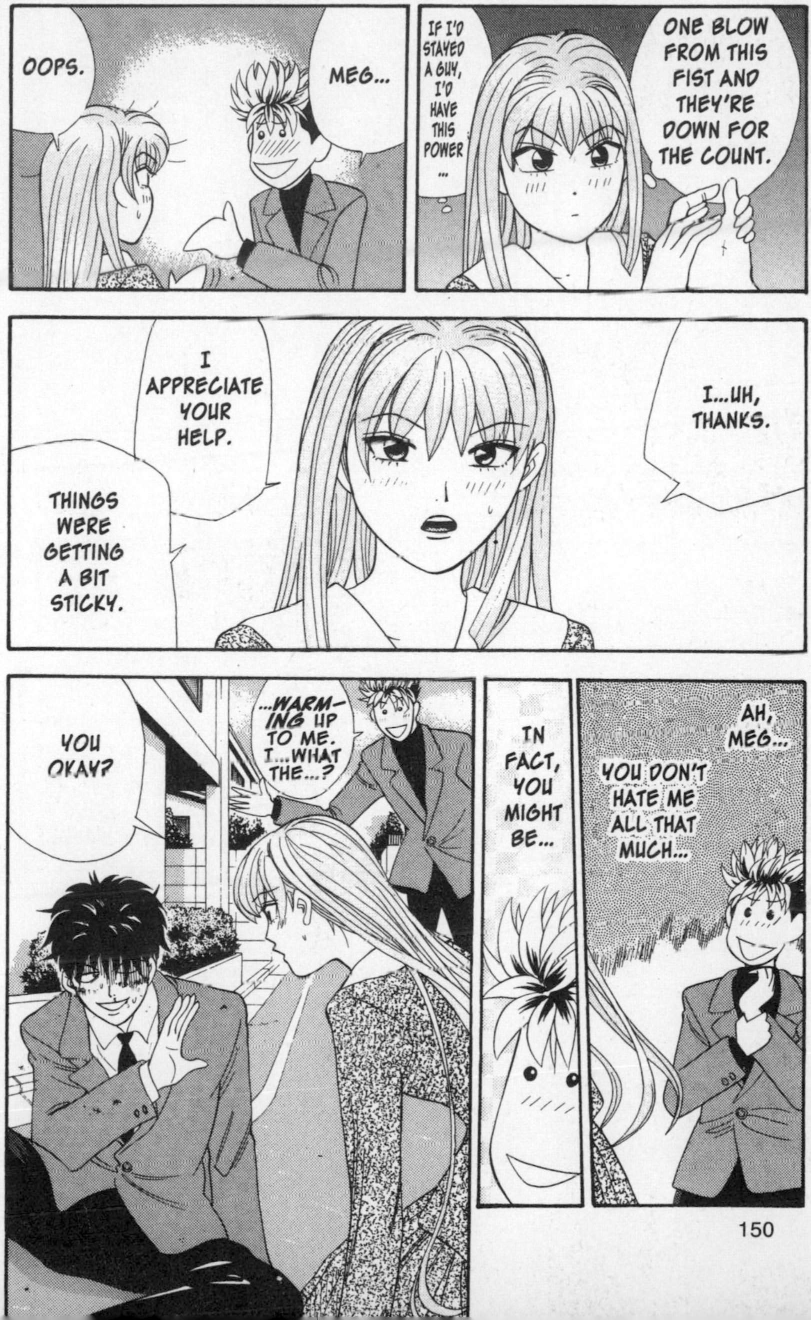
ONE BLOW FROM THIS FIST AND THEY'RE DOWN FOR THE COUNT.
IF I'D STAYED A GUY, I'D HAVE THIS POWER ...
MEG...
OOPS.
I...UH, THANKS.
I APPRECIATE YOUR HELP.
THINGS WERE GETTING A BIT STICKY.
AH, MEG...
YOU DON'T HATE ME ALL THAT MUCH...
IN FACT, YOU MIGHT BE...
...WARMING UP TO ME. I...WHAT THE...?
YOU OKAY?

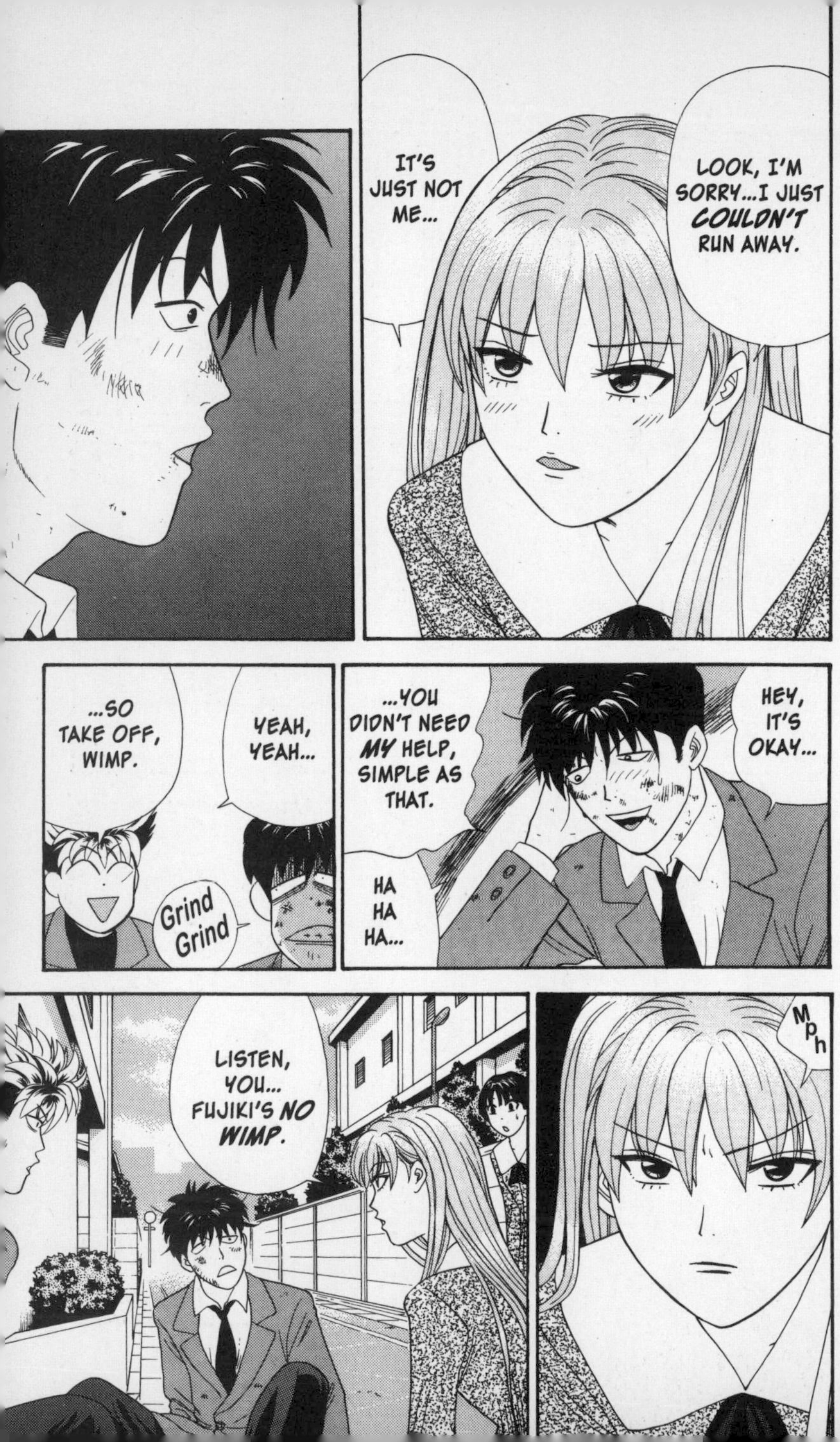
LOOK, I'M SORRY...I JUST COULDN'T RUN AWAY.
IT'S JUST NOT ME...
HEY, IT'S OKAY...
...YOU DIDN'T NEED MY HELP, SIMPLE AS THAT.
HA HA HA...
YEAH, YEAH...
...SO TAKE OFF, WIMP.
Grind Grind
Mph
LISTEN, YOU... FUJIKI'S NO WIMP.

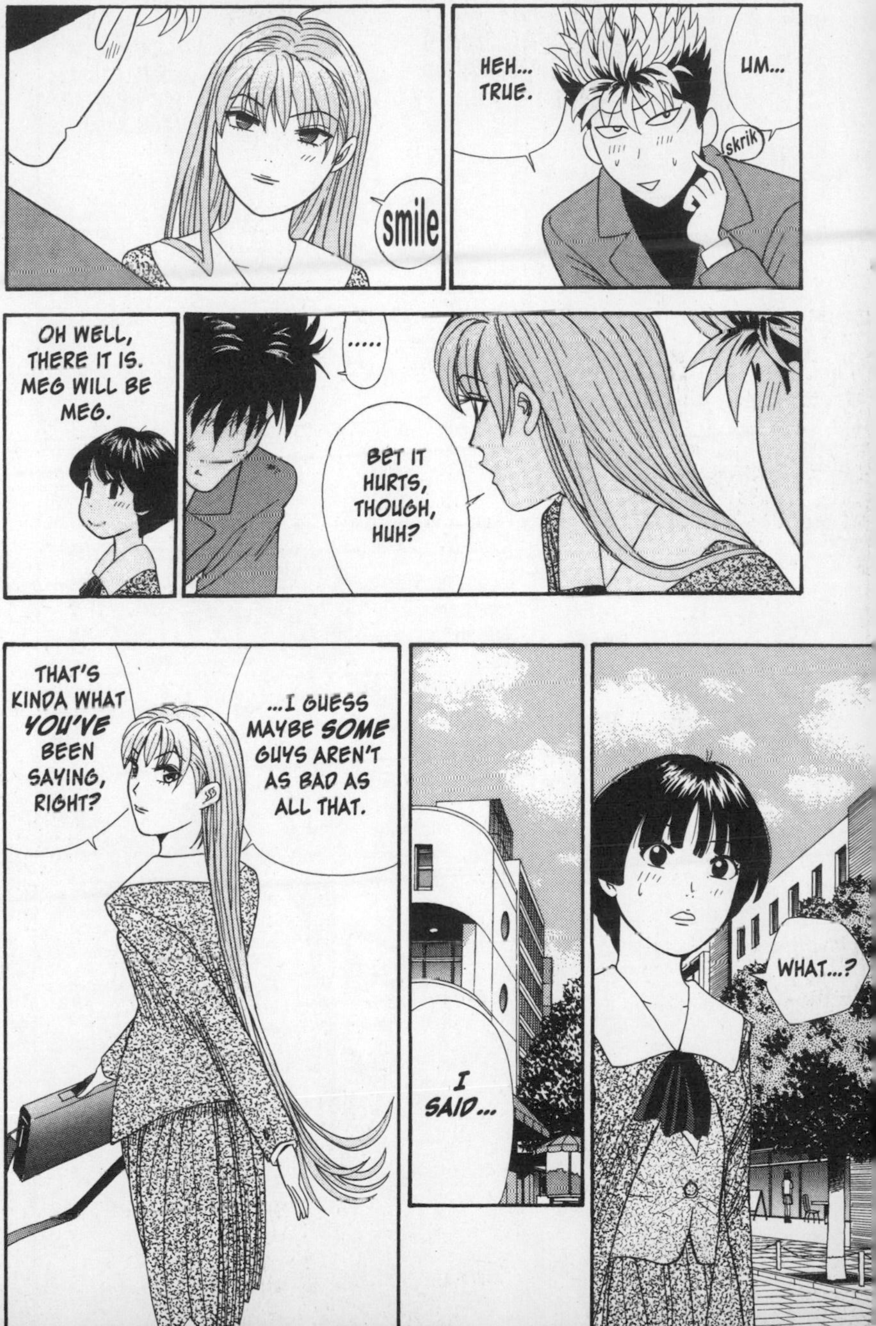
UM...
skrik
HEH... TRUE.
smile
.....
BET IT HURTS, THOUGH, HUH?
OH WELL, THERE IT IS. MEG WILL BE MEG.
WHAT...?
I SAID...
...I GUESS MAYBE SOME GUYS AREN'T AS BAD AS ALL THAT.
THAT'S KINDA WHAT YOU'VE BEEN SAYING, RIGHT?

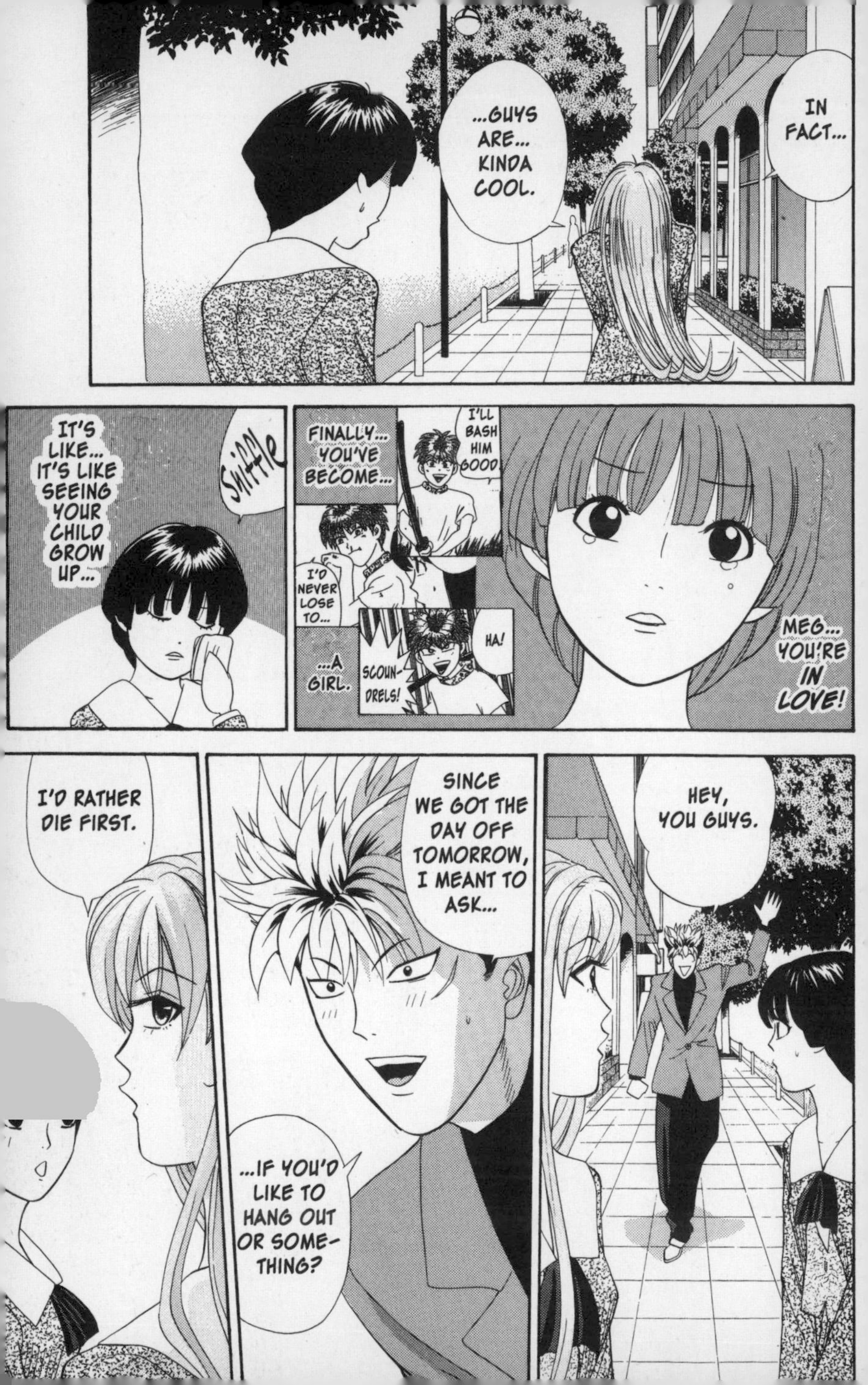
IN FACT...
...GUYS ARE... KINDA COOL.
I'LL BASH HIM GOOD.
FINALLY... YOU'VE BECOME...
I'D NEVER LOSE TO...
HA!
SCOUN-DRELS!
...A GIRL.
MEG... YOU'RE IN LOVE!
Sniffle
IT'S LIKE... IT'S LIKE SEEING YOUR CHILD GROW UP...
HEY, YOU GUYS.
SINCE WE GOT THE DAY OFF TOMORROW, I MEANT TO ASK...
...IF YOU'D LIKE TO HANG OUT OR SOME-THING?
I'D RATHER DIE FIRST.

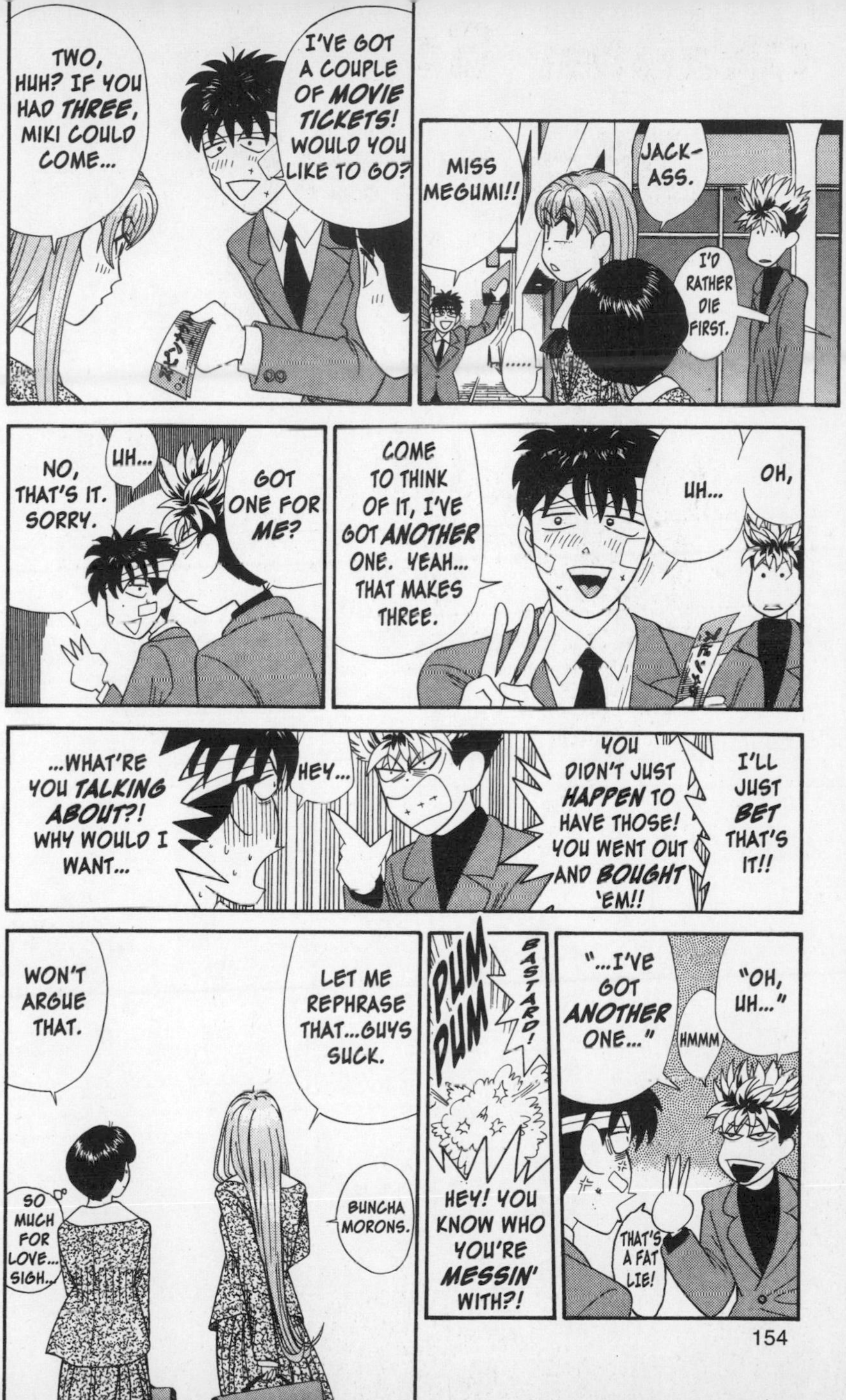
JACK-ASS.
MISS MEGUMI!!
I'D RATHER DIE FIRST.
.....
I'VE GOT A COUPLE OF *MOVIE TICKETS!* WOULD YOU LIKE TO GO?
TWO, HUH? IF YOU HAD *THREE,* MIKI COULD COME...
OH,
UH...
COME TO THINK OF IT, I'VE GOT **ANOTHER** ONE. YEAH... THAT MAKES THREE.
GOT ONE FOR *ME?*
UH...
NO, THAT'S IT. SORRY.
I'LL JUST *BET* THAT'S IT!!
YOU DIDN'T JUST *HAPPEN* TO HAVE THOSE! YOU WENT OUT AND *BOUGHT* 'EM!!
HEY...
...WHAT'RE YOU *TALKING ABOUT?!* WHY WOULD I WANT...
"OH, UH..."
HMMM
"...I'VE GOT **ANOTHER** ONE..."
THAT'S A FAT LIE!
BASTARD!
PUM PUM
HEY! YOU KNOW WHO YOU'RE *MESSIN'* WITH?!
LET ME REPHRASE THAT...GUYS SUCK.
WON'T ARGUE THAT.
BUNCHA MORONS.
SO MUCH FOR LOVE... SIGH...

Chapter 8:
Megumi's Dilemma

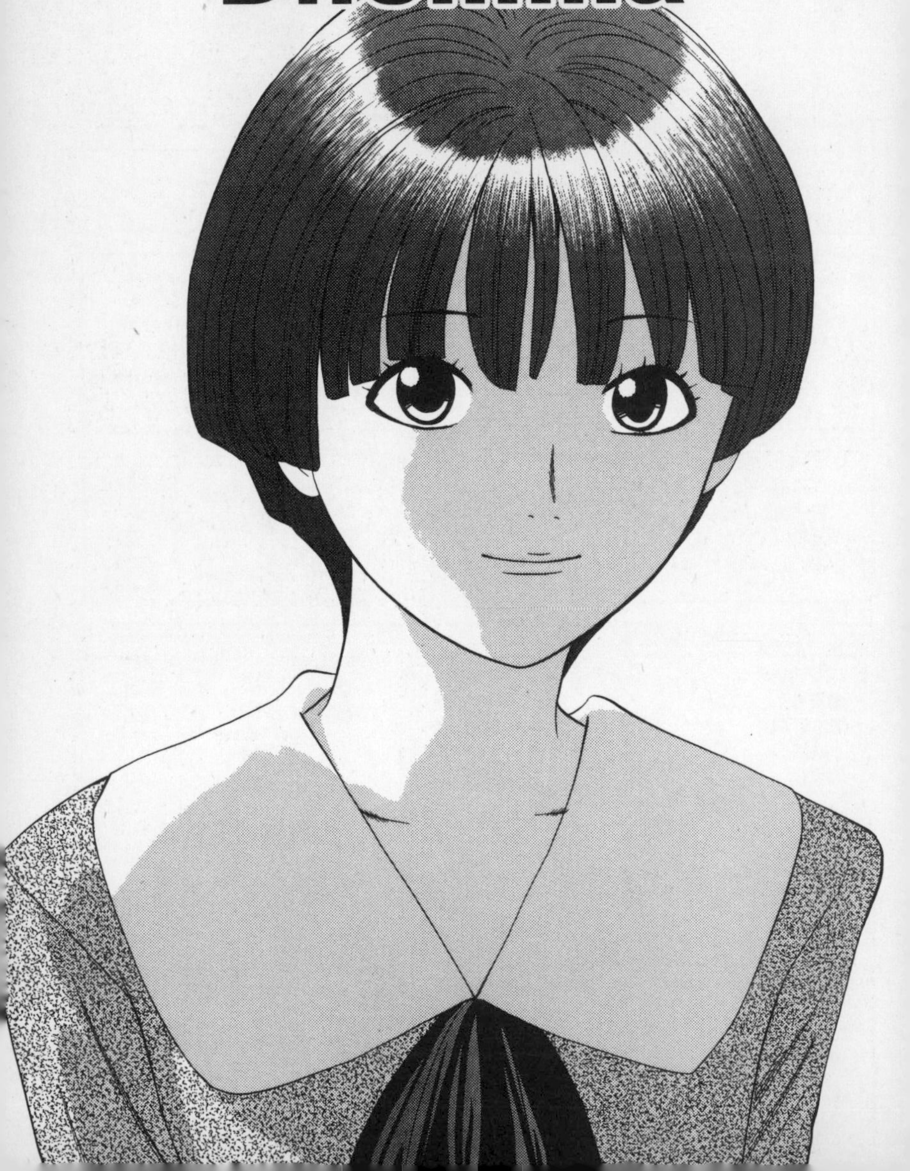

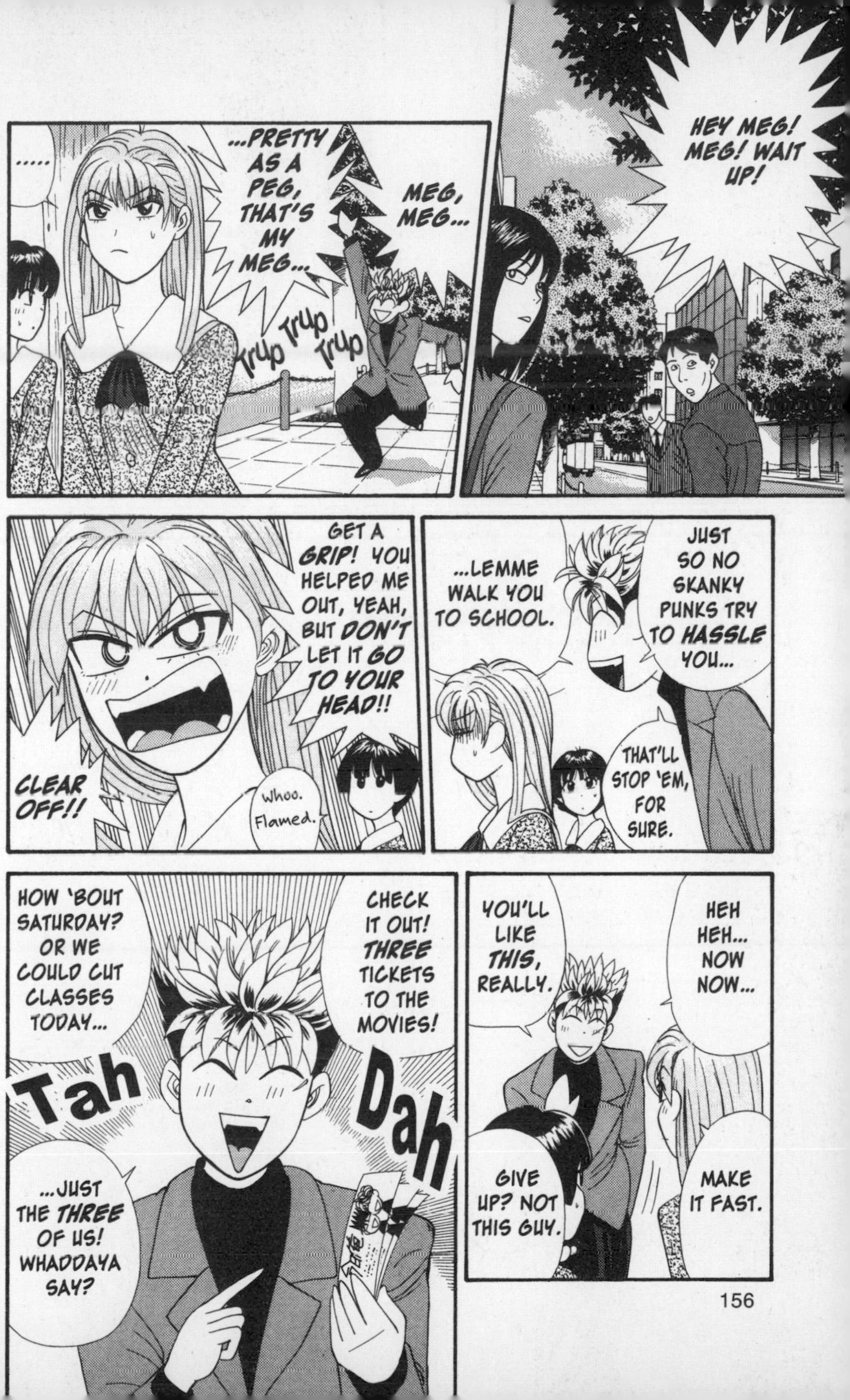
HEY MEG! MEG! WAIT UP!
MEG, MEG...
...PRETTY AS A PEG, THAT'S MY MEG...
.....
Trup Trup Trup
JUST SO NO SKANKY PUNKS TRY TO HASSLE YOU...
...LEMME WALK YOU TO SCHOOL.
THAT'LL STOP 'EM, FOR SURE.
GET A GRIP! YOU HELPED ME OUT, YEAH, BUT DON'T LET IT GO TO YOUR HEAD!!
CLEAR OFF!!
Whoo. Flamed.
HEH HEH... NOW NOW...
YOU'LL LIKE THIS, REALLY.
MAKE IT FAST.
GIVE UP? NOT THIS GUY.
CHECK IT OUT! THREE TICKETS TO THE MOVIES!
HOW 'BOUT SATURDAY? OR WE COULD CUT CLASSES TODAY...
Dah
Tah
...JUST THE THREE OF US! WHADDAYA SAY?

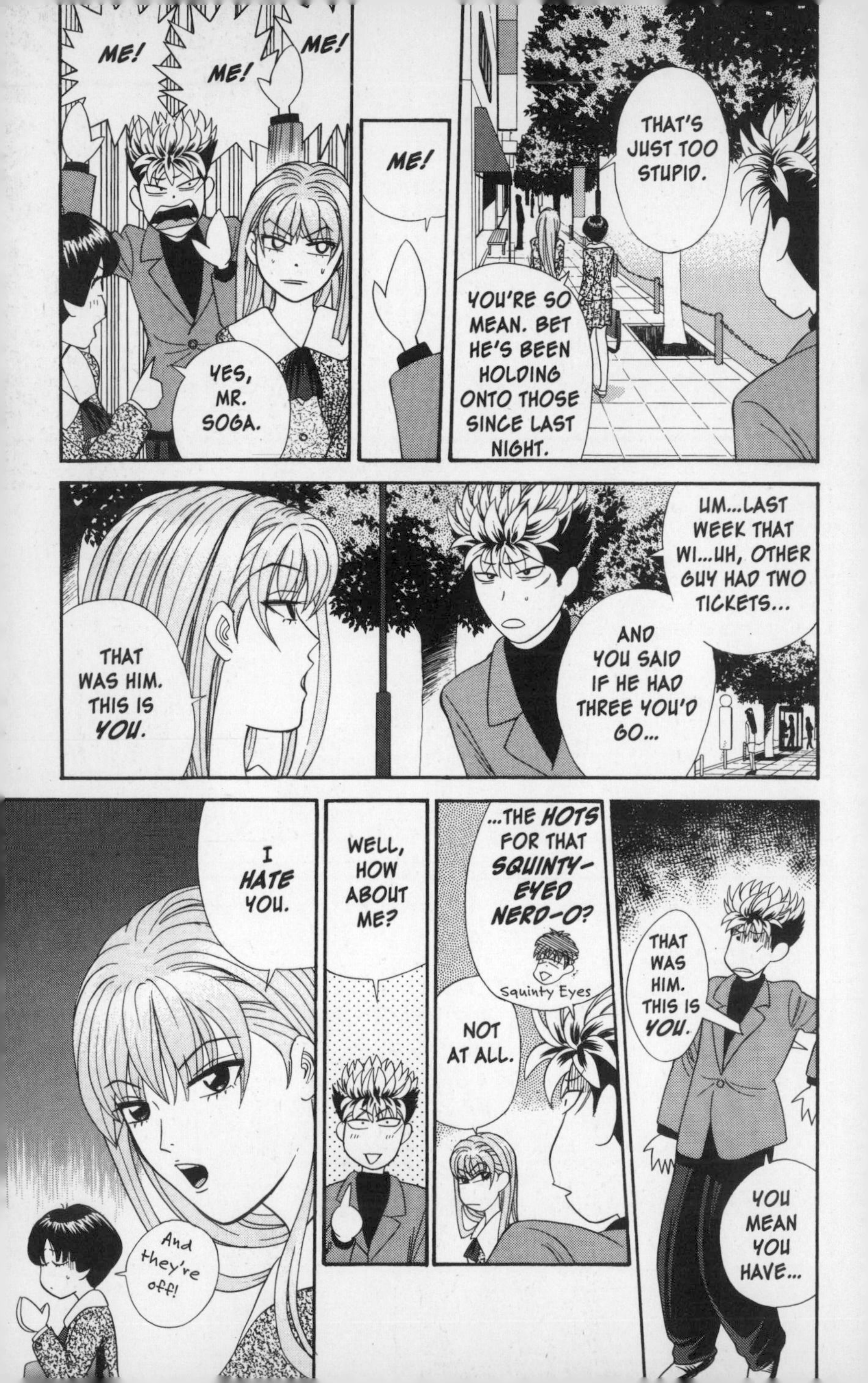

THAT'S JUST TOO STUPID.
YOU'RE SO MEAN. BET HE'S BEEN HOLDING ONTO THOSE SINCE LAST NIGHT.
ME!
ME!
ME!
ME!
YES, MR. SOGA.
UM...LAST WEEK THAT WI...UH, OTHER GUY HAD TWO TICKETS...
AND YOU SAID IF HE HAD THREE YOU'D GO...
THAT WAS HIM. THIS IS YOU.
THAT WAS HIM. THIS IS YOU.
YOU MEAN YOU HAVE...
...THE HOTS FOR THAT SQUINTY-EYED NERD-O?
Squinty Eyes
NOT AT ALL.
WELL, HOW ABOUT ME?
I HATE YOU.
And they're off!

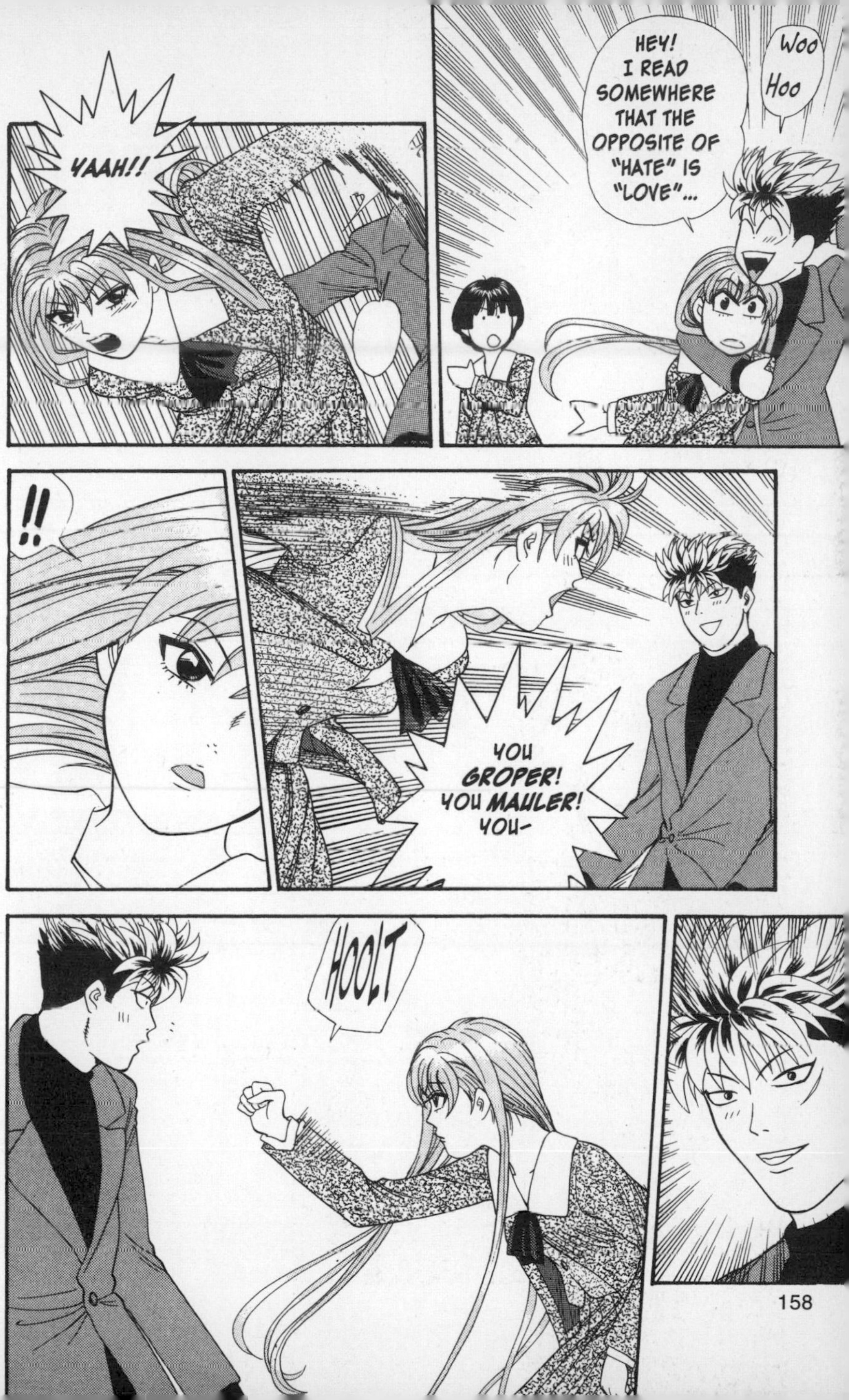
HEY! I READ SOMEWHERE THAT THE OPPOSITE OF "HATE" IS "LOVE"...
Woo Hoo
YAAH!!
YOU GROPER! YOU MAULER! YOU-
!!
HOOLT

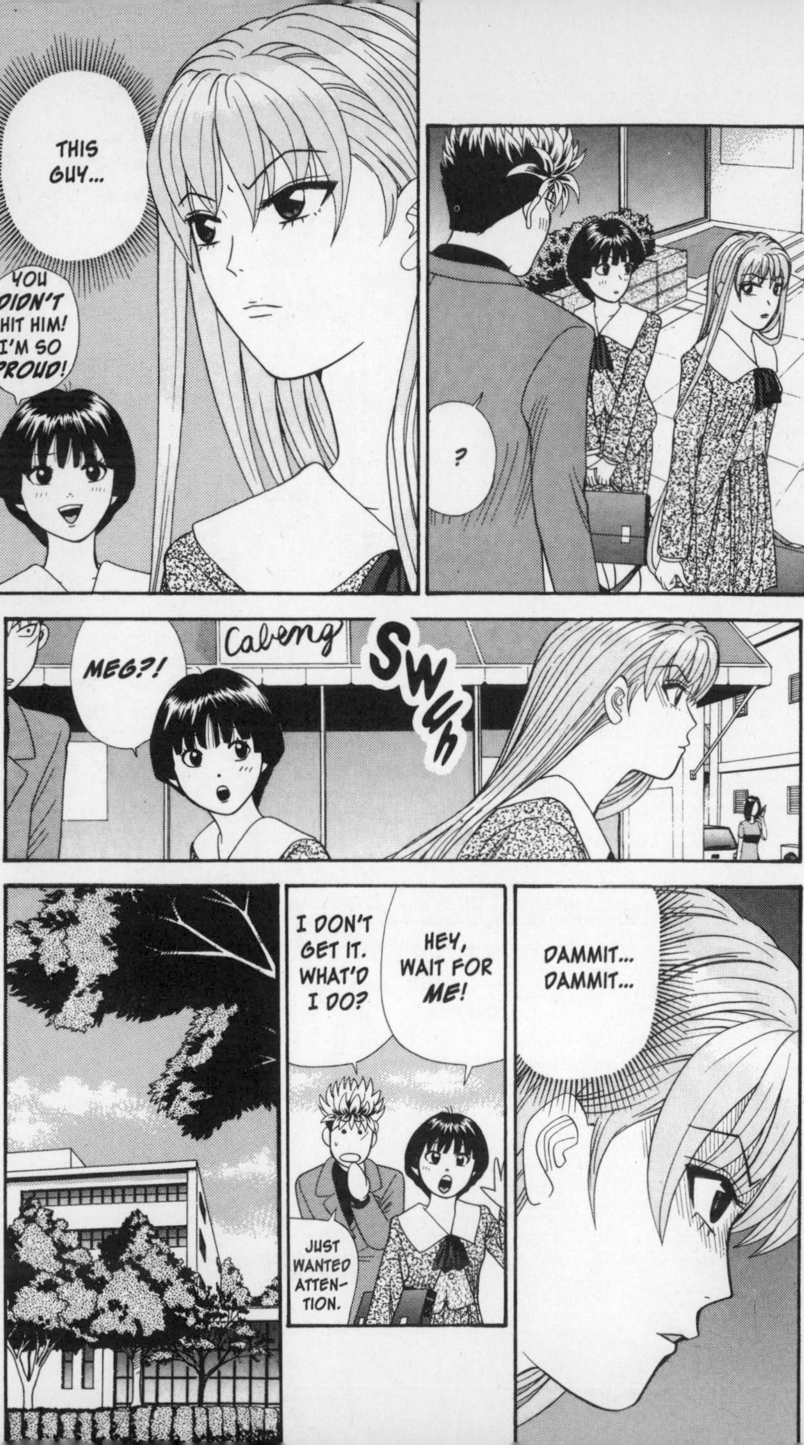
?
THIS GUY...
YOU DIDN'T HIT HIM! I'M SO PROUD!
SWUP
Cabeng
MEG?!
DAMMIT... DAMMIT...
HEY, WAIT FOR ME!
I DON'T GET IT. WHAT'D I DO?
JUST WANTED ATTENTION.

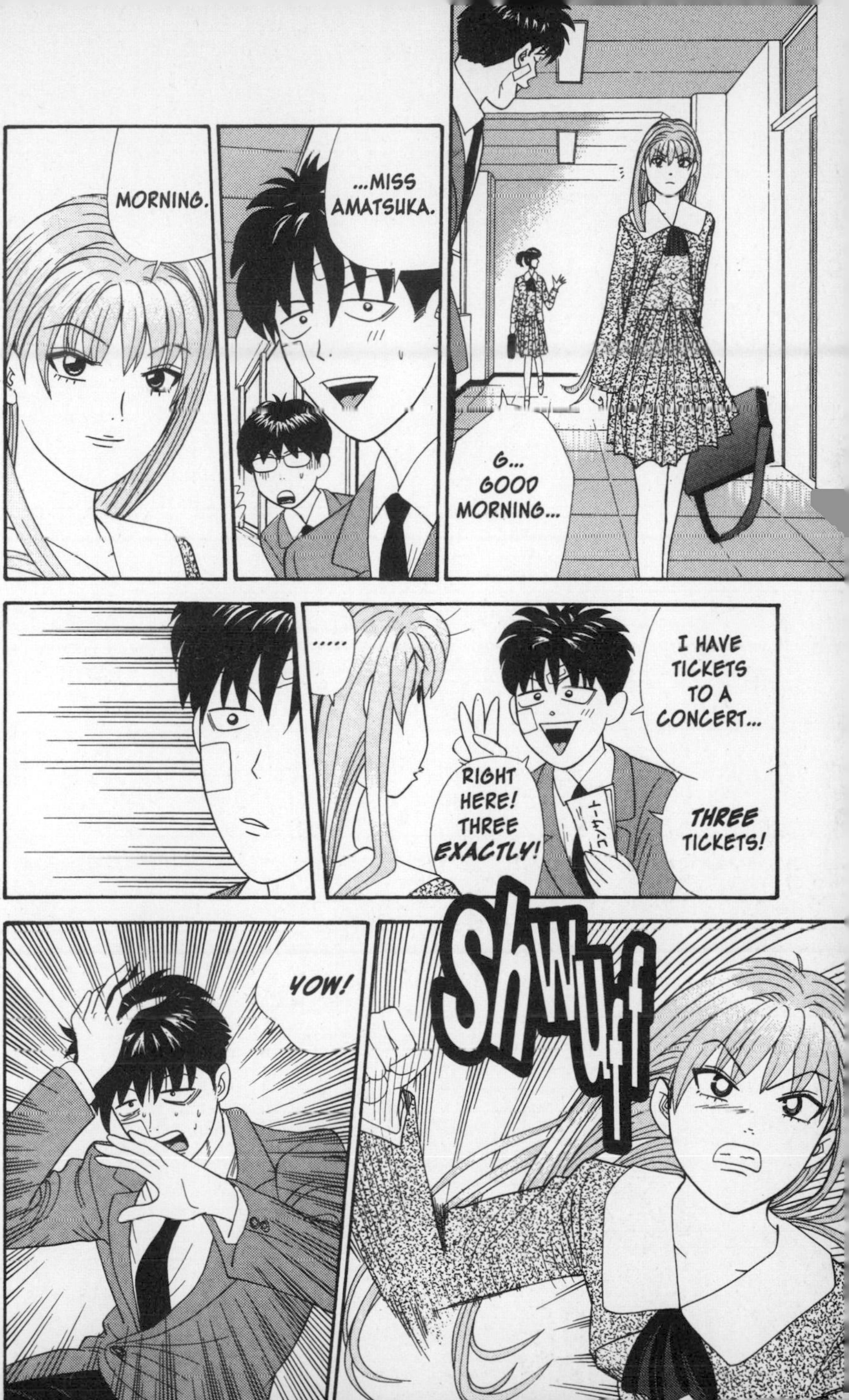
G...
GOOD
MORNING...
...MISS
AMATSUKA.
MORNING.
I HAVE
TICKETS
TO A
CONCERT...
THREE
TICKETS!
RIGHT
HERE!
THREE
EXACTLY!
......
Shwuff
YOW!

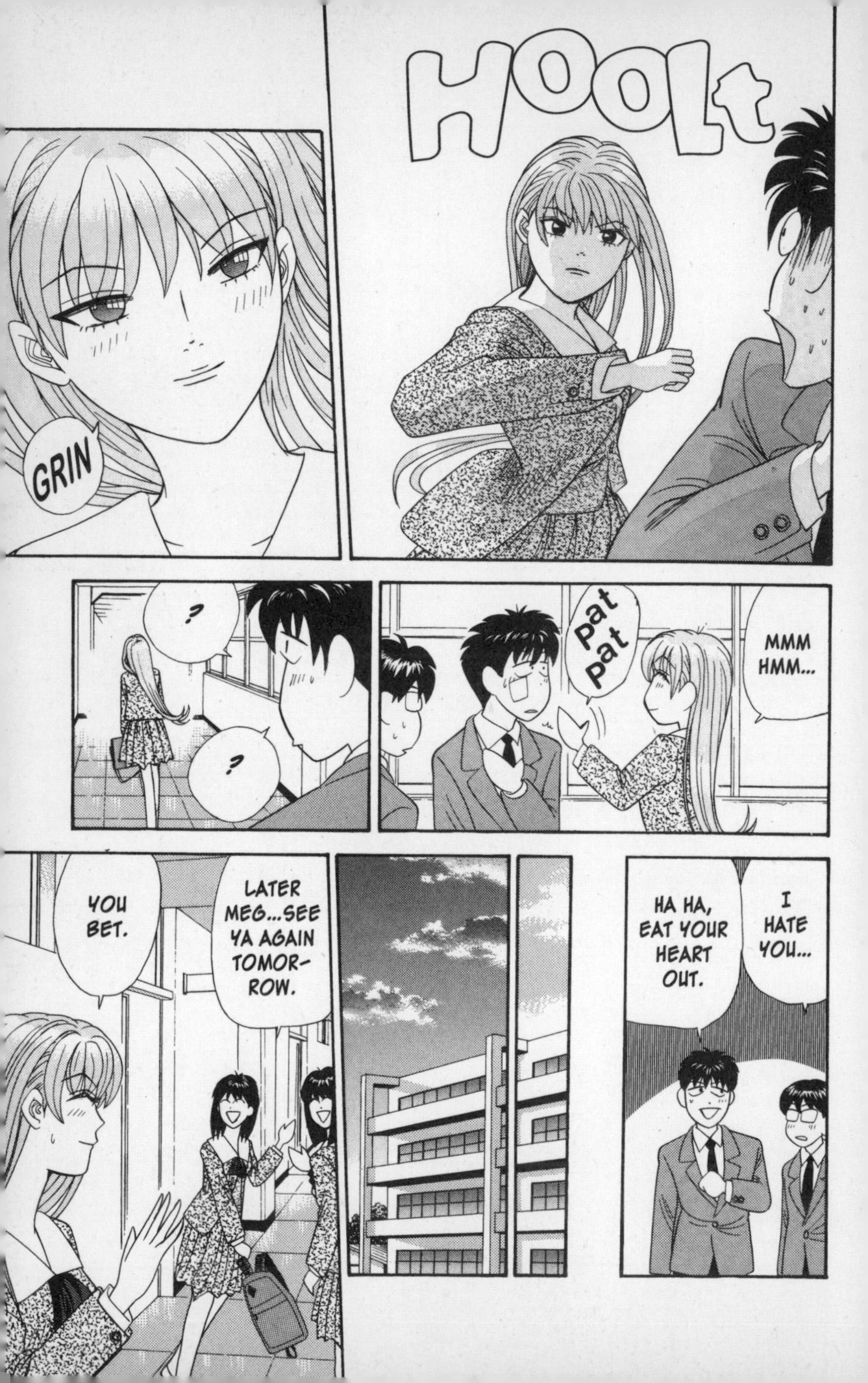
HOOLt
GRIN
MMM HMM...
pat pat pat
?
?
I HATE YOU...
HA HA, EAT YOUR HEART OUT.
LATER MEG...SEE YA AGAIN TOMOR-ROW.
YOU BET.

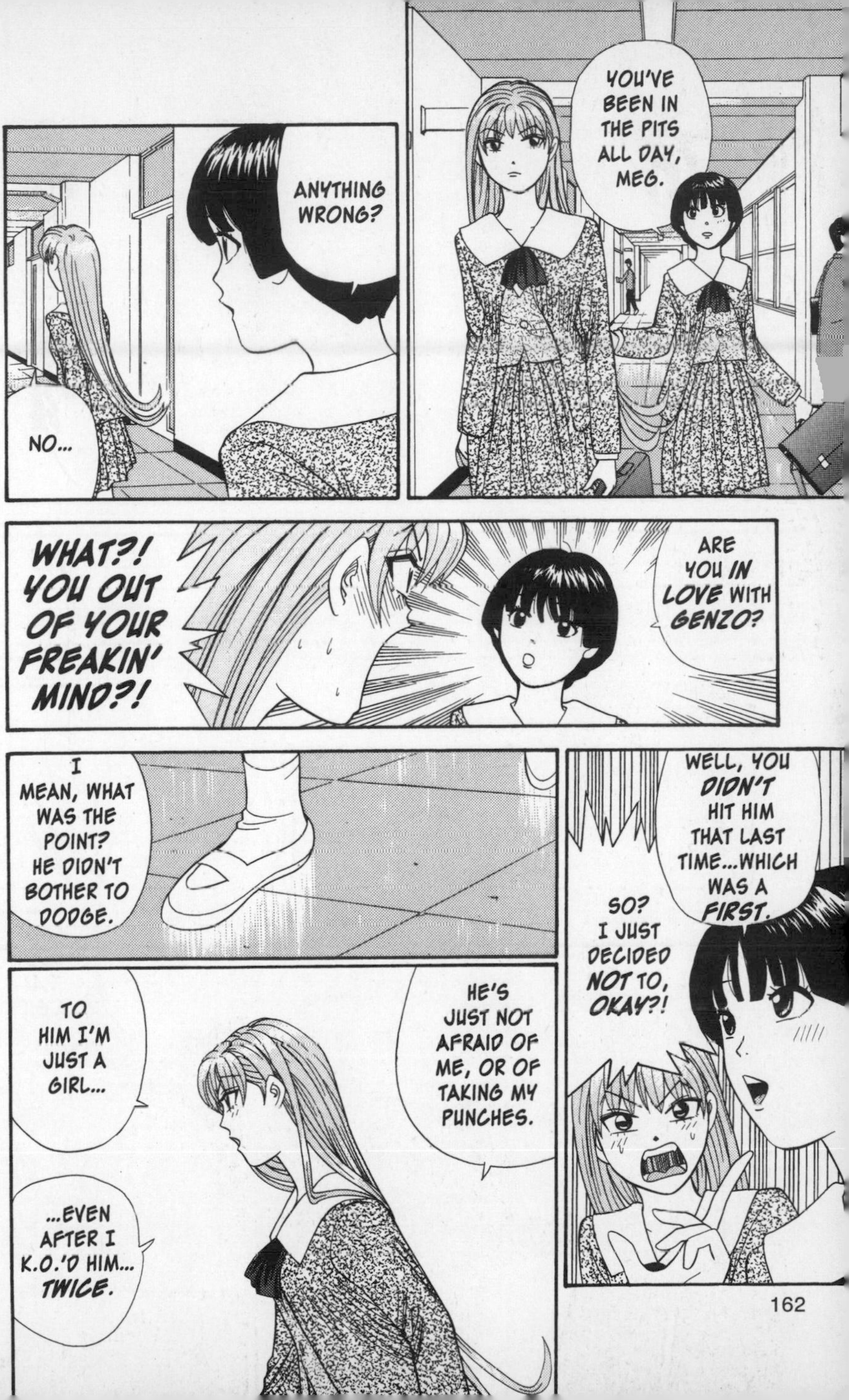
YOU'VE BEEN IN THE PITS ALL DAY, MEG.
ANYTHING WRONG?
NO...
ARE YOU IN LOVE WITH GENZO?
WHAT?! YOU OUT OF YOUR FREAKIN' MIND?!
WELL, YOU DIDN'T HIT HIM THAT LAST TIME...WHICH WAS A FIRST.
SO? I JUST DECIDED NOT TO, OKAY?!
I MEAN, WHAT WAS THE POINT? HE DIDN'T BOTHER TO DODGE.
HE'S JUST NOT AFRAID OF ME, OR OF TAKING MY PUNCHES.
TO HIM I'M JUST A GIRL...
...EVEN AFTER I K.O.'D HIM... TWICE.

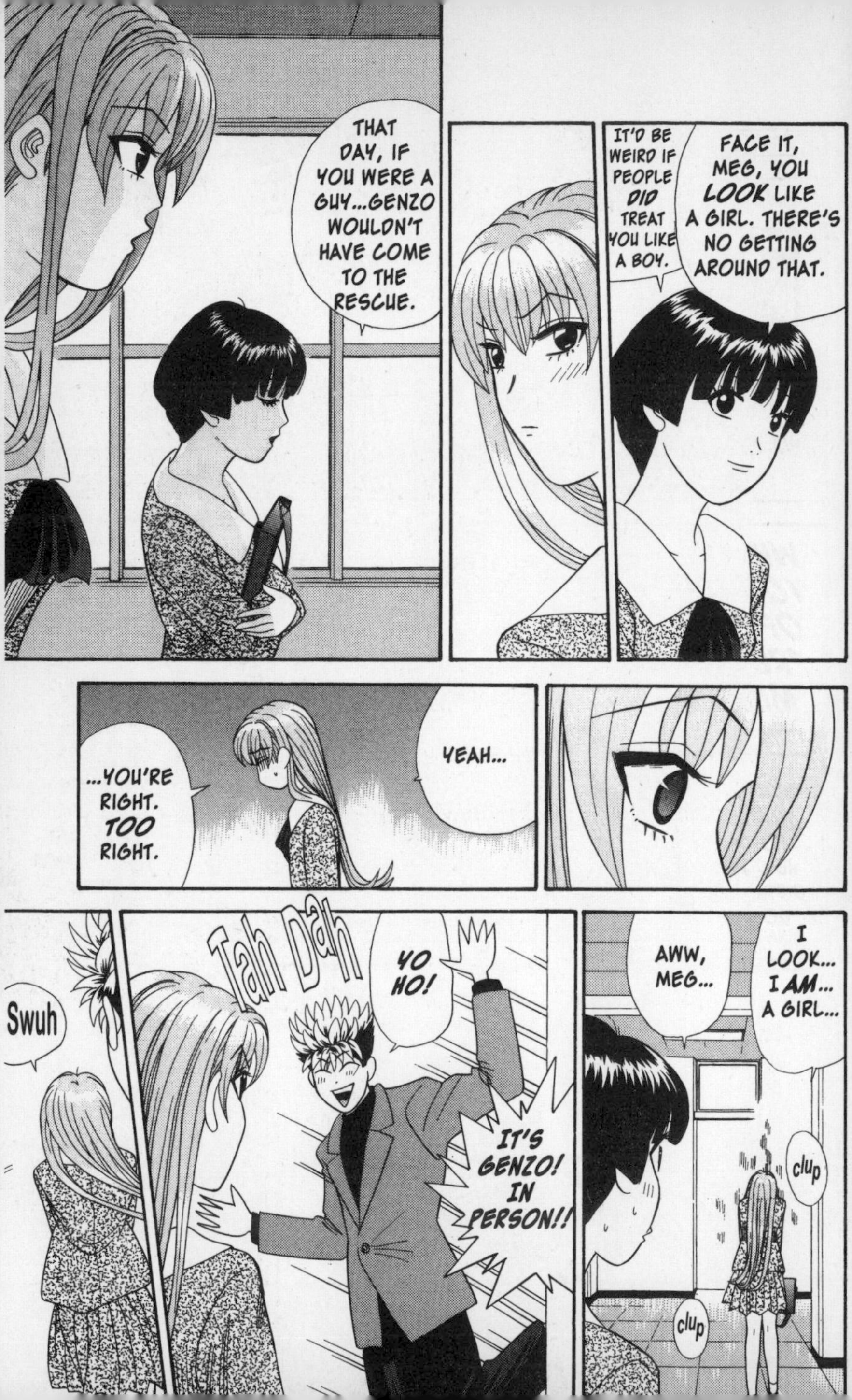
FACE IT, MEG, YOU LOOK LIKE A GIRL. THERE'S NO GETTING AROUND THAT.
IT'D BE WEIRD IF PEOPLE DID TREAT YOU LIKE A BOY.
THAT DAY, IF YOU WERE A GUY...GENZO WOULDN'T HAVE COME TO THE RESCUE.
YEAH...
...YOU'RE RIGHT. TOO RIGHT.
I LOOK... I AM... A GIRL...
AWW, MEG...
clup
clup
Tah Dah
YO HO!
IT'S GENZO! IN PERSON!!
Swuh

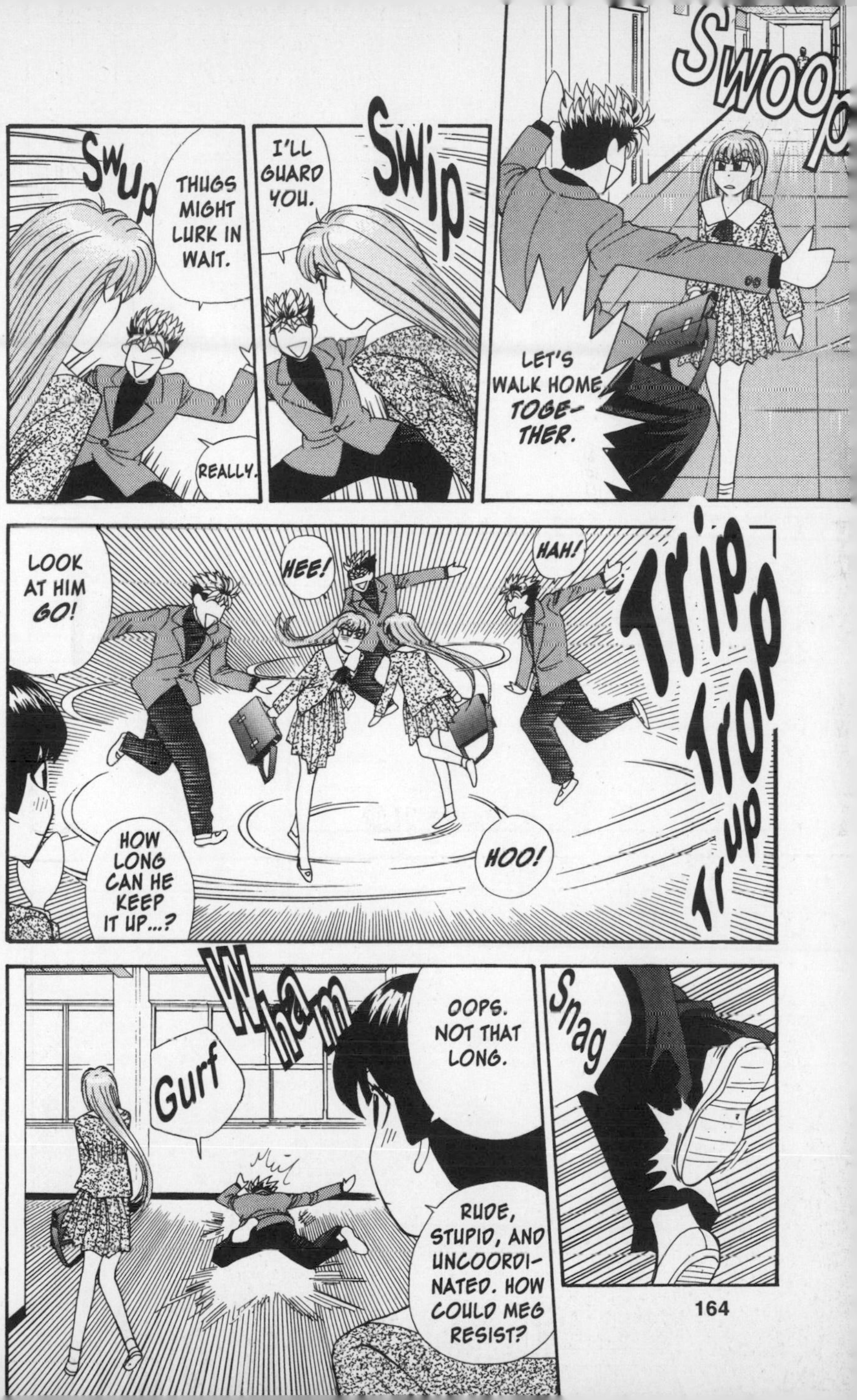
Swoop
LET'S WALK HOME TOGETHER.
Swip
I'LL GUARD YOU.
Swup
THUGS MIGHT LURK IN WAIT.
REALLY.
Trip Trop Trup
HAH!
HEE!
LOOK AT HIM GO!
HOO!
HOW LONG CAN HE KEEP IT UP...?
Snag
OOPS. NOT THAT LONG.
Wham
Gurf
RUDE, STUPID, AND UNCOORDINATED. HOW COULD MEG RESIST?

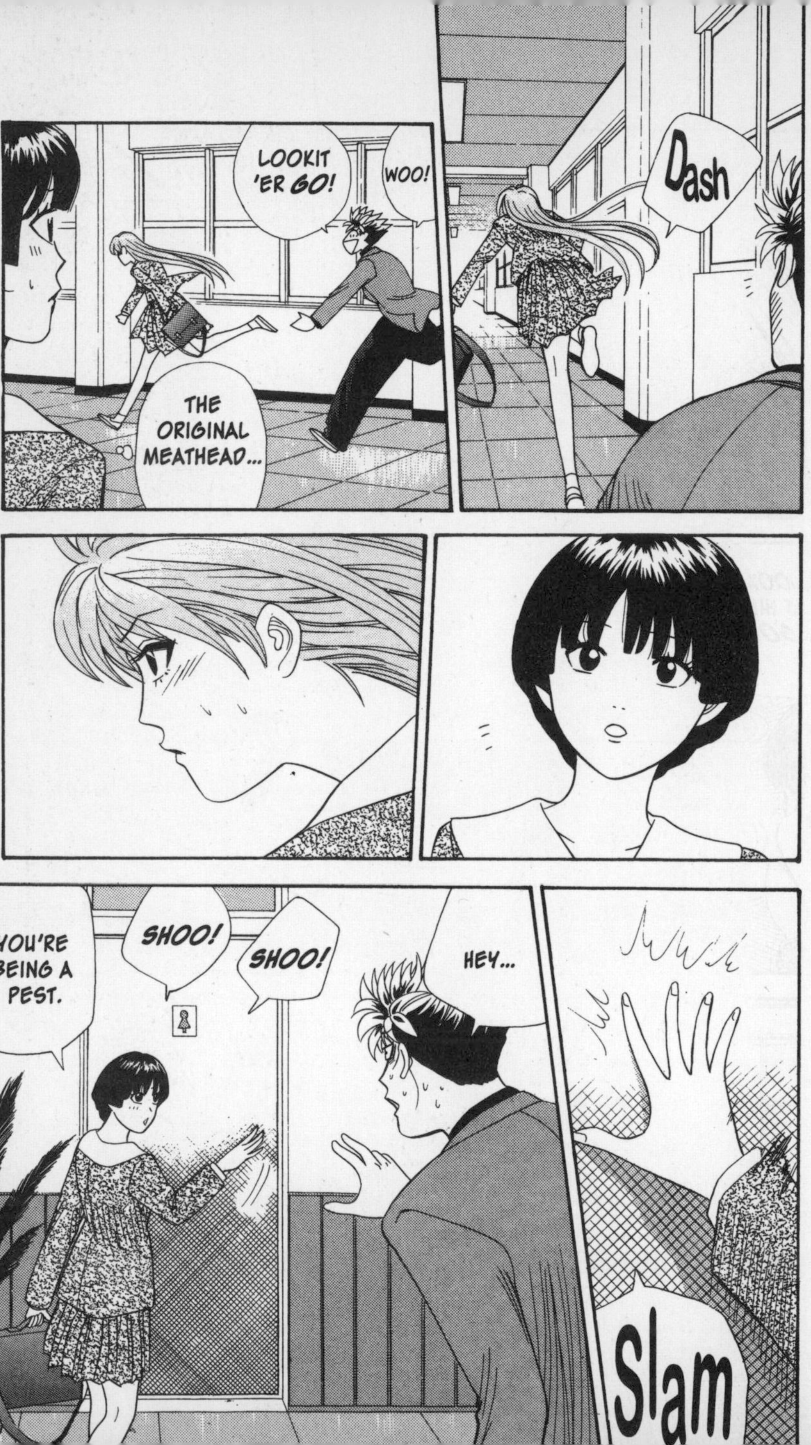
Dash
WOO!
LOOKIT 'ER GO!
THE ORIGINAL MEATHEAD...
Slam
HEY...
SHOO!
SHOO!
YOU'RE BEING A PEST.

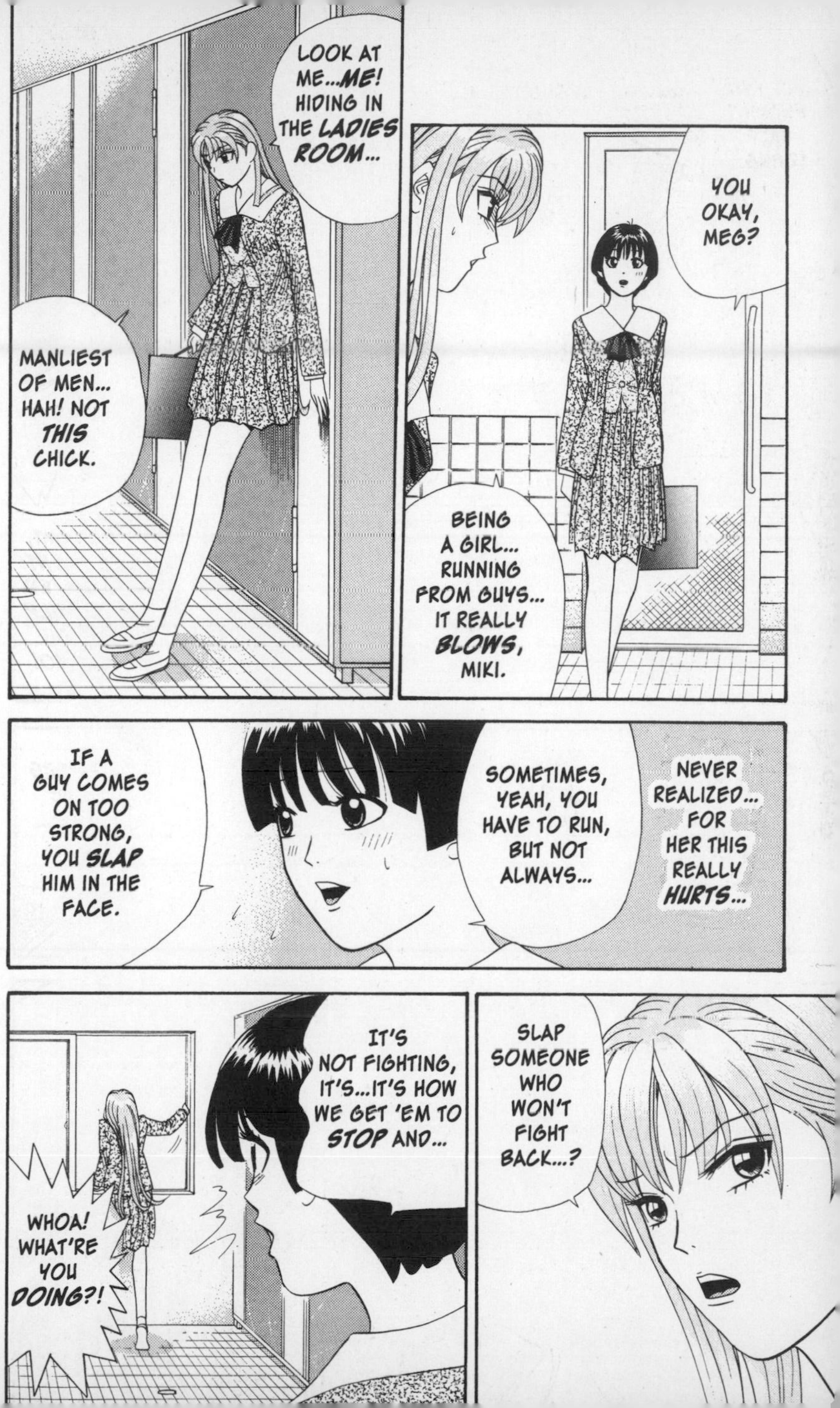

YOU OKAY, MEG?
BEING A GIRL... RUNNING FROM GUYS... IT REALLY *BLOWS*, MIKI.
LOOK AT ME...*ME!* HIDING IN THE *LADIES ROOM*...
MANLIEST OF MEN... HAH! NOT *THIS* CHICK.
NEVER REALIZED... FOR HER THIS REALLY *HURTS*...
SOMETIMES, YEAH, YOU HAVE TO RUN, BUT NOT ALWAYS...
IF A GUY COMES ON TOO STRONG, YOU *SLAP* HIM IN THE FACE.
SLAP SOMEONE WHO WON'T FIGHT BACK...?
IT'S NOT FIGHTING, IT'S...IT'S HOW WE GET 'EM TO *STOP* AND...
WHOA! WHAT'RE YOU *DOING?!*

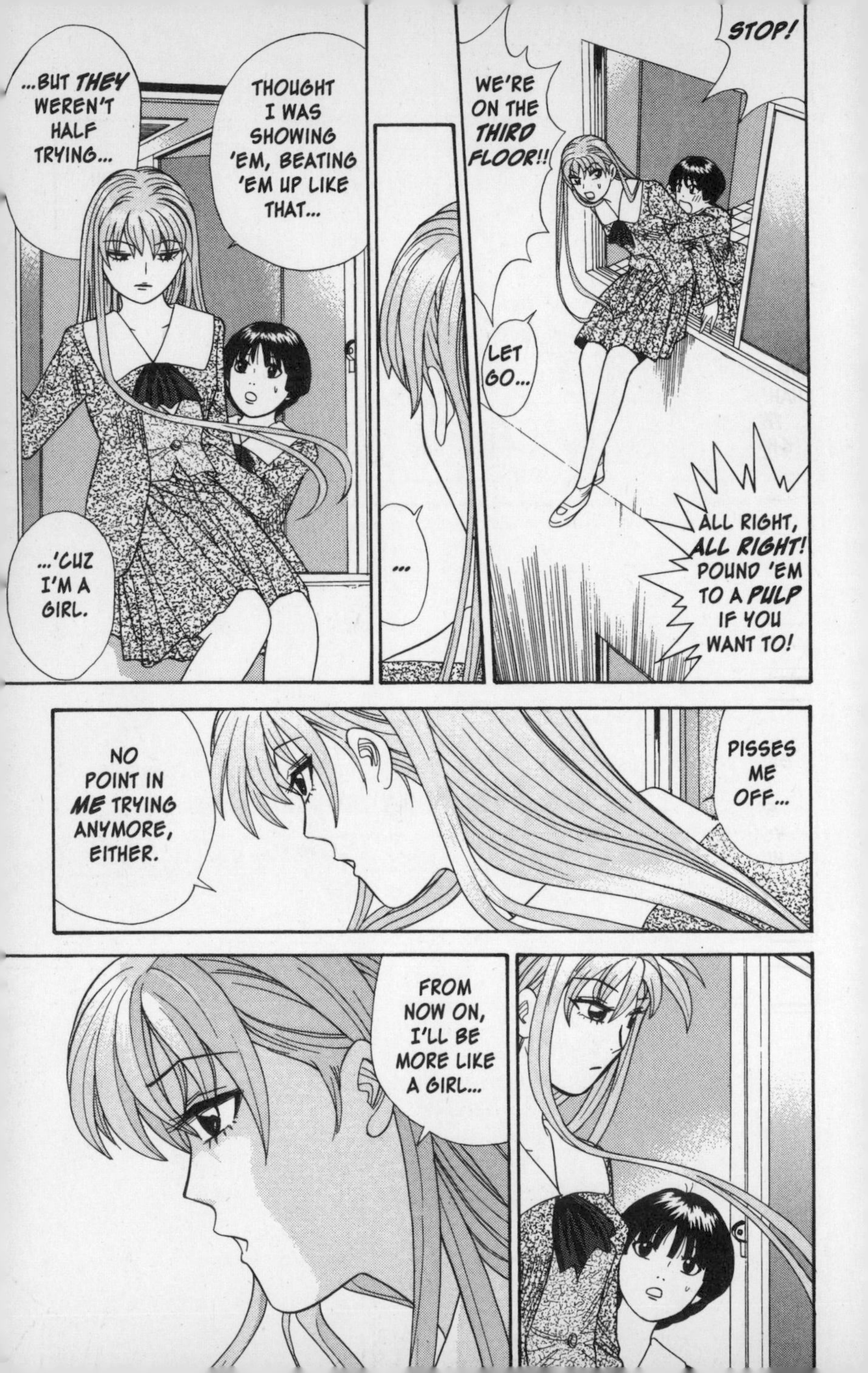
STOP!
WE'RE ON THE THIRD FLOOR!!
LET GO...
ALL RIGHT, ALL RIGHT! POUND 'EM TO A PULP IF YOU WANT TO!
...
THOUGHT I WAS SHOWING 'EM, BEATING 'EM UP LIKE THAT...
...BUT THEY WEREN'T HALF TRYING...
...'CUZ I'M A GIRL.
PISSES ME OFF...
NO POINT IN ME TRYING ANYMORE, EITHER.
FROM NOW ON, I'LL BE MORE LIKE A GIRL...

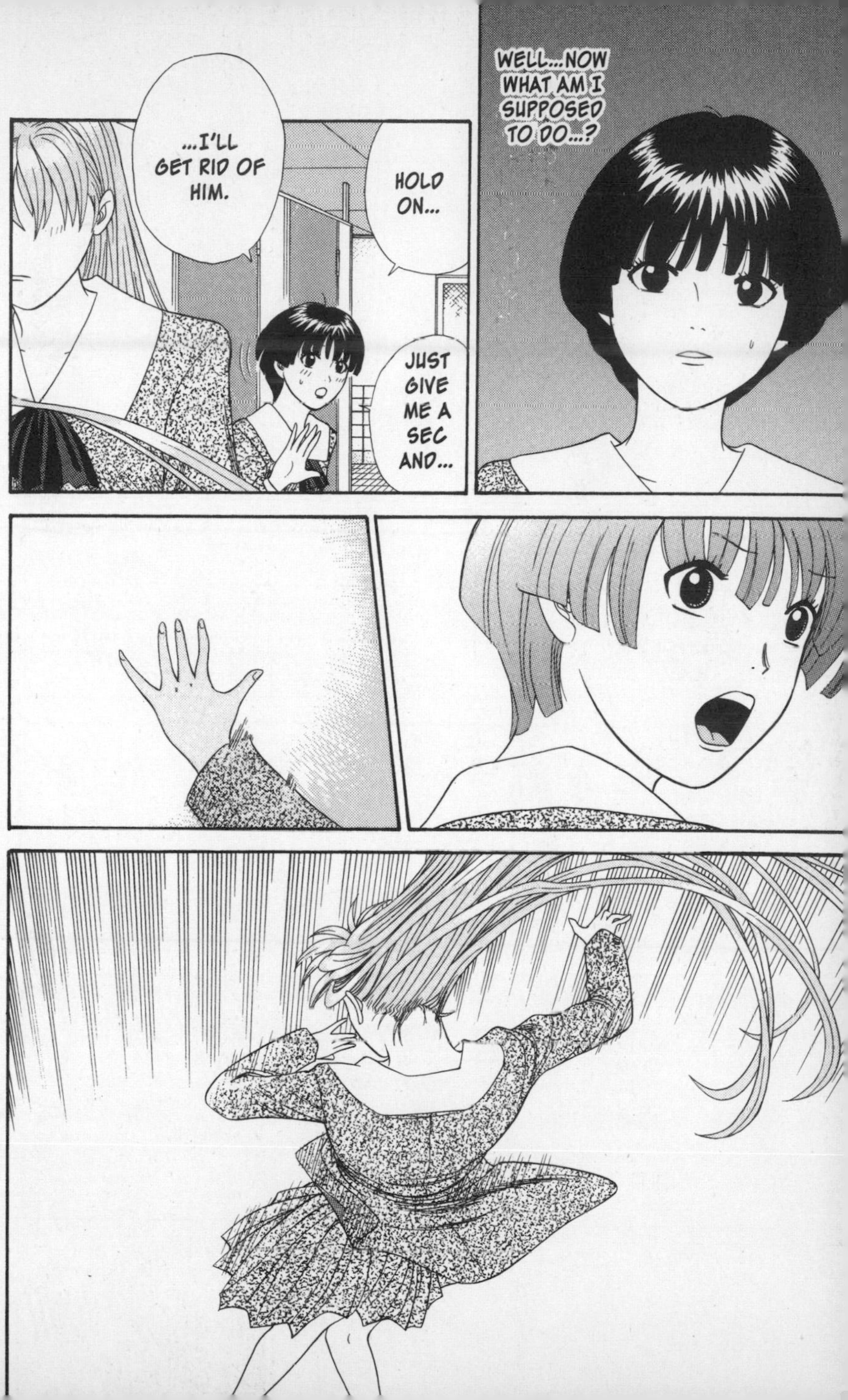
WELL...NOW WHAT AM I SUPPOSED TO DO...?
HOLD ON...
...I'LL GET RID OF HIM.
JUST GIVE ME A SEC AND...

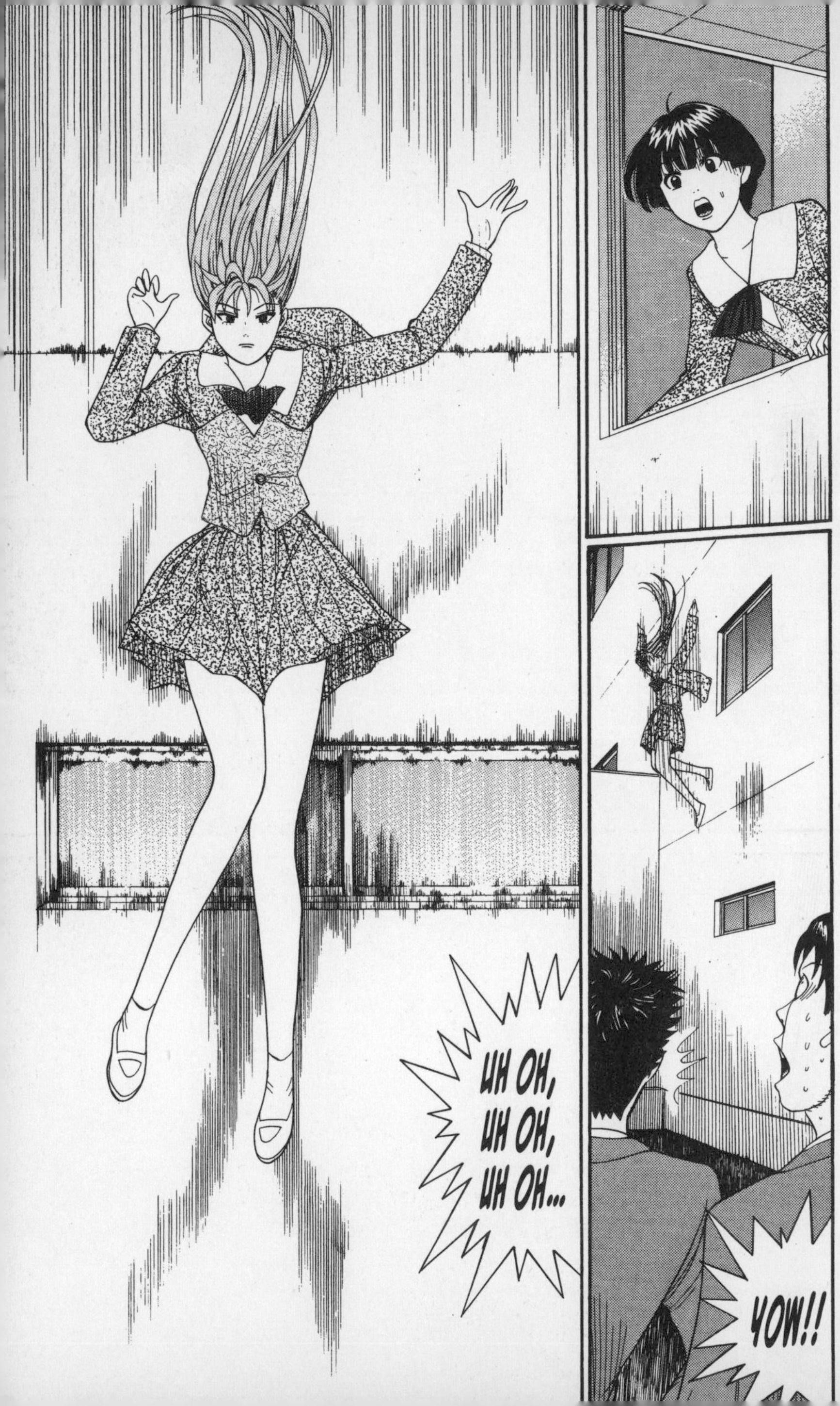
YOW!!
UH OH,
UH OH,
UH OH...

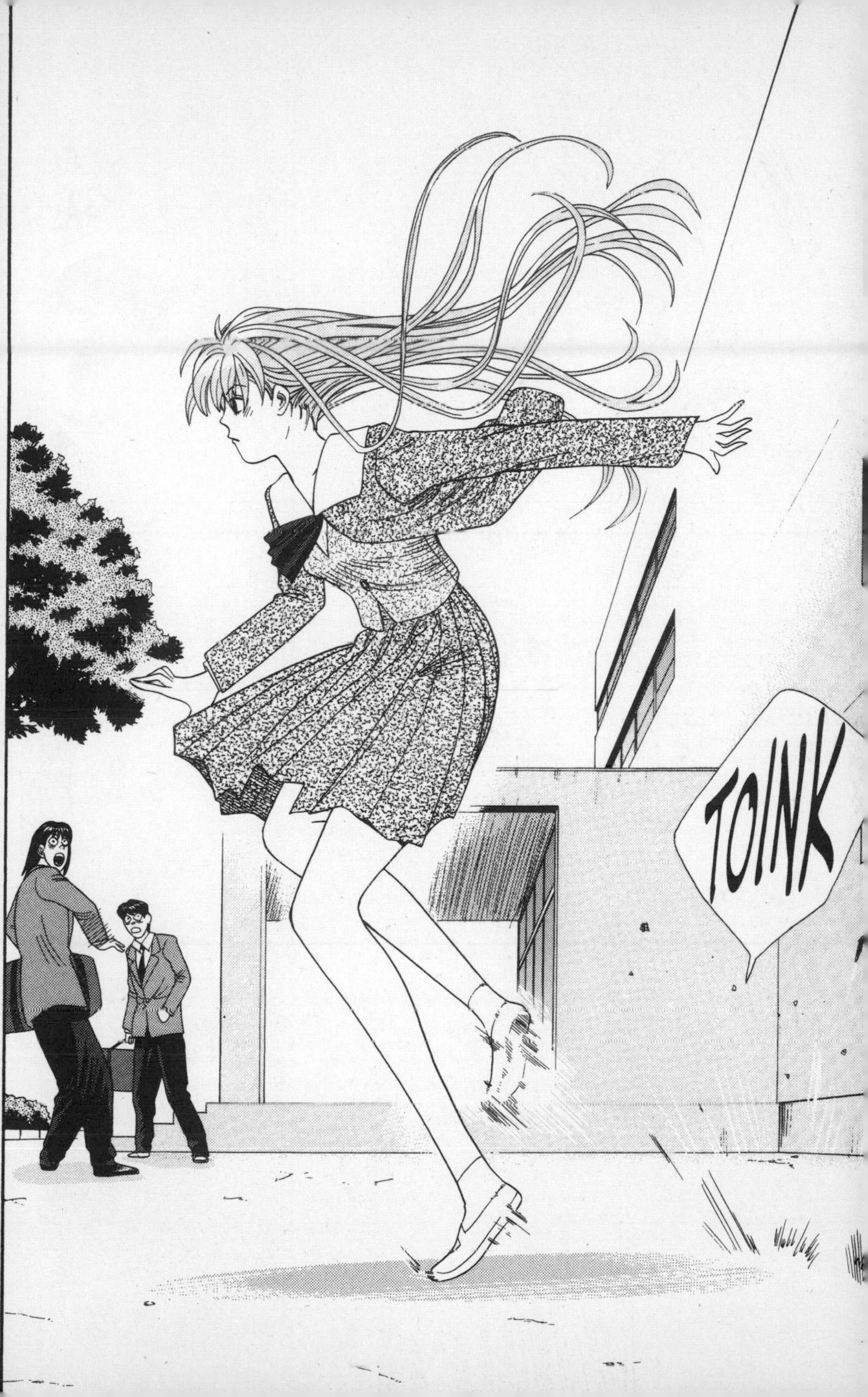
TOINK

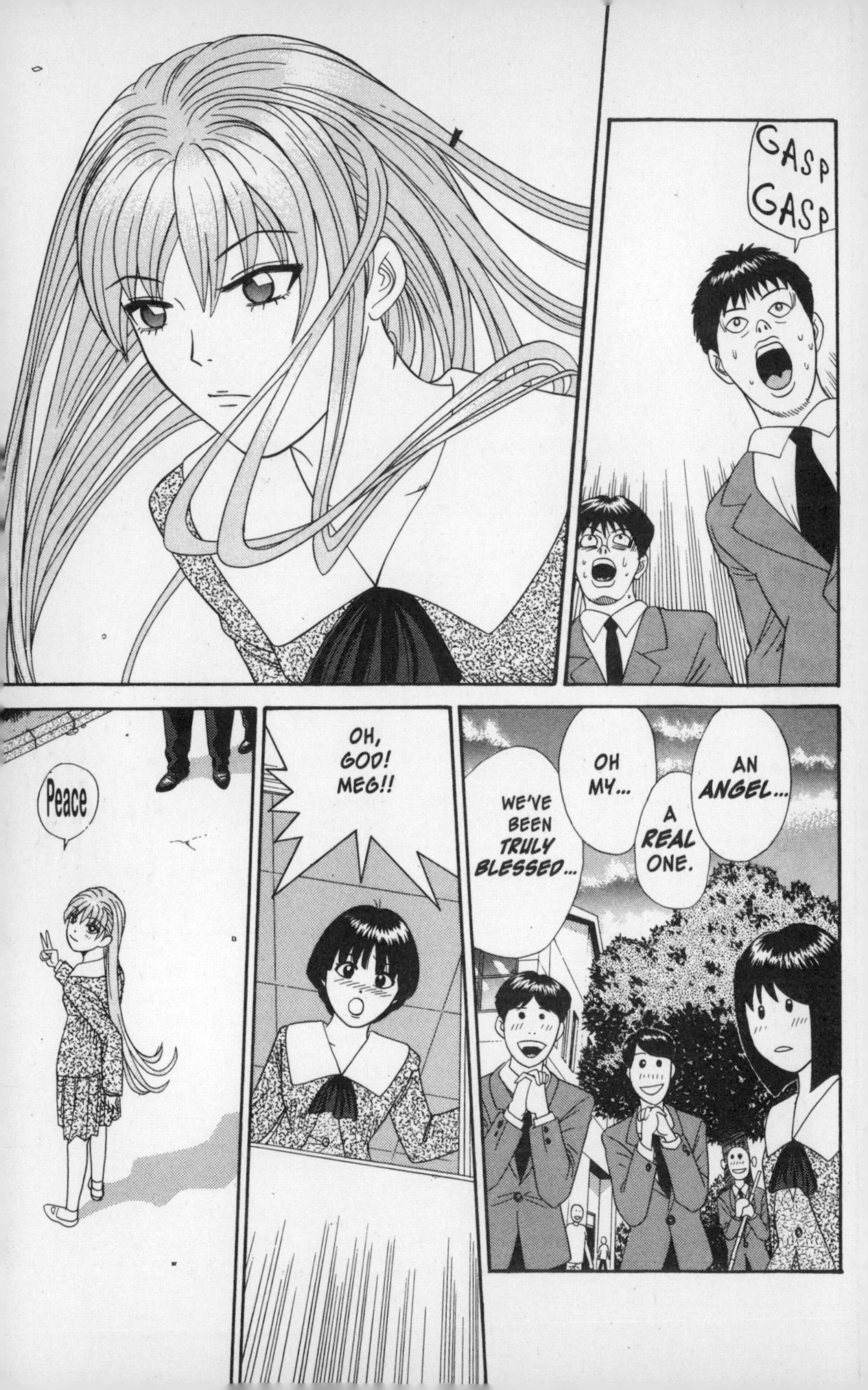
GASP GASP
AN ANGEL...
A REAL ONE.
OH MY...
WE'VE BEEN TRULY BLESSED...
OH, GOD! MEG!!
Peace

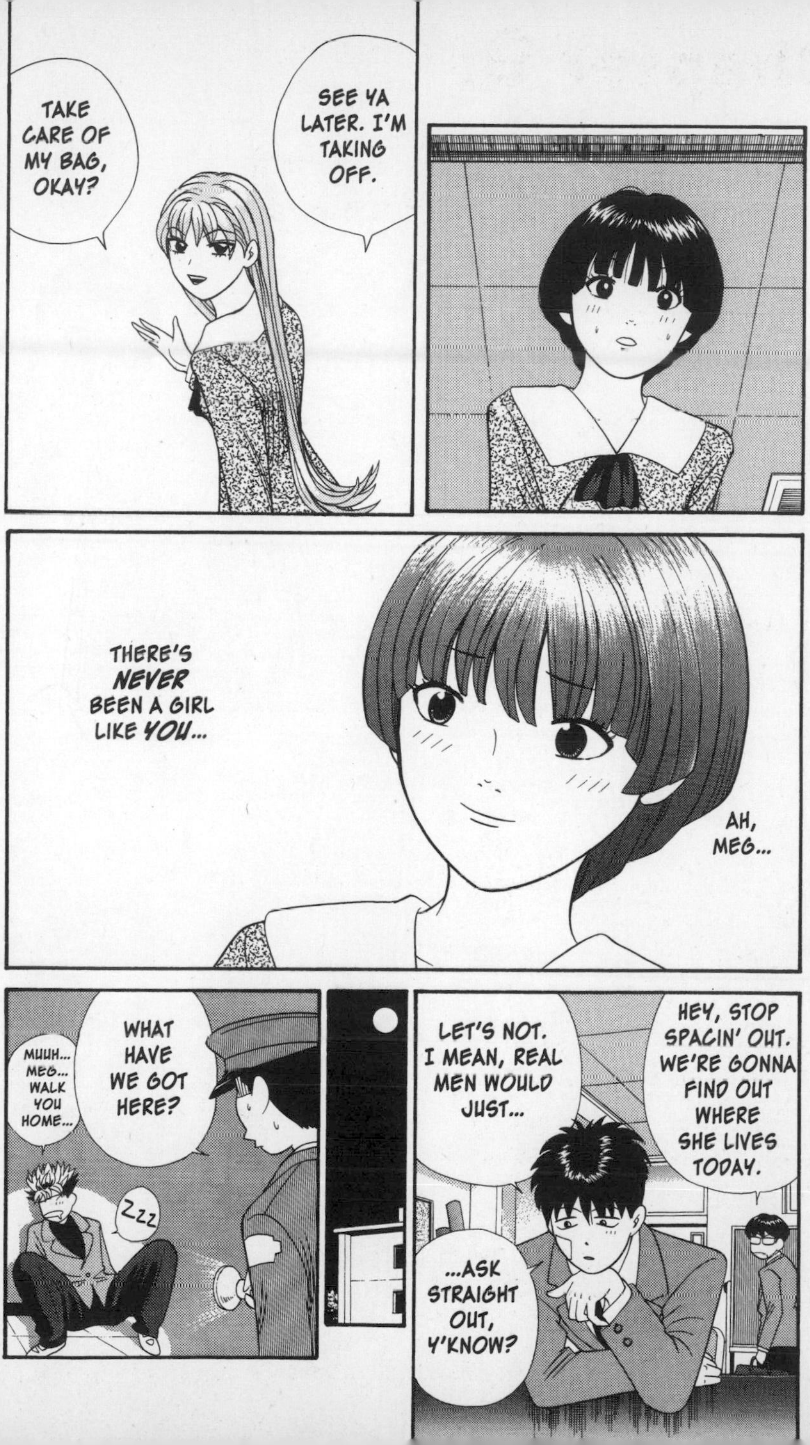
SEE YA LATER. I'M TAKING OFF.
TAKE CARE OF MY BAG, OKAY?
THERE'S *NEVER* BEEN A GIRL LIKE *YOU*...
AH, MEG...
HEY, STOP SPACIN' OUT. WE'RE GONNA FIND OUT WHERE SHE LIVES TODAY.
LET'S NOT. I MEAN, REAL MEN WOULD JUST...
...ASK STRAIGHT OUT, Y'KNOW?
WHAT HAVE WE GOT HERE?
MUUH... MEG... WALK YOU HOME...
Zzz

Chapter 9: Rival...?

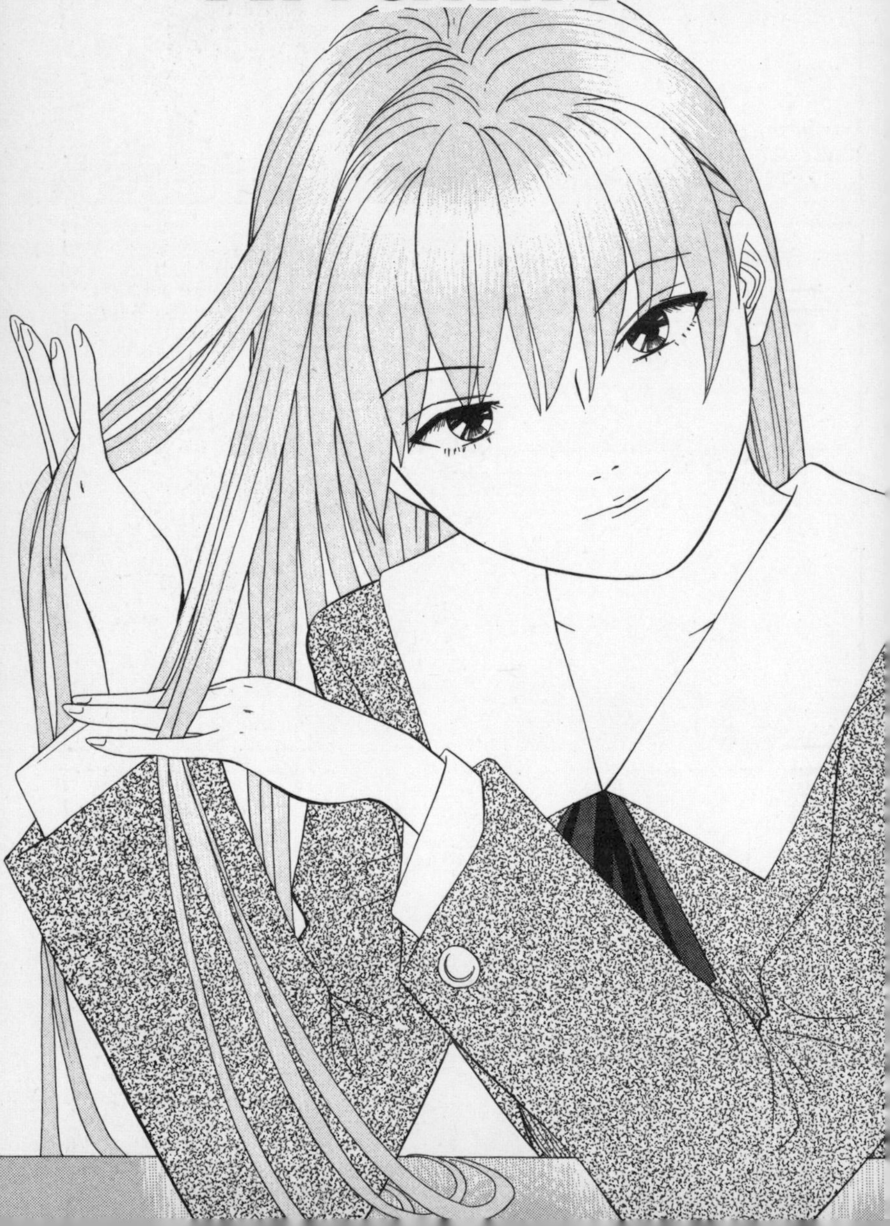

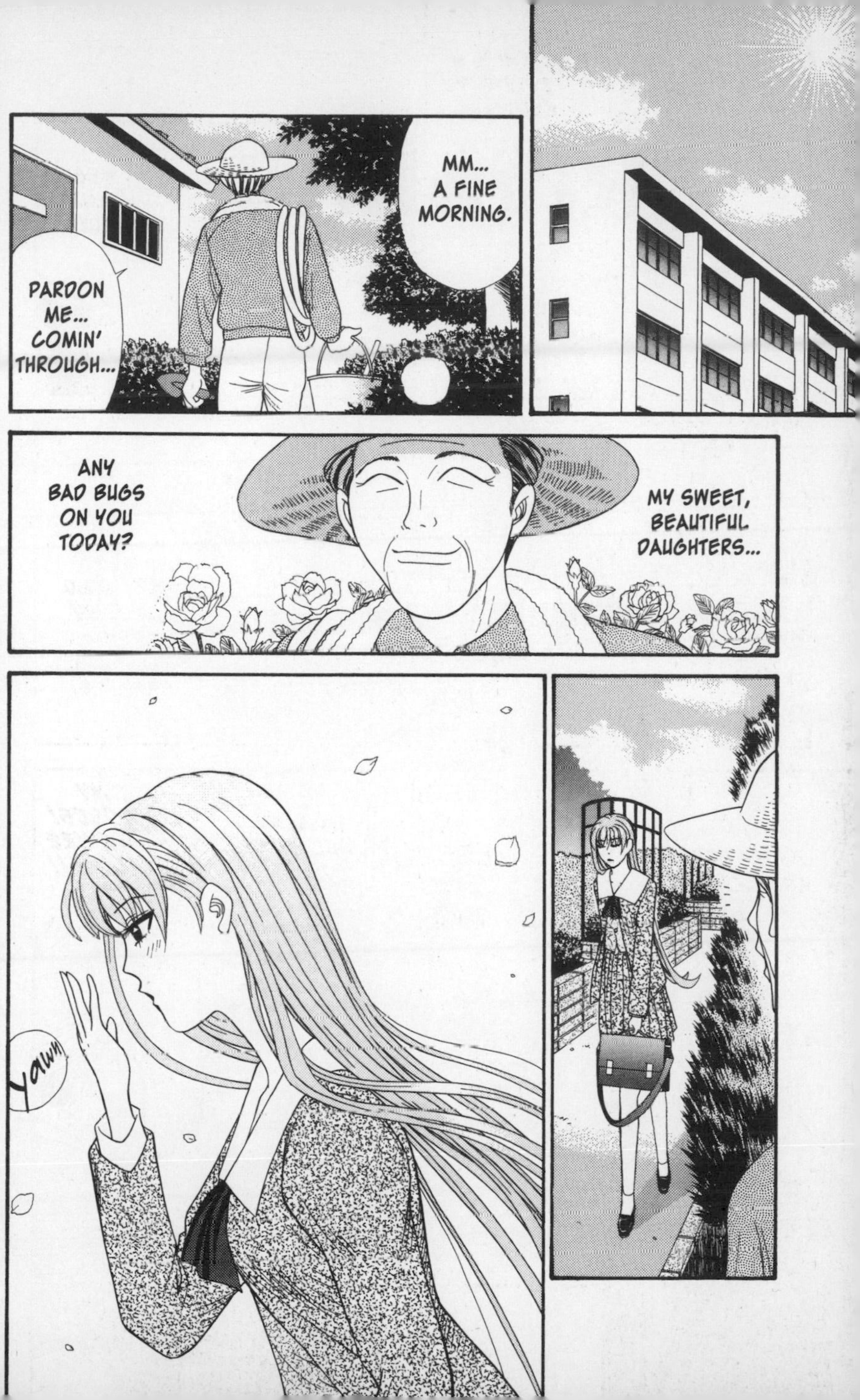
MM... A FINE MORNING.
PARDON ME... COMIN' THROUGH...
MY SWEET, BEAUTIFUL DAUGHTERS...
ANY BAD BUGS ON YOU TODAY?
Yawn

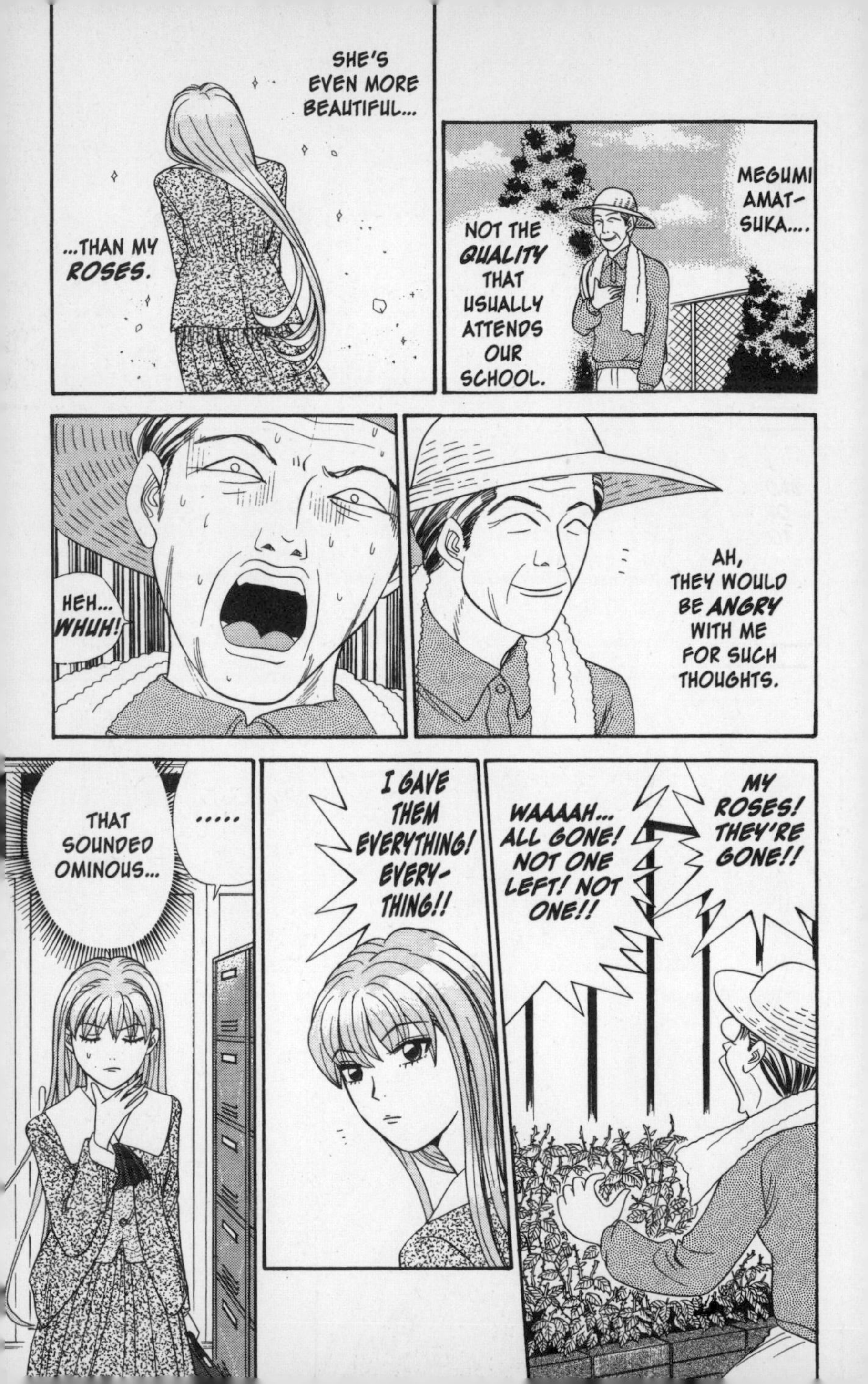
MEGUMI AMATSUKA....
NOT THE QUALITY THAT USUALLY ATTENDS OUR SCHOOL.
SHE'S EVEN MORE BEAUTIFUL...
...THAN MY ROSES.
AH, THEY WOULD BE ANGRY WITH ME FOR SUCH THOUGHTS.
HEH... WHUH!
MY ROSES! THEY'RE GONE!!
WAAAAH... ALL GONE! NOT ONE LEFT! NOT ONE!!
I GAVE THEM EVERYTHING! EVERY-THING!!
.....
THAT SOUNDED OMINOUS...

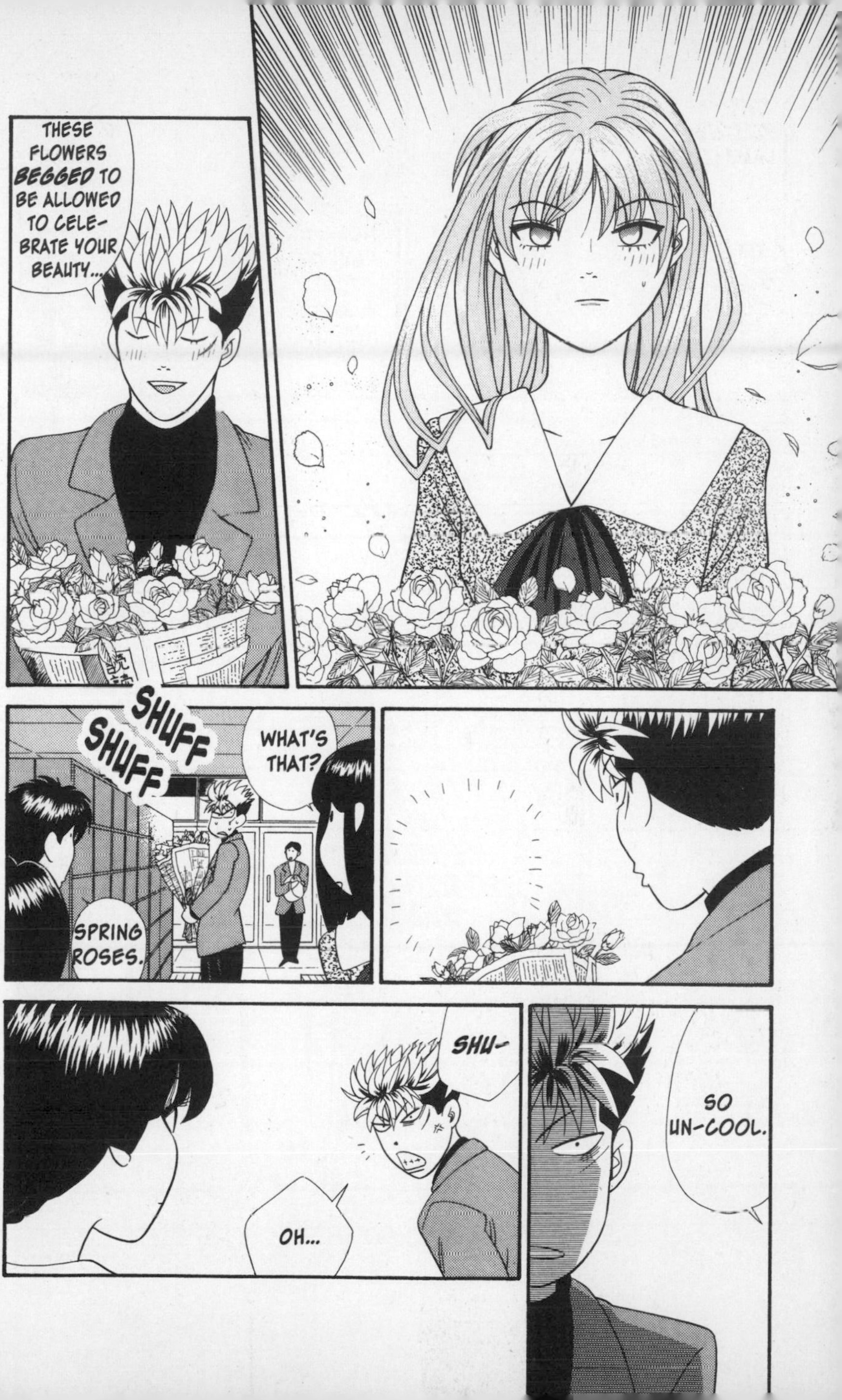
THESE FLOWERS *BEGGED* TO BE ALLOWED TO CELE-BRATE YOUR BEAUTY...
WHAT'S THAT?
SHUFF SHUFF
SPRING ROSES.
SO UN-COOL.
SHU-
OH...

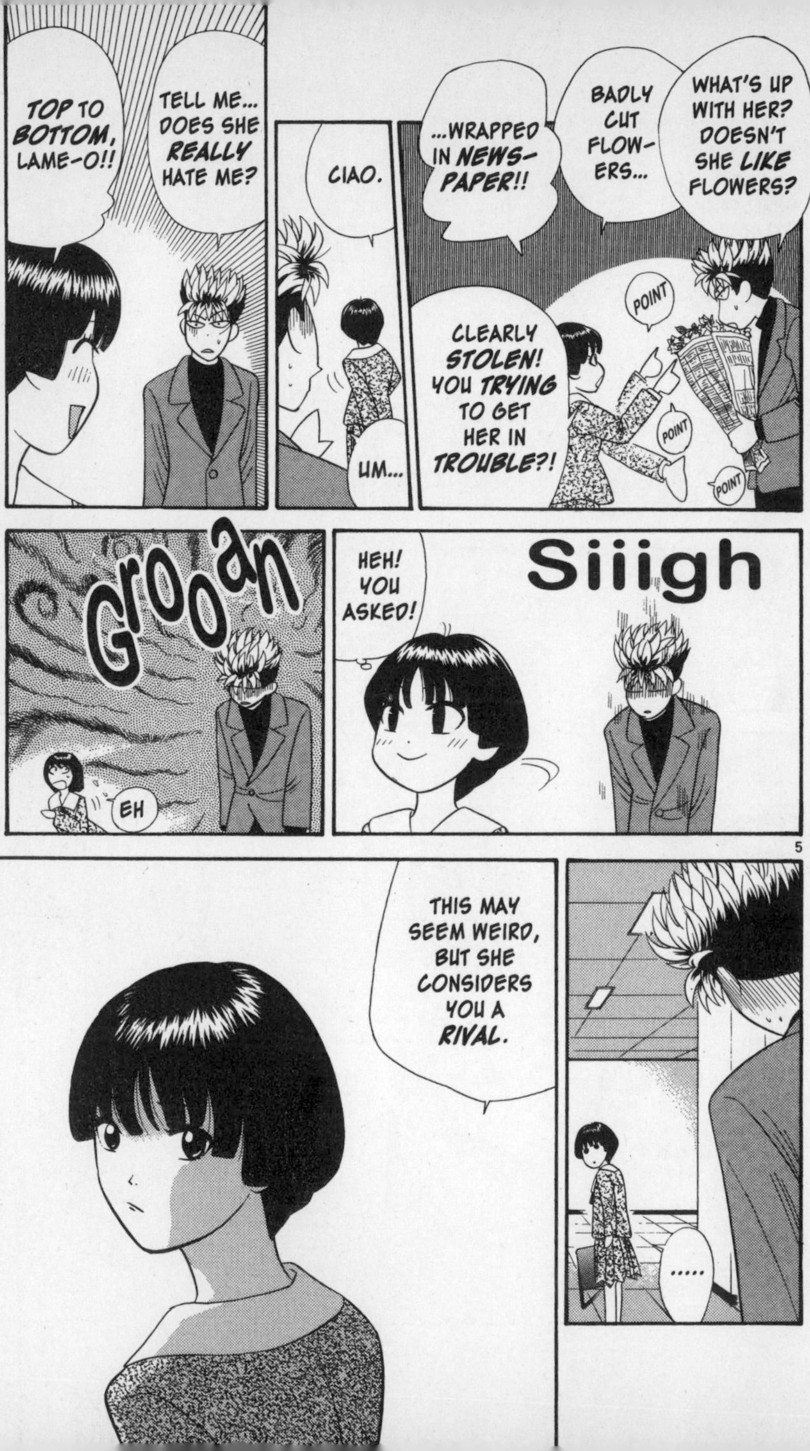
WHAT'S UP WITH HER? DOESN'T SHE LIKE FLOWERS?
BADLY CUT FLOWERS...
...WRAPPED IN NEWSPAPER!!
POINT
CLEARLY STOLEN! YOU TRYING TO GET HER IN TROUBLE?!
POINT
POINT
CIAO.
UM...
TELL ME... DOES SHE REALLY HATE ME?
TOP TO BOTTOM, LAME-O!!
Siiigh
HEH! YOU ASKED!
Grooan
EH
.....
THIS MAY SEEM WEIRD, BUT SHE CONSIDERS YOU A RIVAL.

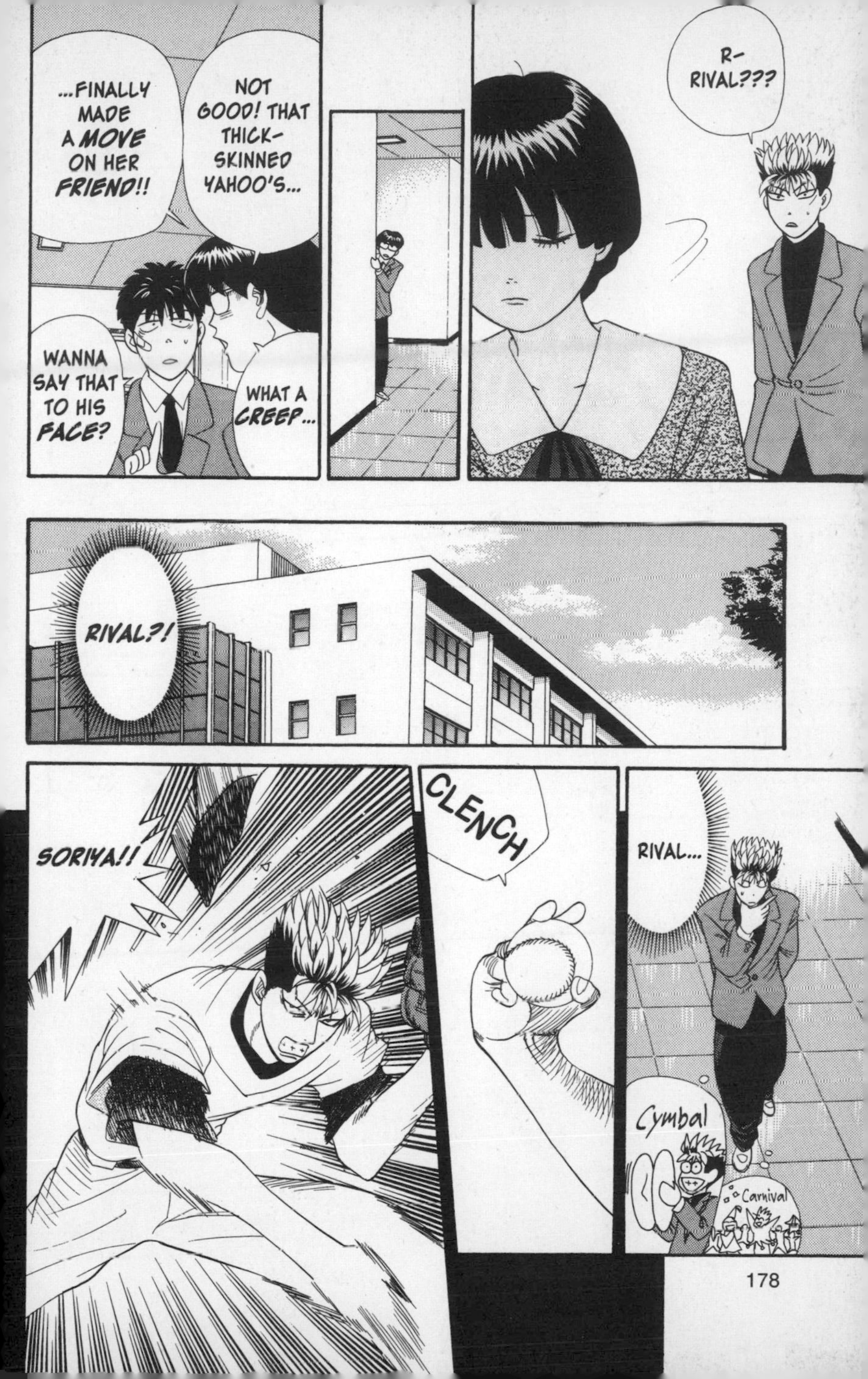
R-
RIVAL???
NOT GOOD! THAT THICK-SKINNED YAHOO'S...
...FINALLY MADE A MOVE ON HER FRIEND!!
WHAT A CREEP...
WANNA SAY THAT TO HIS FACE?
RIVAL?!
RIVAL...
Cymbal
Carnival
CLENCH
SORIYA!!

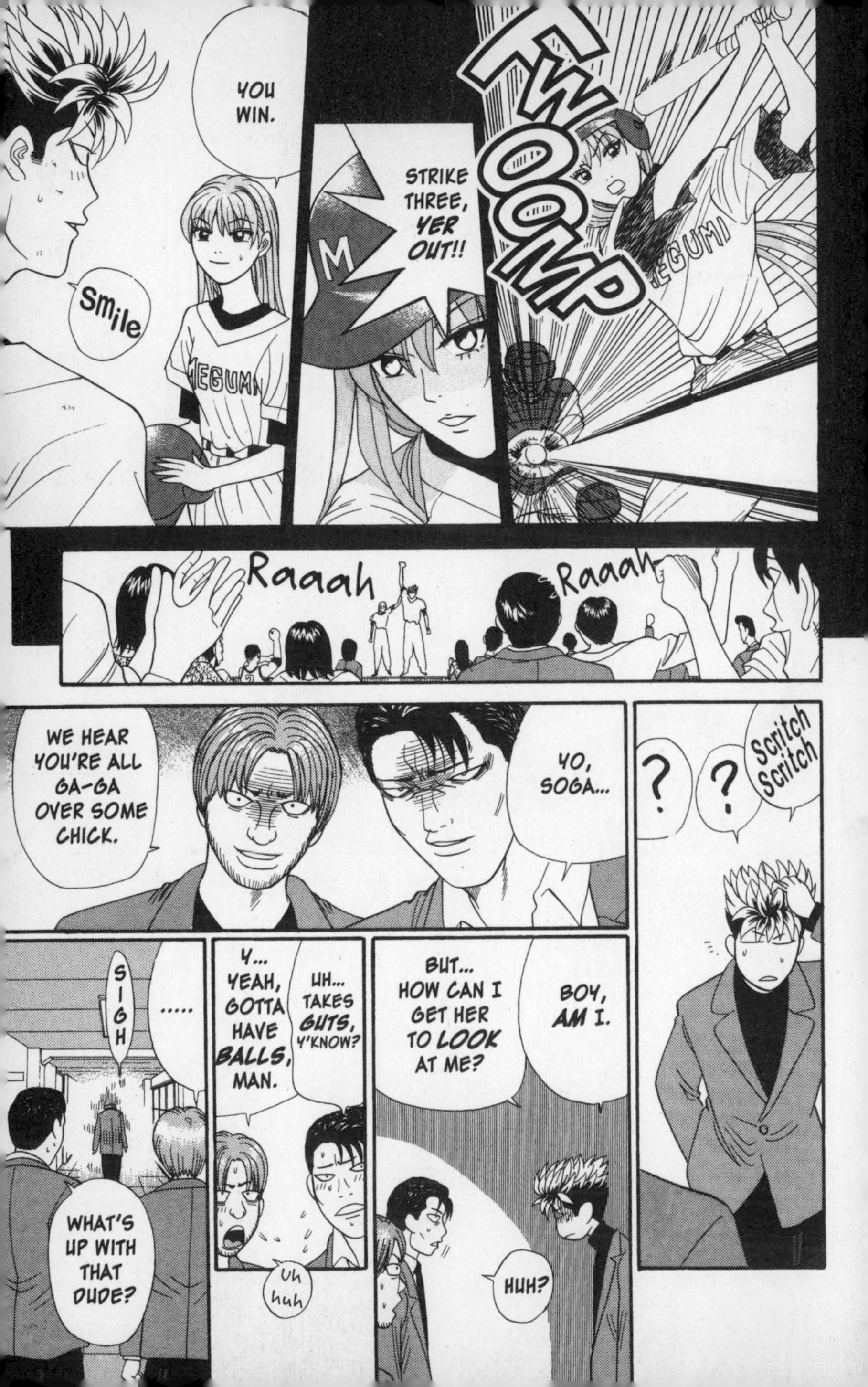
FWOOOMP
STRIKE THREE, YER OUT!!
YOU WIN.
Smile
Raaah
Raaah
? ?
Scritch Scritch
YO, SOGA...
WE HEAR YOU'RE ALL GA-GA OVER SOME CHICK.
BOY, AM I.
BUT... HOW CAN I GET HER TO LOOK AT ME?
HUH?
UH... TAKES GUTS, Y'KNOW?
Y... YEAH, GOTTA HAVE BALLS, MAN.
Uh huh
.....
SIGH
WHAT'S UP WITH THAT DUDE?

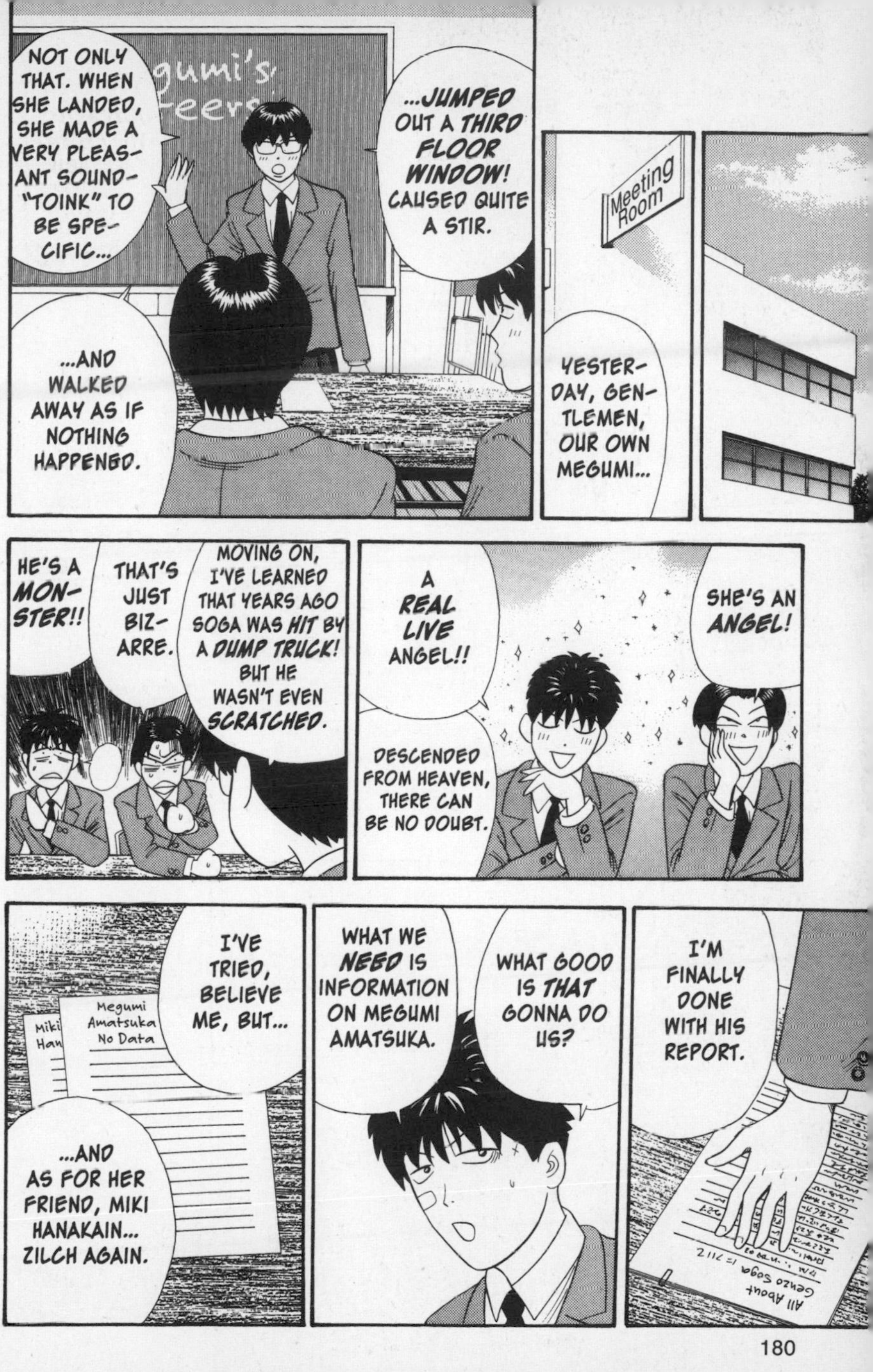
Meeting Room
YESTERDAY, GENTLEMEN, OUR OWN MEGUMI...
...JUMPED OUT A THIRD FLOOR WINDOW! CAUSED QUITE A STIR.
NOT ONLY THAT. WHEN SHE LANDED, SHE MADE A VERY PLEASANT SOUND—"TOINK" TO BE SPECIFIC...
...AND WALKED AWAY AS IF NOTHING HAPPENED.
SHE'S AN ANGEL!
A REAL LIVE ANGEL!!
DESCENDED FROM HEAVEN, THERE CAN BE NO DOUBT.
MOVING ON, I'VE LEARNED THAT YEARS AGO SOGA WAS HIT BY A DUMP TRUCK! BUT HE WASN'T EVEN SCRATCHED.
THAT'S JUST BIZARRE.
HE'S A MONSTER!!
I'M FINALLY DONE WITH HIS REPORT.
All About Genzo Soga
WHAT GOOD IS THAT GONNA DO US?
WHAT WE NEED IS INFORMATION ON MEGUMI AMATSUKA.
I'VE TRIED, BELIEVE ME, BUT...
Megumi Amatsuka No Data
...AND AS FOR HER FRIEND, MIKI HANAKAIN... ZILCH AGAIN.

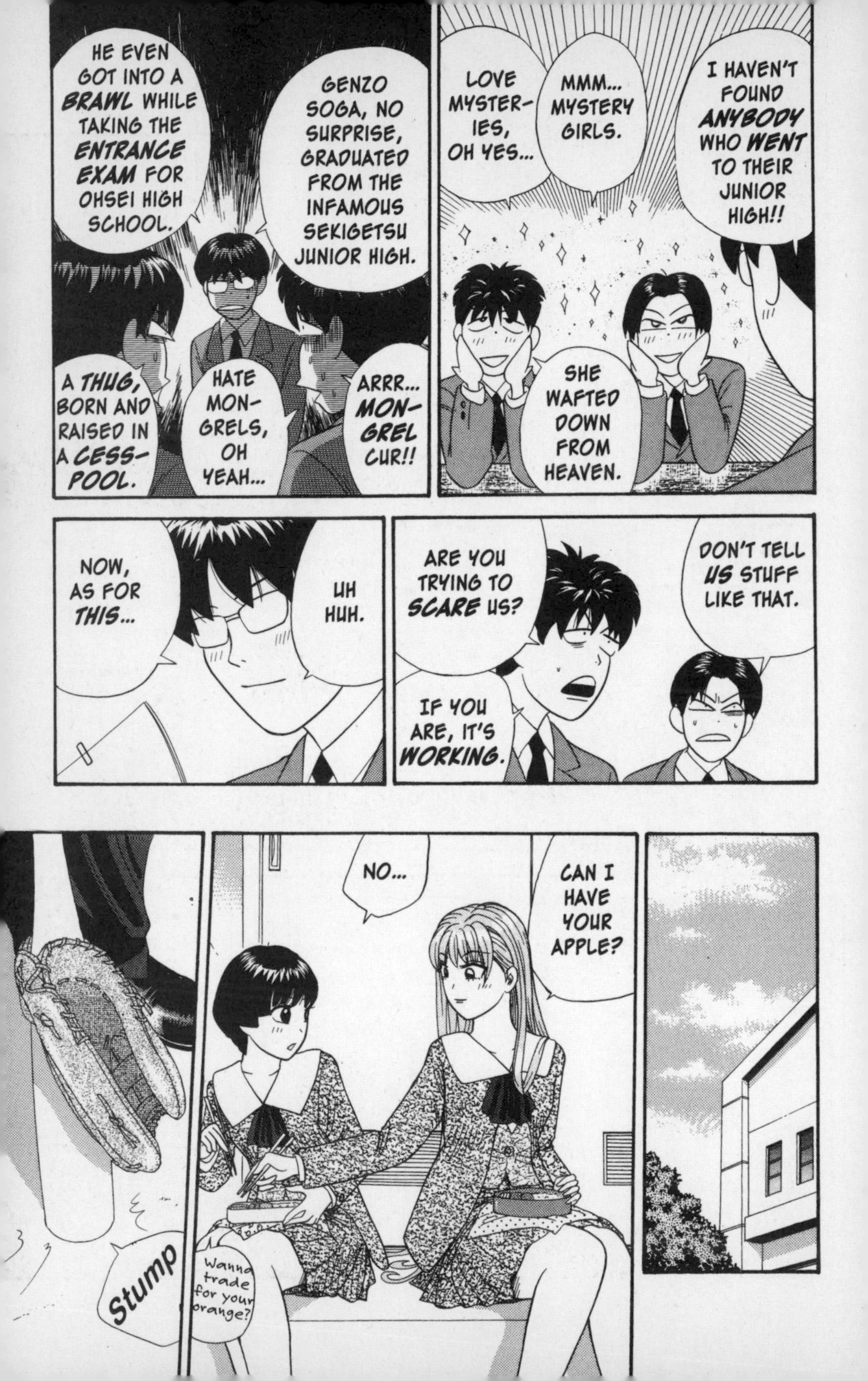
I HAVEN'T FOUND ANYBODY WHO WENT TO THEIR JUNIOR HIGH!!
MMM... MYSTERY GIRLS.
LOVE MYSTER-IES, OH YES...
SHE WAFTED DOWN FROM HEAVEN.
GENZO SOGA, NO SURPRISE, GRADUATED FROM THE INFAMOUS SEKIGETSU JUNIOR HIGH.
HE EVEN GOT INTO A BRAWL WHILE TAKING THE ENTRANCE EXAM FOR OHSEI HIGH SCHOOL.
ARRR... MON-GREL CUR!!
HATE MON-GRELS, OH YEAH...
A THUG, BORN AND RAISED IN A CESS-POOL.
DON'T TELL US STUFF LIKE THAT.
ARE YOU TRYING TO SCARE US?
IF YOU ARE, IT'S WORKING.
UH HUH.
NOW, AS FOR THIS...
CAN I HAVE YOUR APPLE?
NO...
Wanna trade for your orange?
Stump

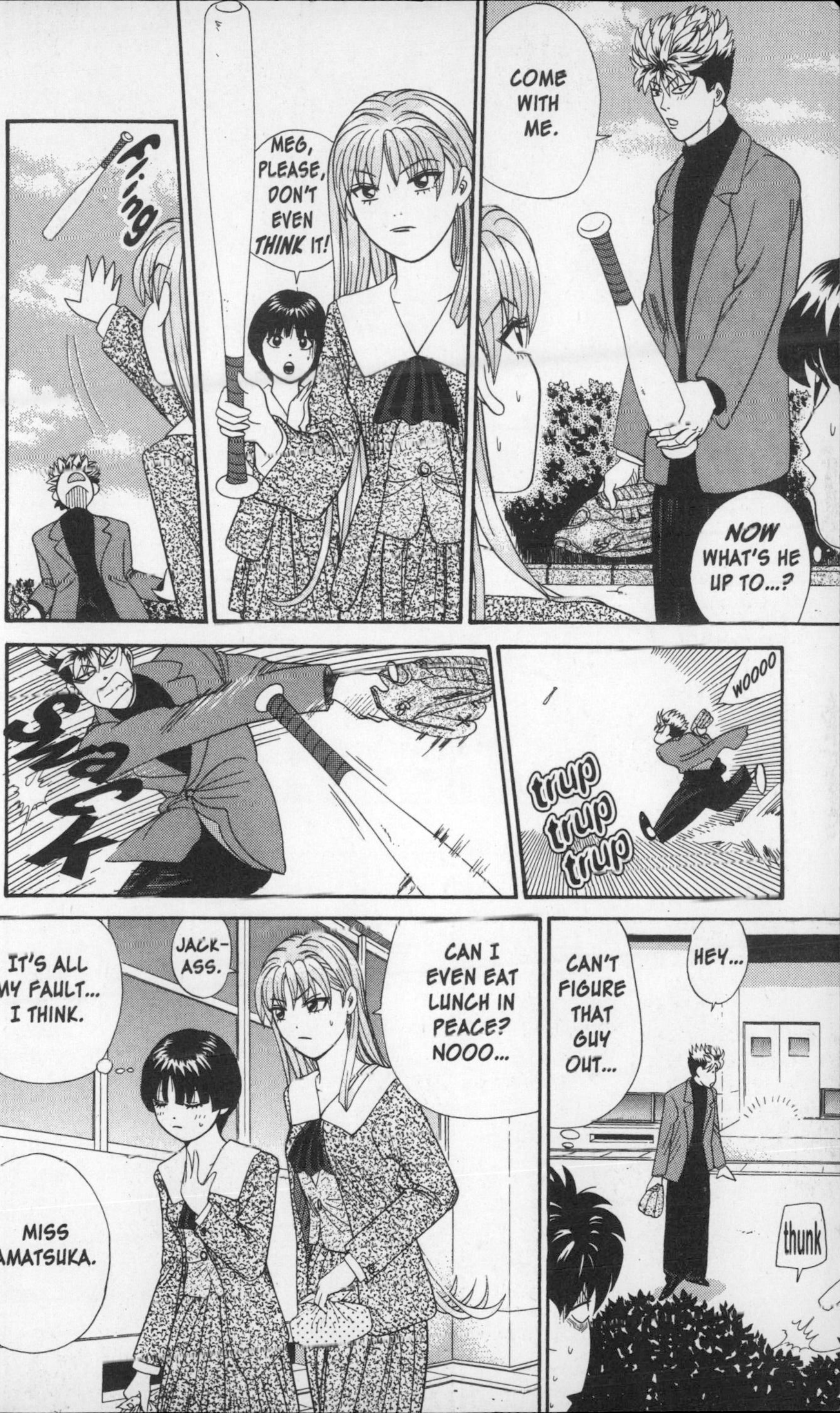
COME WITH ME.
NOW WHAT'S HE UP TO...?
MEG, PLEASE, DON'T EVEN THINK IT!
fling
WOOOO
trup trup trup
SMACK
HEY...
CAN'T FIGURE THAT GUY OUT...
thunk
CAN I EVEN EAT LUNCH IN PEACE? NOOO...
JACK-ASS.
IT'S ALL MY FAULT... I THINK.
MISS AMATSUKA.

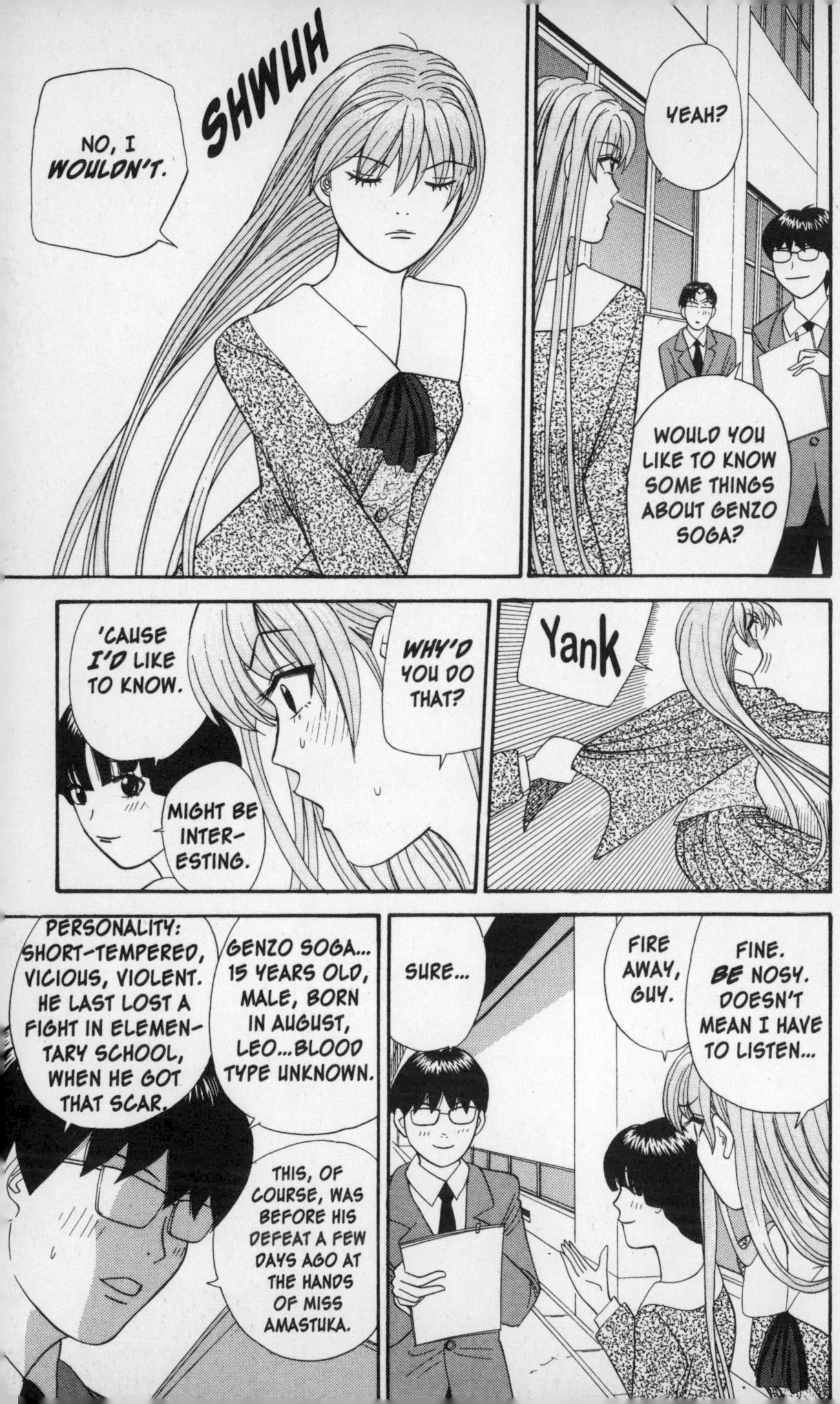
YEAH?
WOULD YOU LIKE TO KNOW SOME THINGS ABOUT GENZO SOGA?
SHWUH
NO, I WOULDN'T.
Yank
WHY'D YOU DO THAT?
'CAUSE I'D LIKE TO KNOW.
MIGHT BE INTERESTING.
FINE. BE NOSY. DOESN'T MEAN I HAVE TO LISTEN...
FIRE AWAY, GUY.
SURE...
GENZO SOGA... 15 YEARS OLD, MALE, BORN IN AUGUST, LEO...BLOOD TYPE UNKNOWN.
PERSONALITY: SHORT-TEMPERED, VICIOUS, VIOLENT. HE LAST LOST A FIGHT IN ELEMENTARY SCHOOL, WHEN HE GOT THAT SCAR.
THIS, OF COURSE, WAS BEFORE HIS DEFEAT A FEW DAYS AGO AT THE HANDS OF MISS AMASTUKA.

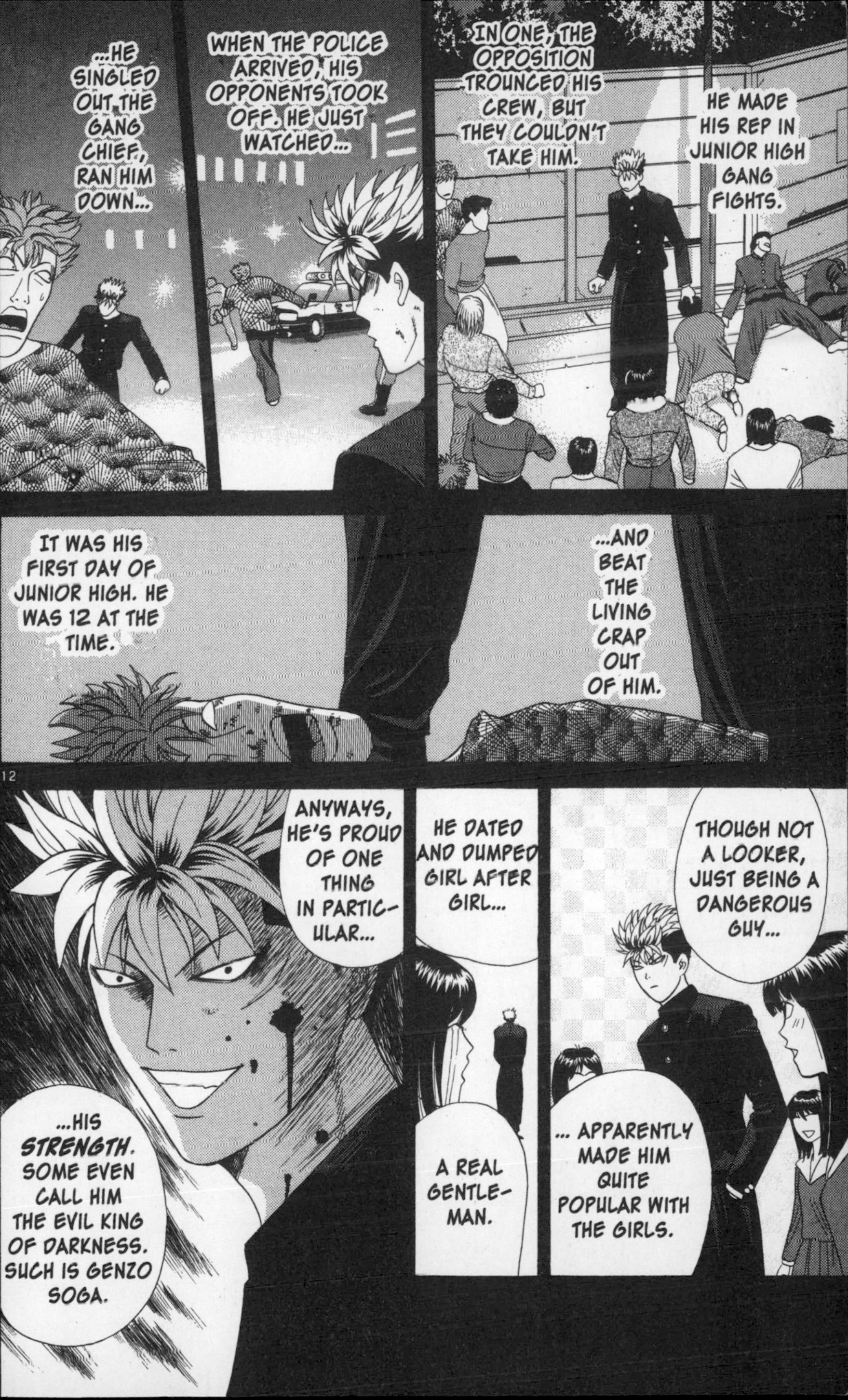
HE MADE HIS REP IN JUNIOR HIGH GANG FIGHTS.
IN ONE, THE OPPOSITION TROUNCED HIS CREW, BUT THEY COULDN'T TAKE HIM.
WHEN THE POLICE ARRIVED, HIS OPPONENTS TOOK OFF. HE JUST WATCHED...
...HE SINGLED OUT THE GANG CHIEF, RAN HIM DOWN...
...AND BEAT THE LIVING CRAP OUT OF HIM.
IT WAS HIS FIRST DAY OF JUNIOR HIGH. HE WAS 12 AT THE TIME.
THOUGH NOT A LOOKER, JUST BEING A DANGEROUS GUY...
... APPARENTLY MADE HIM QUITE POPULAR WITH THE GIRLS.
HE DATED AND DUMPED GIRL AFTER GIRL...
A REAL GENTLEMAN.
ANYWAYS, HE'S PROUD OF ONE THING IN PARTICULAR...
...HIS *STRENGTH*. SOME EVEN CALL HIM THE EVIL KING OF DARKNESS. SUCH IS GENZO SOGA.

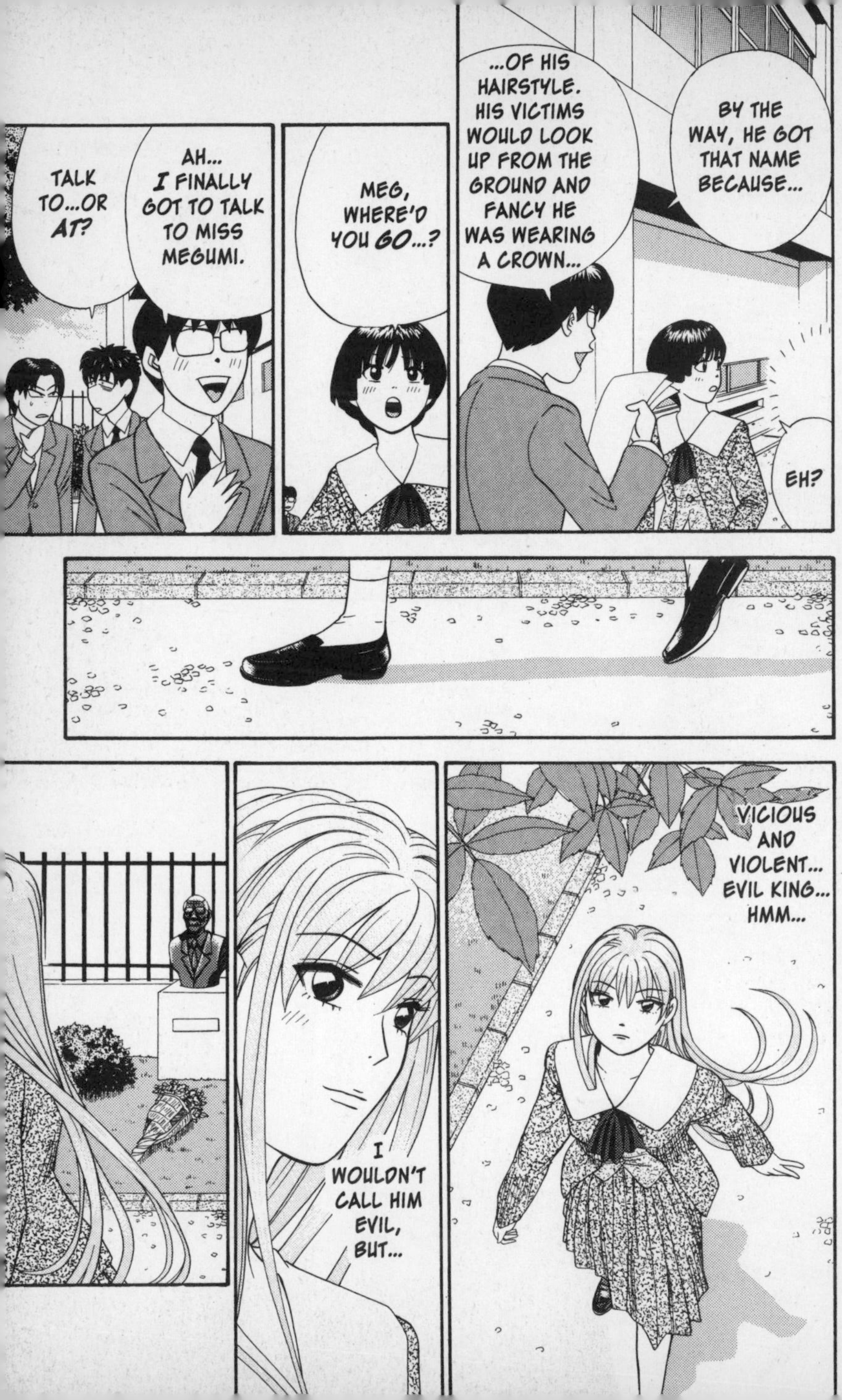
BY THE WAY, HE GOT THAT NAME BECAUSE...
...OF HIS HAIRSTYLE. HIS VICTIMS WOULD LOOK UP FROM THE GROUND AND FANCY HE WAS WEARING A CROWN...
EH?
MEG, WHERE'D YOU GO...?
AH... I FINALLY GOT TO TALK TO MISS MEGUMI.
TALK TO...OR AT?
VICIOUS AND VIOLENT... EVIL KING... HMM...
I WOULDN'T CALL HIM EVIL, BUT...

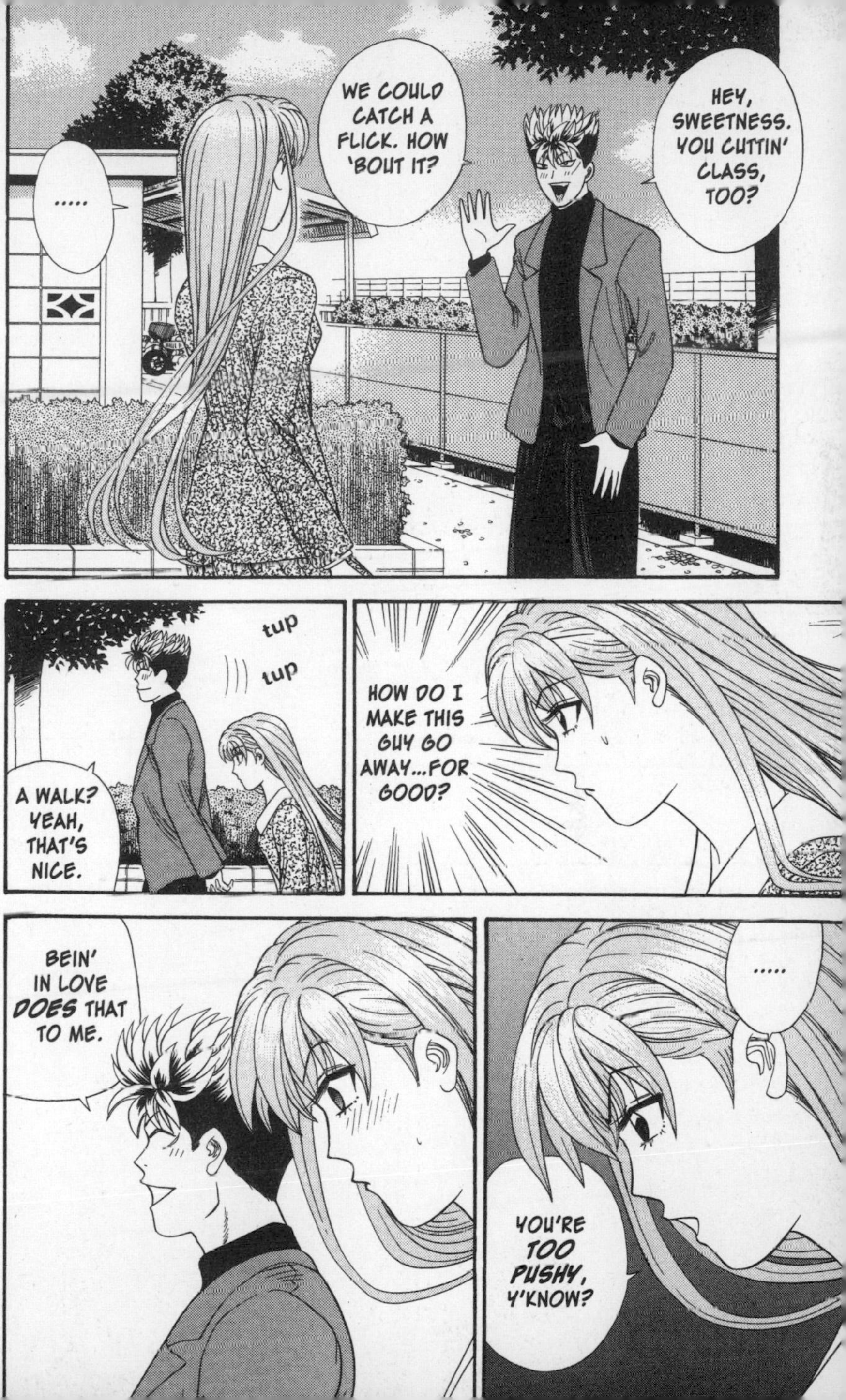
HEY, SWEETNESS. YOU CUTTIN' CLASS, TOO?
WE COULD CATCH A FLICK. HOW 'BOUT IT?
.....
HOW DO I MAKE THIS GUY GO AWAY...FOR GOOD?
tup
tup
A WALK? YEAH, THAT'S NICE.
.....
YOU'RE *TOO PUSHY*, Y'KNOW?
BEIN' IN LOVE *DOES* THAT TO ME.

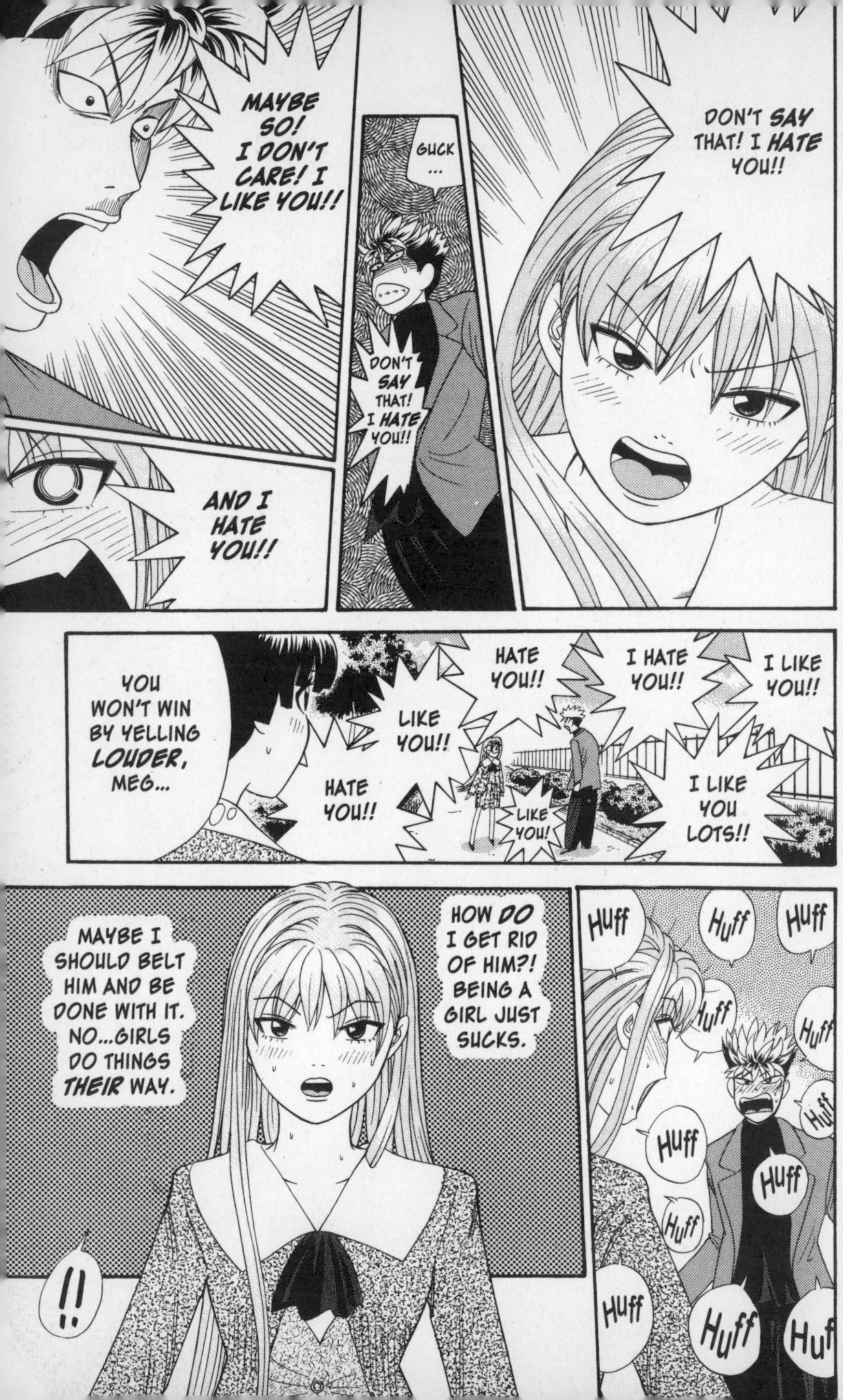
DON'T SAY THAT! I HATE YOU!!
GUCK ...
DON'T SAY THAT! I HATE YOU!!
MAYBE SO! I DON'T CARE! I LIKE YOU!!
AND I HATE YOU!!
I LIKE YOU!!
I HATE YOU!!
HATE YOU!!
I LIKE YOU LOTS!!
LIKE YOU!
LIKE YOU!!
HATE YOU!!
YOU WON'T WIN BY YELLING LOUDER, MEG...
Huff
Huff
Huff
Huff
Huff
Huff
Huff
Huff
Huff
Huff
Huff
Huff
Huff
HOW DO I GET RID OF HIM?! BEING A GIRL JUST SUCKS.
MAYBE I SHOULD BELT HIM AND BE DONE WITH IT. NO...GIRLS DO THINGS THEIR WAY.
!!

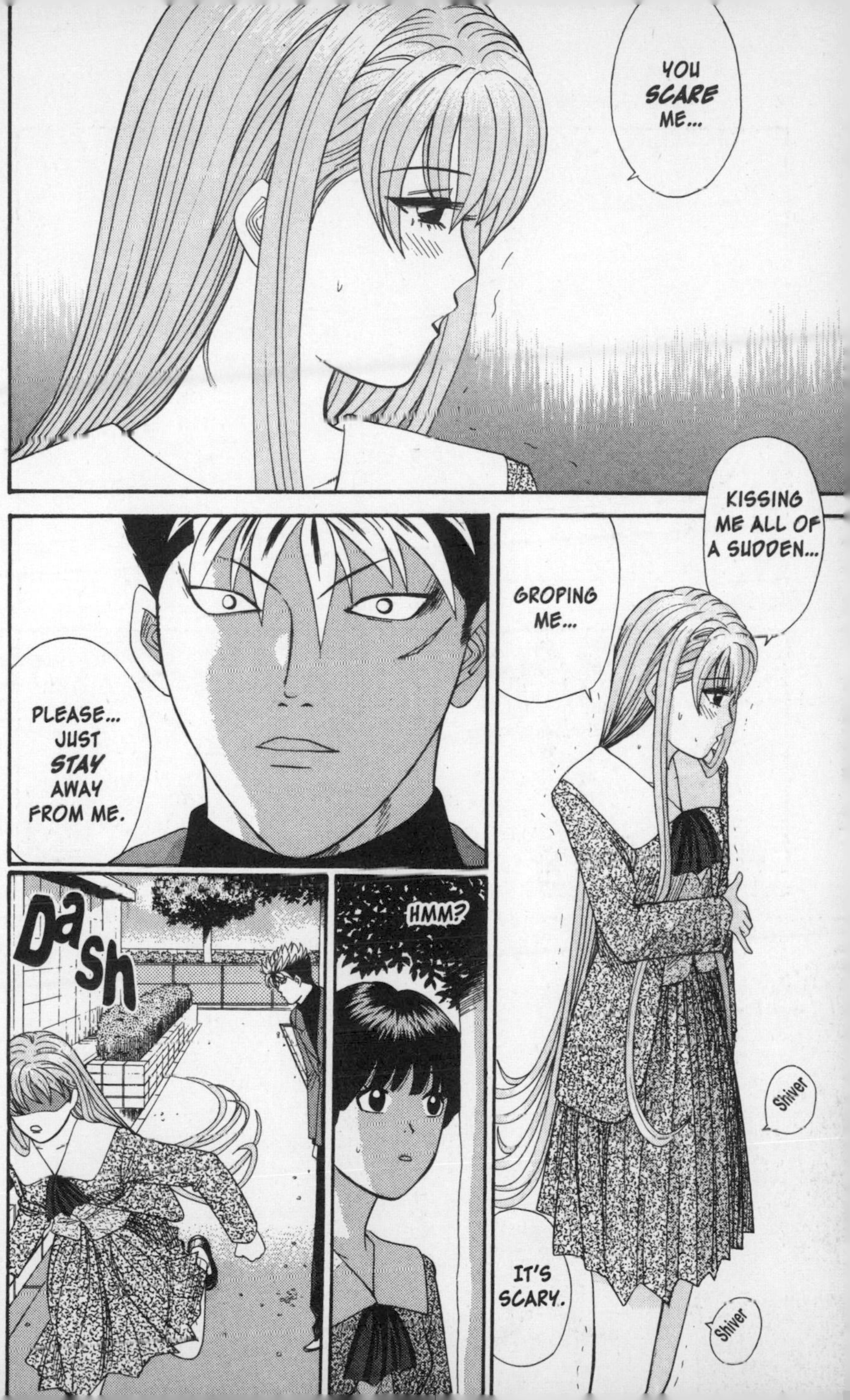
YOU SCARE ME...
KISSING ME ALL OF A SUDDEN...
GROPING ME...
IT'S SCARY.
Shiver
Shiver
PLEASE... JUST STAY AWAY FROM ME.
HMM?
Dash

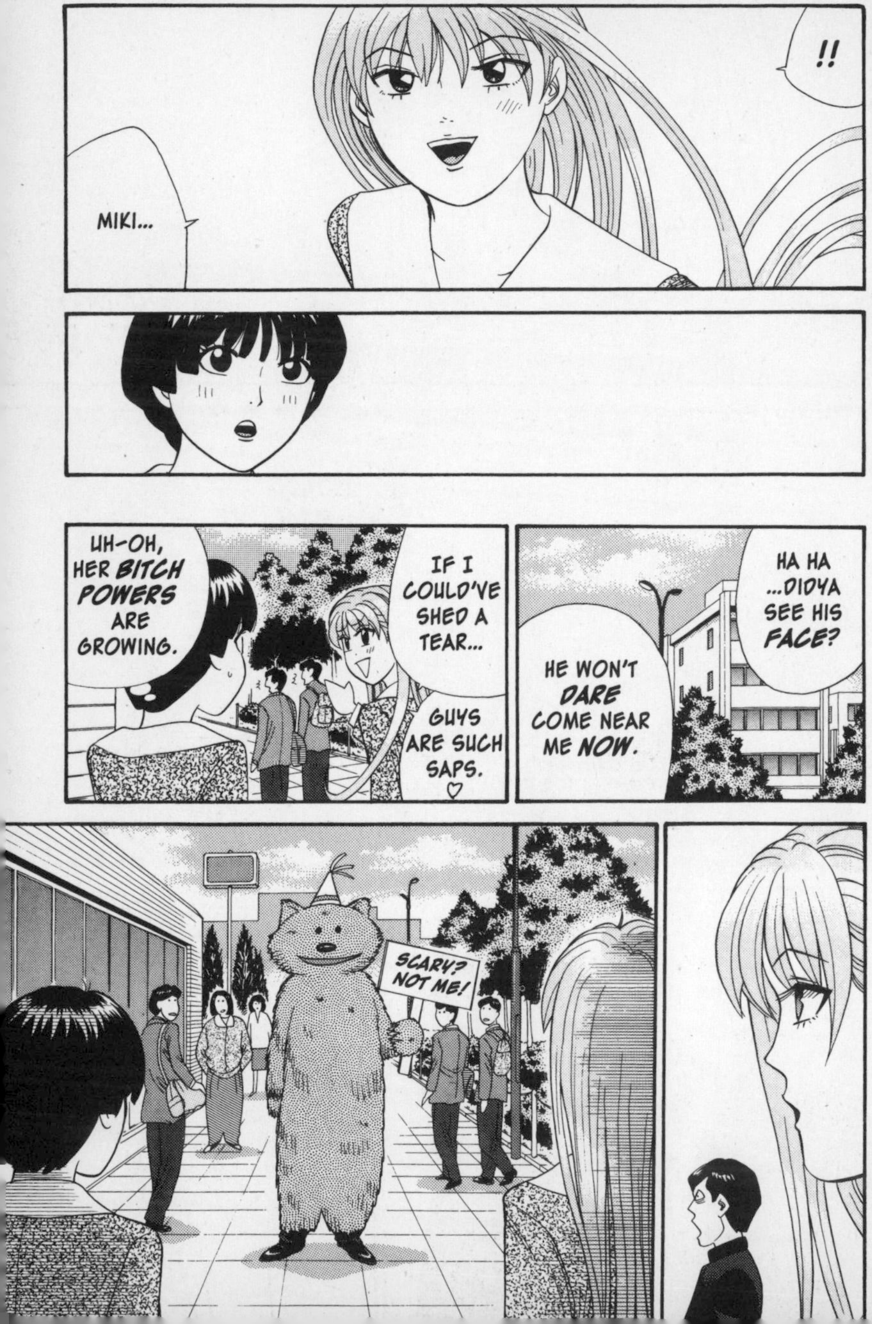
!!
MIKI...
HA HA ...DIDYA SEE HIS *FACE*?
HE WON'T *DARE* COME NEAR ME *NOW*.
IF I COULD'VE SHED A TEAR...
GUYS ARE SUCH SAPS. ♡
UH-OH, HER *BITCH POWERS* ARE GROWING.
SCARY? NOT ME!

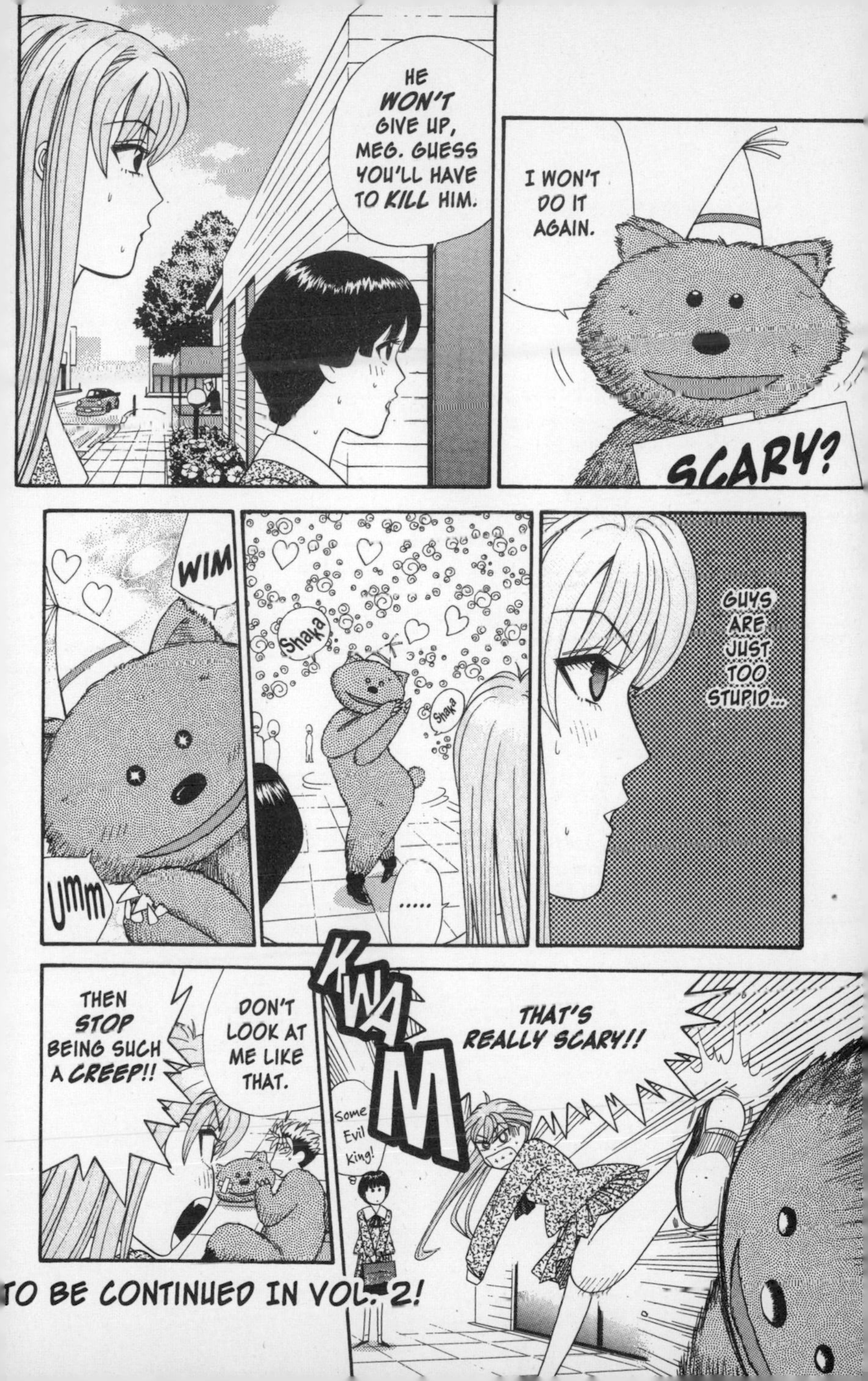

I WON'T DO IT AGAIN.
SCARY?
HE WON'T GIVE UP, MEG. GUESS YOU'LL HAVE TO KILL HIM.
GUYS ARE JUST TOO STUPID...
Shaka
Shaka
.....
WIM
Umm
THAT'S REALLY SCARY!!
KWAM
Some Evil King!
DON'T LOOK AT ME LIKE THAT.
THEN STOP BEING SUCH A CREEP!!
TO BE CONTINUED IN VOL. 2!

Note From the Editor

The age-old caveat "Be careful what you wish for" proves to be an invaluable lesson in CHEEKY ANGEL, a gender-bending manga series from Shogakukan cartoon-prize winner Hiroyuki Nishimori. Also a popular TV anime series in Japan, CHEEKY ANGEL provides high school life as the backdrop for this quirky look at identity crisis amidst a sea of raging hormones and daily struggle for notoriety.

Originally serialized in Japan's manga anthology SHONEN SUNDAY, CHEEKY ANGEL's plot is quite simple—boy (Megumi Amatsuka) asks a playful spirit to make him the "manliest man on Earth," but instead he gets transformed into "the womanliest woman on Earth," and her—I mean his —life is never the same again. And they lived happily ever after...NOT!

Imagine Scenario 1. La-la-la, you're going through life as a boy, climbing trees, getting into fistfights, running around playing all kinds of sports, making model airplanes, having crushes on girls, then all of a sudden, BAM! You've got boobs, a menstrual cycle, and a colorful array of panties in your drawer! You feel a little less agile, you're walking around with a purse, you're shaving your legs, and worst of all, the nasty boys in your class are all mesmerized by your girlish beauty!

But the fun doesn't end there.

What if the transformation is only physical? The anatomy's right, but your mind and heart are still those of a boy? Imagine Scenario 2. You're a boy trapped inside a female body, but you're not gay. Isn't that a kick in the face?

Now, we live in a very modern world. In this day and age, if it were your happiness to undergo any form of transformation—whether cosmetically or gender-wise, provided you had the cash—you're free to do so. Just so long as it's voluntary, right? Sadly, though, that wasn't the case for poor Megumi. He's still "him" inside the hot-mama facade of his current body, and he's got to live with the consequences of his hastily made wish.

For those of us who have, at one time or another, wished for something just for the hell of it and paid for it dearly...

Yeah, I thought so.

Michelle Pangilinan
Editor of CHEEKY ANGEL

EDITOR'S RECOMMENDATIONS

More manga!
More manga!

If you enjoyed this volume of

Cheeky Angel™

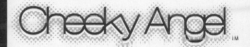

then here's some more manga you might be interested in.

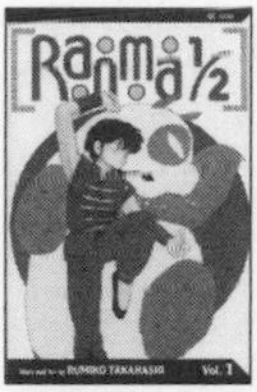
Ranma ½

©1988 Rumiko Takahashi/Shogakukan, Inc.

Ranma 1/2 is one of Rumiko Takahashi's best-selling series in Japan. With the publication of Volume 34 of this series in Japan, Takahashi's total sales passed one hundred million copies of her compiled work. Check out the story of Ranma Saotome, a martial artist who turns into a busty girl when splashed with cold water!

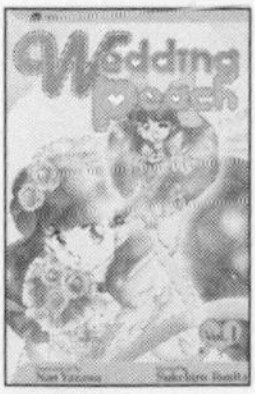
Wedding Peach

©1994 Nao Yazawa/Sukehiro Tomita/Tenyu/Shogakukan, Inc.

Wedding Peach is about a first-year middle-school student Momoko Hanasaki and her friends Yuri and Hinagiku, who transform into demon-slaying supercharged angels when they aren't busy ogling the strapping captain of their soccer team.

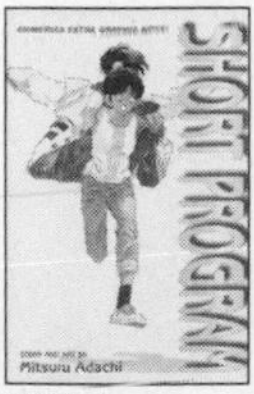
SHORT PROGRAM
Mitsuru Adachi

©1996 Mitsuru Adachi/Shogakukan, Inc.

Short Program is the first graphic novel collecting the short stories of Mitsuru Adachi, one of the masters of the art of storytelling. This graphic novel contains all the *Short Program* installments from *Animerica Extra* Vol. 2, No. 2, to Vol. 2, No. 11.

About the Author

Hiroyuki Nishimori previously wrote
and drew the 38-volume *KYO KARA
ORE WA!!*, which sold 33 million copies
in Japan. Winner of the 46th Annual
Shogakukan cartoon prize, Nishimori's
other works include the two-volume
MAKU KIKEN NA NAMPA DEKA and
the co-creation of the four-volume
series *SPINOUT*.

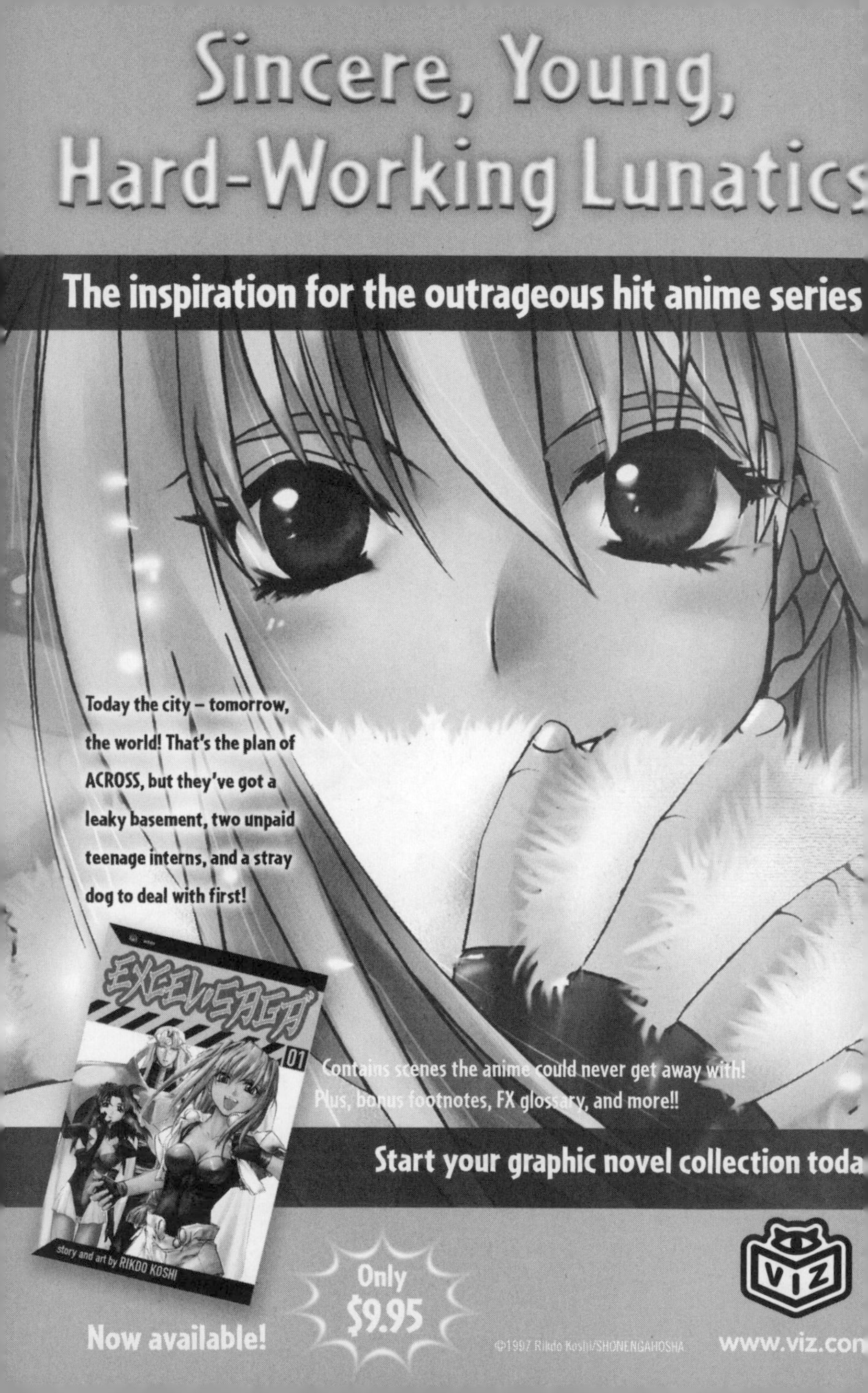
Sincere, Young,
Hard-Working Lunatics
The inspiration for the outrageous hit anime series
Today the city – tomorrow, the world! That's the plan of ACROSS, but they've got a leaky basement, two unpaid teenage interns, and a stray dog to deal with first!
EXCEL SAGA
01
story and art by RIKDO KOSHI
Contains scenes the anime could never get away with!
Plus, bonus footnotes, FX glossary, and more!!
Start your graphic novel collection toda
Only $9.95
Now available!
©1997 Rikdo Koshi/SHONENGAHOSHA
www.viz.co

MEGAMAN
NT WARRIOR ™

Get Connected!

The manga version of the hit TV series on Kids' WB is now available for the first time in English!

Computers have turned the world into a bright and shiny utopia, but there's always trouble in paradise. Can fifth-grader Lan and his NetNavigator, MegaMan, stop a sinister organization from taking over and destroying the world?

www.viz.com
store.viz.com

2001 Ryo Takamisaki/Shogakukan, Inc.
CAPCOM CO., LTD. TM and ® are trademarks of CAPCOM CO., LTD.

MEGAMAN
NT WARRIOR

ONLY $7⁹⁵

Story and art by *Ryo Takamisaki*

Vol. 1

Start your graphic novel collection today!

action

A Ninja Inferno

Armed with the power to control flame, Recca Hanabishi finds himself in an awkward situation when a mysterious older woman pops into his life one day. Is she good? Is she evil? What exactly does she want with the young ninja firecracker?

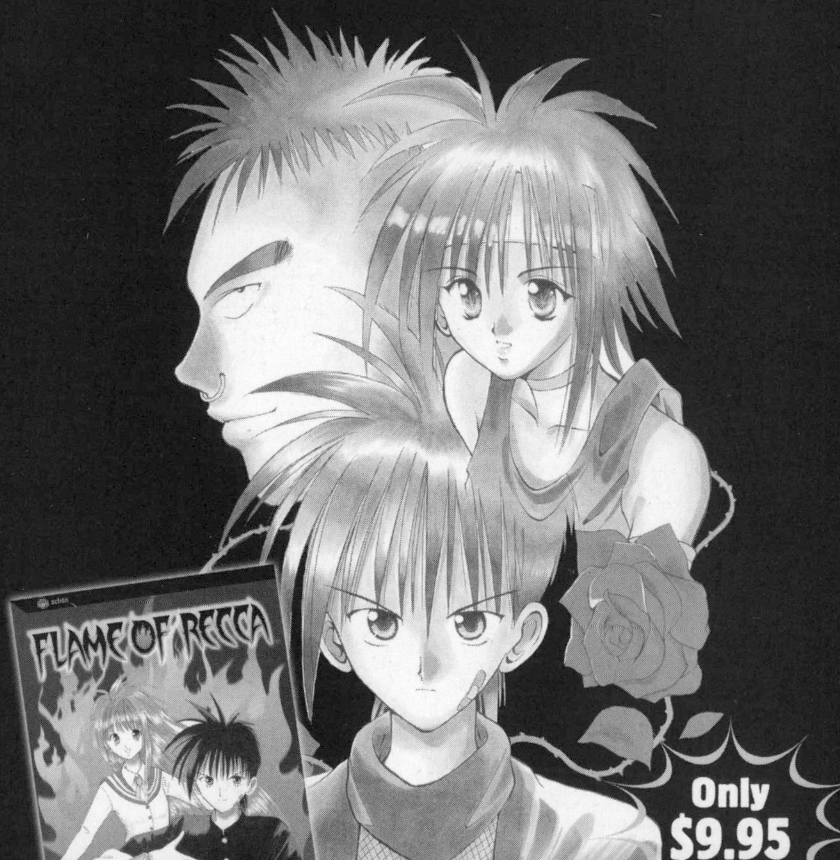
FLAME OF RECCA
Vol.1
Story and Art by
Nobuyuki Anzai
Only
$9.95
VIZ

From the top of the Japanese manga charts comes the inspiration for the hit anime series. Collect the graphic novels today!

www.viz.com

COMPLETE OUR SURVEY AND LET US KNOW WHAT YOU THINK!

☐ Please do NOT send me information about VIZ products, news and events, special offers, or other information.

☐ Please do NOT send me information from VIZ's trusted business partners.

Name: _____

Address: _____

City: _____ **State:** _____ **Zip:** _____

E-mail: _____

☐ Male ☐ Female   **Date of Birth** (mm/dd/yyyy): ___ / ___ / ___   (Under 13? Parental consent required)

What race/ethnicity do you consider yourself? (please check one)

☐ Asian/Pacific Islander ☐ Black/African American ☐ Hispanic/Latino

☐ Native American/Alaskan Native ☐ White/Caucasian ☐ Other: _____

What VIZ product did you purchase? (check all that apply and indicate title purchased)

☐ DVD/VHS _____

☐ Graphic Novel _____

☐ Magazines _____

☐ Merchandise _____

Reason for purchase: (check all that apply)

☐ Special offer ☐ Favorite title ☐ Gift

☐ Recommendation ☐ Other _____

Where did you make your purchase? (please check one)

☐ Comic store ☐ Bookstore ☐ Mass/Grocery Store

☐ Newsstand ☐ Video/Video Game Store ☐ Other: _____

☐ Online (site: _____)

What other VIZ properties have you purchased/own? _____

_____

How many anime and/or manga titles have you purchased in the last year? How many were VIZ titles? (please check one from each column)

ANIME	MANGA	VIZ
☐ None	☐ None	☐ None
☐ 1-4	☐ 1-4	☐ 1-4
☐ 5-10	☐ 5-10	☐ 5-10
☐ 11+	☐ 11+	☐ 11+

I find the pricing of VIZ products to be: (please check one)

☐ Cheap ☐ Reasonable ☐ Expensive

What genre of manga and anime would you like to see from VIZ? (please check two)

☐ Adventure ☐ Comic Strip ☐ Science Fiction ☐ Fighting
☐ Horror ☐ Romance ☐ Fantasy ☐ Sports

What do you think of VIZ's new look?

☐ Love It ☐ It's OK ☐ Hate It ☐ Didn't Notice ☐ No Opinion

Which do you prefer? (please check one)

☐ Reading right-to-left
☐ Reading left-to-right

Which do you prefer? (please check one)

☐ Sound effects in English
☐ Sound effects in Japanese with English captions
☐ Sound effects in Japanese only with a glossary at the back

THANK YOU! Please send the completed form to:

NJW Research
42 Catharine St.
Poughkeepsie, NY 12601

All information provided will be used for internal purposes only. We promise not to sell or otherwise divulge your information.